Dear Dad   Happy Birthday

Love Simon
xxx

17/4/07

A SENSE OF PLACE

West Sussex Parish Maps

KIM LESLIE

west
sussex
county
council

First published in the United Kingdom in 2006 by

West Sussex County Council
County Hall
Chichester
West Sussex
PO19 1RQ

Kim Leslie
West Sussex Record Office
County Hall
Chichester
West Sussex
PO19 1RN

Telephone: 01243 753602
             or
             01243 582424
Fax: 01243 533959
E-mail: kim.leslie@westsussex.gov.uk

British Library Cataloguing in Publication Data
A catalogue record for this book is available from the British Library

ISBN 0-86260-564-4

Front cover: l to r, top: Harting, Stedham with Iping, Bury;
bottom: Poling, Selsey, Highbrook; centre: Petworth
Back cover: Chidham
Dedication page: Highbrook

Design and production: Mike Blacker
Blacker Design
Hillcroft Barn
Coombe Hill Road
East Grinstead
West Sussex
RH19 4LY
info@blackerdesign.co.uk

Retail distribution: Phillimore & Co. Ltd
Shopwyke Manor Barn
Chichester
West Sussex
PO20 2BG
England
Telephone: 01243 787636
E-mail: bookshop@phillimore.co.uk

Printed and bound in China by 1010 Printing International Ltd on behalf of Compass Press

A deep relationship with places is as necessary, and perhaps as unavoidable, as close relationships with people; without such relationships human existence, while possible, is bereft of much of its significance.

Edward Relph, *Place and Placelessness* (Pion, 1976)

Making a Parish Map is about creating a community expression of values, and about beginning to assert ideas for involvement, it is about taking the place in your own hands.

Sue Clifford, 'Places, People and Parish Maps' in Sue Clifford & Angela King (eds.), *from place to PLACE: maps and Parish Maps* (Common Ground, 1996)

Dedicated to

Sue Clifford and Angela King
of
Common Ground
who gave us parish maps

and

Jenni, Victoria and Justin
who – again –
made it possible

Contents

Preface

It all started with four ladies sipping coffee, then we formed a millennium committee and the village set up the Poling 2000 Action Group. But what shall we do to celebrate the millennium? I bumped into Pauline Halls who was producing the Arundel Parish Map and she introduced me to Kim Leslie of West Sussex County Council who came and spoke to an enthusiastic audience in the ballroom at Manor Farm. We decided to make the Poling map.

VALERIE SHEPHERD remembers how it all started for Poling, just one of so many stories of how local people got caught up in the enthusiasm for making maps of where they live. Not ordinary, conventional maps, but maps full of pictures and text in a gloriously colourful and detailed celebration of people and places across the county. This book is in turn a celebration of all that has been achieved in making these highly decorated parish maps in West Sussex over the last few years.

The project, of which Poling is part, has its immediate origins in another book of local maps: *An Historical Atlas of Sussex* published in 1999. In co-editing this volume, a great deal of time was spent working in the cartographic unit at the University of Sussex, a map-maker's paradise. Between concentrated bouts of plotting Sussex history for the atlas, there were tempting moments spent dipping into the university's vast map collection. One chance discovery stood out – a very modern and richly decorated parish map of Charlbury in Oxfordshire. Steeped in detail through delicate pictures and text, it vividly brought to life this little Cotswold town and its surrounding countryside. And it wasn't made by professional map-makers, but local and very talented people who clearly had great affection for where they lived. Maps like this stir the imagination, they urge visits. So going to Charlbury and meeting the map-makers, seeing the original map and the beautiful place it depicts, it wasn't hard to see that here was a type of map – and a community project – with so much to offer. Charlbury's map-makers told of the work of Common Ground, the environmental organisation that has been promoting these maps throughout the UK. Apparently several thousand parish maps had already been made elsewhere. Here was a challenge.

If only we could do lots of Charlburys for West Sussex....

The opportunity soon came when West Sussex County Council started to look around for ideas to celebrate the millennium. Seeing a copy of the Charlbury map, members of the millennium committee at County Hall readily gave their support, some start-up funding was secured, and thus was born the West Sussex Millennium Parish Maps Project.

Whilst the millennium celebrations may well be over, the project continues to spread across the county, having deleted 'Millennium' from its title and now standing as the West Sussex Parish Maps Project. With just over one hundred parishes mapped by the project, a substantial area of the county has already been covered. Hopefully the project will continue into the future until every parish in the county has been mapped in a similar way.

From Charlbury's inspiration the idea of parish mapping came to West Sussex, and from West Sussex our maps have been inspiring similar work and interest as far apart as Cumbria, Monmouthshire, Sweden, Italy, Kobe in Japan and Victoria in Australia. Parish maps are compulsive and compelling.

This book tells the story so far.

Kim Leslie   July 2006
Director
West Sussex Parish Maps Project
West Sussex Record Office

Introduction

SINCE THE EARLIEST Sussex maps were made over four hundred years ago, there have never been maps of the county produced quite like these displayed in this book. They have been made by local people in celebration of where they live, bringing to life their landscapes of home in pictures, words and images, capturing the very essence of the spirit of place. They are community-made maps, and this makes them so different and unusual.

They may be a new type of map, but in their artistry and decoration they have a long pedigree. Modern map-making in this country has its roots in the 16th and 17th centuries with small-scale county maps by Christopher Saxton, John Norden and John Speed, embellished with sea monsters, grotesques, men-of-war, deer in the forests and heraldic devices. Land and sea come alive in a feast of real and imagined imagery with an exuberance characteristic of Renaissance design. Their verve and imagination are echoed in these new parish maps.

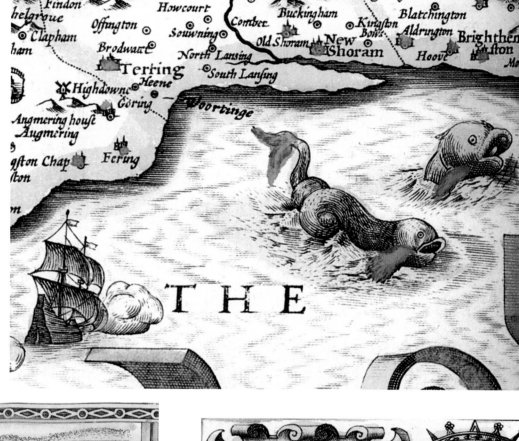

Details from John Speed's map of Sussex, 1610
WEST SUSSEX RECORD OFFICE (WSRO), PH. 19.725

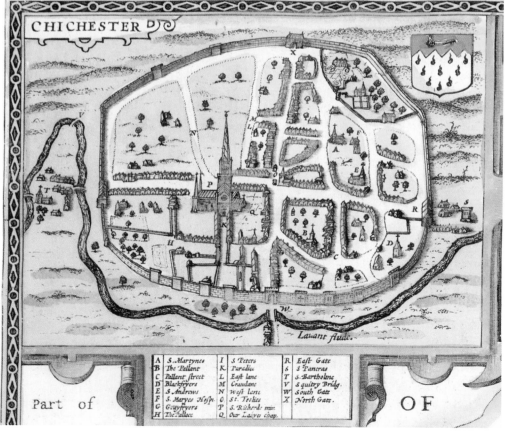

At the same time as the earliest county maps were being produced, Tudor and Stuart landowners were commissioning surveys of their private estates: thus was born the large-scale plotting of farmland, towns and villages 'in perspective view' – their fresh, bright colours bringing to life mansions, farmhouses and cottages, windmills and watermills, churches, trees and hedgerows, even rabbits and sheep in the fields. These parchment landscapes recreate our local past in a riot of vivid and eye-catching detail.

Coloured borders framed the maps and every opportunity was taken to decorate compass roses and scale bars. Lettering and delicate penmanship were elaborate and varied to enhance the pictorial effect.

Cottages at Prinsted in Westbourne by Thomas Kington, 1640   WSRO, Add. Ms. 2857

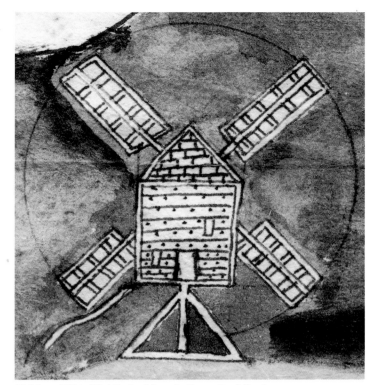

Highdown Mill in West Ferring Manor by George Randall, 1621   WSRO, Add. Ms. 46,862

Shepherd and sheep at Erringham Farm, Old Shoreham by Robert Whitpaine, 1687   WSRO, Add. Ms. 40,625

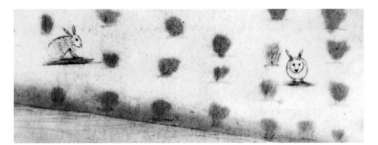

Rabbits at Coates Farm, West Wittering by Nicholas Ayling, 1695
WSRO, E35D/5/1

In these ways early maps are as much triumphs of art as accomplishments of cartography – they are just as much pictures-as-maps as maps-as-pictures. So as well as being geographically valuable they gave, and still continue to give, much aesthetic pleasure. The artistic traditions of these early map-makers carried on throughout the 18th century and into the next, eventually to be superseded by the much more matter-of-fact Ordnance Survey maps that took their place. Improved accuracy at the expense of artistic embellishment revolutionised the science – and presentation – of map-making. Centuries of picturesque mapping came to an end.

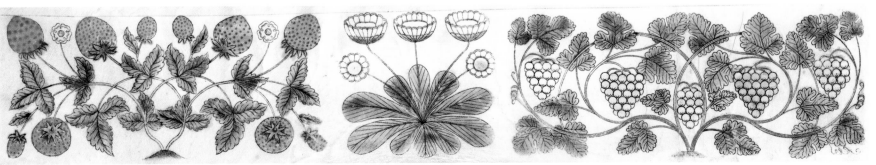

Border detail from a map of Oliver Whitby's lands in Harting by Nicholas Ayling, 1694   WSRO, Add. Ms. 2032

So whilst in one sense the modern parish maps featured in this book actually *revive* the tradition of earlier decorative map-making, yet, in another, they *break* with tradition altogether in that so much mapping in the past was primarily to administer and govern. The reasons for making the earlier estate maps were for plotting ownership and managing the land, and then later the mapping-work of the Ordnance Survey originated as a military survey for purposes of national defence. This is the world of maps dominated by specialists, of maps made as instruments of power and control, the world as seen through the eyes of the official.

Now, in complete contrast, these maps show parishes through the eyes of local people. That's what makes them so unusual and significant. Quite unlike the earlier maps produced for official, business and legal purposes, these are essentially expressions of what people think about the places where they live. They are about peoples' impressions about their locality, giving a bottom-up, rather than top-down, view of the local world, a peoples' view of the county. In this sense they are impressionist maps, maps grounded in personal geographies.

What they clearly affirm is the importance that people attach to living in one very special place, a place with distinct boundaries and separation from elsewhere, where ideas of 'local' can be nurtured and flourish. That's why many Selsey residents have a distinct 'island mentality', so that when they cross the water at the old ferry-point they think of themselves as back home, across a real boundary; it's why the people of South Stoke value their privacy beyond the invisible 'frontier' of the Offham Cut, that steeply-banked dark green tunnel of trees beyond the Arundel tourist beat; it's why Whyke, engulfed by Chichester, is as much a state of mind as streets of houses, whose residents see themselves in their own distinct location, where real things happen in a real community and not in just part of a bolt-on suburb of the city.

That's why making these maps has raised issues about separation and *difference*, with people much more acutely aware of the forces – subtle and overt – that challenge the places they love with unsympathetic change, creating a 'xeroxed' landscape where all places look alike, where places become placeless, where the spirits that give a place its soul have fled in a frenzy of bricks and mortar imposed from above, without any regard for local forms and local feelings. That's why the people of Felpham on their map tell us that 'The battle continues to save the remaining small green areas from bricks, mortar and tarmac'; why Ferring, similarly on their map, express their anxiety 'to preserve the rural character of our village' and why those of Funtington are 'conscious that the whole Parish is a vital part of a Downs View of timeless beauty we should all strive to preserve'. In summing up a

Photo: Nick Birch

Cocking History Column, with one of the two parish maps at the base. A freak snowstorm followed the unveiling in April 2005.

parish, these maps have mobilised opinion in their defence by honouring the *genius loci*, the spirit of place. Understandably these maps are offered to inspectors at planning enquiries, for as convenient shorthand snapshots they don't need any more words or explanations to convey what places mean to local people. As maps are 'abbreviated places', they can bring together a whole parish, with so many layers of meaning conveniently on just one single sheet of paper.

Certainly never before have so many people – and non-professional map-makers at that – got together to map the county in such personal, human terms. Their particular skill is that they know about living in their community, they know about its details, and about its everyday life and main features. If, as has been claimed, maps take their ultimate authority, not from their cartographic accuracy, but from the people who make them, then parish maps reveal a valuable perspective into the hearts, and indeed the minds, of each community depicted.

How did this community map-making all begin? The idea is the brainchild of the environmental organisation Common Ground. Since the mid-1980s it has been encouraging community groups to produce their own maps of their towns and villages as a way of showing *what it is that makes a particular place different and special from elsewhere*. The map-making process thereby encourages people to consider what it is that gives a place its own special identity and distinctiveness that can then be highlighted on the map.

Local identity is made up from so many diverse elements. There is the geographic setting in a place's surroundings and its landscape; there is the natural environment and the teeming wildlife it supports; the jumble of roads and buildings that define our use of the land; as well as the myriad ordinary everyday features that make a place special and different from anywhere else, making a place a definite 'somewhere' rather than just a bland 'nowhere'. But most importantly it is the local people who have made these maps and who know what it is that makes their parishes unique and distinct. That is the special value of these maps.

They have been made in many different media – some are drawn and painted, others woven, or embroidered, some made into photographic collages or ceramic tiles or even spectacularly cast in bronze as part of the column of history at Cocking. One Sussex map has even been made as a public garden, its outline formed by the shape of the town, its colours changing with the seasons. There is no end to the inventiveness that can be used for this type of mapping. These are no ordinary maps.

The area covered is usually the parish, but it doesn't have to be. The territory may be an ancient ecclesiastical parish or the more recent civil parish, or it may perhaps be even more localised and concentrate on the centre of a place, or a single neighbourhood, or even just one single street. As Sue Clifford puts it in Common Ground's handbook on parish maps, the essence is:

> *. . . to focus on locality, the smallest arena in which life is played out. The territory to which you feel loyalty, which has meaning to you, about which you share some knowledge, for which indignance and protectiveness is easily roused, the neighbourhood of which you have the measure, which in some way helps to shape you. . . It is in this sense of a self-defined small territory, that Common Ground has offered the word* parish, *implying people and place together. . . .*

And so 'parish' in terms of 'parish maps' is used generically as a convenient handle for maps covering a wide variety of territory. They are really 'homeland' maps in the sense that they embody not only physical locality but also more personal feelings deriving from familiarity, identification and belonging; where people feel *of* rather than merely *at* a particular place, encapsulating the idea of attachment to an area people call home. This sense of belonging to one special location creates powerful emotions, for having a home territory is surely at the very foundation of personal identity, 'home' such a basic need of the soul. To be 'inside' a place is to belong to it and the more deeply inside we are – physically and spiritually – the stronger is our identity with place. The fence all around Shipley's map takes on new meaning when seen as a symbol of division, between inside and outside.

Copthorne's map makes a tree a metaphor for the community – the mighty oak symbolising the strength of community spirit, the shape of the tree creating the map itself, the village its branches. The roots beneath the tree feature family names, so that just as its roots nurture growth so the people themselves make the community; and as the tree brings forth its fruit as acorns, so these fruits encase the harvest of talent in the form of clubs and societies. This is a brilliant conception. As Sue Clifford has said, 'people and place together'.

The process of making a map of this type inevitably leads to some deep-searching discussion about what a place really *is*. How might we define a place in some form of graphic and pictorial shorthand, a whole parish compressed onto one piece of paper? The questions raised in doing this – and the answers – can reach into the very roots of how we perceive the patch – the parish – or wherever we live.

West Sussex County Council first took up the idea of parish mapping as one of several ways to celebrate the new millennium in 2000. Parish maps were felt to be ideal for making a permanent record – a snapshot in

Detail from Copthorne Parish Map, 2000

time – of places and people in the county at this key moment in the calendar. The idea proved so successful that the project has continued, and is continuing, to spread across the county. Each year more maps are being added, so that at the time of writing (in summer 2006), just over a hundred parishes have been covered. More are in the pipeline.

This book reproduces seventy-five of these parish maps, each accompanied by supporting text, written neither as a guide to the maps nor a history of each parish. The commentary is more a series of personal views and feelings to try and capture the spirit or sense of each place, about what it is that gives a place its distinct atmosphere. And, as with the maps, these are highly personal statements. In the end this approach is all about understanding the distinction between 'looking' and 'seeing' – in 'reading' a place at its many different levels. So in this way this is no conventional atlas-guidebook to the county, but a celebration of West Sussex towns and villages through this community-mapping enterprise. Hopefully, maps and text together will encourage readers to explore some of the byways of the county and perhaps even see the county in a new light.

Certainly some fascinating information has come to light, revealing all sorts of oddities in the landscape: the location of Vesuvius and Misery; the local swan called Pooh who lent his name to that most famous fictional bear in the world, Winnie; the village that moved six miles; the centre of fictional crime in a real downland setting; the village road lost daily under the tides; the beach that inspired Eric Coates to write *By the Sleepy Lagoon*; the West Sussex village that sent its name to Penang; the site of Pig City UK.

That even now some of these new maps are historic records soon after they were made is commentary enough on their value. Change creeps along our High Streets: the fascia boards of shops and businesses exquisitely painted around Henfield's map catch a glimpse of village trade that has already moved on since the millennium. And since Selsey's map was made, fields to the north-east, on the map delicately hedged, ploughed and under grass, have fallen to a flood of concrete and brick, a new gateway to this little peninsular town as it pushes towards its extremities. The Horse and Groom on Clapham and Patching's map, well-known roadside pub from coaching days and lately abandoned by the new highway, is now by-passed and marooned, and – with a new twist – re-created as the Worlds End. Peter Jerrome takes a realistic stand on his home ground: 'Even five years on there will be changes. It doesn't matter. Petworth, like anywhere, must balance change and permanence. . . . Petworth changes and will change.' Graphically we can see what has been lost as tales of our time pour from these parish maps.

Other clues hint at change in the countryside at yet another, and more discreet, level. Some of our parish maps meticulously record their distinctive field-names, like Eel Pie in Donnington, Little Earwig in Sidlesham and Bare Shins in Burpham. Local historians might assume that the names on these new maps are those documented by that major source for field-names – the tithe maps of the late 1830s and early '40s where nearly every parcel of land is given some descriptive name relating to past events or the landscape. But just as some field-names changed before tithe-map times, so some of those recorded on parish maps are a new-generation of names introduced since the early Victorian period. In Lavant the fields on both sides of the main road by the Chichester boundary are given names on the parish map not found on the tithe map of 1840. Another spot-check reveals new names on the Madehurst map, again not on the earlier tithe map of 1841. Maybe a search in other parishes would find similar changes. In little ways like this our modern parish map-makers have added to the store of local history.

Detail from Felpham Parish Map, 2000

Behind all these tales and the finished maps is the story of how some two thousand West Sussex volunteers – listed at the back of the book – came together in what continues to be one of the most remarkable community heritage projects ever undertaken across the county and how, through international conferences, its influence has spread abroad, particularly to Italy in the making of *mappe di comunità*.

What has been remarkable has been the way the project has touched so many lives. It has been the *process* of making these maps, as much as the maps themselves, that has been significant both in personal and community terms.

New facts, new skills and new horizons have been opened up, pride and local affection for the community have been raised, selling prints of the original maps has not only made thousands of pounds for good causes but turned them into excellent ambassadors for these West Sussex parishes both at home and abroad. Prints of these maps have been sent all over the country as well as to Europe, Australia, New Zealand, Japan, Canada and the United States. We know that a print of the parish map for Parham hangs somewhere on the faraway island of St Helena in the South Atlantic.

And making parish maps has been a spring-board into further action. Some groups haven't wanted to disband after finishing their maps and have kept together by starting other activities. As one group leader put it: 'It was such fun and I'm so sorry the map is finished!' One group started oral history recording, others have published books, another parish started a newsletter, one went on to create a village heritage trail, another has formed a local art society. As a stage forward from the parish map, several groups have since embarked on yet another Common Ground initiative, creating their own pictorial parish ABC through the challenge of discovering twenty-six local features that give meaning to each community.

Parish mapping in West Sussex has been an enormously liberating exercise, releasing a great deal of energy across the county. On a personal level, Fiona Gowar of Easebourne says it began a new phase in her career as an artist, starting her off in taking on commissions for portraits of houses and cherished classic cars. Pat Kettle of Redford, encouraged by the reception of her paintings for the Woolbeding and Linch map, embarked on a card and notelet business. In ways like these, the project has produced so much more than the maps themselves.

Something of the story about the project, how it worked and some of its consequences, and then its extension abroad, is outlined in appendix two towards the end of the book.

Meanwhile enjoy poring over these beautiful maps and their mass of detail and it shouldn't be hard to agree with Robert Louis Stevenson in his introductory note to *Treasure Island* that in maps there 'is an inexhaustible fund of interest for any man with eyes to see'. These maps certainly hold the key to so much West Sussex treasure right on our own doorsteps. When visitors saw them exhibited in Worthing Art Gallery a few years ago they left their comments behind: 'amazing . . . stunning . . . makes me proud to be Sussex born and bred . . . I am so pleased to live here among these lovely people and places . . . these maps deserve to be presented in book form'.

Well, in answer to all the encouragement received, here they are! We offer this book as an attempt to convey something of what has been achieved by the county's two thousand parish map-makers.

KIM LESLIE

Thanks

A SHARED ENTERPRISE of this magnitude owes much to many different people. Across the county so much goodwill has been generated over the years in making these wonderful maps – from artists, researchers, organisers and technical experts. Homes have been invaded as makeshift studios, storage areas and meeting places for months and months on end. Lives have been turned upside down as 'the map' took over. No wonder one local organiser felt lost after her map was finally unveiled. 'Every now and then this week I've had the feeling that one of the family is missing. But we're all here. What's missing is the map!' An enormous bond was created between maps and map-makers – their finished work presented here is testimony to all the thousands of hours given in love and devotion to this project that owes its origin to the work of Common Ground and its two founders, Sue Clifford and Angela King. Their tireless work throughout the UK in raising awareness about the need for local identity and local distinctiveness, through all manner of community projects, not just parish maps, has been incalculable. Our own West Sussex project is grounded in their inspired work.

I first came across parish maps when working on another mapping project at the University of Sussex. Working with cartographer Sue Rowland, the power of this type of mapping first took hold on my own imagination. Sue was firmly committed to what they stood for. She showed me Charlbury's map and then spoke of her plans for helping with one for her own East Sussex parish of Hamsey. The rest – for West Sussex – is history, thanks to Sue.

This book would certainly not have been possible without the interest of Margaret Johnson, Chairman of West Sussex County Council. She personally secured the funding necessary for its production and throughout has given her wholehearted support. With funds assured, it was then necessary to find a design team and this was eventually located through the good offices of County Councillor Phillip Coote who introduced us to Blacker Design of East Grinstead. With so many fine art books to their name, their input guaranteed the book's success from the very start. Throughout the book's preparation I have worked closely with Elwyn, Mike, Simon and David Blacker and Cindy Edler in their studio, and thank them for their constant hospitality and for all their work in ensuring the book's fine quality.

Designed in East Grinstead, much of the writing and editing took place in West Sussex Record Office at County Hall in Chichester. The facilities made available through Richard Childs, County Archivist, have been most appreciated. Especial thanks must go to Clare Snoad and David Milnes for all their scanning and computer wizardry and to my two personal assistants, firstly Janet Stevens and then later, Rosie Ritchie.

At County Hall a number of key officers have given advice and information, particularly Dr John Godfrey, then Head of Secretariat, who gave so much help and ensured that the Parish Initiatives Fund never closed its doors on the project. Chris Cousins, Head of Planning Services,

and Bob Connell, Principal Planner, discussed parish maps and how they could be used as a way of achieving community involvement in the preparation of parish plans under new planning procedures. Bob, in a very perceptive document, drew attention to the potential value of the mapping project in terms of much wider issues such as local character studies and community-managed landscapes. Keith Hardman, Senior Planner, helpfully responded to my requests for up-to-date statistical information. Sarah Burnett, our Principal Application Specialist, kindly negotiated the new Ordnance Survey composite licence to reprint parish maps previously licenced individually.

The County Library Service and University of Chichester have tracked down difficult titles and obscure articles. There are quite a lot of references to Sussex-based fiction in the text. One local author's books proved so elusive, with her nostalgic schoolgirl novels of the 1930s–50s amazingly fetching anything up to £300–£400 each. Through my sister, Jill, Ros Bayley of the Elsie Oxenham Appreciation Society put her valuable collection at my disposal so I could see what I was writing about. Shaun Cooper threw valuable light on his father, science-fiction author Edmund Cooper.

Two significant stages in the project have been the Worthing exhibition in 2001–2 and then, as a direct consequence, its dissemination in Italy. By all the reports the exhibition was a winner. It took over more than its originally allotted space and brought thousands of visitors from near and far. Much was owed to the hard work and enthusiasm of Emma Ball and Laura Kidner who were always such a delight to work with.

One very special visitor to Worthing was Donatella Murtas of the Istituto di Ricerche Economico Sociali (IRES) del Piemonte in Turin. She came to investigate the potential use of these maps in her work for the ecomuseum movement in Italy. (Ecomuseums are about living/working landscapes and local identity.) Donatella was so impressed by the work that a request was made to send the exhibition to Italy. The logistics made this out of the question, but copies of the maps were supplied and

Donatella Murtas at Pietraporzio

Photo: Kim Leslie

an exhibition, based on reproductions, was later set up in Turin and then in Pietraporzio, a small mountain village high in the Italian Alps, to inspire local people to make their own map. Encouragement for all this involvement with West Sussex owed much to Donatella's IRES director, Maurizio Maggi, and has led to my

xiii

delivering papers on the West Sussex project to conferences in Turin, Biella, Genoa and Argenta. In turn these opportunities have led to a growing network of Italian contacts all willing to share their expertise and experience. For some very fruitful discussions at meetings we have had in Chichester and Italy, particular thanks must go to Fiorenza Bortolotti, an *ecomuseo* facilitator promoting *mappe di comunità* in Trentino and Umbria.

One very special feature of the project has been the vast amount of goodwill there has been in encouraging the spread of parish mapping across the county. A vital stage in its early progress was the very successful Parish Maps Conference held in Haywards Heath in May 1999, organised jointly between West Sussex County Council, Mid Sussex District Council, Green Willow Arts Consultancy and the Sussex Wildlife Trust, all welded together by Susan Wilson of the Sussex Local Environmental Action Forum. It brought parishes together, setting up an informal network of support and mutual help that has been a key characteristic of the whole enterprise. For example, notes about making the Fernhurst map by John Tucker, and by David Morton and Roger Putnam in making their map of Walberton, circulated practical guidance and advice to any parish in need of help. Elly Spilberg and Pru Hart of Graffham organised pub meals and meetings to discuss matters of mutual mapping interest with neighbouring parishes. County Councillor Tex Pemberton used his influence to bring together parishes around Midhurst.

As with funding for this book, so funding has been necessary to underpin the whole project. Each parish needed money for materials and framing – expensive when framed to conservation standards – and as most of the map groups wanted to publish copies of their original maps, so there were printers' costs to be raised.

To make all this possible grants were made available by West Sussex County Council and by most district and parish councils. Substantial grants were made by the Millennium Festival Fund for All and its successor, Lottery Grants for Local Groups – Awards for All, Help the Aged Millennium Awards, Shell Better Britain Campaign, Rural Action for the Environment, and the Local Heritage Initiative of the Countryside Agency. Other sources were tapped, especially local business sponsorship. There were many other fund-raising initiatives. One parish raised over £3,000 through a skittles evening, turkey hunt, treasure hunt, plant sales, cream teas, a summer fête, a party and disco. The work needed to raise such substantial sums of money has meant persistence and masses of form-filling. People have given generously of their time to bring in the money. Certainly without the generous financial support of so many official bodies, private companies and individuals, the project would never have got off the ground in the first place. Their support is acknowledged on each parish map.

Whereas the majority of the book's text is mine I approached some key individuals – some professional writers in a few cases and others well-connected to where they live – asking them to add their special feel to the book. Their own personal thoughts in defining a sense of place are most valued.

Throughout the whole project my own family, Jenni, Victoria and Justin, have given an enormous amount of time and help with their opinions and comments, coming to so many parishes to help me with talks, presentations, exhibitions and unveilings as well as joining me on a great many of the enjoyable explorations needed for the preparation of this book; then, at the end, in giving some fresh eyes for all the checking, proof-reading and indexing. As ever, they have been my best support and best critics.

KIM LESLIE

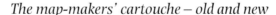

The map-makers' cartouche – old and new

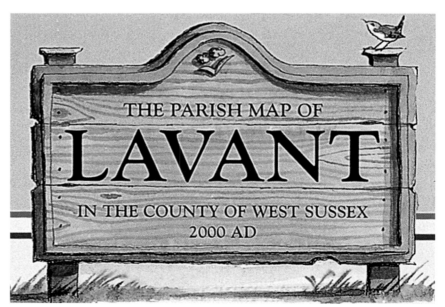

Gilded birds decorate a map of Woodmancote and Upper Beeding by Richard Dendy, 1756
WSRO. Add. Ms. 173

List of Contributing Writers

Caroline Adams is senior archivist at West Sussex Record Office, specialising in outreach activities; she is investigating hospitality in Elizabethan England for a higher degree and is part of a team preparing a new history of her own parish of Fishbourne.

Cliff Archer is a long-standing resident of Chidham actively involved in community affairs, currently as a school governor, parish councillor and parish plan co-ordinator.

Angela Bromley-Martin is Bosham's local historian; she has written several books on the history of her home parish as well as a book on Chichester Harbour.

Peter Browne has lived in Highbrook for thirty years where he works as a silversmith; as a trustee of the Highbrook Charitable Trust he organises local support for a village in Sri Lanka devastated by the recent tsunami.

Pam Bruce, author of *Northchapel: A Parish History*, researches with the Wealden Buildings Study Group and is developing a database of parish officers for West Sussex/Surrey border parishes in the 17th and 18th centuries.

Pat Carroll is a retired occupational therapist living in Hunston where she is involved in church and village affairs; she supports Chichester Harbour Conservancy as a volunteer in its educational and environmental work.

Kay Coutin has a special interest in historic buildings and their context and has recently edited *Out and About in West Hoathly West Sussex from Early Days to Modern Times* for the West Hoathly History Group.

Robert Elleray, a retired local studies librarian, is an active conservationist, vice-president of the Worthing Society and author of books on Brighton, Eastbourne, Hastings and his home town of Littlehampton, the Victorian churches of Sussex and a forthcoming publication about Sussex theatres.

Claire Foster is policy adviser to the Archbishop's Council of the Church of England, deputy director of St Paul's Institute and lay canon of St Paul's Cathedral as well as being actively involved in her local community at Highbrook.

Dr John Godfrey has lived in Arundel for more than thirty years, served as a former chairman of the Arundel Society, has written the Sussex volume in the New Shell Guides series, and has a specialist interest in landownership and agriculture on the South Downs in the 19th and 20th centuries.

Chris Hare is a West Sussex adult education manager and local historian; he lectures and has written several books on the county, including Burpham and Washington and his home town of Worthing.

Jeremy Hodgkinson, who wrote the article on Crawley Down, is a school teacher, a former parish councillor, vice-chairman of the Wealden Iron Research Group and chairman of the trustees of East Grinstead Museum.

Bridget Howard edits *Midhurst Heritage* for the Midhurst Society to which she contributes her local research, as well as having written elsewhere on Cornish beam engines, iron mining and Victorian company scams.

John Hurd of Billingshurst is a retired educational adviser and a former non-stipendary curate in the parish where he has been researching local history for some thirty years.

Peter Jerrome, MBE, chairman of both the Petworth Society since 1978 and of the Petworth Cottage Museum, is the author of some dozen books on Petworth and district.

Gaynor Marsh is a professionally-trained artist living and working at Offham, South Stoke, where she finds much of her inspiration from the surrounding countryside.

Len Milsom has lived in Loxwood for twenty-two years where he is involved in conservation and amenity work as co-chairman of the Loxwood Society.

Deborah Mitchelson is a Fine Artist who lives and works in St John's Street, Chichester. Her semi-abstract paintings of landscapes explore colour and space – see **www.deborahmitchelson.com**

Dr Ian Nelson of Hurstpierpoint is a retired dentist and the author and editor of local history books; he was awarded a postgraduate degree for his research into the poor law in mid Sussex.

Mike Oakland settled in Lurgashall ten years ago where he has been clerk to the parish council; he delights in the birdsong, wildflowers and walks of green Sussex and is currently researching into the local soldiers commemorated on the parish war memorial.

Sue Ogden started her career in journalism as a Bow Street court reporter and now, living in Heyshott, writes for the parish magazine about life and work throughout the seasons on the two local farms.

Val Porter of Milland is a professional writer and author of some forty books on countryside matters; she recently produced two volumes about the history of Milland.

Sue Ray, who did the research for the parish map of Staplefield, found this the perfect opportunity for using the skills she learnt whilst working on the landscape studies course at the University of Sussex.

Sandra Saer, a lifelong wordsmith, is a local historian, editor, bookseller and published writer and poet; under the SMH Books imprint she has published country and Sussex books and her award-winning children's book, *The Giant and the Mouse*.

Andrew Shaxson has always lived and worked in Elsted. Previously in farming, he is now fully occupied with the Environment Portfolio for Chichester District Council as well as writing regular local history articles for his parish magazine.

Dr Spencer Thomas, who has written the articles on Aldwick and Pagham, was Head of Geography between 1968 and 1996 at what is now the University of Chichester. He is the author of several school textbooks and articles for academic journals as well as *West Sussex Events: Four Centuries of Fortune and Misfortune* and a forthcoming study of settlement patterns of Sussex villages.

Michael Tibbs, OBE, has served in the Royal Navy, the Sudan political service and the AA and is a former Secretary of the Royal College of Physicians. With his wife, Anne, he has written two books on Lynchmere and one on the Sudan.

Janet Valentine has lived in Slinfold for seventeen years where she has served on the parish council for seven years, two of them as its chairman.

Heather Warne is an archivist and local historian who has lived in Worlds End, Burgess Hill, for forty years, where she has raised her family; she is president of Burgess Hill Local History Society and the archivist at Arundel Castle.

Jane Weeks, who has lived in Chichester since 1982, trained as an archaeologist and has worked in museums for more than twenty-five years.

Geoff Westcott writes a regular feature on local history for *Yapton News and Views* and is chairman of the Yapton and Ford Local History Group.

Richard Williamson managed Kingley Vale National Nature Reserve between 1963 and 1995. Author of four books and over 2,500 wildlife and other articles for the local papers, plus TV scripts and documentaries, he is the president of the Henry Williamson Society that celebrates the life and work of his father. He wrote the articles on Itchenor and Rogate.

Map-makers' corner pieces – old and new

Gilded quarter-compass from map of East Woolves in Ashington, Washington and Buncton by Samuel Jenner, 1724   WSRO. Add. Ms. 2033

'Summer' from Poling Parish Map by Valerie Shepherd, 2000

Aldwick

JUST OVER A CENTURY AGO Aldwick was being described as a 'small quiet watering place whose prosperity solely depends upon its visitors being enabled to allow their families and children to walk about on the sands and seashore and elsewhere in the locality unattended without the fear of molestation'. This idyll was still evident in February 1929 when King George V heeded the recommendation of his medical advisers to convalesce where there was a combination of sea air with a southerly exposure, protection from strong winds, privacy and reasonable access to London. These attributes, along with a reputation as a sun-trap and level ground, attracted a monarch, discerning holidaymakers and permanent residents to Aldwick.

The impetus generated by the publicity surrounding the King's convalescence in 1929 at Craigweil House, the home of Sir Arthur du Cros, pioneer of the pneumatic tyre and founder of the Dunlop Rubber Company, transformed Aldwick. As Lady Diana Cooper, the socialite whose family home was at nearby West House, wrote in her autobiography: 'soon afterwards the cornfields gave way to villadom'. The villas were rather superior structures, more accurately described as mansions, coating Aldwick with a veneer of prestige, respectability and class. Her husband – statesman and diplomat Duff Cooper who was raised to the

The Duck Pond

peerage in 1952 as the 1st Viscount Norwich of Aldwick – considered it his 'terrestrial paradise' and with his neighbours comprised a veritable 'hustings' of MPs. The 'West End' of Bognor Regis retains the aura of eminence and desirability ingrained by its early aristocratic and parliamentary residents.

At the time, Barrack, Dark, Fish and Gossamer were leafy, winding, hedge-rimmed country lanes radiating from the village core. Today, although primarily traffic arteries, they are still instantly recognisable, revealing agreeable surprises around each corner. Communal green spaces may have contracted, but Rose Green and Aldwick Green, both once much more extensive than at present, and former roadside wastes such as Trendle Green, all survive. Preservation and conservation societies protect the shrunken remnants and combat pernicious pressures threatening to violate a special environment and destroy a precious heritage. Pocket parks, areas of special character and tree wardens have been introduced to keep the characteristics that attracted the early visitors and more recent newcomers – access to the sea, trees, greenery, seclusion.

Ghosts of the former, bucolic village – green, pound, duck pond, Hundred House and rookeries stalk the streets, while blue plaques locate them and perpetuate their memories.

The Grange

Rowland Rank Centre

The Grange, Aldwick, Pryors, Willowhale and Tithe Barn farms are commemorated by road names or camouflaged as a garage or converted to apartments. Old families such as Rose, Malmayne, Blondell, Stapleton and others live on as addresses. The family of Rowland Rank, of the flour milling family – brother of J. Arthur Rank of the giant film company – lived at Aldwick Place, gifting the community a typical Sussex flint barn that now serves as a community centre. Together they constitute an indispensable catalogue of a distinctive milieu.

In the late 1920s a disciple of the Garden City Movement applied its principles and developed the Aldwick Bay Estate as an enclave for a well-to-do clientele. Generous plots, manicured verges, palm trees, weatherboarded and thatched cottages 'like overblown strays from an Essex village', and a social club in the renovated Tithe Barn, attracted an eclectic mixture of patrons. It achieved exclusivity 'in a peaceful neighbourhood not invaded by trippers and charabanc parties ... free from bands, pierrot parties and ... noise and hustle'. Changing fashions have altered the social and spatial mosaic but the aspiration, advertised in the prospectuses, 'to be like a miniature Bournemouth', remains.

Ditches and watercourses which once drained this 'fenland' sidle sinuously out of sight along roadsides, verges and back gardens only to revive during periods of exceptionally heavy rainfall. Wells that supplied drinking water have been capped. The fertile soil, a rich

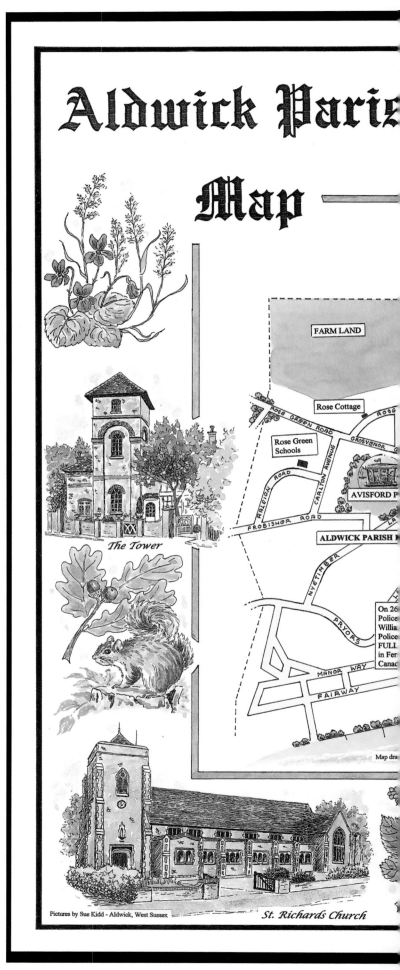

Aldwick Parish Map

FARM LAND

Rose Cottage

ROSE GREEN ROAD

Rose Green Schools

GROSVENOR

AVISFORD P

The Tower

ALDWICK PARISH

On 26 Police Willia Police FULL in Fer Cana

PRYORS

MANOR WAY

FAIRWAY

Map dra

St. Richards Church

Pictures by Sue Kidd - Aldwick, West Sussex

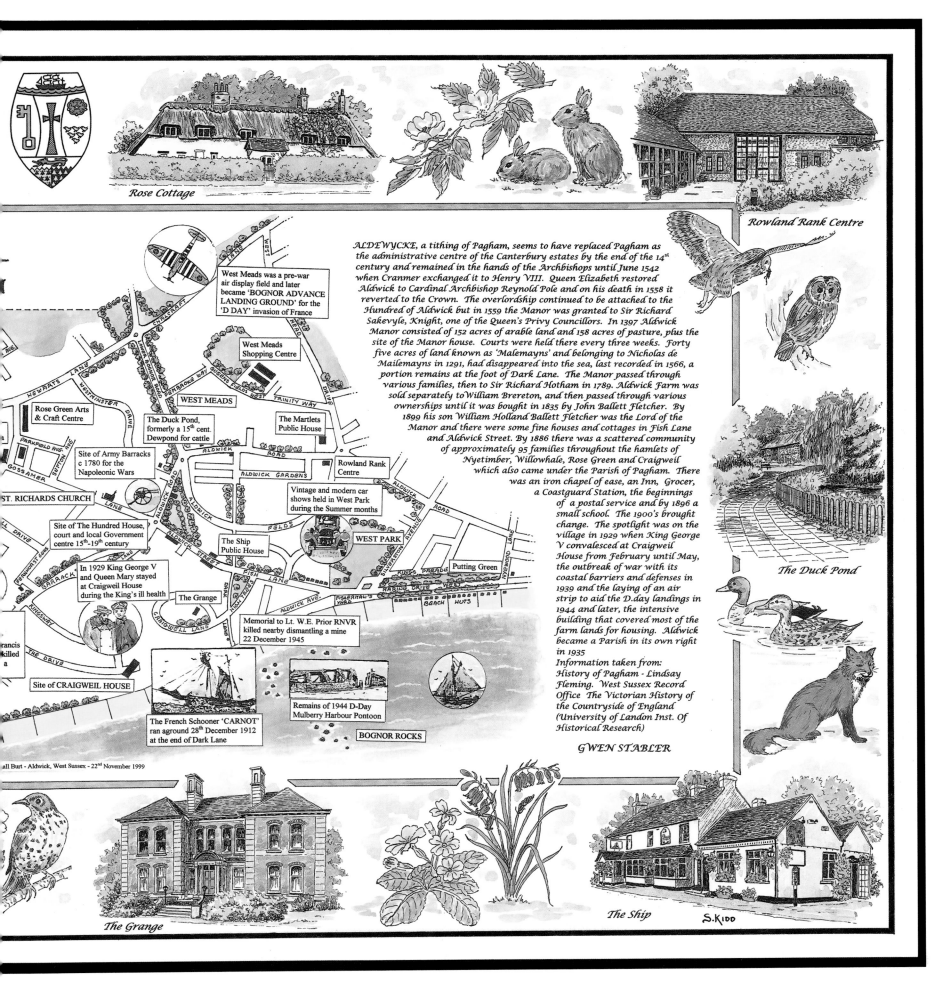

Rose Cottage

Rowland Rank Centre

West Meads was a pre-war air display field and later became 'BOGNOR ADVANCE LANDING GROUND' for the 'D DAY' invasion of France

West Meads Shopping Centre

WEST MEADS

Rose Green Arts & Craft Centre

The Duck Pond, formerly a 15th cent. Dewpond for cattle

The Martlets Public House

Site of Army Barracks c 1780 for the Napoleonic Wars

ST. RICHARDS CHURCH

Rowland Rank Centre

Vintage and modern car shows held in West Park during the Summer months

Site of The Hundred House, court and local Government centre 15th-19th century

The Ship Public House

WEST PARK

Putting Green

In 1929 King George V and Queen Mary stayed at Craigweil House during the King's ill health

The Grange

Memorial to Lt. W.E. Prior RNVR killed nearby dismantling a mine 22 December 1945

Site of CRAIGWEIL HOUSE

Francis killed a

The French Schooner 'CARNOT' ran aground 28th December 1912 at the end of Dark Lane

Remains of 1944 D-Day Mulberry Harbour Pontoon

BOGNOR ROCKS

all Burt - Aldwick, West Sussex - 22nd November 1999

ALDEWYCKE, a tithing of Pagham, seems to have replaced Pagham as the administrative centre of the Canterbury estates by the end of the 14th century and remained in the hands of the Archbishops until June 1542 when Cranmer exchanged it to Henry VIII. Queen Elizabeth restored Aldwick to Cardinal Archbishop Reynold Pole and on his death in 1558 it reverted to the Crown. The overlordship continued to be attached to the Hundred of Aldwick but in 1559 the Manor was granted to Sir Richard Sakevyle, Knight, one of the Queen's Privy Councillors. In 1397 Aldwick Manor consisted of 152 acres of arable land and 158 acres of pasture, plus the site of the Manor house. Courts were held there every three weeks. Forty five acres of land known as 'Malemayns' and belonging to Nicholas de Mailemayns in 1291, had disappeared into the sea, last recorded in 1566, a portion remains at the foot of Dark Lane. The Manor passed through various families, then to Sir Richard Hotham in 1789. Aldwick Farm was sold separately to William Brereton, and then passed through various ownerships until it was bought in 1835 by John Ballett Fletcher. By 1899 his son William Holland Ballett Fletcher was the Lord of the Manor and there were some fine houses and cottages in Fish Lane and Aldwick Street. By 1886 there was a scattered community of approximately 95 families throughout the hamlets of Nyetimber, Willowhale, Rose Green and Craigweil which also came under the Parish of Pagham. There was an iron chapel of ease, an Inn, Grocer, a Coastguard Station, the beginnings of a postal service and by 1896 a small school. The 1900's brought change. The spotlight was on the village in 1929 when King George V convalesced at Craigweil House from February until May, the outbreak of war with its coastal barriers and defenses in 1939 and the laying of an air strip to aid the D.day landings in 1944 and later, the intensive building that covered most of the farm lands for housing. Aldwick became a Parish in its own right in 1935

Information taken from:
History of Pagham - Lindsay Fleming. West Sussex Record Office The Victorian History of the Countryside of England (University of London Inst. Of Historical Research)

GWEN STABLER

The Duck Pond

The Grange

The Ship

S. Kidd

St Richard's Church

legacy deposited by the retreating ice sheet at the end of the Ice Age, underpinned a vibrant agricultural economy for hundreds of years and now deceives enthusiastic gardeners into believing that it is their green fingers that are responsible for luxuriant gardens and impressive entries for the Aldwick in Bloom competition.

The ancient territorial division of Aldwick Hundred attests to its antiquity, but its existence as a parish, independent of neighbouring Pagham, only dates from 1934 when St Richard's Church – 'beautiful' in the eyes of the Bishop of Chichester at the service of dedication, 'horrible' according to Ian Nairn in Pevsner's *Buildings of England* – replaced a little wooden-walled, tin-roofed chapel to serve the expanding community.

By The Sleepy Lagoon, a laconic melody composed by Eric Coates when he lived within sight of the shimmering blue crescent of Aldwick Bay, is germane to the allure of the parish. The tang of the salty, tonic air; the sound of breaking waves rolling stones up and down the beach until their rough edges have been smoothed into rounded pebbles; the ghostly presence of a cold fret periodically blanketing the coastline, floating inland and wrapping itself around you; the 'ocean' acting as a huge storage radiator absorbing the sun's rays in summer and releasing its accumulated heat ensuring mild winters; a water table fluctuating with the tides; lop-sided trees stripped of their seaward-facing foliage by the prevailing south-westerly winds; and the taunting

screeches of gulls seeking sanctuary from storms, all are integral to the rhythm of life in Aldwick.

The bite of the sea is fiercer than its bark. Sea Lane and Dark Lane once met at the tithing of Charlton, but both are now sawn off at the knees, leaving their feet paddling in Aldwick Bay searching for the lost village. The coastline has capitulated to incessant, insidious and occasionally violent attack by the sea. It is retreating in the face of a relentless enemy reinforced by global warming.

Preventive stations, coastguard cottages, Napoleonic barracks, horse-racing stables, greyhound kennels which once housed Rotten Row, winner of the coveted Waterloo Cup, and the Ship Inn, defer to a more racy side. Soldiers, smugglers, gamblers and house parties hosting the likes of Noël Coward, Cecil Beaton and Evelyn Waugh have all contributed to refining the personality of the parish.

From the moment it cut the umbilical cord with its parent parish of Pagham in 1934, Aldwick has lived out its biblical lifetime of three score years and ten, during which it severed its intimacy with its rural past, matured to absorb and integrate an expanding Bognor, and retired into old age with its growing pensioner population. Elderly residents remember Aldwick 'in the old days as one big happy family making our own enjoyments'. The traditional, self-contained, introspective, nostalgic Aldwick might only ever have existed in the imagination, but the qualities which conjured up that image have endured. Despite the inevitable changes, a piece of paradise has been preserved. As Richard Dally concluded in his local guide of 1828, 'Aldwick will be ever loved and admired'.

SPENCER THOMAS

The Ship

Apuldram

APULDRAM IS A VERY SPECIAL PLACE, still a little withdrawn from the modern world, like one of the minor parishes of Barsetshire. The homes of its few inhabitants are mostly scattered loosely over the flat, sweeping landscape with its beautiful cornfields and pastures, its glimpses of harbour and cathedral and the distant downs. Its village is a ghost, its little common no more. Its sturdy little church, sitting quietly like a hen on its nest . . . William Ryman's old grey tower house rising above its orchard, intriguing and mysterious, suggest memories of far off times and tales. The Manor Farm might recall the Abbey Mill Farm in Jane Austen's Emma. The hamlet and anchorage of Dell Quay with its pleasant inn and few houses speak of ancient voyages and once active trade. . . .

So the preface to Father Richard Ratcliff's parish history entices us to a landscape thick with atmosphere. Flat and watery, this harbourside parish is all about wide-open spaces, distant views and vast tracts of sky, ingredients for a moody elemental place. A striking feature of this low-lying harbour country is in the backdrop towards the rising Downs, Chichester Cathedral its focal point punctuating our mid-horizon. Hills and cathedral are a constant presence, at a distance, yet an integral part of this immediate countryside as major reference points beyond these coastal flatlands. We might be *in* Apuldram – but we are always visually within a much wider world enclosed by the distant Downs.

Writing a hundred years ago, the naturalist W. H. Hudson made the point about the 'always present' cathedral spire from here; the one feature that 'pulls' the scene together with such 'unity and distinction'. And what to him made the soaring spire of such account in the

Dell Quay

Apuldram Rose Garden

landscape was always 'The line of the downs . . . beyond'. He goes on to notice that 'Perhaps the most beautiful effect is an afternoon or evening . . . when there are clouds, but in the east and north a pale clear sky, against which the grey spire and distant downs appear sharply outlined; the earth green, but the hills in shadow deepest indigo blue'. Ever-changing colours under ever-changing skies are intensified from these wide-open spaces.

St Mary the Virgin's Church

Apuldram looks two ways, inwards as a place of the soil with its farming and famous roses, outwards as a place of water, to the seaward life, towards Chichester Harbour and its long twisting fingers linking the open sea to these more protected inland waters.

Rymans

Inward-looking Apuldram, once a thriving village, was deserted centuries ago and is now little more than a cluster of three ancient buildings – church, manor house and bulky Rymans, said to be more like a Northumbrian tower-house – its old streets nothing more than footprints in the fields, its modern population now widely scattered around the parish.

Outward-looking Apuldram is called Dell Quay, the parish's maritime quarter, once with important legal status as the Port of Chichester, shipping cargoes of farm produce, fish and oysters, timber, stone, coal and grain. Some of the last recorded shipments were from the *Will Everard* bringing in tons of oil cake and flour from London in 1935. One of four

Dell Quay: still in commercial use in the 1930s

identical sailing barges built in steel in Great Yarmouth in the 1920s, they were the largest ever built at 97 feet long, 22 feet in breadth and an internal depth of nearly 10 feet, a massive size for the little port.

Sailing at Dell Quay

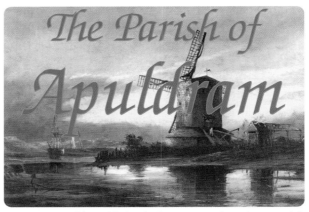

The Parish of Apuldram

Sailing at Dell Q

The Dell Quay Boat Club was formed after a gale in August 1925 wreaked havoc with moored boats. Owners struggling to refloat their craft realised that co-operation would ease the task, and later made their association permanent. The 25 founder members adopted a yellow and red burgee and had a boathouse on the quay for storing their gear.

In 1934 the burgee was registered at Lloyds, 300 yards of saltings were leased from the Ecclesiastical Commissioners, and the name was changed to The Dell Quay Sailing Club.

The following year the Club joined the Chichester Harbour Federation, leased a clubroom on the first floor of the Crown and Anchor, and held its first regatta, with prizes for swimming, diving and three sailing events. There was also reference to the first Club trophy, the 'Mr Williams Cup', now called the 'Bransby Williams Trophy.' Later that year the first commodore presented the 'Burnard Trophy', a model of the Chichester Harbour 12 Foot Restricted Class, a

In Saxon times, and for a while after the Norman conquest, the parish was part of the Manor of Bosham, and there is no separate entry in the Domesday Book. In about AD 1125 Henry I gave the demesne to the Abbot and Brethren of Battle in exchange for Reading, and in AD 1197 Battle granted possession to Sir Michael de Appeltrieham, Sheriff of Sussex. Perhaps the parish took its name from him. Old records show many different spellings - Apulderham, Apeldreham, Appeltrieham, Appledrum, but for several centuries the spelling used by the church has been Apuldram.

The parish reverted to the crown following the Dissolution of Monasteries, and in AD 1580 Elizabeth I made a grant to William, Baron Howard of Effingham. On his death it passed to his son Charles, who was Lord High Admiral and commanded the fleet that defeated the Spanish Armada.

Research by John Magilton and aerial photography for the Archaeology Database for Chichester has suggested that the Roman Stane Street originally ran from Pulborough to a Roman port at Copperas, and then on to the deep water anchorage off Bracklesham. The suggestion is that Stane Street was built to link the important trading centre at Pulborough with the port and deep water anchorage, and that the extensions from Pulborough to Dorking and from Dorking to London came later. Another interesting suggestion is that the Roman Town Noviomagus Regnensium (Chichester) was also built later with the south-east section of the city walls alongside and enclosing the road.

In the middle ages Dell Quay was the major landing place for the port of Chichester, which was reckoned the seventh in importance in all England. The navigable channel deteriorated in the 17th century, and in AD 1680 Dell Quay was the limit for sea going vessels, but coastal craft carrying corn could still reach Fishbourne, where there were several active mills.

The area of the parish is 1111 acres, and at the census in AD 1991 the population of the parish was 165.

The picturesque Crown & Anchor inn was [...] crews and stevedores working on the qua[...] villagers at Apuldram and people using the [...] As with many waterside inns of this perio[...] that candles were placed in the windows s[...] story goes that two excise men were hange[...] only five foot of headroom. A priests hole, [...] likely to have been used for hiding contraba[...] one time the local vicar was reputedly the le[...] The original very popular game of ringing th[...]

RAF Apuldram was an active airfield from May 1943 to November 1944. The runways were made of large grip metal mesh laid on grass. Sheep kept the grass short and were hopefully rounded up before aircraft took off or landed. Three squadrons of Typhoon fighter-bombers arrived first, attacking targets in Northern France. In April 1944, three Czech squadrons of Spitfires arrived and were active over France before covering the allied invasion on D-Day. The Apuldram squadrons sadly lost 16 pilots during the Normandy campaign. A Polish squadron of Spitfires arrived in June for two weeks, and the airfield was finally closed in November.

The HQ and control room were at New Barn, and the main access was via Oak Street.

The painting, by Hoffmann, shows Typhoons of 181 Squadron. The building on the left is the Black Horse.

The Salt Industry

Salterns Copse, by Chichester Marina, takes its name from the salt pans which at one time were located nearby. The Domesday book records 285 salt pans on the Sussex coast. As the tide rose, sea water was collected in shallow square pans with clay bottoms and was reduced by the sun to strong brine, which was boiled in shallow iron vessels. The salt crystals in the residue were used medicinally and to preserve meat and fish.

Seventeenth century legislation protecting North-country salt killed off most of the Sussex industry. Apuldram survived until mid nineteenth century, when free trade laws opened the market to continental imports.

The Last Cargo Leaves Dell Quay
Loading Sugar Beet from Apuldram Manor Farm in 1934

RULES & REGULATIONS
To be observed by Masters of Ships and Vessels coming to load and unload at

DELL QUAY

1.– Before coming alongside Masters shall apply to the Quay Master for a berth and shall anchor, moor and place the Ship or Vessel as the Quay Master may direct.

2.– All Ships and Vessels coming to load or unload at the Quay shall take their turn in regular rotation of arrival, and if required by the Quay Master shall shift their berths when partly unloaded and remove to other Quay berths, or lie in a second or third tier when the Quay Master shall deem it absolutely requisite.

3.– Masters and their mates lying at the head of the Quay shall at high water time be ready when required to slack their chains and warfs, and to have their jib and mizen booms and running bowsprits rigged close in to allow free egress and ingress to the side berths.

4.– Immediately a Cargo is discharged Masters shall haul out from the Quay berths, unless specially allowed to remain by the Quay Master or compelled by stress of weather.

5.– Traders desiring to deposit goods will be allowed to do so on the bay made for the purpose at a charge of 1d per ton per week or any part of a week, but no goods on any pretext, will be allowed to remain longer than ten days.

BY ORDER S. SIMMONDS Quay Master

TO THE PUBLIC.
William Penn
...
Now selling at 36s per Chaldron,
...
Chichester, March 10, 1817.

Apuldram – the old village

In the 10th century, during the reign of Edward the Confessor, one of the six canons of the College of Bosham was Prebend of Apuldram, and paid a deputy (vicar) to live in and care for the parish, so it seems reasonable to suppose that there was a village with a church at that time.

Rent lists dated 1321 and 1432 show about 30 dwellings in Apuldram. Both lists refer to the streets shown on the map, though the references are not easily interpreted.

There is little difference in the number of villagers before and after the arrival of the Black Death in England in 1349, so it seems that it was not the direct cause of the later desertion of the village. Only the church, the Manor and Rymans now remain.

The Parish Church of St Mary the Virgin

The church in its present form was built in the middle of the thirteenth century as a chapel of ease by the monks of Bosham, who said daily services, for which they received seven shillings and sixpence per year.

The chancel has beautifully proportioned triple lancet windows with Purbeck marble shafts and stone mouldings. Behind the pulpit is part of a stone staircase, which once led to a rood-loft, a narrow gallery across the church.

The altar stands on Victorian tiles, but those in the first pavement by the rails are mediaeval with some modern replacements. A crusaders floor slab lies on the south side of the sanctuary.

The south aisle was added a hundred years later and has a squint cut near the organ. The wooden screen by the door is 15th century. The porch east window has a scratch sundial; the window jamb acted as the sundial style until the outer flintwork and stone surround were added, when the window was glazed. The font is 12th century: its centre shaft is the original; the others are later replacements. The handsome oak pews are modern.

The entire roof was restored in 1870 and further complete re-tiling was completed in 1999.

Apuldram Manor

The north face of this early seventeenth century house has a picturesque Dutch gable, rare in this part of the country at that time. Soon after its construction it was bought by William Smyth of Binderton. It passed, via his great-grand-daughter Mary to her husband William Hamilton and stayed in that family for a century and a half. The house was owned at one time by Sir William Hamilton, Ambassador to the Court of Naples, whose wife was Emma, Lady Hamilton, Lord Nelson's paramour. The property was bequeathed in AD 1872 to the Lord Bishop of Winchester, and now belongs to the Church Commissioners.

Apuldram Rose Garden

Transformed over fifteen years from an orchard, the rose garden at Apuldram Manor contains over 300 different varieties, including ramblers, climbers, shrub roses, tea roses, floribundas and miniatures.

Rymans

At the end of the twelfth century Sir Michael de Appeltrieham owned several hundred acres of the parish, including this property. The earliest recorded house on the site was built for Chauns in the thirteenth century, and at the beginning of the fifteenth century William Ryman added the three storey tower and the south wing shown in the picture. Despite many later demolitions and additions, William Ryman's house was probably much the same size as it is to-day.

Ryman was a prominent lawyer and his son, Sir William Ryman, was Sheriff of Sussex. The Ryman family held the estate for nearly two centuries until it was bought in AD 1619 by William Smyth of Binderton. After a suit in Chancery it was divided in AD 1730 between the two daughters of George Smyth: Rymans and some three hundred acres went to Barbara, wife of the Rev Walter Barttelot; the Manor and the same amount of land went to Mary, wife of William Hamilton. The lovely gardens are opened to the public several times a year.

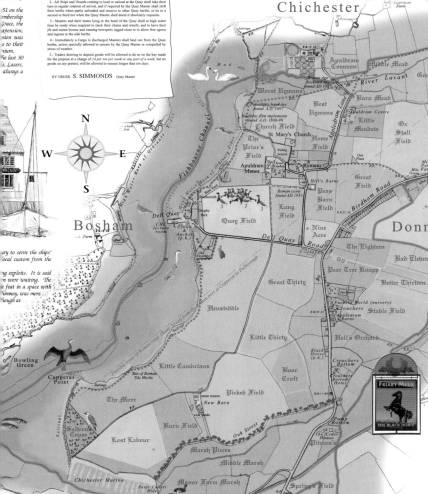

The Peter Catlett Memorial Hide

Apuldram Manor Farm Marsh lies between Oak Street and the Canal, and is a nesting site and haven for a variety of bird and other wild life. The hide, overlooking the marsh, was built in 1997 by the Friends of Chichester Harbour, as a memorial to their former Chairman, Peter Catlett, naturalist and environmentalist.

Bird Watching

The Great Fight

"This morning, at an early hour, The road was covered with vehicles of every description, and the numerous barouches and four were filled with swells of the first quality." So wrote the reporter of the Sussex Chronicle on June 8, 1824, describing the prelude to a unique day in the annals of Chichester. The prize ring championship of All England was to be held in Apuldram. The champion, Tom Spring, was to meet the Irish challenger, John 'Pat' Langan.

The rules of the prize ring allowed wrestling as well as bare knuckle fighting. The fight was held in a field, now known as Spring's Field, bordering the Chichester Canal. The location was kept secret until the last moment for fear that the law would intervene.

The fight lasted 77 rounds and one hour forty minutes! The two were evenly matched at first. Round 13 - both men were sick. Round 19 - Spring's left hand was injured, and Langan got ready for the kill. Round 30 - an hour had passed, and betting was now on Spring. Round 46 - Langan was exhausted but wouldn't give up. Round 75 - Langan was unable to see, but battled on. Round 77 - The umpires said it would be cruel to go on, and declared Spring the winner.

HISTORY OF THE GREAT FIGHT BETWEEN Spring & Langan, FOR THE CHAMPIONSHIP OF ENGLAND, AND One Thousand Sovereigns, ON Tuesday, June 8, 1824;
TO WHICH IS ADDED, THE WHOLE OF THE CORRESPONDENCE RELATIVE TO THE DISPUTED POINTS ON THEIR FIRST BATTLE; WITH THEIR LIVES AND PORTRAITS.
London: PRINTED BY AND FOR HODGSON & CO. No. 10, NEWGATE-STREET.
One Shilling.

0   1 km   1 mile

Based on Ordnance Survey six inch to the mile maps, revision 1938.

The presence or absence of a detail on the map should not be taken as evidence of a right of way, a boundary or other feature. Efforts have been made to update the information shown, but there has been no detailed survey and private property has not been entered.

Sponsors: Help the Aged; West Sussex County Council; Chichester District Council.

Contributors: Fred Dickin; Jill Dickin; Suzanna Gayford; John Gostling; Sylvia and Christopher Hoare; Chris Keville; Ian Manning; Bill Mason; Sally Mason; Di Sawday; Lorraine and Matthew Sawday; Linda Wilkinson, Rymans Riding School; Bob Clark, Blacksmith; Crown & Anchor public house.

Cartographer: Nathalie Johns McGinty.

Artists: Jill Dickin; Tom Groom; Hoffman; Ian Manning; Harold Nibbs.

Editor: Ian Manning.

Printed in April 2000 by: the Print Unit, the Tannery, Westgate, Chichester PO19 3RH

Prepared by the Apuldram Millennium Group as part of the West Sussex Millennium Map Project.

The Crown & Anchor

Great opportunities for bird watching

Such commerce is long dead and gone, the old sailing ships and chugging steamers no more, replaced by very different craft, the yachts and dinghies that make this a sailors' paradise. More people than ever come here, for Dell Quay is one of Chichester Harbour's magnets with its waterside pub, sailing club, launching facilities and boatyards. It's the birthplace of the famous *Dell Quay Dory*, the amazingly popular little boat that has taken the name of this tiny place all around the world. The Quay is also home to Chichester Harbour Conservancy's Education Centre where all sorts of courses on the appreciation of wildlife and ecology make it the gateway to learning about this inspirational environment. Children and adults love this place alongside the mud and water.

And what of these two names themselves, Dell Quay and Apuldram? Names as picturesque as their setting, they invest these special places with so much historical meaning and understanding. The channel leading up to Fishbourne was once known in 13th-century documents as 'La Delle', and on Saxton's Sussex map of 1575 is marked as 'Delle flu', from the Latin meaning flow or river. Place-name specialists suggest that the Dell element might refer to the dip in the channel bed that made navigation over these shallow waters possible. Then there's Apuldram, probably meaning the village of apples. Originally Saxon, the name metamorphosed down the centuries as Apeldreham, Appeldoreham, Apultreham, Apuldreham, before more modern standardisation took over. But unlike most other places there's not even agreement today. Whilst the church, the parish meeting and most local people insist its Apuldram, others, such as the district council, persist with Appledram. Confusingly we find Apuldram Manor House in Appledram Lane. Who owns and controls the place name? The little matter shows up two quite different perceptions about local identity. . . .

KIM LESLIE

Dell Quay

Arundel

ARUNDEL IS A HILL TOWN – and that's something you can easily miss on an aerial photograph. Arundel's millennium 'map' is actually a photograph of the town and its surroundings from the air. Whilst this graphically illustrates the compactness of the place and the greenness of its setting, it conceals the essence of the town's appeal deriving from its position on a bluff of the South Downs with its characteristic, almost French, skyline of castle, church and cathedral commanding the valley of the river Arun.

The old town occupies much the same boundaries as it did a thousand years ago, when a settlement developed around the castle originally built by Roger de Montgomery, William the Conqueror's lieutenant, to defend his lands in western Sussex. Roger built the castle here because of the strategic importance of the site: from the high ground rising from the river valley he could control the road crossing the Arun, England's second fastest flowing river, at the point nearest the sea at which it could conveniently be forded or bridged.

Arundel and the Arun are indivisible. No-one knows whether the town derives its name from the river, or the other way round. The very ambiguity serves to emphasise the bond between the two. The main coast road through

Sussex, probably developed originally by the Romans, crosses the river here and the river itself was of vital importance for transport and trade, large masted ships plying upstream to the busy wharves of the port of Arundel until late in the 19th century, exchanging coal and manufactured goods for corn, wool, timber and hides.

No wonder then that a location of such strategic and commercial importance has enjoyed a long association with one of the

most powerful aristocratic families of England. The Dukes of Norfolk have owned the castle, much of the town and the surrounding agricultural estate since the 16th century and are still resident in Arundel today. The original stone castle built in the reign of Henry II was largely destroyed during the English Civil War in the 1640s when Arundel was held for the king. The castle we see today, and many of the buildings in the town, are much more recent than they seem, and date from the late 19th century.

Each age has contributed to the urban fabric of Arundel. The parish church of St Nicholas was built in the 14th century, many timber-framed houses in the Conservation Area date from the 16th and 17th centuries and the fine gentlemen's houses and the Norfolk Arms coaching inn from the 18th century. The contribution made in the 19th century, under the direction of Henry, the 15th Duke, was of particular importance. Henry rebuilt the castle and built what is now the Roman Catholic cathedral, the Catholic and Church of England schools, the imposing post office at the junction of the High Street and Mill Road, and the new tree-lined avenue which he laid out from the heart of the town to Swanbourne Lake in the castle park.

Downriver from the old town bridge

Post Office and Castle

Chequerboard-patterned gable in the High Street

Statue of the 15th Duke's patron saint, the Emperor Henry II, in Maltravers Street

Many of the most attractive domestic and agricultural buildings in the town and on the estate, with their characteristic steeply-pitched roofs and colour-contrasting brickwork, were the work of father and son team, George and Walter Heveningham, successively clerks of works to the estate in the late 19th century. Others were the responsibility of nationally-known architects, including Joseph Hansom who designed the famous horse-drawn cab.

All this went on within the old urban core of Arundel, in what is now the Conservation Area. To the west, between the Ford and Chichester roads, an area of new housing developed in the early 20th century, partly in the adjoining parish of Tortington. Large villas first appeared on the heights of Torton Hill, commanding views of the castle and town, later complemented by more modest private and social housing on the lower slopes. The area was incorporated within the parish of Arundel in the 1980s and features quite rightly on the millennium map. But as the map shows very clearly, the old town and the new remain divided by the busy A27 trunk road, with severe congestion at peak times.

The historic town huddles the river

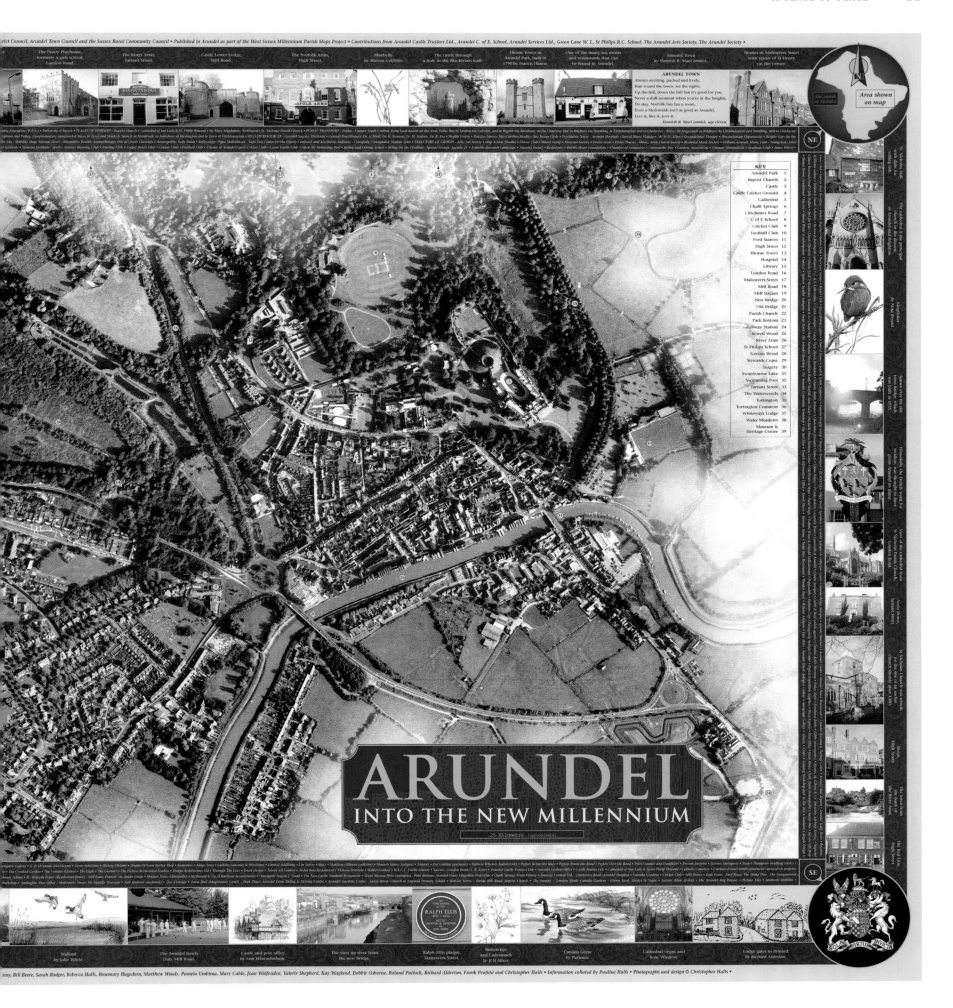

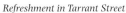
Refreshment in Tarrant Street

The French-gothic Cathedral of Our Lady and St Philip Howard

Nevertheless, Arundel – and in particular the Conservation Area – is an immensely attractive place in which to live, a fact reflected in the cost of property in the town. The place is small enough for people to know one another and to share their common love for the town. Creative people have been drawn to Arundel over the years and the cultural activity of the town is celebrated during the annual summer festival. Antique shops have proliferated, art galleries have opened up and there are plenty of places where visitors can find a cup of tea. Arundel has a successful monthly farmers' market and is rapidly establishing itself as a centre for specialist shopping and good restaurants and bars. With so many businesses keeping open on a Sunday, the town is particularly lively with visitors when most other small towns are shut up and silent.

To climb up Parson's Hill to school or cathedral on a frosty morning, to watch cricket in the summer on the castle ground as the Duke of Norfolk's XI takes on the touring side, to stroll down Mill Road in the calm of a summer evening, to shelter under rugs and waterproofs in the open-air theatre, to enjoy a pint of *London Pride* in the King's Arms, these are all pleasures which Arundel has to offer. The Duke and Duchess invited the whole town to join them in the castle on the first day of January 2000 to celebrate the new millennium. As we enjoyed their generous hospitality and each other's company, many would have agreed with Hilaire Belloc that Arundel and the Arun Valley are indeed 'a jewel for which the whole county of Sussex was made'.

JOHN GODFREY

Balcombe

PEOPLE MATTER! There's no other West Sussex map making the point in such a lively pictorial way: that a place is defined as much by its people as the environment in which they live. Buildings, scenery and landscape are crucial in the make-up of any place, but the contribution of people in bringing it alive is the one vital ingredient transforming a 'place' into a 'community'. Maybe this goes without saying, but it's unusual to be emphasised like this on a parish map.

So with fifty people chosen to represent Balcombe as a community, here's a massed portrait of village people at the millennium. (To identify them all with names, even down to Tigger the dog out with the ramblers, a chart hangs next to the framed original in the Victory Hall.)

As people are such a major feature of Balcombe's map, this is the opportunity to mention some other key figures: the artists who gave form to all the ideas that came out of the map team's deliberations.

Three local artists created this three-sectioned map. Michael Noble did two thirds: the people on the left side, and the parish map itself on the right. On the people-side the idea was to celebrate the parish as a thriving and diverse community and give a good indication of contemporary fashions and village activities. Those shown represent nearly all the clubs, societies and essential services in the village.

On the map-side are the main landscape features of the parish, plus the village-centre inset highlighting shops, services and – unusually for a parish map – the location of some significant occupations such as three artists, two airline pilots, one teacher and a nurse. Michael's work for this type of detail built on forty years as a freelance, illustrating TV magazines like *TV21* and *Look-in* with series that became household names. *Thunderbirds, Captain Scarlet, Worzel Gummidge* and *Follyfoot Farm* were all commissions executed in his Balcombe studio. More recently he designed the parish flag symbolising the ancient iron industry, Balcombe Viaduct, Balcombe Lake and Balcombe Forest. For the church he designed both a new lychgate and a stained glass window to remember local people who have given service to village and country.

Tessa Land-Smith worked on the central framework of local flora and fauna. Life in the sky includes a jet from Gatwick – the village is right under a flight-path and is seconds from the runway. Produce from local gardens is in the trug – a special wooden basket traditionally made in Sussex – and there is jam and home-made baking. Her two sons, William and Jonathan, can be found in the leaves and tree. Tessa is a freelance artist and magazine illustrator.

Within Tessa's decorative framework are some of the main buildings around the village centre by Roger Reese, Head of Design and

Post Office

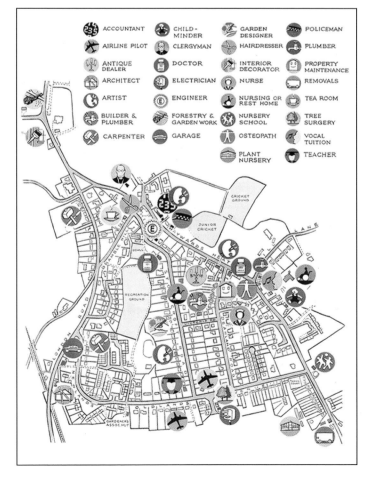

Victory Hall

Technology at Angmering School where he specialises in teaching art. He says that drawing and painting keep him sane! Conveniently, Roger was Chairman of the Balcombe Footpaths and Countryside Association that ran the map project on behalf of Balcombe Parish Council.

Their huge map is not the first local art work to find a permanent home in the Victory Hall. Around the hall's interior walls are three massive frescoes on the theme of War and Peace painted just after the First World War by

Neville Lytton who lived at nearby Crabbet Park. The single dead soldier carried by the stretcher party against a background of desolation, of broken and scarred trees, is emblematic of the horrors of the trenches he knew from personal experience in Flanders. In poignant contrast is the hope of peace – of music and dance amongst the healthy growth of Wealden oak trees with a familiar backdrop: the South Downs crowned by its clump of beeches at Chanctonbury. On one side is

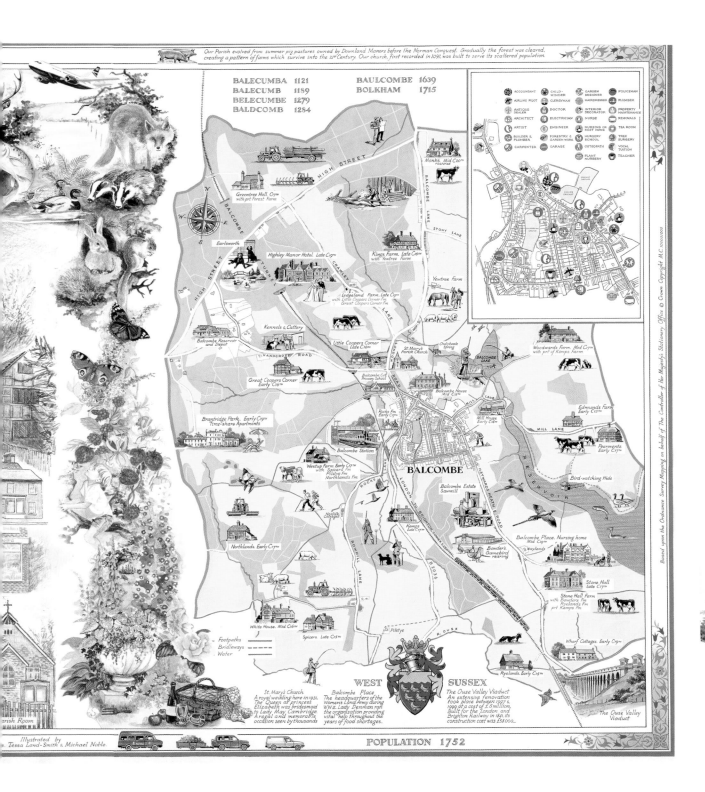

Balcombe church, on the other, men at work building Balcombe's memorial to the war – the Victory Hall. Several well-known local people are distinguishable. The lady looking at the architect's plans for the new hall is Lady Denman.

Lady Denman (1884–1954) is one of the legends of Balcombe, whose wealth, generosity and kindness are still remembered with great affection. Her father, Viscount Cowdray, gave her the three thousand-acre Balcombe Estate

where she did do so much for her tenants and the village. Her enthusiasm, influence and money ensured the completion and decoration of the Victory Hall. On the national stage of public affairs, she was the driving force behind the National Federation of Women's Institutes as its first chairman for thirty years – hence their college near Abingdon is named in her memory as Denman College. Her other claim to fame is that she led the Women's Land Army as its director throughout the Second World

CLUBS AND ORGANISATIONS

St Mary's Parish Church
United Reformed Church
Catholic Church
'61 Club
Badminton   Davis
      "   Minton
      "   Ladies Aft.
      "   Social Club
Balcombe Care Group
Balcombe Estate
Balcombe Forest W.I.
Balcombe W.I.
Balcombe School
Bowls Club
B.W.T.A.
Cranbrook Nursery Sch.
Christmas Tree Society
Cricket Club & Juniors
Cubs
District Councillor
Flower Club
Football Clubs

Footpaths & Countryside
   Association
Gilletts Surgery
Gardeners' Association
Honeywood Playgroup
Junior Church
Middy Village News
Mother & Toddler Group
Mothers' Union
Neigbourhood Watch
Parish Council
P.T.A.
Rapha House Surgery
Rifle & Pistol Club
Royal British Legion
School of Dance
Scouts
Social Club
Stoolball Club
Tennis Club
Victory Hall Man. Com.
Yoga Class

War, making its headquarters at Balcombe Place where her home became offices and home for fifty staff. Throughout the war the Land Army's equipment and uniforms were all stored here and distributed nationwide as railway freight from Balcombe. Through her two great national organisations, plus all her other good works, she really put Balcombe on the map.

Just as the Victory Hall was being finished in 1923, another personality of the day was expressing his own joy for Balcombe and its country life. This was E.V. Knox – known as 'Evoe' – writer and then editor for *Punch*. The strains of London urged him to find a place in the country where he could keep hens, grow vegetables and put up a swing for the children, and yet still be within a train's ride of his office. He found Balcombe, on the main London-Brighton line, settling at Trent House by the village green. His pen never still, Evoe put together a little book, *An Hour from Victoria* (1924), made up of conversation pieces that had previously appeared in *Punch* about village and country life in and around Balcombe, thinly disguised as 'Bittleigh'. The nation knew all about life in Bittleigh with its Sussex yokels stuck in the countryside with all their odd ways.

Just as it had brought new possibilities into Evoe's life, so it was the railway that transformed the village into prime commuter territory. Local symbols of this great transport revolution are in two massive Victorian railway works below and above the parish. Balcombe Tunnel drives the line deep under the forest; Balcombe Viaduct soars gracefully across the Ouse Valley, one of the finest in the country, an ornament in its natural setting. This much photographed viaduct is yet one more fitting tribute to the endeavours of so many talented people, past and present, who have left their mark so strongly on Balcombe's life. As this map emphasises, people matter!

KIM LESLIE

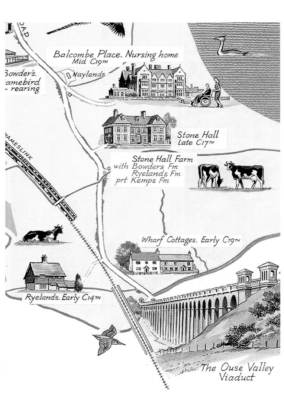

Balcombe Place. Nursing home Mid C19th
Wayland's
Bowder's gamebird-rearing
Stone Hall Late C17th
Stone Hall Farm with Bowders Fm Ryelands Fm prt Kemps Fm
Wharf Cottages. Early C19th
Ryelands. Early C14th
The Ouse Valley Viaduct

Balcombe Station

Billingshurst

BILLINGSHURST IS AN ANCIENT, scattered parish straddling the Adur-Arun watershed. Within its bounds are the hamlets of Five Oaks, Parbrook, Adversane, Newbridge and Coneyhurst. Some of our ancient farms still occupy boundaries established before the Norman Conquest. Most of the older houses are not visible from any road. There is evidence of a Mesolithic community thriving some nine thousand years ago on a sandy hill overlooking the river Arun. Bronze Age axes have been found here. Our High Street is part of the Roman road, Stane Street, built from Chichester to London in the first century of the first millennium. Some of our old footpaths may even pre-date this road.

The parish is still largely farmland, but very few residents now work in agriculture or related services. Local commerce and industry grew from the boost given by the Wey and Arun Canal, opened in 1816, and the coming of the railway in 1859. Today people commute to London, Crawley and Gatwick Airport. Many of our local businesses are in highly specialised activities, including toolmaking, like our Mesolithic forebears.

Despite new housing developments, local people are still very aware of belonging to a recognisable community. The range of clubs and societies testifies to this. Until fairly recently we were quite sure that we lived in a village. Now Billingshurst is coming to terms with being a small town. The population in 2001 stood at 6,531, but is now nearer eight thousand with the massive house-building that has followed the opening of the new bypass. We wanted our map to capture not only the *look* but also the *feel* of the place, especially at a time when our sense of place seemed to be threatened. Indeed to create this sense of place was our chief objective in making the map. Are we a big village, or a small town? Whatever we are, we want to try and preserve as much as we can of the good points of our older environment as we are inevitably pushed towards even more development.

We also wanted to inform and delight and show the full extent of the parish served by the parish council. We wanted old residents to recognise their own experiences, hoping that the hundreds of new ones would be able to sense something of the richness of the growing community.

A small team set out to gather the names of all the businesses in the parish, a mammoth undertaking. They are all recorded on the border of the map. Also included are the names of some of our farmers. Contacting

High Street

New bypass

River Arun at Newbridge

each of the clubs and societies, asking each for a logo, took persistence, but proved fruitful. One of the artists visited the playgroups and schools to ask pupils how they would like to be represented. Their wishes were met and we added the names of the heads and chairs of governors. We were able to add the names of all the children who started in the infants school in 2000. There are also many more names – our MP, county, district and parish councillors, firemen, doctors, dentists and library staff, as well as the parish map team, with a special thank-you to our sponsors. This was our way of seeing that the map was as much about people as about buildings.

Another team was that of the artists who did the paintings especially for the map. There are buildings from every century and every style. Since we were marking a point in time we also put in all the public clocks dating from the early 18th century to the most modern one, set above a new shop in Jenger's Mead just days before the map went to the printer.

BILLINGSHURST at the MILLENNIUM

Map labels (place names):

LEVERANGE · SPURLAND · POUNDS · RIDGES · WINSTRILLS WOOD · GOLDINGS · GRAININGFOLD · BUCKMANS · SLINFOLDLAND · OKEHURST · COPPID HALL · JEFFRIES · SUMMERS · WOOD DALE · LAYHOLD · TEDFOLD · FRATTS · ROWNER · TOWNLAND · HILLAND · WOODHOUSE · EATONS · PRIORS · EAST LAND · GUILDENHURST MANOR · WOODISHANS · DUCKMORE · HOILE · ROWFOLD · WILDERN · HOOK · PRATTS · DAUX · DIGGLES · ROSIER · DUNCANS · FEWHURST · PALMERS · NARBROOK · ANDREWS · GILMANS · KINGSFOLD · JEFFRIES · SLAUGHTERS (Court Farm) · LORDINGS · BEEK · FOWLERS · FRITHWOOD FARM · CAPLINS · SOUTHLANDS · MARRINGDENE · SOUTHHOUSE · COOMB LAND · LEE PLACE · HADFOLD · WELLERS · JACKMANS · CROUCHLAND · BRIGGS · HIGHFURE

THE KINGS ARMS · SIX BELLS · THE RAILWAY INN — WHITBREAD — WINES·SPIRITS·BAR·GAMES · CRICKET CLUB · LOCAL HISTORY SOCIETY · WI MARKETS · BILLINGSHURST SOCIETY · BILLINGSHURST IN BLOOM · GROUP HEDGE DATING

N 2000

1 MILE

Millennium Map celebrates our past & present & is dedicated to the future. ∞ The work was done by local people – we did not have space to include all the ideas. ∞ The information refers to January 1st 2000. ∞ We hoped to include every society & business & apologise to anyone we have missed.

Billingshurst Population	
1641	est 1003
1801	1164
1851	1458
1901	1591
1951	2955
1981	5425
2001	6000+

Billingshurst is in the County of Sussex. in the low clay Weald Forest. Clay is very good for oak, trees. ∞ Before the canal in the 18th century and the railway in the 19th century, travel was difficult for many months in the year. Perhaps this is why nothing spectacular happened here & nobody very famous lived here. ∞ Some footpaths & lanes probably date from the Saxon period – some may be much older than Roman Stane Street. ∞ Some hedges are rich in species & may be 1000 years old. ∞∞∞∞

We included our fire engine, milk float, dustcart and post-people. Although some had doubts, we included our 'Tardis' public lavatory and our newly-issued wheelie bins. There are a few 'hidden' references – for example a Land Rover, without any information that it was the brainchild of a Billingshurst man.

The library very kindly helped to sell copies of the map and the local bookshop took a large stock without any profit to themselves, all receipts going to a local medical charity. Maps were sold at village fêtes and at every local function generous enough to offer us a facility. The map was well received. We were very pleased that all the work, including the printing, was carried out in Billingshurst.

The original map was accepted by the parish council for permanent display in the new village hall and then the affairs of the map group were wound up. Its funds were given to medical charities, various children's groups, including the schools, youth projects, and the Scouts and Guides. The largest single donation went to upgrade recreational facilities at the Women's Hall for mothers and toddlers. The remaining stock was given to Billingshurst Rotary for its charitable fund-raising.

Copies of the map have been sent to every continent, and sent as gifts to Billingshurst's German twin town, Scheinfeld. Perhaps the most satisfying remark came from a long-standing resident when she said that she found something new every time she looked at it. Another lady said 'It makes me smile!' and one little boy who saw the map on sale at the village fête announced that his name was on the map – perhaps he will show it to his grandchildren! One copy was sealed in Horsham District Council's 'Time-Capsule 2000' with other local artefacts and placed under the sundial centrepiece of Horsham's new Forum.

Making the map started us all thinking about Billingshurst's local character, especially about building styles used around the parish. We weren't at all happy at the prospect of more and more development having little or no regard to the locality. One of our map team, a district councillor and her husband, decided to draw up their own design brief which was eventually accepted by the principal developer of many of the new houses. Most of us now feel that these houses sit well on what used to be old cow pastures. This then led on to influencing the design of other development in the High Street, so in its own way the map has played its part in Billingshurst's more modern look.

JOHN HURD

Streele

Lakers Meadow

Bolney

Bishop of Chichester presents Sussex's First Parish Pump Priming Award

These were the headlines from David Bellamy's Conservation Foundation reporting the award it made to the Bolney Local History Society for its Jubilee Parish Map in November 2002.

Launched just months earlier, these Parish Pump Priming Awards represent a brand new initiative aimed at supporting local community projects. It put Bolney amongst the first half-dozen parishes in the UK singled out for one of these awards. They have been given to help a great many projects, from making a rope bridge for squirrels, to tree maintenance, nest boxes for sparrows, repairing a windmill and churchyard restoration. Bolney's award for £500 was the first in the country given for a parish map, highlighting the potential of this type of map for raising awareness about the local environment.

On presenting the award to Bryan Davies, leader of the map team, the Bishop of Chichester, the Right Reverend John Hind, said that it gave him 'huge pleasure to present the Parish Pump Priming Award to Bolney. As a village you have so much to offer from the perspective of historic, social and commercial interests. In somewhat fancy modern parlance that is part of what is meant by biodiversity. Bolney's identity ranges from the mixed woodland of the High Weald to low-lying mill ponds and streams and if you look carefully at the Jubilee Parish Map you will see how much

this particular parish has to offer both as regards public and more secret treasures.'

Bolney's treasures spread across the whole map. Its wildlife – trees, flowers, birds, butterflies, fungi and fish – point to a rich countryside of ancient woodland, mixed farmland of arable and pasture (differentiated by a coloured key) and a string of ponds. Landscape variety is the keynote; quite significantly the High Weald Landscape Trail (ninety miles from Horsham to Rye) is routed right through the parish.

So many of its buildings are treasured because they sit so comfortably within the landscape that made them, constructed centuries ago from local materials – of timber and brick and roofed in tiles or massive Horsham slabs – made of the very earth from which they have sprung. That's why the main street is so attractive. Beyond the village core are some outstanding specimens of historic houses; over forty are listed buildings. One exceptional example is timber-framed Homewood House, now deceptively tile-clad on the exterior. Dating from about 1300–30, this is one of the earliest medieval houses in Sussex. More apparent in its use of great timbers is the Bolney Stage pub and restaurant, dating from about 1500. Then there is Bolney's most outlandish pile, once used as a film set for Hammer Films' horror movies – the turreted French château-style Wykehurst Park built in the 1870s for Austrian merchant banker Henry Huth.

The Eight Bells and Long House

Homewood House

Wykehurst Park

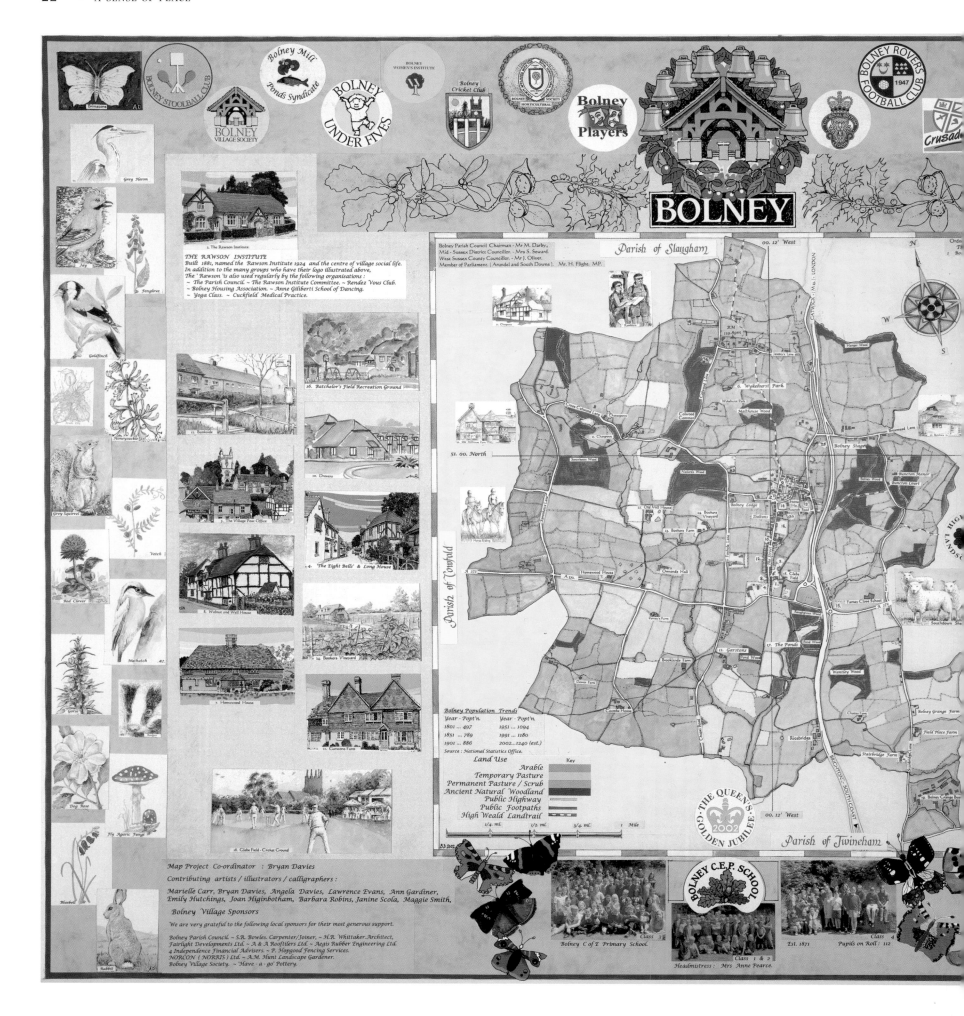

BOLNEY

THE RAWSON INSTITUTE
Built 1881, named the Rawson Institute 1924 and the centre of village social life.
In addition to the many groups who have their logo illustrated above,
The 'Rawson 'is also used regularly by the following organisations :
~ The Parish Council. ~ The Rawson Institute Committee. ~ Rendez Vous Club.
~ Bolney Housing Association. ~ Anne Giliberti School of Dancing.
~ Yoga Class. ~ Cuckfield Medical Practice.

Bolney Parish Council Chairman - Mr M. Darby.,
Mid - Sussex District Councillor. - Mrs S. Seward.
West Sussex County Councillor. - Mr J. Oliver.
Member of Parliament. (Arundel and South Downs). Mr. H. Flight. MP.

Parish of Slaugham

Parish of Cowfold

Parish of Twineham

Bolney Population Trends
Year - Popt'n.   Year - Popt'n.
1801 ... 497   1951 ... 1094
1851 ... 789   1991 ... 1180
1901 ... 886   2002...1240 (est.)
Source : National Statistics Office.

Land Use
Key
Arable
Temporary Pasture
Permanent Pasture / Scrub
Ancient Natural Woodland
Public Highway
Public Footpaths
High Weald Landtrail
1/4 mi.   1/2. mi.   3/4 mL.   1 Mile

THE QUEEN'S GOLDEN JUBILEE 2002

Map Project Co-ordinator : Bryan Davies

Contributing artists / illustrators / calligraphers :

Marielle Carr, Bryan Davies, Angela Davies, Lawrence Evans, Ann Gardiner,
Emily Hutchings, Joan Higinbotham, Barbara Robins, Janine Scola, Maggie Smith,

Bolney Village Sponsors

We are very grateful to the following local sponsors for their most generous support.

Bolney Parish Council ~ S.R. Bowles. Carpenter/Joiner. ~ H.R. Whittaker Architect,
Fairlight Developments Ltd. ~ A & A Rooftilers Ltd. ~ Aegis Rubber Engineering Ltd.
4 Independence Financial Advisers. ~ P. Hopgood Fencing Services.
NORCON (NORRIS) Ltd. ~ A.M. Hunt Landscape Gardener.
Bolney Village Society. ~ 'Have - a - go' Pottery.

BOLNEY C.E.P. SCHOOL

Bolney C of E Primary School
Est. 1871   Pupils on Roll : 112
Headmistress : Mrs Anne Pearce.

Bennetts

Bankside

The small estates called Bennetts, Drovers and Bankside represent modern Bolney, accounting for much of its recent growth. Predictably the population has been ever upward – 1801= 497; 1901= 886; 2001= 1,209. These figures actually show a slight slowing down in growth as the proportional increase during the last century has been less than over the previous hundred years. So Bolney's essential character as a small village has so far been preserved.

This might not have been the case. Plans that could have wiped it out altogether as a village make for one of the 'might-have-beens' of local history. Imagine the Crawley New Town/Gatwick Airport complex centred on Bolney. This might easily have been the case, for a new 'Garden City' of two thousand houses plus an 'aeroplane landing ground and aerodrome'

Cricket has been played at Bolney since at least 1718

Bolney Grange Business Park

The Bolney Stage

Bolney Flyover

complete with flying school, air taxi base, clubhouse, hangars and public enclosure were planned for Bolney in 1933–4. Served by the main London-Brighton road that conveniently carves its way through the parish – and seen in the light of yet another 'might-have-been', a railway planned for Bolney years before – here was a possible combination of factors that could have obliterated Bolney village as we know it today. One of the parish council's objections was that 'low flying machines will disturb and frighten cattle, horses & sheep'. For what they have been spared, Bolney and its animals can count their blessings.

The other great blessing is the Bolney Flyover taking the east-west A272 under the London-Brighton A23. The junction, as an old-fashioned crossroads, was once one of the most notorious accident blackspots in the south, again and again widely publicising Bolney's good name as just another scene of roadside carnage. Opened in 1972, the flyover immediately made an enormous difference to those catching the train or shopping in Haywards Heath; now it's taken for granted and Bolney's name has disappeared from the travel bulletins.

A more cheerful roadside advertisement for Bolney is its colourful village sign by the side of the A272. Incorporating the church's lychgate, its peal of bells and branches of fruiting cherry, the design was originally made by Lawrence Evans specifically for the parish map.

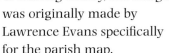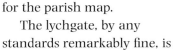

Honeysuckle

The lychgate, by any standards remarkably fine, is one of the best in the county, built entirely of Sussex materials and paved with millstones from the old Bolney watermill. In bell-ringing circles Bolney has been long-famed for its peal of eight bells, the first to have this number in the county, even before Chichester Cathedral. Cherries were chosen to decorate the sign as the parish was once well-known for its summer cherry fairs. Just as the new village sign is a direct spin-off from the title-piece of this map, so the same design has been also taken over as the parish council's logo for its notepaper and website.

Yet another beneficial outcome of the parish map was the discovery of numerous artists in the village who now meet regularly in the Eight Bells pub. The map built on the Local History Society's millennium history book, both projects so successful that another book has been produced, this time on Bolney in the Second World War. The map has played its part in being a really positive influence in the village. As a Golden Jubilee map marking the 2002 celebrations, a copy was fittingly sent to the Queen at Buckingham Palace.

Goldfinch

KIM LESLIE

Bosham

BOSHAM IS UNIQUE. At least that is what the locals think. It is neither a typical Sussex village nor a south coast seaport. The writer Arthur Stanley Cooke considered it 'one of the most interesting spots in Sussex . . . the artist lingers in and about it for months; and the antiquarian seldom tires of visiting it . . . . It has a touch of Venice in its colour, and, with the estuary on both sides of it, more than a touch of Holland in its situation.'

Even the pronunciation of the name is a conundrum – anyone calling the place Bosh-am will incur the wrath of the locals. It is Bozz-am, but as there have been some twenty-eight different spellings over the centuries one can perhaps understand how much confusion there must always have been. The name probably came from an amalgamation of the Roman word 'boscus' for wood and 'ham' for hamlet – the hamlet in the woods. In Roman times the whole area was covered by oak woods, some of which survive on the peninsula to this day.

This is a village which has gone from one extreme to another. The Romans inhabited the area, making use of the little port; it was the sixth most important *town* in the 8th century; it was part of the story of events leading to the Norman invasion in 1066; it was one of the wealthiest manors in England according to the Domesday survey in 1086; and after Henry

VIII had finished looting the church, one of the poorest, to retire almost into insignificance during the following five centuries. It then came into its own again in June 1944 when pontoons for the Mulberry Harbours were assembled here for the D-Day Normandy landings.

Bosham's wealth can be gauged by the regular looting of the place by the Vikings, the Danes and the Saxons. King Canute, Earl Godwin and King Harold (of 1066 fame) all had homes here – it was one of the many places where Canute attempted to turn back the tide; he probably did no more than build a rather ineffective dyke to reclaim more land for growing corn. There would have been everything here for which these great men could have wished: a safe, deep-water anchorage, a plentiful supply of timber for building their ships, excellent soil in the surrounding area to grow the corn, while the seas held ample fish stocks. With the prevailing south-westerly wind, it would have been a comparatively easy boat journey to and from Normandy. That Bosham played a vital part in the story of the events leading up to the Norman Conquest is demonstrated by its inclusion in the Bayeux Tapestry. Three

The Quay

Bosham views were stitched into the needlework: King Harold, last of the Saxon kings, praying in Bosham church; feasting in a grand house; and embarking for Normandy on the fateful journey which was to lead to his defeat at the Battle of Hastings. So much of importance has happened here that Sussex writer S.P.B. Mais claimed that Bosham was 'richer in historical association than any other place of a similar size in the country'.

So much of this rich past is told in stone, through the story of Bosham's church, that Simon Jenkins ranks it as one of England's thousand best churches, so atmospheric that 'the interior seems of a piece with its royal genesis. On a quiet evening, when the yachtsmen have departed and the wind is heard in the sycamores, the shouts of arriving

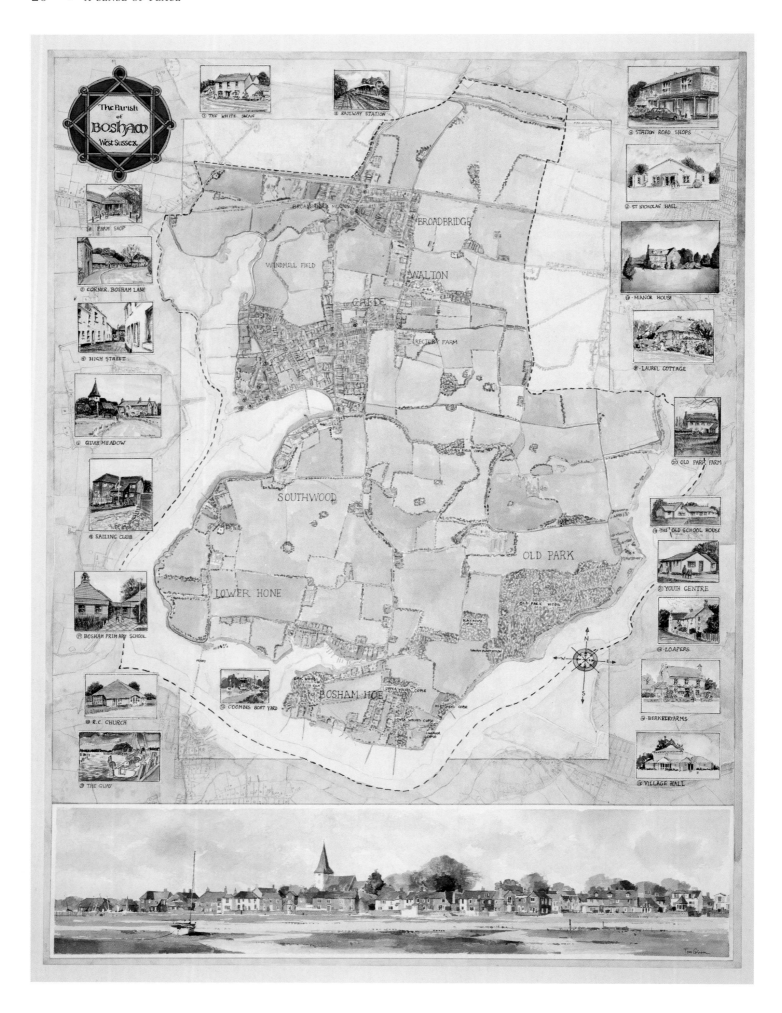

Saxons and the clatter of armour might almost be heard through the door.' For here is a Saxon church of great note. It is built unusually on the footprint of a Roman basilica; Roman tiles and bricks are embedded in the walls; it has one of the best Saxon arches in England, made famous by being featured in the Bayeux Tapestry. A flight of stone steps leads down into the crypt – even more atmospheric in its simplicity and solitude. It may well be built over the cell of Dicul, the monk whose little 7th-century monastery at Bosham marks the earliest Christian site in Sussex. For this it finds an honourable place in Bede's *History of the English Church and People*, the nation's first history book written in the 8th century. Bosham is hallowed ground.

Much later, church lands in Bosham were gifted by King Edward the Confessor to the bishops of Exeter in the 11th century. Here they established a college of canons, with the chancel of the parish church made into their chapel. All sorts of friction arose with the bishops of Chichester within whose diocese Exeter now intruded. And over the centuries, reports on the canons' behaviour were far from satisfactory: they were frequently absent from their duties, they failed to keep the fabric of the church in good repair, so the roof collapsed, nor did they hold the mass on time, while one was dismissed for living in sin with a widow. Perhaps Henry VIII had a point in dissolving the college! From then on the church suffered, and in order to keep it standing, the cathedral authorities in Chichester had to fork out and pay some of the bills for the next few hundred years.

Bosham reverted to being a little fishing village with the fishermen going out in their boats for days on end, selling their catches in such places as Portsmouth and Southampton. It would not appear that the Danes or Vikings left their physical marks on the village – there are few fair-haired blue-eyed people here, but there are many good-looking, dark-haired and swarthy-skinned locals. With Bosham oyster shells found in Rome, the Bosham oystermen bringing the young molluscs from the shores of Normandy to fatten in Chichester Harbour, and with trading schooners landing their cargoes on Bosham Quay, it would be surprising if there are not a few people in the village descended from foreign stock. Once the Romans had left these shores, the roads over the Downs and through the Weald became at times almost impassable. It was far quicker to get to the Seine by sea than London by land.

But history has since turned full circle. The fishing and

Sailing Club

Quay Meadow

trading boats have gone, to be replaced by cruising yachts and racing dinghies. The fishermen have left their shore-side cottages to live elsewhere and find other ways of earning their living. With no sandy beaches or large hotels to attract the crowds, Bosham has become one of the leading sailing centres on the south coast. Gone are the bearded sea captains and the strong-armed sailors. Today, along with the enthusiastic racing sailors of every age pushing boats and heaving sails, are the thousands of visitors who come to this attractive spot on the shores of Chichester Harbour.

As the best known village around the harbour, Bosham is one of the 'musts' for anyone touring around Sussex. It's the waterside that draws. By the Raptackle and old watermill is Quay Meadow owned by the National Trust, surely one of the most unusually sited village greens to be seen anywhere. Shore Road, east from here, is impassable twice a day when high tide in the harbour laps under the windows of the little cottages along the shoreline. Leave a car here at the wrong time and 'the Bosham car-wash' teaches a costly lesson! This is a village road unlike any other along the entire Sussex coast. Then, apart from the normal daily tides, there is the twice-yearly threat from the high spring tides in April and September that can reach further inland up into the High Street. This is why the steps into the gardens and houses are over low walls to keep out the sea water. Every yard of any walk around Bosham gives a constant reminder that this is a most unusual water-girt village.

ANGELA BROMLEY-MARTIN

High Street

Boxgrove

UNVEILED BY A DUKE and launched with a bang at Christmas time, the parish map was given a memorably noble birth. The Duke of Richmond performed the ceremony, accompanied by festive fireworks, on 20 December 2000, just in time for the new millennium's first Christmas. There was an appropriateness in asking the Duke. Not only has his family's Goodwood Estate been closely interwoven with Boxgrove's history, it has also been closely associated with map-making through the 3rd Duke in the 18th century. He set up the Ordnance Survey in the 1790s. The maps that he commissioned for his Goodwood lands – including Boxgrove – are some of the finest estate surveys ever produced in this country. Two hundred years on, Boxgrove's parish map, designed by Vera Quinton and her WI team, is the latest in a long tradition of local map-making.

We see the parish almost cut in half by Stane Street, the Roman road linking Chichester with London. Wedged tightly between this ancient highway and the modern A27, as if neatly caught in the pincers of a nutcracker, lies the village itself, bypassed, but never far from traffic. Boxgrove clusters around its chief glory, the priory church of St Mary and St Blaise; he was patron saint of wool-combers and weavers, very fitting for this South Downs sheep country.

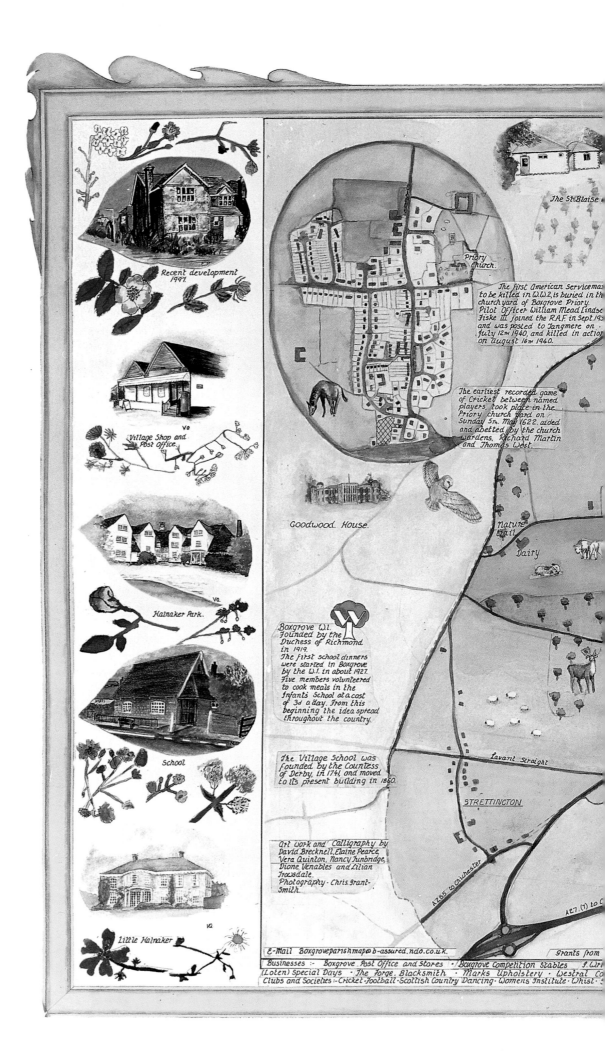

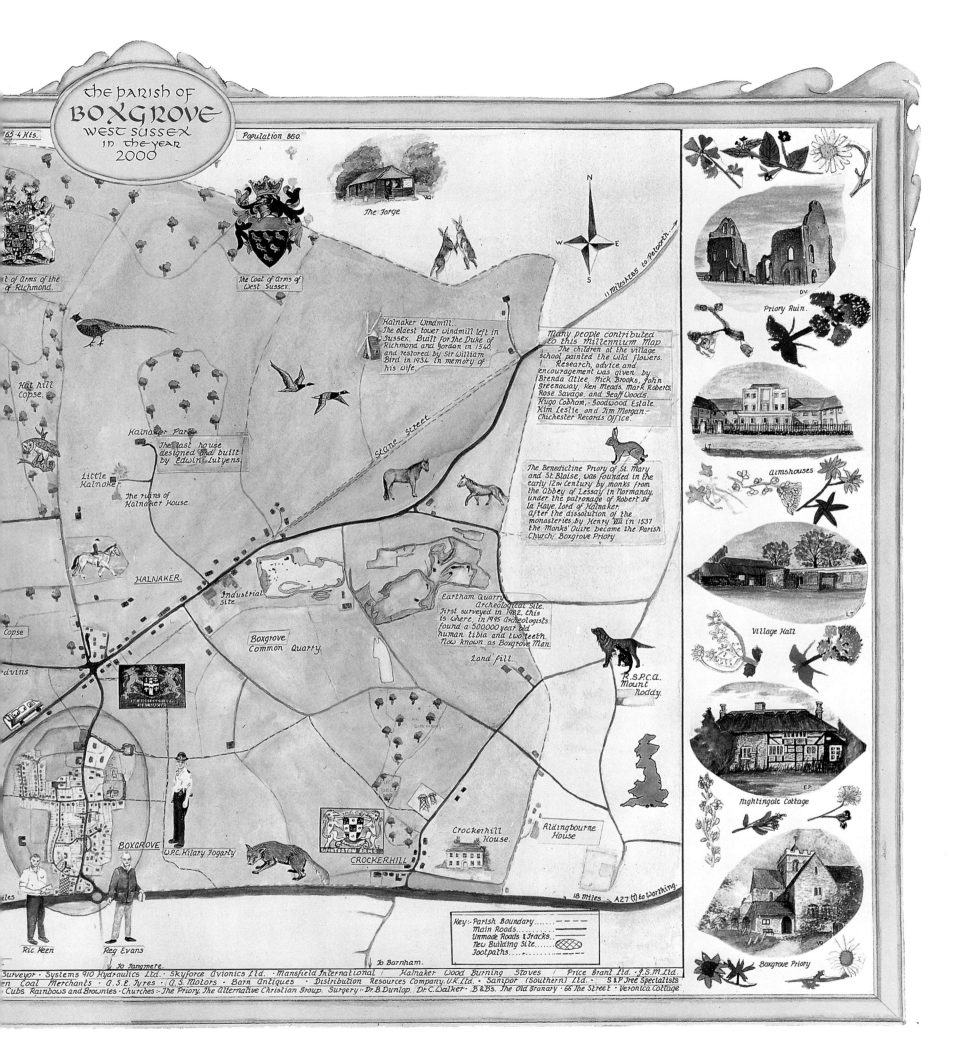

Boxgrove Priory

Go into the south-east corner of the churchyard to see the grave of Billy Fiske, born in Chicago in 1911, killed in the Battle of Britain in 1940 when stationed at RAF Tangmere. He is said to have been the first American serviceman to die in the Second World War. The same churchyard is famed in the history of cricket as the scene of two games in 1622. On one occasion men from the village were accused of 'playing at crecket in the churchyard', breaking windows and 'that a little child had like to have her braynes beaten out with a cricket batt'. From out of their sins we have one of the earliest references to cricket not only in Sussex but in the whole country.

The priory church is one of the glories of Sussex, second only to Chichester Cathedral. So big for a village this size, it's been likened to a 'half-size cathedral'. Unmistakably French in its exterior, Boxgrove was a daughter foundation of the Abbey of Lessay in Normandy where its mother church can be found. Within its magnificent interior, arches and columns lead the eye to Boxgrove's two Tudor treasures, the de la Warr chantry tomb and the nave's painted ceiling. One of the chantry's carvings (on the north-east column) shows boys raiding a fruit tree, a girl holding her skirt to catch the spoils. In the painted ceiling (second central boss from the east end) is a curious carving with eight faces. Each face has two eyes, and yet there are only eight eyes altogether – a Tudor puzzle picture.

Priory Ruins

Boxgrove is steeped in history as a village walk soon reveals, from the priory ruins and church, the 18th-century Derby almshouses – still performing their original function – to homely cottages in brick, timber, flint and thatch. Nightingale Cottage, by the school, is the oldest house in the village. The present owners are intrigued by their very deep well. No matter what goes down – one old gardener used to fill it up with garden rubbish – everything disappears, suggesting a powerful underground stream at the bottom.

Within the parish boundary is Eartham Quarry, for years scooped deeply for its gravel. Here, in 1993, archaeologists found a human shin-bone half a million years old, reaching back to the very

Nightingale Cottage

origins of mankind. This one fragment led to the reconstruction of 'Boxgrove Man', a giant of a man over 6 feet tall and weighing about 13 stone. Hailed at the time as 'the oldest man in Europe . . . a prehistoric heavyweight', he represented a major advance into what we know of early man, putting Boxgrove firmly on the worldwide archaeological map.

Boxgrove's well-known landmark is Halnaker Mill, high on the edge of the Downs, the oldest brick tower mill in Sussex dating from the late 18th century. A hundred years ago it was falling down and famously used by Hilaire Belloc as a symbol of what he saw as England's decay:

Ha'nacker Hill is in Desolation:
Ruin a-top and a field unploughed ...
Spirits that call and no one answers;
Ha'nacker's down and England's done ...

Several restorations since – it is now looked after by West Sussex County Council – the mill, even without its machinery, is in fine shape. If Belloc was right about the bad times it augured in his day – his poem was written just before the First World War – then maybe its proud sight today foreshadows hopeful times for the future. Pilots flying back to base at Tangmere during the Second World War saw it from afar as their symbol of safety and home.

And as a home today, Boxgrove scores highly. Despite its growth, expansion has been in a fairly tight envelope around its ancient core without overwhelming its rural and historic setting.

Village Stores and Post Office

New houses and new people have kept the place alive with a happy blend of young and old. As a community Boxgrove has a lot going for it.

The stores and post office is a major part of village life. The debt the village owes to those who give their services, come rain or shine, is acknowledged on the map by the inclusion of four named individuals: postmen Ric Keen and Colin Harris, milkman Reg Evans and local policewoman Hilary Fogarty, a goodly reminder that it is people who make communities. Parish maps rarely give named individuals.

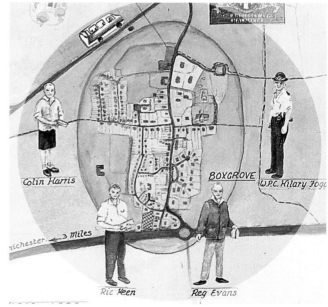

Boxgrove's two schools, the nursery and primary, both thrive. The primary school is planning to build anew on land donated by the Goodwood Estate. The village hall is to be rebuilt, even the recreation ground is to be enlarged, thanks again to Goodwood. The parish church has its new St Blaise Centre and the village is home to RELIC – Rural E-Learning Information Centre – a government- and local authority-funded initiative bringing computer training into the countryside. This is a village moving forward. Brenda Atlee, who led the map team, says she's 'proud to see this wonderfully ancient village keeping so abreast of modern times'.

KIM LESLIE

Recent development
1997

Bramber

Bramber is the filling in a sandwich of which Steyning and Upper Beeding are the slices of bread – what slices, what a filling, a quarter of a mile of sweet and savoury pleasures starting with a Norman castle.... And all along the way are other delightful tasting ingredients, such a charming little church, good restaurants and a welcoming pub, a handsome 14th-century jettied house, St Mary's, famed throughout the world.

Put this way by John Batten in the *West Sussex Gazette*, Bramber sounds quite a feast. No wonder tourists have been tempted here for years, and for much more than on this menu. River trips used to come up from Shoreham for the funfair and teas in the castle grounds – the village was well-known for its tea gardens: 'a tea-party paradise' was how one writer described it. For amusement there was the famous Potter's Museum of stuffed birds and animals, with its tableaux of 'The Death of Cock Robin' and 'The Kittens' Tea and Croquet Party' that lasted for over a hundred years until 1970. Then the House of Pipes took over, telling the story of smoking – '38,000 items from 180 countries'.

The National Butterfly Museum had its home in the village from 1979 to 1982. Bramber was well and truly on the map, but all have now gone except for St Mary's as its one big visitor attraction. It's one of the outstanding medieval houses in Sussex.

St Mary's House

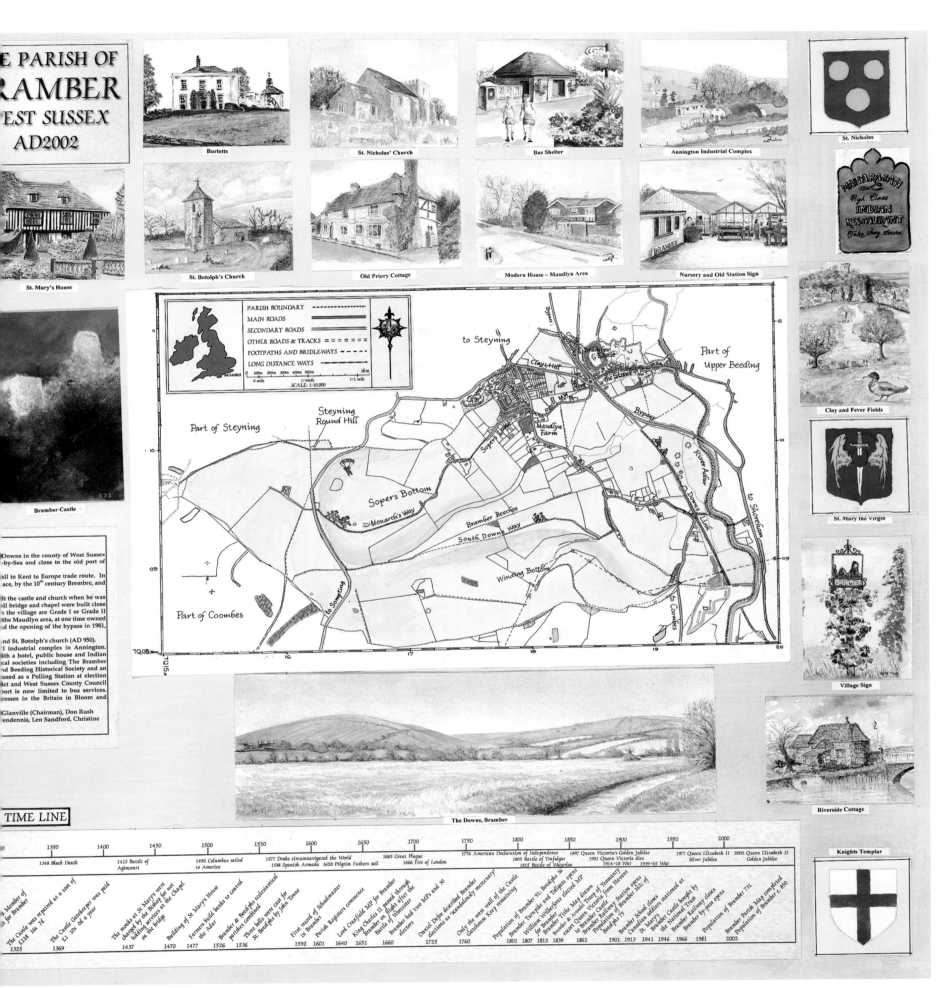

THE PARISH OF BRAMBER
WEST SUSSEX
AD2002

Burletts

St. Nicholas' Church

Bus Shelter

Annington Industrial Complex

St. Nicholas

St. Mary's House

St. Botolph's Church

Old Priory Cottage

Modern House – Maudlyn Area

Nursery and Old Station Sign

MAHARAJAH High Class INDIAN RESTAURANT Take Away Service

Bramber Castle

Clay and Fever Fields

St. Mary the Virgin

Village Sign

Riverside Cottage

Knights Templar

The Downs, Bramber

PARISH BOUNDARY
MAIN ROADS
SECONDARY ROADS
OTHER ROADS & TRACKS
FOOTPATHS AND BRIDLEWAYS
LONG DISTANCE WAYS

SCALE: 1:10,000

to Steyning

Part of Upper Beeding

Bramber Castle

Clays Hill

The Street

Part of Steyning

Steyning Round Hill

Bypass

Maudlyn Farm

Sopers Lane

River Adur

Downs Link

to Shoreham

Sopers Bottom

Monarch's Way

Bramber Beeches

South Downs Way

Bramber Beeches

Winding Bottom

Part of Coombes

to Steyning

to Coombes

...Downs in the county of West Sussex
...-by-Sea and close to the old port of
...all to Kent to Europe trade route. In
...ace, by the 10th century Brembre, and
...lt the castle and church when he was
...ll bridge and chapel were built close
... the village are Grade I or Grade II
...the Maudlyn area, at one time owned
...d the opening of the bypass in 1981,
...nd St. Botolph's church (AD 950).
...l industrial complex in Annington.
...with a hotel, public house and Indian
...cal societies including The Bramber
...nd Beeding Historical Society and an
...used as a Polling Station at election
...ct and West Sussex County Council
...port is now limited to bus services.
...cesses in the Britain in Bloom and

...Glanville (Chairman), Don Rush
...endennis, Len Sandford, Christine

TIME LINE

1350 1400 1450 1500 1550 1600 1650 1700 1750 1800 1850 1900 1950 2000

1348 Black Death
1415 Battle of Agincourt
1492 Columbus sailed to America
1577 Drake circumnavigated the World
1588 Spanish Armada 1620 Pilgrim Fathers sail
1665 Great Plague
1666 Fire of London
1776 American Declaration of Independence
1805 Battle of Trafalgar
1815 Battle of Waterloo
1897 Queen Victoria's Golden Jubilee
1901 Queen Victoria dies
1914–18 War
1939–45 War
1977 Queen Elizabeth II Silver Jubilee
2002 Queen Elizabeth II Golden Jubilee

1325 1369 1437 1470 1477 1526 1536 1592 1601 1640 1651 1660 1725 1760 1801 1807 1812 1839 1861 1901 1913 1941 1946 1966 1981 2002

What went on in the past here means a lot to the village. The time line at the foot of the map – the only West Sussex parish map to have one – tells a great deal about how the parish sees itself against the highlights of its own history.

As a garrisoned castle, Bramber was the 'capital' of its own jurisdiction, giving its name to the swathe of countryside it controlled – the Rape of Bramber – one of six rapes – or divisions – the Normans established in Sussex, each with a castle to defend routes between the sea coast

Bramber roundabout

Bramber Castle

and London. It was granted market status, was a port for sea-going vessels and stood astride the great medieval highway between Canterbury and the west that crossed the Adur here. For centuries Bramber was of such importance that it had two members of parliament. But even by the first national census in 1801, Bramber had only ninety-one people and was still being represented by two MPs, whilst huge places like Manchester had none at all. Bramber was a nest of corruption in a scandal-ridden system, and alongside similar decayed places with a more glorious past was known as a 'rotten borough'.

Once it had its own railway station, but even that's now gone. Bramber's story is very much about what has gone

and passed away – the past is a constantly-felt backdrop, its old heart still dominated by castle and church at the end of the village street. Since the bypass came in 1981, with some fairly effective traffic-calming measures, memories of noise and fumes make the present even more attractive. And as a linear village hugging the main street, the countryside is literally right on the doorstep.

Bramber is very much a village of the countryside, the built-up parts around the street, and the more modern housing at Maudlyn, taking up a very small proportion of the total parish area. The elongated rural parish runs from its low-lying end by the river right up to its sharpened westward end at a lonely spot high on the Downs called No Man's Land – the meeting place of four parishes. The Bramber boundary takes in the ancient settlements of Annington and Botolphs with its medieval church at a former crossing of the Adur. No doubt prayers were said here before the perils of the journey across the river,

Modern Bramber – at Maudlyn

St Botolph's Church, Botolphs

Victorian terrace

Botolph being a patron saint of travellers and river crossings. Today many walkers come through the parish following three long-distance footpaths: the South Downs Way between Winchester and Beachy Head, the Monarch's Way between Worcester and Shoreham – Britain's second-longest signposted walking trail – and the Downs Link connecting the North and South Downs.

Come to Bramber at the height of the summer for an overwhelming sight – flowers cascading along the street, in tubs, planters and baskets. It's in the premier league in the flower world: seven awards since 1994 in the South-East in Bloom Competition; a national finalist in the 1999 Britain in Bloom Competition; holder of the Premier Award Trophy for small villages from the Royal Horticultural Society in 2003.

The parish council supplies the containers and pays for the plants. The success of the whole exercise has depended entirely on the enthusiasm of residents to keep the plants in good condition by individuals 'adopting a lamp post'. Watering can be a thankless task. Strong support has always been given by the pub, hotel and restaurants, all major contributors in making the centre a real showpiece.

Parish councillor Ted Jones takes up the story from here as the flowers give an interesting extra to community life: 'The decision by the parish council to enter into the South-East in Bloom Competition had an unexpected knock-on effect. A suggestion was made that there might be a strictly informal – buy your own beer – gathering at the Castle Inn to discuss the practical arrangements. This developed into a regular meeting for all residents on the first Friday of the month as an opportunity to meet neighbours, chat about

village activities and propose social events. All this has helped to bring residents together on speaking rather than the usual nodding terms!' The informal group turned itself into the Bramber Society. One group of villagers, mostly non-churchgoers, has taken on the maintenance of the churchyard. As external church supporters they call themselves appropriately The Flying Buttress Club. In 2003 they were given a special award by the South-East in Bloom Competition.

Bramber's parish map was completed to mark the Queen's Golden Jubilee in 2002, with district councillor Alan Fisher at the helm of twenty-six artists and researchers. A separate leaflet was produced detailing all the paintings arranged around the map. The original is in St Mary's, with a print on display in the church porch.

KIM LESLIE

Flowers cascading along the street . . .

Burgess Hill – Worlds End

ORLDS END IS AN OLD HAMLET on the north-east edge of Burgess Hill, from which it was once distinct. But the two communities have been joined up by the spread of housing during the 20th century. Old lanes, now suburban roads, bring us into Worlds End; or we can use the railway, alighting at a station inappropriately called 'Wivelsfield'. Why this name? Having lived near the station since 1967, I have often helped perplexed travellers needing to get to Wivelsfield village, a good two miles away. I would tell them, sympathetically, that the name 'Worlds End' was avoided, all down to religious sensitivities in 1886 when the station was first opened. For its first ten years it was called 'Keymer Junction'.

Wivelsfield is in East Sussex whilst Worlds End, since local government reorganisation in 1974, is in West Sussex. Or, at least, most of it is! With a proper, but misplaced acknowledgement of history, the new county boundary was drawn partly along the ancient parish boundaries of Wivelsfield and Keymer, thus inconveniently casting part of Worlds End into a different county. Worlds End was also partly in Ditchling, another East Sussex parish, but this part was later taken into Burgess Hill and thence came into West Sussex in 1974. The corner of the Recreation Ground marks the spot where the three old parishes meet – a place so central to the community that in 1989 it was chosen by our Residents Association for the planting of six thousand crocuses given to us by Mid Sussex District Council. Yes, we have a strong sense of place and were determined to take part in the millennium map project with this collage – another Residents Association initiative – despite the minor inconvenience of not actually being a parish.

Keymer and Ditchling are the parent parishes that spawned the early community at Worlds End. With little room for expansion near the villages themselves, people looked towards the woods and commons on the clay towards the north of their parishes. Here they might take in a few acres, grow a few crops, offer their labour and craft skills to the larger farmers in the neighbourhood and generally lead a reasonably independent life style.

New communities need a focus. Ours was Valebridge Common, not only the centrifugal point but also a general name for the locality. The name 'Worlds End' came later. The old lanes that led into the common – Lye Lane (now Leylands Road), Cants Lane (now Junction Road) and Janes Lane, were each flanked by small cottages dotted around. Some of these were put up in the 17th century, others earlier. One of them, put up in 1655,

was transferred to the officers of Keymer parish in 1685 to give shelter and work for the poor. The site now accommodates Manor Court, our warden-assisted flats for the elderly, at the heart of Worlds End. Keymer Manor also had a role in the early community because the manorial beadle lived at Bedelands Farm, whose last farmer, William Courage, is featured on the map. The beadle was both a local farmer and an agent for the lord of the manor, informing people of meetings and collecting their rents. This thread of local government carries on today. The Friends of Bedelands Local Nature Reserve work in voluntary partnership with the district council in managing the reserve.

The Oakwood Veterinary Clinic was the site of our first pub, around 1860, or so I was told by old Johnny Ashdown whose family used to run the greengrocer's shop (which now sells riding equipment). They, and Mr Stubbings at the newsagent's shop next door, were 'real' old Worlds Enders. Ashdown and his old mum and his brother, and many odd hangers-on who helped out a bit, used to bag up your potatoes whilst delivering all the local news and gossip in a constant flow, whether you wanted it or not. But usually you did. It made you feel connected. They once told me that their family had given the land so that the entrance to the Recreation Ground could be built. They must have felt very connected too.

The Watermill Inn was built in the 1880s after the railway station had opened and most of the housing had come. Its name commemorates Valebridge Mill, a 17th-century watermill that ground corn until the 1960s when it was pulled down. Like the former windmill out on St John's Common to the south-west – also commemorated in a local pub name – it succumbed to hard commercial pressures of the urban spread. But our local butcher and baker carried on until the 1990s. Jim and John Thwaites at the post office stores kept up the exchange of local news and views after the Ashdown family had all died off.

In the centre of Worlds End, with its rows of 1880s terraced houses for workers in the nearby brickyards and railway, lie the Victorian buildings of the Junction Road Schools – now Manor Field Primary School. Yet there is another, smaller, building at the heart of the community that had a parallel role. Somers Clarke put it up in 1887 as a reading room for working people, as part of an early adult education movement. Now trading as Kanine Clips and the Worlds End Angling Centre (formerly Exotic Pets), it was also once used as a mission house until a proper church, St Andrew's, was completed in 1904, a short distance away in Junction Road. The plain, but appealing, interior of St Andrew's rises in local brick and terracotta to open rafters whose excellent acoustics provide us with the best concert hall for miles around.

The great changes of the 19th century brought us our modern identity and our name. Valebridge Common, enclosed in 1828, was turned from open gorse into new fields, and a few years later accommodated the new

London to Brighton railway. This was built northwards from Brighton using chalk, and southwards from Haywards Heath in other materials, boldly spanning the Adur Valley in red brick at the Eight Arches Viaduct. The two projections met up in what must have seemed to the navvies a most god-forsaken place in the middle of nowhere. Might they perhaps have said 'And where, b'Jesus, is this place indeed? Sure, t'is the very world's end'. Local legend gives us this story and reason does not contradict it. The name 'Worlds End' was first recorded in an electoral roll in 1865, about twenty-five years after the coming of the railway, perhaps the right time-span for a new name to blossom forth in print.

Nowadays the old chemist's shop is the vet's surgery and the fish and chip shop offers Chinese take-aways. Patterns of shopping have changed and we no longer buy many of our essentials locally. But the specialist traders who have come to Worlds End soon learn that they are part of a locality with its own sense of purpose. They join the Residents Association and support its endeavours. The Patel family, who have taken over the post office stores, warmly welcomed our carol singers last Christmas and brought their new baby downstairs to see and listen. We are all part of a continuum and a community which, though called Worlds End, to us is rather a central place in our lives.

HEATHER WARNE

WORLDS END 2000

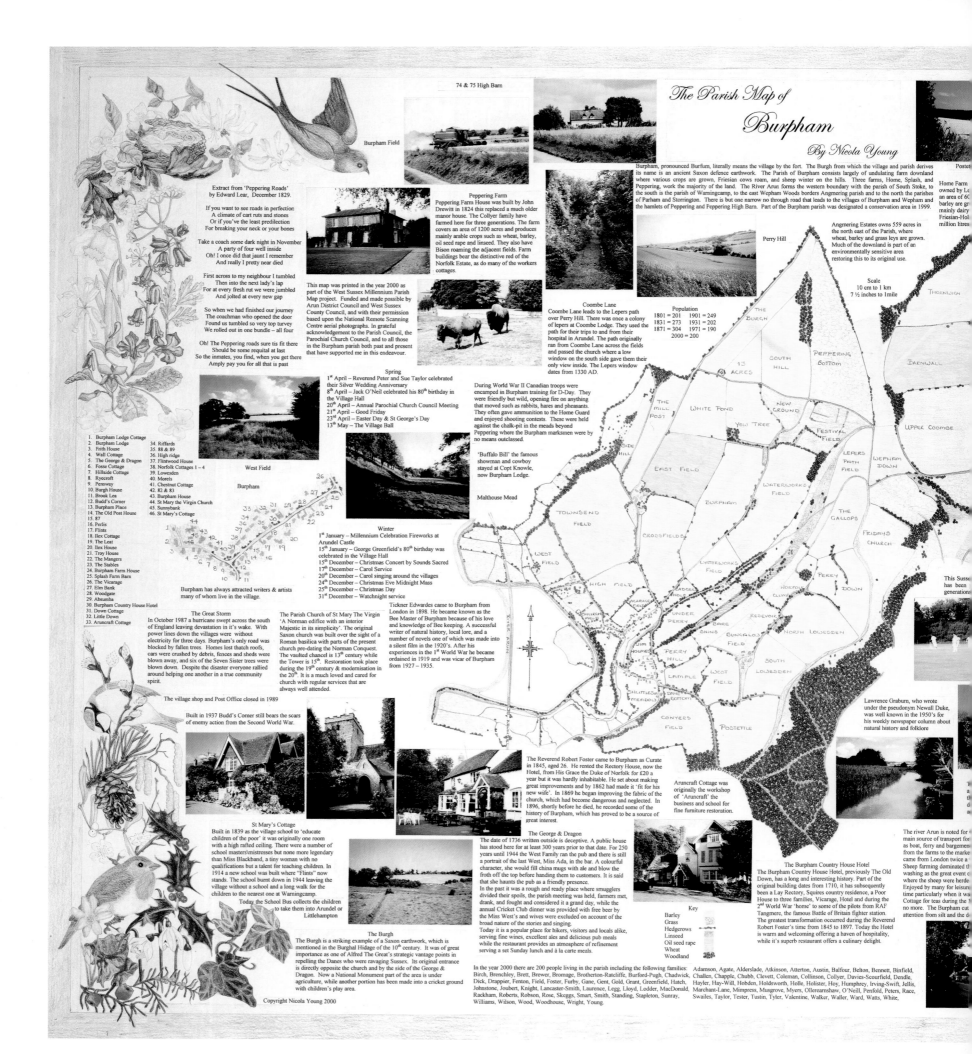

74 & 75 High Barn

Burpham Field

The Parish Map of
Burpham
By Nicola Young

Postern

Home Farm
owned by Lu
an area of 60
barley are gr
mainly dairy
Friesian-Hol
million litres

Burpham, pronounced Burfum, literally means the village by the fort. The Burgh from which the village and parish derives its name is an ancient Saxon defence earthwork. The Parish of Burpham consists largely of undulating farm downland where various crops are grown, Friesian cows roam, and sheep winter on the hills. Three farms, Home, Splash, and Peppering, work the majority of the land. The River Arun forms the western boundary with the parish of South Stoke, to the south is the parish of Warningcamp, to the east Wepham Woods borders Angmering parish and to the north the parishes of Parham and Storrington. There is but one narrow no through road that leads to the villages of Burpham and Wepham and the hamlets of Peppering and Peppering High Barn. Part of the Burpham parish was designated a conservation area in 1999.

Peppering Farm
Peppering Farm House was built by John Drewitt in 1824 this replaced a much older manor house. The Collyer family have farmed here for three generations. The farm covers an area of 1200 acres and produces mainly arable crops such as wheat, barley, oil seed rape and linseed. They also have Bison roaming the adjacent fields. Farm buildings bear the distinctive red of the Norfolk Estate, as do many of the workers cottages.

Extract from 'Peppering Roads'
by Edward Lear, December 1829.

If you want to see roads in perfection
A climate of cart ruts and stones
Or if you've the least predilection
For breaking your neck or your bones

Take a coach some dark night in November
A party of four well inside
Oh! I once did that jaunt I remember
And really I pretty near died

First across my neighbour I tumbled
Then into the next lady's lap
For at every fresh rut we were jumbled
And jolted at every new gap

So when we had finished our journey
The coachman who opened the door
Found us tumbled so very top turvey
We rolled out in one bundle – all four

Oh! The Peppering roads sure tis fit there
Should be some requital at last
So the inmates, you find, when you get there
Amply pay you for all that is past

This map was printed in the year 2000 as part of the West Sussex Millennium Parish Map project. Funded and made possible by Arun District Council and West Sussex County Council, and with their permission based upon the National Remote Scanning Centre aerial photographs. In grateful acknowledgement to the Parish Council, the Parochial Church Council, and to all those in the Burpham parish both past and present that have supported me in this endeavour.

Angmering Estates owns 559 acres in the north east of the Parish, where wheat, barley and grass leys are grown. Much of the downland is part of an environmentally sensitive area restoring this to its original use.

Perry Hill

Coombe Lane
Coombe Lane leads to the Lepers path over Perry Hill. There was once a colony of lepers at Coombe Lodge. They used the path for their trips to and from their hospital in Arundel. The path originally ran from Coombe Lane across the fields and passed the church where a low window on the south side gave them their only view inside. The Lepers window dates from 1330 AD.

Population	
1801 = 201	1901 = 249
1831 = 273	1931 = 202
1871 = 304	1971 = 190
2000 = 200	

Scale
10 cm to 1 km
7 ½ inches to 1mile

Spring
1st April – Reverend Peter and Sue Taylor celebrated their Silver Wedding Anniversary
8th April – Jack O'Neil celebrated his 80th birthday in the Village Hall
20th April – Annual Parochial Church Council Meeting
21st April – Good Friday
23rd April – Easter Day & St George's Day
13th May – The Village Ball

During World War II Canadian troops were encamped in Burpham training for D-Day. They were friendly but wild, opening fire on anything that moved such as rabbits, hares and pheasants. They often gave ammunition to the Home Guard and enjoyed shooting contests. These were held against the chalk-pit in the meads beyond Peppering where the Burpham marksmen were by no means outclassed.

'Buffalo Bill' the famous showman and cowboy stayed at Copt Knowle, now Burpham Lodge.

Malthouse Mead

West Field

Burpham

1. Burpham Lodge Cottage
2. Burpham Lodge
3. Frith House
4. Wall Cottage
5. The George & Dragon
6. Fosse Cottage
7. Hillside Cottage
8. Ryecroft
9. Pensway
10. Burgh House
11. Brook Lea
12. Budd's Corner
13. Burpham Place
14. The Old Post House
15. 87
16. Perlis
17. Flints
18. Ilex Cottage
19. The Leat
20. Ilex House
21. Troy House
22. The Mangers
23. The Stables
24. Burpham Farm House
25. Splash Farm Barn
26. The Vicarage
27. Elm Bank
28. Woodgate
29. Absumba
30. Burpham Country House Hotel
31. Down Cottage
32. Little Down
33. Aruncraft Cottage
34. Riffards
35. 88 & 89
36. High ridge
37. Flintwood House
38. Norfolk Cottages 1 – 4
39. Lowesden
40. Morels
41. Chestnut Cottage
42. 82 & 83
43. Burpham House
44. St Mary the Virgin Church
45. Sunnybank
46. St Mary's Cottage

Burpham has always attracted writers & artists many of whom live in the village.

Winter
1st January – Millennium Celebration Fireworks at Arundel Castle
15th January – George Greenfield's 80th birthday was celebrated in the Village Hall
15th December – Christmas Concert by Sounds Sacred
17th December – Carol Service
20th December – Carol singing around the villages
24th December – Christmas Eve Midnight Mass
25th December – Christmas Day
31st December – Watchnight service

The Great Storm
In October 1987 a hurricane swept across the south of England leaving devastation in it's wake. With power lines down the villages were without electricity for three days. Burpham's only road was blocked by fallen trees. Homes lost thatch roofs, cars were crushed by debris, fences and sheds were blown away, and six of the Seven Sister trees were blown down. Despite the disaster everyone rallied around helping one another in a true community spirit.

The Parish Church of St Mary The Virgin 'A Norman edifice with an interior Majestic in its simplicity'. The original Saxon church was built over the sight of a Roman basilica with parts of the present church pre-dating the Norman Conquest. The vaulted chancel is 13th century while the Tower is 15th. Restoration took place during the 19th century & modernisation in the 20th. It is much loved and cared for church with regular services that are always well attended.

Tickner Edwardes came to Burpham from London in 1898. He became known as the Bee Master of Burpham because of his love and knowledge of Bee keeping. A successful writer of natural history, local lore, and a number of novels one of which was made into a silent film in the 1920's. After his experiences in the 1st World War he became ordained in 1919 and was vicar of Burpham from 1927 – 1935.

The village shop and Post Office closed in 1989

Built in 1937 Budd's Corner still bears the scars of enemy action from the Second World War.

The Reverend Robert Foster came to Burpham as Curate in 1845, aged 26. He rented the Rectory House, now the Hotel, from His Grace the Duke of Norfolk for £20 a year but it was hardly inhabitable. He set about making great improvements and by 1862 had made it 'fit for his new wife'. In 1869 he began improving the fabric of the church, which had become dangerous and neglected. In 1896, shortly before he died, he recorded some of the history of Burpham, which has proved to be a source of great interest.

Aruncraft Cottage was originally the workshop of 'Aruncraft' the business and school for fine furniture restoration.

Lawrence Graburn, who wrote under the pseudonym Newall Duke, was well known in the 1950's for his weekly newspaper column about natural history and folklore

St Mary's Cottage
Built in 1839 as the village school to 'educate children of the poor' it was originally one room with a high rafted ceiling. There were a number of school masters\mistresses but none more legendary than Miss Blackband, a tiny woman with no qualifications but a talent for teaching children. In 1914 a new school was built where "Flints" now stands. The school burnt down in 1944 leaving the village without a school and a long walk for the children to the nearest one at Warningcamp.

Today the School Bus collects the children to take them into Arundel or Littlehampton.

The George & Dragon
The date of 1736 written outside is deceptive. A public house has stood here for at least 300 years prior to that date. For 250 years until 1944 the West Family ran the pub and there is still a portrait of the last West, Miss Ada, in the bar. A colourful character, she would fill china mugs with ale and blow the froth off the top before handing them to customers. It is said that she haunts the pub as a friendly presence.
In the past it was a rough and ready place where smugglers divided their spoils, the parish meeting was held, farmers met, drank, and fought and considered it a grand day, while the annual Cricket Club dinner was provided with free beer by the Miss West's and wives were excluded on account of the broad nature of the stories and singing.
Today it is a popular place for hikers, visitors and locals alike, serving fine wines, excellent ales and delicious pub meals while the restaurant provides an atmosphere of refinement serving a set Sunday lunch and à la carte meals.

The Burgh
The Burgh is a striking example of a Saxon earthwork, which is mentioned in the Burghal Hidage of the 10th century. It was of great importance as one of Alfred The Great's strategic vantage points in repelling the Danes who were ravaging Sussex. Its original entrance is directly opposite the church and by the side of the George & Dragon. Now a National Monument part of the area is under agriculture, while another portion has been made into a cricket ground with children's play area.

This Susse
has been
generations

The river Arun is noted for
main source of transport for
as boat, ferry and bargemen
from the farms to the marke
came from London twice a
Sheep farming dominated th
washing as the great event of
where the sheep were herde
Enjoyed by many for leisure
time particularly when it wa
Cottage for teas during the M
no more. The Burpham cut
attention from silt and the de

The Burpham Country House Hotel
The Burpham Country House Hotel, previously The Old Down, has a long and interesting history. Part of the original building dates from 1710, it has subsequently been a Lay Rectory, Squires country residence, a Poor House to three families, Vicarage, Hotel and during the 2nd World War 'home' to some of the pilots from RAF Tangmere, the famous Battle of Britain fighter station. The greatest transformation occurred during the Reverend Robert Foster's time from 1845 to 1897. Today the Hotel is warm and welcoming offering a haven of hospitality, while it's superb restaurant offers a culinary delight.

Key
Barley
Grass
Hedgerows
Linseed
Oil seed rape
Wheat
Woodland

In the year 2000 there are 200 people living in the parish including the following families: Birch, Brenchley, Brett, Brewer, Bromage, Brotherton-Ratcliffe, Burford-Pugh, Chadwick, Dick, Drappier, Fenton, Field, Foster, Furby, Gane, Gent, Gold, Grant, Greenfield, Hatch, Johnstone, Joubert, Knight, Lancaster-Smith, Laurence, Legg, Lloyd, Lodder, MacDonald, Rackham, Roberts, Robson, Rose, Skeggs, Smart, Smith, Standing, Stapleton, Sunray, Williams, Wilson, Wood, Woodhouse, Wright, Young.

Adamson, Agate, Alderslade, Atkinson, Atterton, Austin, Balfour, Belton, Bennett, Binfield, Challen, Chapple, Chubb, Clevett, Coleman, Collinson, Collyer, Davies-Scourfield, Dendle, Hayler, Hay-Will, Hobden, Holdsworth, Holle, Holister, Hoy, Humphrey, Irving-Swift, Jellis, Marchant-Lane, Mimpress, Musgrove, Myers, Ollerearnshaw, O'Neill, Penfold, Peters, Race, Swailes, Taylor, Tester, Tustin, Tyler, Valentine, Walker, Waller, Ward, Watts, White,

Copyright Nicola Young 2000

Burpham

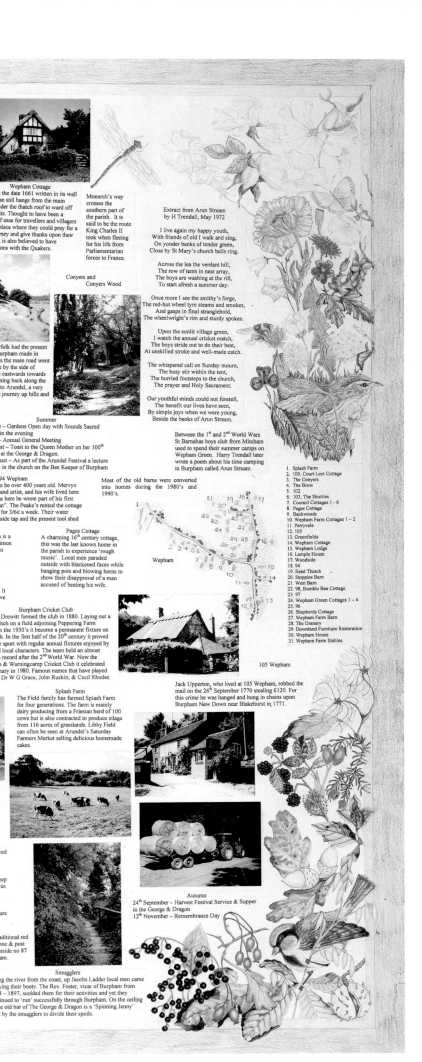

Wepham Cottage
This has the date 1661 written in its wall and Gorse still hangs from the main rafter under the thatch roof to ward off evil spirits. Thought to have been a chapel of ease for travellers and villagers alike, a place where they could pray for a safe journey and give thanks upon their return. It is also believed to have associations with the Quakers.

The Duke of Norfolk had the present main road into Burpham made in 1883. Prior to this the main road went along Green Lane by the side of Wepham Cottage eastwards towards Poling before turning back along the Worthing road into Arundel, a very long and difficult journey up hill and over dales.

Summer
11th June – Gardens Open day with Sounds Sacred Concert in the evening
8th July – Annual General Meeting
4th August – Toast to the Queen Mother on her 100th birthday at the George & Dragon.
30th August – As part of the Arundel Festival a lecture was held in the church on the Bee Keeper of Burpham.

94 Wepham
...pham is thought to be over 400 years old. Mervyn ...the author, poet, and artist, and his wife lived here 1940-1942. It was here he wrote part of his first ...book, "Titus Groan". The Peake's rented the cottage ...the Norfolk Estate for 3/6d a week. Their water ...was from the outside tap and the present tool shed ...r privy!

...niture Restoration is a ...iness owned by Simon ... studied his craft in ...aruncraft".

Pages Cottage
A charming 16th century cottage, this was the last known home in the parish to experience 'rough music'. Local men paraded outside with blackened faces while banging pots and blowing horns to show their disapproval of a man accused of beating his wife.

...tion in Burpham. It ...20's by successive

Burpham Cricket Club
Dawtrey Drewitt formed the club in 1880. Laying out a cricket pitch on a field adjoining Peppering Farm House. In the 1930's it become a permanent fixture on the Burgh. In the first half of the 20th century it proved a popular sport with regular annual fixtures enjoyed by colourful local characters. The team held an almost unbeaten record after the 2nd World War. Now the Burpham & Warningcamp Cricket Club it celebrated its centenary in 1980. Famous names that have played here are, Dr W G Grace, John Ruskin, & Cecil Rhodes.

Splash Farm
The Field family has farmed Splash Farm for four generations. The farm is mainly dairy producing from a Friesian herd of 100 cows but is also contracted to produce silage from 116 acres of grasslands. Libby Field can often be seen at Arundel's Saturday Farmers' Market selling delicious homemade cakes.

...ttage
...e where centuries ...Presided over by ...the village they ...ettled disputes, ...rs.

...perch. It was the ...with many employed ...carrying produce ...lso lighters that ...y goods. ...r months with sheep ...t into the river, was ...ities. ...as a popular past ...Mrs Wakeham's ...teas and cottage in ...great need of

The traditional red telephone & post box outside no 87 Burpham.

Smugglers
Along the river from the coast, up Jacobs Ladder local men came carrying their booty. The Rev. Foster, vicar of Burpham from 1854 – 1897, scolded them for their activities and yet they continued to 'run' successfully through Burpham. On the ceiling in the old bar of The George & Dragon is a 'Spinning Jenny' used by the smugglers to divide their spoils.

Conyers and Conyers Wood

Monarch's way crosses the southern part of the parish. It is said to be the route King Charles II took when fleeing for his life from Parliamentarian forces to France.

Extract from Arun Stream by H Trendall, May 1972

I live again my happy youth,
With friends of old I walk and sing,
On yonder banks of tender green,
Close by St Mary's church bells ring.

Across the lea the verdant hill,
The row of tents in neat array,
The boys are washing at the rill,
To start afresh a summer day.

Once more I see the smithy's forge,
The red-hot wheel tyre steams and smokes,
And gasps in final stranglehold,
The wheelwright's rim and sturdy spokes.

Upon the sunlit village green,
I watch the annual cricket match,
The boys stride out to do their best,
At unskilled stroke and well-made catch.

The whispered call on Sunday mourn,
The busy stir within the tent,
The hurried footsteps to the church,
The prayer and Holy Sacrament.

Our youthful minds could not foretell,
The benefit our lives have seen,
By simple joys when we were young,
Beside the banks of Arun Stream.

Between the 1st and 2nd World Wars St Barnabas boys club from Mitcham used to spend their summer camps on Wepham Green. Harry Trendall later wrote a poem about his time camping in Burpham called Arun Stream.

Most of the old barns were converted into homes during the 1980's and 1990's.

Wepham

105 Wepham
Jack Upperton, who lived at 105 Wepham, robbed the mail on the 26th September 1770 stealing £120. For this crime he was hanged and hung in chains upon Burpham New Down near Blakehurst in 1771.

Autumn
24th September – Harvest Festival Service & Supper in the George & Dragon
12th November – Remembrance Day

1. Splash Farm
2. 100, Court Leet Cottage
3. The Conyers
4. The Brow
5. 102
6. 103, The Shuttles
7. Council Cottages 1 - 6
8. Pages Cottage
9. Backwoods
10. Wepham Farm Cottages 1 – 2
11. Perryvale
12. 105
13. Greenfields
14. Wepham Cottage
15. Wepham Lodge
16. Lample House
17. Woodside
18. 94
19. Reed Thatch
20. Stopples Barn
21. West Barn
22. 98, Bumble Bee Cottage
23. 97
24. Wepham Green Cottages 1 – 4
25. 96
26. Shepherds Cottage
27. Wepham Farm Barn
28. The Granary
29. Downland Furniture Restoration
30. Wepham House
31. Wepham Farm Stables

YOU CAN LITERALLY 'read' this map because of the enormous amount of information spread right across it. There's so much history interwoven with all sorts of present-day facts about local happenings and about the people and wildlife that share the parish together. There are even two little 'postman's maps' showing named and numbered properties, such a boon in a jumbled-up sort of country place that this is. An amazing amount of information makes it as much an encyclopaedia as a map. With the bonus of its fine photographs, even a complete stranger can readily gauge the feel of the place before setting foot here. The map speaks, concisely and vividly, for all the thousands of words in all the dozens of Sussex books describing Burpham, for this is one of those villages regularly earmarked by writers for lavish praise. 'The most peaceful village within fifty miles of London' wrote E.V. Lucas in *Highways and Byways of Sussex* many years ago, and it's still much the same today.

For time has dealt gently with Burpham and its sister Wepham, its little hamlet on the hill opposite. Their simple secret is that they're at the end of the road, a narrow lane ending in a farmtrack high on the Downs, and then going no further. The winding road from Arundel cuts through the hills for three miles, then the village lanes rise and fall, twist and turn through a contorted figure-of-eight. Their special treat is that they're all on different levels with constant surprises across rooftops and fields, one minute looking up from the little valley around Splash Farm and then up to magnificent vistas across the Arun and

Number 87, Burpham

The River Arun

distant downland in all directions. Views of the countryside dominate all around the village, so it's quite inseparable from its landscape.

Because it links people to this landscape, the most fitting companion to go with this map is Roger Coleman's beautiful book of earthy watercolours called *Downland: A Farm and a Village*. The farm is Splash, the village Burpham, a perfect combination, and yet bizarre in that the book was published in New York and never widely available in Sussex. He tells what it's like to live in the deep country, the effect of the seasons not just on the landscape but on people and their feelings, of the 'demanding and functional relationship of man and the earth', reminding us that out here the sense of loneliness is never far away. There is much 'silence . . . darkness . . . inexplicable noises' to get used to. His is very much the realist's philosophy of the life behind these images across the map. Burpham has been well served by creative people like Roger who have warmed to this landscape and feel it in their bones.

Nicola Young, who made this outstanding map for Burpham Parish Council, is again in the long tradition of creative people who have settled here, drawn to the place by its very special qualities. Near where the original hangs in the village hall is her other great work, a coloured copy of the tithe map showing all the parish properties in 1840. This is of enormous value to the local historian and now gains so much more with her millennium survey made in 2000. For comparative purposes these two maps belong to each other. Future historians will bless people like Nicola. They are already in her debt with her detailed survey and recording of all the graves in the churchyard, captured before even more precious detail is lost to weather and time.

Perhaps the most well-known name in the churchyard is Mervyn Peake (1911–68) who is buried here with his wife, painter and writer Maeve. They lived at 94, Wepham (still using the old Norfolk Estate numbering). With its views across to Arundel Castle it's thought that this was his inspiration in creating the brooding gothic setting of *Gormenghast*, quite imaginable when its stark silhouette across the river is seen at dusk. We know that his long downland walks up and along the Lepers Path were inspirational, where his son Sebastian says he had his 'imaginings', and where he came up with those idiosyncratically-exotic names that run through the trilogy, with characters like Flay, Swelter and Prunesquallor made up on the way. His startling 'Dead Rat' poem came out of a Burpham walk.

Close by in the churchyard is another name whose clutch of more than a dozen books has spread Burpham's inspiration far and wide. An odd mix, for he was a naturalist as well as a romantic novelist, Tickner Edwardes (1865–1944) lived here in his earlier years, later returning as the vicar. His novels were based around the village, with *Tansy*, the story of a love-torn shepherdess, made into an early silent film on the Burpham hills

St Mary the Virgin's Church

The George & Dragon

Peppering Farm House

and shown in cinemas here and abroad. An authority on bee-keeping, his classic work *The Lore of the Honey Bee* (1908) went through impression after impression, twelve by 1923. Wildlife and the open air were celebrated in *A Country Calendar* (1928) and *A Downland Year* (1939), all based on his Burpham observations. In *Neighbourhood: A Year's Life in and about an English Village* (1911) we soon recognise Windlecombe as Burpham:

> *But there is no way through ... therein lies Windlecombe's chiefest blessing. Windlecombe wears the quiet of the hills about it like a garment.... How wild and quiet the place is you can only realise by living in it from year's end to year's end....*

A blue plaque on Burpham's little country hotel, the former vicarage where he did so much of his writing, was unveiled in 1994 by crime-writer Simon Brett. Simon lives by the pub in a

house once occupied by novelist John Cowper Powys, perpetuating the village's tradition of being something of a literary haven. Simon's characters have the run of these hills. In *Death on the Downs* (2001), Burpham lightly masquerades as Weldisham, hiding its dark secrets beneath its outer peace and inspirational countryside. Simon is very conscious of his settings, rooted in the real landscape he knows so well.

Burpham's special landscape is the stimulus behind much of the writing that has come from this peculiarly creative place. Even Edward Lear, of 19th-century nonsense-verse fame, came to Peppering – 'my favourite abode ... with its sprain-ancle road' – where he 'Gobbled enough to choke a Goliath'. Lear, with his love for the absurd, would have delighted in Peppering's exotic bison – see top left of the parish map – Burpham's oddest sight in a village full of surprises.

KIM LESLIE

Burpham's harvest

Peppering's bison

Bury

Dunnell · Barbara Godwin · Ron Kirby · [...] Reynolds · Jan Sitwell · Gwen Squire · [...] Briggs · Calligraphy ~ Melanie Ward ·

THE PARISH OF BURY 2000

Population of Bury 1991 Census – 690 · Popul... Millennium Green Play Area · Village shop Published in June 2001 as part of the W...

RABBITS OUTNUMBER people in this riverside, downland parish. Rabbits, scores of them, each individually painted and no two quite the same, lollop, thump and nibble their way around an endless border. They surround a roll call of village surnames – the names of all the families living here in the year 2000, just like a modern form of Domesday. The map gives 690 residents to 690,000 rabbits! Enormous colonies have burrowed into the side of the Downs, multiplying as only they know how, nibbling the turf flat as they eat their way through the parish. They have been on these slopes for centuries. Once a staple for fur and food, when acres and acres of downland like this were enclosed as rabbit warrens, they were commercially farmed and controlled. Now seen as a pest rather than as a resource, their vast numbers are out of control – the hills and gardens of Bury must be a rabbit's paradise. Just look at them in all their detail in the wonderfully expressive frieze right around the map. Certainly few maps could ever have celebrated the rabbit with such humour.

Bury's other wildlife have a much more welcome presence. From the Arun and its low-lying wetlands up to the dry chalklands of the Downs above, this is a nature lover's heaven, captured by the colourful vignettes scattered around: birds, butterflies, animals and insects, fungi, flowers and trees. In their due season they can all be spotted somewhere in this richly-endowed parish, making a walk here such a joy. All the footpaths interlacing the parish are marked on the map, pointing the way through the village, along the river and up onto the hills.

Many people visiting Bury for the first time stand outside what used to be the old village shop, gazing in surprise at the odd-looking carvings decorating its outside walls. They are always known locally as 'The Gargoyles'; (more properly they are 'grotesques'). Apparently when the property was being rebuilt in 1898, the builder got them from a worker on the Norfolk Estate who was 'acquiring' them from Arundel Castle during rebuilding operations. He brought them over the hill to Bury and they've been here ever since. Two are shown as corner-pieces to the map. There are men smoking pipes – with smoke carved into the stone – a women with a fruit in her mouth, one with her tongue lolling out, a friendly-looking lion and a horse. They must be Bury's oddest sight.

THE PARISH OF
BURY 2000

There's always been a lot of good humour in the village, kept alive from old times by the Women's Institute in their village scrapbook. One story goes that one day old Noggie Mann, the local roadman, arrived at the shop, asking for a pound of cheese. This was in the days when 'tasters' were given out, with consequent holes left in the cheeses waiting to be sold. As the cheese started to be cut, old Noggie said 'Aint gooin' ter 'ave that 'un'. 'Why?' asked the querulous shopman. 'She's got 'oles in 'er', said Noggie. 'What's the matter, they don't weigh anything', came the reply. 'No, and yer caan't eat 'em neither', was Noggie's po-faced reply.

The original village shop was a real old-fashioned store. One day BBC comediennes Elsie and Doris Waters – 'Gert and Daisy' who used to live at Steyning – came into the shop. They liked the atmosphere so much that it inspired them to dream up their radio shop-comedy called *Floggits* in the 1950s. The old store has closed, but it's been replaced by a small shop and post office in the village hall. Both are key centres in the community where clubs and organisations all help to bring the village together. Some of their badges are grouped together on the map showing the range of interests.

The antics of the Amateur Dramatic Society would have delighted Bury's one-time famous

resident. This was John Galsworthy (1867–1933), playwright, novelist and creator of *The Forsyte Saga* that gave him such success in his lifetime and worldwide fame long after his death when adapted for television. His last seven years were spent at Bury House, the stateliest looking house in Bury, solid and stylish mock-Tudor of 1910. A blue plaque commemorates his stay here. He was a most generous man, buying up all the cottages he could get hold of in the village – nine in all – for staff and other working people, and then actually reducing the rents. Three local house names perpetuate Bury's connection with the Forsyte books: Robin Hill, shown on the map, next door is Jolyon (built by the author) and then, appropriately, Forsytes. Galsworthy loved the village, wrote with the Downs as his constant backdrop and when he knew the end was near willed that his ashes be scattered from the top of Bury Hill.

There is some beautiful older property in the village, a good number pictured around the edge of the map. Their local materials have been cut and quarried close at hand: timber, flint, some clunch from the Downs (hard chalk suitable for building) and a type of sandstone known as upper greensand. Right under the Downs it might be expected to find more buildings in flint and clunch but the sandstone

13. Village Hall and post office

10. Bury House.

has been used a lot as most of Bury is built on this greensand ridge that runs all along the foot of the chalk. Some of these houses are said to be built directly on solid rock foundations. Local materials for local houses, that's why these old houses have so much appeal.

The half-timbered Fogdens Barn in The Street with its eyebrow windows in its thatched roof, is late medieval – an outstanding example of its type – one of the best in the village. Bury's oldest house is Bury Manor, tucked behind the church. It now houses Dorset House School that claims to be one of the oldest preparatory schools in the country, described as a 'paradise for young boys' in its lush parkland setting down by the river. Annually the school hosts the village summer fête in late July, drawing in visitors from miles around. Everyone loves its old-world villagey feel, stalls piled high, a brass band and delicious cream teas. One July an American was heard to comment: 'This is exactly how I pictured England!'. Perhaps one entry in the visitors' book in the church says it all: 'Such a beautiful little village, everything is so pleasant, peaceful and very calming'.

Its grounds border the Wharf from which a ferry used to take passengers across the Arun to the Amberley side: 'one penny for parishioners and tuppence for strangers'. The ferryman was grandly called the harbour-master, directing operations when barges arrived from Littlehampton and Arundel loaded with coals and freight for the village.

32. Wildbrooks, The Floods, 2000

On a beautiful day this spot is one of those backwaters to bottle for its memories – lazy days by the river against the backdrop of the Wildbrooks and Amberley Mount, an artist's heaven.

High above the map's soaring birds there is plenty more aerial activity – hot-air ballooning and gliding: by conventional glider (from nearby Parham airfield), and para- and hang-gliding because Bury is the home of world champion John Pendry whose flying skills were learnt on the Downs. For his achievements in these two sports he was awarded the Gold Medal of the Royal Aero Club. Perhaps not surprisingly these little paintings of John in the skies were by proud mother Tess Pendry, who also did the amazing frieze of rabbits.

Ranged right across the map of Bury there is a tremendous mix of information, the old and new side by side – the present interwoven with the past. To many local people it sums up what is meant by living here in this riverside arcadia beneath the hills.

KIM LESLIE

16. Fogdens Barn

Chichester – St John's Street

WHEN WE SAW KIM LESLIE's article in the *Chichester Observer* encouraging parishes in West Sussex to create parish maps to celebrate the millennium, we were keen to participate.

Living in Chichester, our first step was to define the area to cover – for these maps this is usually, but not necessarily, the parish. The territory may be the ancient ecclesiastical parish or the more recent civil parish. Firstly we considered representing the parish of St Pancras; we thought also about taking the whole of the south-east quarter of the city. Then we looked at a publication produced by Common Ground, the environmental organisation that developed the idea of parish mapping. In terms of defining the parish, Sue Clifford suggested 'trying to focus on locality, the smallest arena in which life is played out. The territory to which you feel loyalty, which has meaning to you, about which you share some knowledge, for which indignance and protectiveness is easily roused, the neighbourhood of which you have the measure, which in some way helps to shape you. . . . It is in this sense of a self-defined small territory, that Common Ground has offered the word *parish*, implying people and place together. . . .'

St John's Street lies in the south-east quadrant of Chichester, within the city walls. By day it's noisy with busy car parks on both sides. Predominantly residential, there are a few businesses including a long established estate agent and auction house, a solicitors' office, chartered surveyors and a sandwich shop. Originally within the grounds of the Blackfriars friary, St John's Street was developed in the 19th century. There are a few 20th-century additions. The street is dominated by St John's Chapel, an elegant early 19th-century evangelical preaching house with an impressive three-decker pulpit, tall enough for the preacher to see each one of his flock below or in the galleries surrounding him above. With the altar almost hidden behind the dominant pulpit, the layout reflects the importance the evangelical

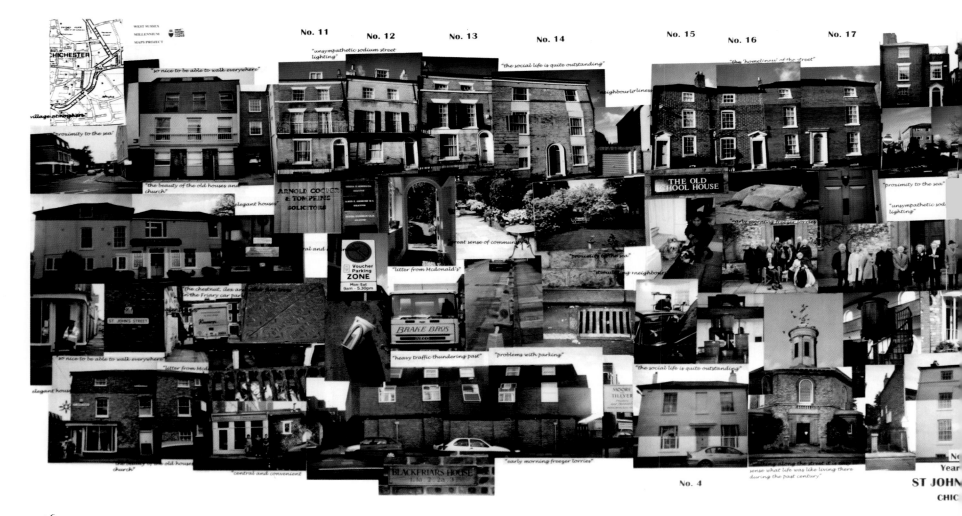

movement gave to sermons and reading from the scriptures, rather than communion.

It's people that make a community. We were both struck by the strong sense of community in the street. So we decided to focus on the people more than the buildings, flora or fauna. We began by giving each resident a questionnaire, asking: ' What is important to you about living in Chichester?'; 'What do you like and dislike about living in St John's Street?'; 'What would you like to see recorded on a map?'. The answers were inspirational and in some cases unexpected. Some of the comments were incorporated on the map. Some were very positive: 'the social life is quite outstanding'; 'so nice to be able to walk

everywhere'; 'you feel you are living in the country'; 'the secret gardens behind the houses'. Others were more negative: 'the heavy traffic'; 'unsympathetic street lighting'; 'litter from McDonald's'.

We felt an urban environment required a different approach. We looked at other examples of city maps such as the parish map created by Vizability Arts with the Easton community in Bristol, where the map-in-the-making was taken round on a double-decker bus to encourage all residents to participate. We also looked at East London where an artist and a photographer produced an installation 'London Fields – The Ghetto 1994' documenting the homes and lifestyles of a community of

squatters occupying an area of Hackney under threat from re-development. David Hockney's photo collages of a Paris street were also instrumental in our decision to record the street and its people in photographs.

We organised a group photograph outside St John's Chapel on a bitterly cold Sunday in February – a key has been made giving their names – and took hundreds of photographs of individual houses in the street, including details of their fabric, like red brick and flint. We also reflected negative aspects: parking cones, lorries and litter from McDonald's. The finished map (stored in West Sussex Record Office) is enormous – some 8 feet long by 2.5 feet high. It was launched with a party

that everyone in the street attended. Demand for copies of the finished artwork was high.

Looking at the map five years later we realise what a snapshot in time it was. November 2001 saw the Lavant burst its

Miles of pipework saved the city from the floods

banks and flood the city; the collage includes photos of the sandbags and the elaborate pipework that prevented our houses from being deluged. Inevitably since then, some of the people have gone. Neighbours have moved, some have died and a few houses redeveloped. McDonald's has now closed on the corner of East Street, the international publishing company of John Wiley has relocated in the city, replaced by Thomas Eggar, the solicitors, and St John's Chapel, somewhat dilapidated in

Secret Gardens

St John's Chapel

2001, has been restored to its former glory. Stride's estate agency and auctioneers, one of the city's oldest family businesses, keeps its traditional place amongst us, its Southdown House a good visual stop at the street's southern end.

Looking back, what would we have done differently in making the map? We should have planned ahead and taken more photographs in the summer, we should have considered making a video capturing the life of the street, preserved residents' memories and perhaps have tried to record the height and type of local trees.

When you embark on making a parish map – in whatever form – the possibilities are endless. We would have liked to have known much more about the street a hundred years ago. What did it look like then? What did the people look like? What did they wear? Did they feel the same sense of community as we do? In another hundred years, the residents of St John's Street will know some of the answers to these questions by looking at our collage-map, a glimpse of life in the years 2000 and 2001.

DEBORAH MITCHELSON and JANE WEEKS

'. . . on a bitterly cold Sunday in February'

Chichester – Whyke

THE TWO CHICHESTER MAPS – of Whyke and St John's Street – demonstrate just how elastic the definition of a parish map can be. Unlike so many community-made maps, they both make the point that the area chosen doesn't have to cover a whole parish, but can be narrowed down to a town or village centre, a particular neighbourhood, or even just a single road or street. Whatever their boundaries, what they all have in common is that they are about the territory people call home. The two Chichester maps share another similarity – they are both photographic. Geoff King, who masterminded this aerial-view map with Pauline Newton, feels that this type of map has the edge on the two-dimensional plan as it gives a touch of reality – 'the sense of place that we strive for' he says.

Whyke's map is of a neighbourhood forming the south-eastern part of Chichester. To those living here it has a character and spirit all its own that the Whyke Residents Association was set up to protect and enhance. Those who really care about these things don't want to see Whyke's identity lost. George Appleby, its chairman, said the association owed its motivation to 'the distinctiveness of the area. Not just that it is close to the city centre, pleasingly and variously built, has open spaces, trees and plenty of friendly residents; it has a history which gives it a character of its own.'

This history gives Whyke its meaning. Look up Whyke in any Victorian *Kelly's Directory* and you won't find it; if you don't know the locality it would be like trying to discover the name of Rumpelstiltskin in the fairy story. So search in the directories for an equally tortuous and heavy-sounding name – Rumboldswyke – and there's the answer – described as both a village and parish in its own right. The church and the little street of cottages were surrounded by fields growing grass, wheat and barley, and there were even two quite separate hamlets, Hornet and Wickham. It was a tiny country village, on Chichester's doorstep, but physically quite separate and distinct, the only parish with its village centre so close to the city. That's why its history has given it a far greater diversity and varied character unlike any other community around the city margins.

Rumboldswyke's historic footprint can still be discovered, pinpointed on the map by numbered features that link with little drawings and watercolours. The first is for the oldest building, the redundant church of St Mary, a thousand years old, its walls embedded with re-used Roman bricks and tiles. In pre-Reformation days it held the clue to the origin of the parish's name. In the church was a chapel to St Rumbold – whoever he was, for there were two Rumbold saints, one English, one Irish – to whose memory the pious gave gifts.

Chichester High School for Boys

Chichester High School for Girls

Rumboldswhyke Church of England Infants School

St George's Church, Cleveland Road

St Mary's Church, Whyke Road

Richard Barnam gave fourpence for 'the maynteynyng of the Light of Saint Romboltes Chapel in the parish of Wyck' in 1525. For centuries the place was variously called Wyck (meaning a settlement), sometimes Rumboldswyke (thus specifying the settlement and distinguishing it from nearby Shopwyke), but both spelt in all sorts of fractured ways. Now almost everyone calls and spells it Whyke, but the infants' school in Rumbolds Close clings to the more historic 'Rumboldswhyke' for its name.

Priest's House, Whyke Road

By the church is the next oldest building, the Priest's House, thatched (unusual for Chichester now), and so tiny, probably dating from the 16th century. They are at the end of what was once a pathway that made a straight line across the fields linking two parish churches – St Pancras in Chichester with St Mary's, the route still traceable between the twitten in the Hornet and along the route of Whyke Lane. (A twitten is a Sussex word for a very narrow passage-way.) This ancient way is still a main route between the city and the heart of the old parish. On the map the route is shown between numbers 16 and 3. In parts it has to be a pedestrian way, not only because of the twitten, but also because the railway line makes its ruler-like print across the face of Whyke. It cut the parish into two unequal parts when built in the mid-1840s.

Whyke Lane – the twitten

Rumboldswyke's other major artery, and once its main street, is Whyke Road, where five detached houses (numbers 13–17) are some of Whyke's best Victorian properties with their beautifully worked flint fronts, knapped (cut with a flat face) and galleted (little flakes of flint used in the mortar joints). Numbers 18 and 19 show another way of using local flint, here in their uncut pebble form, again with galleting. Two of Whyke's notable houses are

This is our community of Whyke in the first year of the third millennium AD, and from an aircraft a camera has captured our small piece of England.

The buildings here date from Saxon times to the present day. You can still see a site where the Romans may have watched their gladiators, and another where a Saxon king is believed to have lived. The earliest surviving structure, St Mary's church in Whyke Road, is of Saxon origin with 13th century additions. It was formerly known as St Rumbold's, hence the village name of Rumboldswhyke. Listed as 'Wiche', the village appears in the *Domesday Book* of 1086.

Rumboldswhyke was a small settlement around the church, separated from Chichester by farmland and orchards. In 1846 the railway cut through the village from east to west, and rapid commercial and housing expansion followed. In 1893 the parish of Rumboldswhyke became part of the city of Chichester, and was thereafter known as Whyke. The old church proved inadequate for the growing population, and in 1901 the much larger St George's church was built north of the railway. By the early 1950s the last major public housing development – the Whyke Estate – was completed.

Quarry Lane light industrial estate was developed on the site of a filled-in gravel pit, bringing much valued employment and services plus wholesale and retail shopping to complement our community stores and post office. The cattle market, opened in 1871 to take animals off the city streets, ceased trading in 1990. The site became a car park, but a general market is still held there twice weekly. Last year saw the start of a farmer's produce market.

Whyke is not a dormitory community. We live, work, learn and play here. We enjoy the vibrancy of commerce and the lively presence of primary and secondary schools, youth and church groups, and the many students from Chichester's two Colleges who live here; there is also a valued community policeman. The least popular feature for many people on this photograph is the noisy, busy, dangerous by-pass on our southern boundary. This aside, Whyke remains a popular and pleasant place to live.

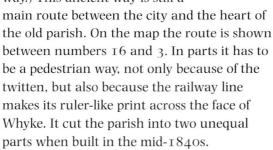

Top: 11. Whyke Estate Shops. *Centre:* 12. Lindwhyke Stores, Whyke Lane. *Bottom:* 13. Post Office & Stores, Cambrai Avenue.

THE NE

From left: 14. Bull ring in market wall.
15. New market entrance.
16. Whyke Lane twitten.
17. Market stall.

Clockwise from top left:
18. The Crown Inn, Whyke Road. 19. The Four Chesnuts, Oving Road. 20. The Wickham Arms, Bognor Road. 21. The Mainline Tavern and Whyke Road Level Crossing.

Left above: 1. St Mary's Church, Whyke Road.
Right above: 2. St George's Church, Whyke Road.
Left: 3. The Priest's House, Whyke Road

7. Wellington Terrace, Caledonian Road.

Top: 4. Portfield Mercedes, Quarry Lane.
Centre: 5. Covers, Quarry Lane.
Bottom: 6. The Forum, Stirling Road.

Top: 8. Fishing at Whyke Lakes.
Centre: 9. Guide Hut, Whyke Lane.
Bottom: 10. Scout Hut, Whyke Road.

CHICHESTER

WHYKE

¼ km – ¼ mile

Rumboldswhyke Church of England Infants' School

KINGSHAM C.P. SCHOOL
KINGSHAM COUNTY PRIMARY SCHOOL

...th the aid of grants from West Sussex County Council, ...ncil and the Millennium Festival Awards for All Fund.

Illustrations contributed by Barbara Booth, Roger Clark, Jose Denton, Marigold Durnford and Jo Patten. Historical notes were supplied by Monica Maloney, Katherine Slay and Bunny Williams. The project was coordinated for the Whyke Residents' Association by Geoff King and Pauline Newton.

...RHOOD OF WHYKE   WITHIN THE PARISH OF RUMBOLDSWHYKE   west sussex county council in the same road: Trimmers House (opposite the Scout Hut), with its Dutch-style stepped bricks over the porch, and at number 29, by the York Road corner, with all the elegant simplicity of Georgian architecture.

One of the most extraordinary uses of pebbles is Wellington Terrace in Caledonian Road where their protrusion beyond the mortar line gives an unusual finish, and notice the huge egg-shaped pebble under Wellington's bust. All

Wellington Terrace

around there is a profusion of styles and materials: not only in flint, but stucco and painted brick as well as bricks in yellow and shades of red. There are many delightful features. For example in Lyndhurst Road, the little pointed gothic-style windows and crenellations at 40 and 41; the Edwardian balconies at numbers 67–69; some interesting use of corrugated iron for the canopy linking 16–21; on the corner by number 16 is a boundary wall with sunflower decoration. At every turn there are interesting roof finials, date stones, chimney pots and pretty Victorian gable-boards.

Whyke's more modern development dates from the 1920s when the city council built in Pound Farm Road. This was followed by the private enterprise of Frederick Keates in the '30s, whose road names were memorials to his own family: Cambrai after the famous tank battle of World War One where Keates fought and where his brother was killed; Ormonde after

Post Office and Stores, Cambrai Avenue

the French place where they both stayed just before the battle; Velyn after his daughter, Evelyn, who died in childhood; and more happily Winden, combining the name of his surviving daughter, Winifred, with that of her husband Denis.

Whyke's largest housing estate came in the heady days of post-war reconstruction after 1945. South of the railway

line the city council developed the massive Whyke Estate with flats, houses and bungalows around a huge central green, still its dominant feature. One nice little touch is Kingsham Primary School's drawings burnt into the tops of the wooden seats around the green – a butterfly, tortoise, fish, girls skipping, a witch on her broomstick, and many more, a little bit of fun and fantasy in the search for something special for this big open space.

As flint has made such a major contribution towards Whyke's distinctiveness, it's good to see modern architects using this traditional local stone. The 1982 house at 49 Lyndhurst Road, the extension to Walnut Tree Cottages in Cleveland Road and the Linden houses in Old Bakery Gardens are model examples of what can be achieved in making new work so harmonious in its surroundings.

When the Residents Association recently published *Aspects of Whyke Through the Ages*, Katherine Slay wrote about why it was such a pleasant place in which to live. Wildlife is one major feature, the gravel-pit lakes and St Mary's churchyard its two most important habitats. 'Seventy-one different species of wild flowers were recorded in the churchyard ... together with 12 species of butterflies. Yew, cherry, elder, blackberry, rosehip and beech provide food for birds. Slow worms may be found under gravestones, and the nearby lakes mean that there are

Gravel-pit fishing

damselflies and dragonflies darting around the churchyard during the summer and autumn.' Listing some of Whyke's mature trees she says that Whyke has its own tree warden [Geoff King]'concerned not just with existing trees, but with planting new ones in consultation with those living nearby'.

Katherine concludes that it's 'an attractive and flourishing area of Chichester' where there is plenty going on. And as the map says 'Whyke is not a dormitory community. We live, work, learn and play here.' To residents it's a vital place, certainly not just a bolt-on suburb of the city.

KIM LESLIE

Chidham

WE JUST HAD TO INCLUDE the famous Chidham Wheat with a field mouse as part of our title-piece. Within these ears of wheat are the names of the three villages associated with the parish – Chidham, Hambrook and Nutbourne. Enthusiasts from all three banded together to make the parish map. The inspired suggestion from Caroline Davis that the map should be of fabric was at first received with some timidity, but under her tuition and leadership the thirty-strong group finished the map in record time. Fabric painting, patchwork, embroidery and appliqué were all involved, so it was with a mixture of relief and pride that the volunteers saw its final completion in 2001.

The parish has seen an upsurge of pride in the community over the last few years. A parish photobook was prepared at the same time as the parish map and these have been followed by a parish plan looking at environmental and planning issues we face in the future. To illustrate the parish plan we used elements taken from the map. The map itself is proudly displayed in St Mary's Church.

Chidham is a small rural parish five miles west of Chichester. When the parish council chose to produce a map as one way to celebrate the millennium, there was an immediate difficulty. The parish boundaries do not encompass all of the area many people thought should be covered by the map. After much discussion a consensus was reached; purists can look for the red dashed line showing precisely the area within the civil parish. The map also shows three important physical features: the A27 trunk road, the railway line and the A259. The map group used the railway line to especially good effect. Many local people, not in the group, decried their own ability with needle and thread, but were each cajoled by Caroline into putting just one railway sleeper onto the map, thus making their mark for posterity! Making the map provided much fun and enjoyment for many members of the community.

No photograph could do full justice to our map. You will have to visit the church to appreciate its warmth, texture and size. The map hangs in a side chapel dedicated to St Cuthman. This is particularly appropriate because the map shows Cuthman pushing his mother in a barrow from Chidham to Steyning – for details about this legend see Christopher Fry's play *The Boy with a Cart*.

We think that the map combines a firm overall structure with fine detail. Birds and animals, wild flowers and plants are shown. A watercress plant represents the watercress beds of Hambrook. See whether you can find the ladybird on an oak leaf. Leaves of local trees are a particular feature. The inner border shows leaves in each corner,

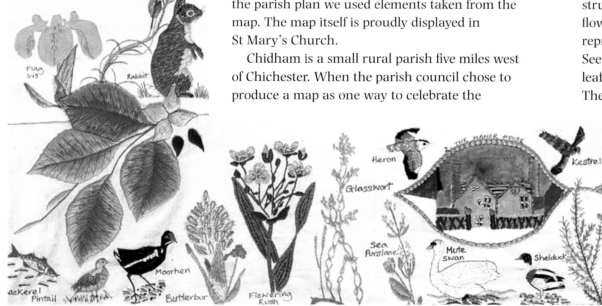

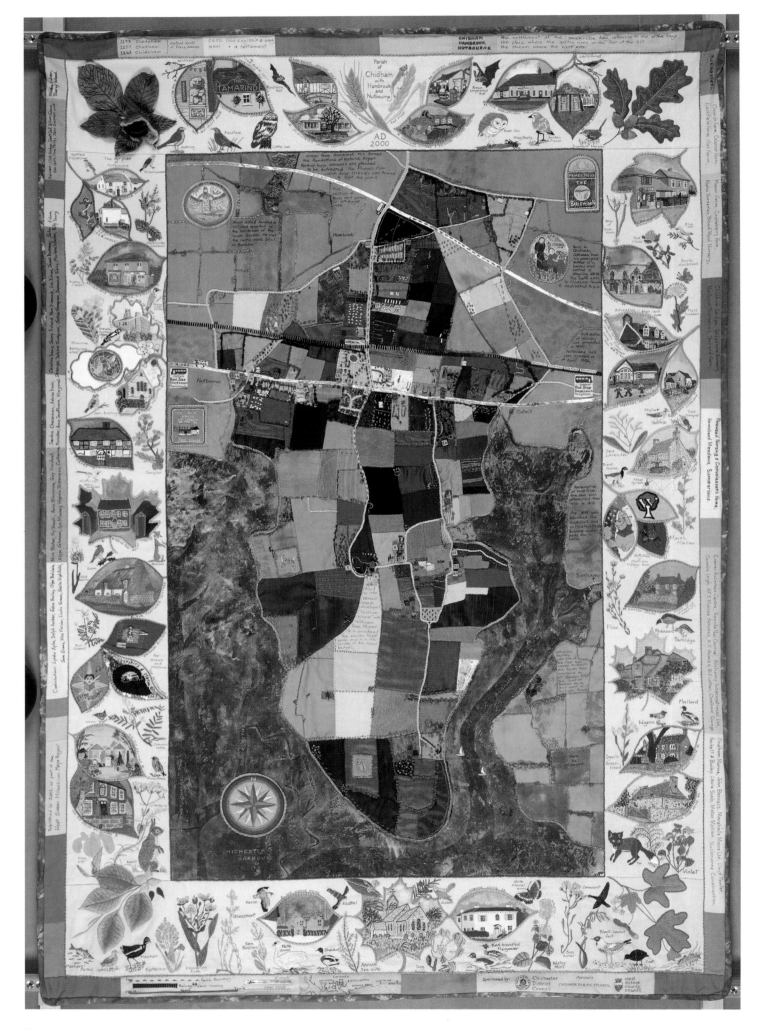

work. The map group decided not to cover the map, but to allow children (and adults!) to touch it for its wonderful feel. We did not want a museum piece; we appreciate that it has a finite life and realise that when it becomes worn it will need to be removed.

Aficionados of the art of patchwork will be interested in the stitch-and-flip method used in making the individual fields. Timid volunteers soon mastered this esoteric technique, and now proudly point to 'their' group of fields, each matched to the correct colour and texture revealed by an aerial photograph. The inter-tidal waters of Chichester Harbour around the Chidham peninsula are a haven for wildlife. Low tide exposes mud flats and these are represented, using fabric paint, in rich, glowing colours.

and aspects of the parish, such as buildings and organisations, have each been stitched within a leaf outline. The outer border tells us about the people who worked on the map, local businesses, sponsoring authorities and the derivation of the local place names. 'The place where the spring rises at the foot of the hill' – i.e. Hambrook, provides a reliable source of clean water for watercress, still in commercial production.

The large central panel holds the map itself. Deciding which features to show and then how to highlight them was a source of lengthy debate. We did not shy away from relatively modern features; you will see the cars in a car-recycling business and caravans in a holiday camp, ingeniously illustrated by the use of coloured beads. The fierce battle against proposals to extend the gravel pits on Hambrook Hill – once used as a source of material for the foundations of Gatwick Airport – is mentioned in the text at the top of the map.

Long-standing residents of Nutbourne talk wistfully of their much-loved pubs that have now disappeared, shown just beneath the splendid three-dimensional horse-chestnut in the top left corner of the map. The chestnut itself has special significance for the parish. In days gone by, magnificent chestnut trees lined parish lanes. Disease and concern over their safety led to their loss, but in more recent times re-planting has started to work its magic – leafy shade is now returning to the lanes.

Our map acts as a magnet for all visitors to St Mary's Church. Children in particular are drawn to it and gaze in awe at its intricate

Chidham's map was accepted for *Stitch 2000* – the National Needlework Record's database set up to record and study community-made needlework created for the millennium. Needleworks that are part of this project will be the subject of research studies; they will record their life histories and monitor their future physical state in terms of the environment in which they are displayed.

You will have gathered that we are all very proud of our 'different' parish map. Would we have the courage to do it all again? We think we would, but not for a few years, please!

CLIFF ARCHER

Clapham and Patching

A S BUDA IS TO PEST so is Clapham to Patching, locked together like pieces of a jigsaw, inseparable Sussex twins separated by little but a road with the most lovely name, the Long Furlong, that here begins and ends its snake-like journey across the hills. Richard Williamson put it beautifully in the *West Sussex Gazette*, calling them 'the heavenly twins, like Castor and Pollux, set near the haven of the high Downs'. How fittingly that *Under the Heavens* gives the title for a book about life in the local countryside by Bunny Austin (once-famous 1930s Davis Cup player who married into a Clapham family).

Twins in such close proximity have necessarily much in common: their downland setting, farmland behind each village street, a goodly mix of older housing in local flint, brick and timber, a few thatched, most tiled, neatly intermingling with newer development, narrow lanes ending abruptly in gated-fields and medieval churches. They share virtually all the same clubs and societies, the same village hall, school, post office/shop, and rector, both churches united as long ago as 1874 – two villages yet one community across the dividing road.

In 2000 they shared their millennium celebrations, jointly producing both a parish map and compendious tome on local history, *Bricks & Water: 100 Years of Social History in Clapham and Patching Villages.* Its double-edged

Waterworks, Long Furlong

The Old Tollgate, Long Furlong

title neatly conveys two essential differences: the dependence on one industrial business, the Clapham Common Brick and Tile Company, for much of last century; Patching drawing much of its prosperity from arable and sheep farming between the Downs and Patching Pond – the 'Water' of the title. Industrial one side, downland farming on the other. The brick and tile works has closed, but heavy commercial use persists with a building supplies merchant and a county council highways and transport depot responsible for a large part of West Sussex. Patching continues its long tradition of rural woodcrafts, but now with a changed emphasis – no longer hurdles, sheep feeders and wheelwrighting but modern joinery in the France Lane Woodyard and Seth Evans' Joinery Shop on the Long Furlong road where they made the kiosks for the London Eye.

Walking sticks – a local craft

The Horse & Groom

The Millennium Book

Children's Cycle Track, Clapham

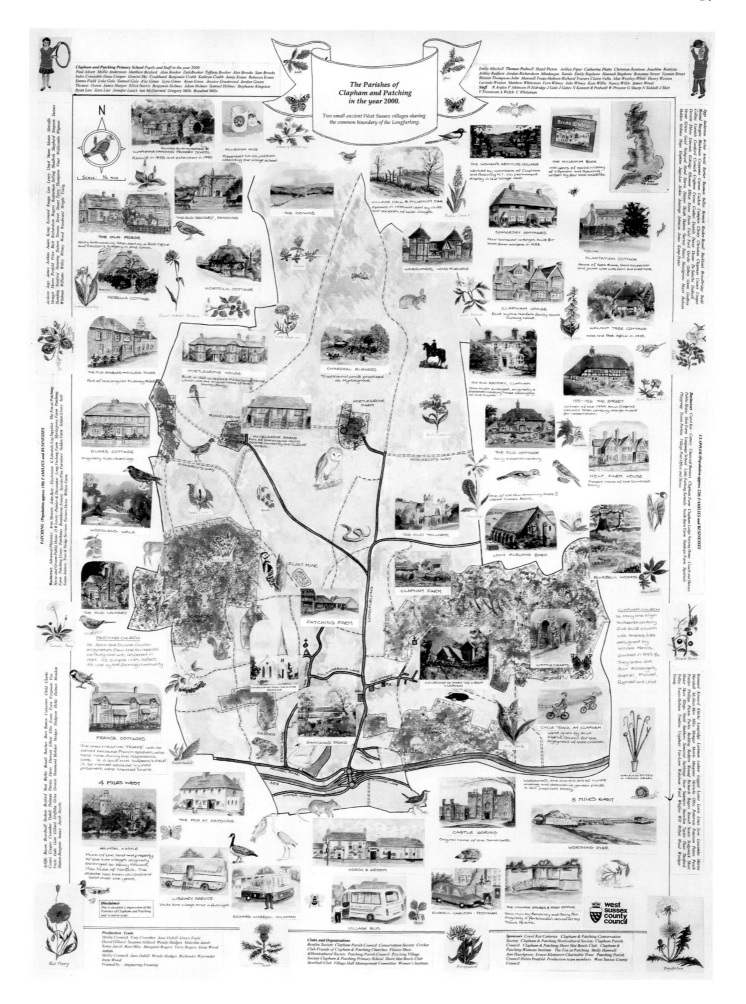

The Downs

The Old Rectory, Clapham

Richard Warren, milkman

Village bus

Russell Carlton, postman

Both villages are gateways to two quite different types of countryside: Patching onto open Downs and the summits of Blackpatch and Harrow, pock-marked by prehistoric flint-mines, and with fabulous views; Clapham leading into a myriad of tracks through the darker enclosed depths of Clapham Woods.

Clapham Woods

These woods can cast their magic as they did on Elsie Oxenham (1880–1960), whose tales of jolly gym-slipped heroines captured a vast schoolgirl market. Living in Worthing and using Sussex backdrops for her girls' adventures, she knew Clapham Woods well, bringing her Camp Fire Girls (a bit like the Girl Guides) for camping and exploration. *New Girls at Wood End* (1957) gathered inspiration from the

Clapham School of Nature Study and Gardening run by the redoubtable Miss Collins and Miss Cracknell – 'Collie and Crackie' – in their home at the former Rectory from 1911 until 1936. More like a bucolic finishing school for thoroughbreds, their young ladies wore Land Army-style uniforms with breeches and brown Liberty-linen smock tunics. They studied by oil and candlelight – two candles a week each for their bedrooms – worked on the land, tended the livestock and, as one student remembers when the urgent jobs were done, 'Collie took us into the woods and taught us to turn over stones and pieces of bark' for nature studies. Bunny Austin was as entranced as Elsie Oxenham by this place, immortalising these two lady teachers in their big house in *Under the Heavens*, published in 1936:

> I can only say that in England alone can such a house be found; only English genius can create its character, and only an English village can form its setting. . . . old and grey, instinct with calm and quiet comfort, with security and peace. . . . Such houses are the essence of all that is best in the English character – simplicity and sanity and unselfconscious goodness. And Miss Millicent and Miss Olive are two ladies whom, travel the wide world, you will find nowhere but in such a house.

St John the Divine's Church, Patching

St Mary the Virgin's Church, Clapham

They and their Clapham house reminded Bunny Austin of Rupert Brooke's lines of '. . . sights and sounds . . . /in hearts at peace, under an English heaven'.

If Clapham and Patching's countryside is one way to heaven, then another sure way is up the lanes to their churches – and what a contrast there is. Patching plain and simple, its spire soaring to the skies on the very edge of the Downs, sitting almost in a farmyard and called by one local resident 'the farmers' church'; the other at Clapham, the 'landlord's church', its squat tower crouched low in its woodland camouflage.

Historically Clapham's church has long been a shrine to its squires and is still intimately linked with the Somerset family and their Castle Goring Estate, whereas Patching has always been more remote from its Arundel landlord, the Duke of Norfolk, so tenant farmers have held sway here. Traces of Daniel Dulaney's property – the major tenantry – survive as integral parts of the village: a remnant of the big house and its outbuildings – The Old Coach House and its clocktower, The Old Laundry opposite, Dulaney Lodge in France Lane, the ice house still seen from along Coldharbour Lane. 'But Patching never had a squire of its own in the twentieth century to match the Somersets in Clapham', according to *Bricks & Water.*

Echoing its wealthy landlords' tastes, Clapham church positively glows from its rich decorative brasswork, the setting for an impressive display of William Morris tiles surrounded by a vast family of Shelley memorials – forty-six ancestors of the poet commemorated in brass and stone. They lived in some splendour at nearby Michelgrove, now a downland ruin, later building Castle Goring, an astonishing two-faced mansion by the A27, flint-gothic one side, stone-classical on the other. Clapham church played its part in the 1992 celebrations for the bicentenary of the Sussex-born poet, Percy Bysshe Shelley.

Castle Goring

The church is watched over by Clapham's wild Rev. He's the white shirt-fronted ginger tom who attends worship, sleeps in his house by the graveyard hedge and eats by the porch. A much-loved custodian of the church, he's a bit of a charity cat, that's why his bowls are always there. Over at Patching the village is looked over by three high-flying black cats, all very territorial amongst the roofs. They're easier to find than the Rev!

KIM LESLIE

Village Hall and Millennium Oak

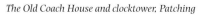
The Old Coach House and clocktower, Patching

Cocking

IF EVER THERE WAS a *Guinness Book of Records of Parish Maps* then Cocking's place in it would be assured. Cast in bronze, its two maps – not just one – make an extraordinary and unique contribution to parish mapping. The maps are literally monumental, part of a 15 feet high, three-quarters of a ton column of history inspired by Trajan's Column in Rome. Just as this was for a celebration two thousand years ago – for Roman victories – so Cocking celebrated the new millennium with its own spectacular monument. In itself the Cocking History Column creates a new focus of deep meaning within the landscape it so powerfully depicts.

The story started with Juliet Kay, her enthusiasm for a parish map reaching fellow Cocking resident Philip Jackson, one of the foremost sculptors working in bronze today, renowned for his equestrian sculpture of the Queen in Windsor Great Park, Sir Matt Busby at Old Trafford, Manchester and other high-profile commissions around the world. When he learnt that Cocking wanted to be part of the West Sussex project and might be making a paper map, Philip suggested raising the stakes, offering his skills for something quite different. As ever, his ambition was visionary.

His inspiration galvanised the Cocking History Group into action, first of all under Juliet's leadership in researching the parish's history and then working under Philip to model forty-eight low-relief panels graphically illustrating Cocking's past and present through pictures and lettering. These would wind their way down the height of the column in a spiral band recording ancient history from the Bronze Age at the top down to the millennium at the bottom. Twisting around the column between these panels would be a narrow ribbon of national history giving overall context to what was happening in Cocking through the centuries. Beneath, on a Portland Stone base, would be the two parish maps by Juliet Crawford.

Planning Stage – some of the panel-makers discussing their work with Philip Jackson

Photo: Tony Heller

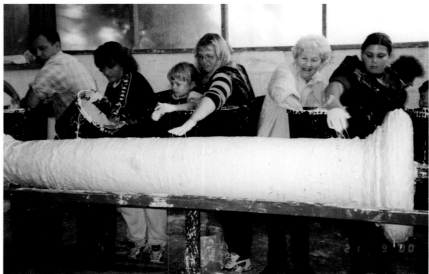

Spinning the Column – the column rotates whilst plaster is applied by hand, 'a gloriously messy business'

Photo: Tony Heller

Carving the Plaster – Myfanwy Rogers carves the lettering for a plaster panel

Photo: Tony Heller

*Working in Wax –
Juliet Crawford applies the
finishing touches to the wax
relief model for one of the
parish maps*

Photo: Tony Heller

Photo: Diana Zeuner

*Cocking in 2001 –
one of the finished parish maps cast in
bronze, now on the base of the column*

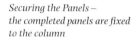

*Securing the Panels –
the completed panels are fixed
to the column*

Photo: Tony Heller

*Casting at Lasham –
the molten bronze
reaches 1,200°C*

Photo: Tony Heller

Philip taught the skills of working in wax for low-relief modelling and letter carving to a group of twenty-eight volunteers, few of whom had any experience in this field. They each worked at home, everyone devising their own favourite way of making it pliable, like warming it with a hair dryer, and each finding their own favourite tools like old dentist's equipment and even a potato peeler. Slowly the panels took shape and the column was eventually ready to go to the foundry at Lasham in Hampshire for casting. This too was another intricate and complicated process starting with a sectionalised mould, then the production of a wax positive, then ceramic dipping and finally the excitement when the molten bronze was poured and the column finally born.

After six years of planning, research and production, the column was unveiled on a beautiful spring morning on 15 April 2005 by Lady Cowdray – herself one of the modellers – then blessed by Cocking's vicar, Colin Bradley. Just three hours later one freakish storm-cloud hurled snow and hail onto the village with such ferocity that life froze to a standstill. This was Cocking's storm alone, column and storm captured beautifully on Cocking's website – www.cocking.org – that went live the very same day. The column site overlooks the Downs as its backdrop, testimony to Philip's belief that placing, setting and atmosphere are all crucial in making a sculpture work.

Photo: West Sussex Gazette

Unveiling the Column –
Lady Cowdray performs the ceremony;
note the parish map at the base

As the research team gathered such an enormous amount of historical information it was decided to go a step further, to publish a parish history that was launched on the same day at the unveiling party. *A Short History of Cocking* by Naomi Barnett, Juliet Kay and Myfanwy Rogers and designed by Jean Jackson, Philip's wife, tells the story of the parish for the first time with many previously unpublished photographs. A copy has been sealed within a lead-wrapped time capsule beneath the column. Column and book, created in tandem, are a remarkable achievement, together an outstandingly imaginative contribution to the West Sussex Parish Maps Project.

KIM LESLIE

Photo: Nick Birch

Interweaving Local and National History –
details on the bronze column

Photo: Nick Birch

Coldwaltham, Watersfield and Hardham

ONE POINT THAT STANDS OUT SO impressively from Coldwaltham's Millennium Map is that the parish is shaped like a peninsula – three-quarters surrounded by the waters of the rivers Rother and Arun. And at least half the remaining quarter is bordered by trees on its western side. The map has made people more aware of our boundaries and our setting.

Much more apparent is the presence of the A29 London to Bognor road cutting right through the centre of Coldwaltham. Many years ago, members of the parish council held a meeting at Hardham Bridge to see for themselves the dangers of the bottleneck created at this point. They were nearly run down, the meeting abandoned! Tom Barber, who instigated the meeting, won his point, and a parallel pedestrian bridge was duly erected – long known as 'Barber's Bridge'.

Thankfully the main road does not dissect the parish's heart, which has long beaten in the widespread community spirit we have

here. It must be said that people have lived around the locality for a very long time as Coldwaltham seems to have been an area of human habitation since prehistoric times. So the community element is nothing new.

The modern civil parish unites three communities: the two ancient ecclesiastical parishes of Coldwaltham and Hardham and the hamlet of Watersfield.

Coldwaltham has its lovely church dedicated to St Giles, patron saint of the infirm – and blacksmiths. There was probably a small chapel here in Saxon times; certainly the evidence for the site's antiquity is its yew tree, estimated at an amazing three thousand years old. It's one of the oldest yews in the country. Of the original medieval church little remains except for the tower, unusually half-timbered under a pyramid-shaped cap looking distinctly like a Welsh-borders church. St Giles was for long the heart of all the social life in the village – not just from Sunday to Sunday, but from day to day. Perhaps one day that will again be the case.

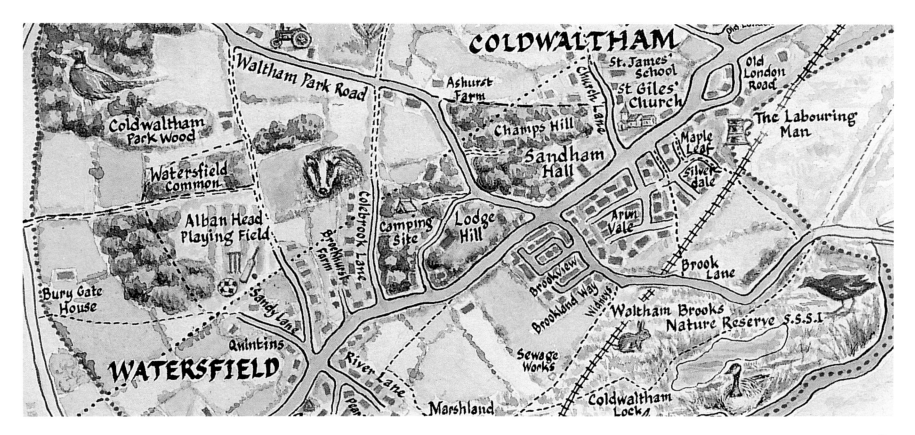

Hardham's little church, dedicated to St Botolph, patron saint of travellers and river crossings, is one of the notable Saxon churches of England, famed for its medieval wall paintings, a 'superb gallery of Norman art' in the opinion of Simon Jenkins in *England's Thousand Best Churches*. That of St George is the earliest known representation of him in the country. Less describable is the atmosphere of serenity that pervades the place, thankfully left stranded on a loop of the old road and separated from the traffic-filled A29.

Much of the heart of the parish comes from St James' Church of England School. It's hard to believe that it was almost closed down in 1986 for lack of pupils. Since then it has gone from strength to strength. The annual summer fête held in the school grounds brings together teachers, parents, pupils and community in an especially close way. There has long been discussion over one of Coldlwaltham's curiosities: why does the church school have St James as its patron when it is run under the auspices of St Giles' Church? One suggestion is that St Giles, patron of the lame and infirm, is hardly suitable for a school for lively youngsters!

Time marches on. Recent changes have included the building of Chapel Close in Watersfield, and a housing-association complex, Piers Secombe Close, in Coldwaltham. The demolition of both the pub and the garage in the heart of Watersfield was watched with horror. Both were at the very centre of local life. The modern garage had long replaced the Croft Garage, owned until 1945 by Moses Harris. It was no more than a shed where young Stanley Ruff (later to become the third generation

St James' C of E School Coldwaltham, opened in Church Lane in 1848, has been much extended and improved since the original School House was built. A thriving place for its young pupils and teachers, it boasts a strongly supportive Parent Teachers' Association

A Council House on the 1930s estate which comprises Brook View, Brook View South and Brookland Way. Many of these houses are now privately owned

A bungalow on the Arun Vale housing estate, built in 1963, two years before Silverdale housing estate. Both private estates, these house a goodly number of Coldwaltham residents

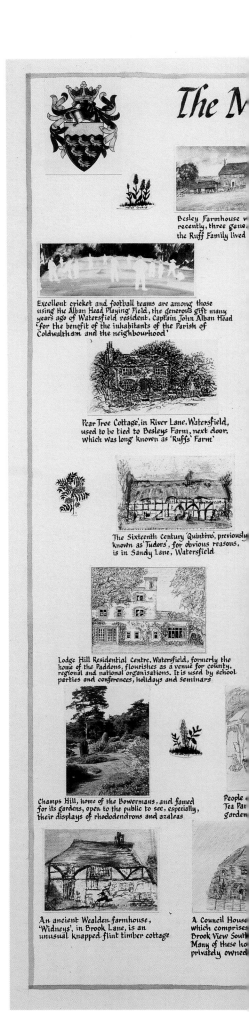

The M

Besley Farmhouse w recently, three gener the Ruff Family lived

Excellent cricket and football teams are among those using the Alban Head Playing Field, the generous gift many years ago of Watersfield resident, Captain John Alban Head 'for the benefit of the inhabitants of the Parish of Coldwaltham and the neighbourhood'

Pear Tree Cottage, in River Lane, Watersfield, used to be tied to Besleys Farm, next door, which was long known as 'Ruffs' Farm'

The Sixteenth Century 'Quintins', previously known as 'Tudors', for obvious reasons, is in Sandy Lane, Watersfield

Lodge Hill Residential Centre, Watersfield, formerly the home of the Paddons, flourishes as a venue for county, regional and national organisations. It is used by school parties and conferences, holidays and seminars

Champs Hill, home of the Bowermans, and famed for its gardens, open to the public to see, especially, their displays of rhododendrons and azaleas

People Tea Par garden

An ancient Wealden farmhouse, 'Widneys', in Brook Lane, is an unusual knapped-flint timber cottage

A Council House which comprises Brook View Sout Many of these ho privately owned

nium Map of Coldwaltham, Watersfield and Hardham 2001

View over Watersfield

Coldwaltham Parish's Millennium Sign

Waltham Brooks Nature Reserve, granted SSSI (Site of Special Scientific Interest) status in 1987

PULBOROUGH

The Ruins of the Chapter House at Hardham Priory, founded during the reign of Henry III for the Black Canons of the Order of St Augustine

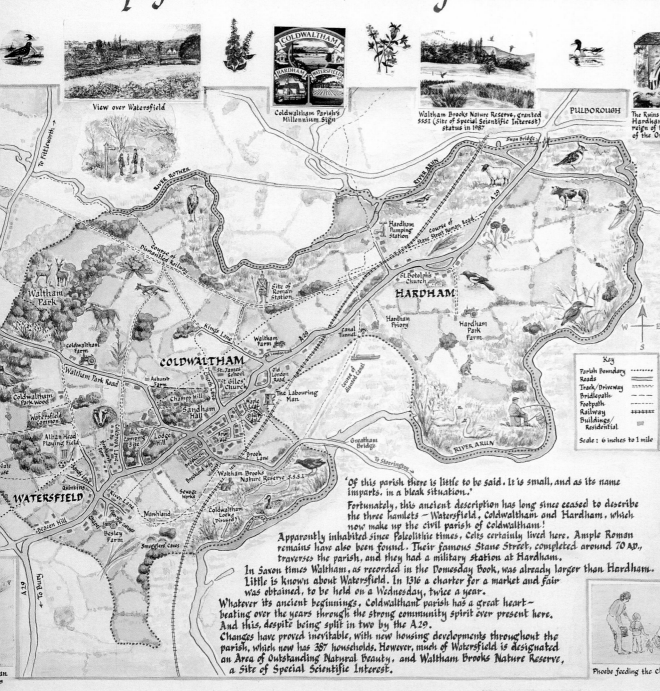

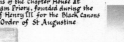

Winter's Farm, built c.1500, originally belonged to Hardham Priory, and is the last house in the parish before reaching Pulborough causeway

Hardham Pumping Station, on the east side of the River Rother, serves the Horsham and Crawley areas, along with Pulborough and Coldwaltham parish and other areas as required. Its current maximum output is 75 million litres

Hardham Church, built about 1050 AD, is thought to be the oldest Saxon Church in the country. It was dedicated to St Botolph, the Saxon patron of ports and river crossings

A remarkable feature of Hardham Church is its almost complete series of Romanesque wall paintings, which date from shortly after 1100 AD

Key

Parish Boundary	
Roads	
Track/Driveway	
Bridlepath	
Footpath	
Railway	
Buildings/Residential	

Scale : 6 inches to 1 mile

'Of this parish there is little to be said. It is small, and as its name imparts, in a bleak situation.'

Fortunately, this ancient description has long since ceased to describe the three hamlets – Watersfield, Coldwaltham and Hardham, which now make up the civil parish of Coldwaltham!

Apparently inhabited since Paleolithic times, Celts certainly lived here. Ample Roman remains have also been found. Their famous Stane Street, completed around 70 AD, traverses the parish, and they had a military station at Hardham.

In Saxon times Waltham, as recorded in the Domesday Book, was already larger than Hardham. Little is known about Watersfield. In 1316 a charter for a market and fair was obtained, to be held on a Wednesday, twice a year.

Whatever its ancient beginnings, Coldwaltham parish has a great heart – beating over the years through the strong community spirit ever present here. And this, despite being split in two by the A29.

Changes have proved inevitable, with new housing developments throughout the parish, which now has 387 households. However, much of Watersfield is designated an Area of Outstanding Natural Beauty, and Waltham Brooks Nature Reserve, a Site of Special Scientific Interest.

Phoebe feeding the chickens

The Labouring Man, now the only public house and eating place in the parish, was first built in Edwardian times, burned down in 1906, and then re-built

A bungalow on the Arun Vale housing estate, built in 1963, two years before Silverdale housing estate. Both private estates, these house a goodly number of Coldwaltham residents

Sandham Hall was built in 1902, as a practical memorial to the Rev'd James Sandham. Many of the parish's social events, as well as the Coffee Shop are held here, and it now also houses a useful Sub-Post Office

The weekly Coffee Shop in the Sandham Hall is well patronised by parishioners, who meet for a chat with friends and buy local produce and other requisites

St James' C of E School Coldwaltham, opened in Church Lane in 1848, has been much extended and improved since the original School House was built. A thriving place for its young pupils and teachers, it boasts a strongly supportive Parent Teachers' Association

Coldwaltham Parish Church, dedicated to St Giles, the Patron Saint of cripples, beggars and blacksmiths, dates back to the early 13th Century. In the Churchyard stands a yew tree more than 3000 years old and one of the twelve oldest in the country

The Old Priest House, built about 1220 by Hardham Priory to house the priests serving Coldwaltham Church, is now a restaurant, part time

of his family to farm in Watersfield) mended bicycles. A more than adequate petrol pump served drivers' requirements, as well as the Ford belonging to Captain Alban Head, kept clean and gleaming by Moses, who also chauffeured him wherever he wanted to go.

Among the other legendary characters some still remember 'Darkie' Pollard who used to say that he was apprenticed to a duck-shoe-er. When pressed he would reveal, with a twinkle, that this meant helping a man to shoo ducks in the right direction!

Watersfield's pub used to be housed in what is now called the Old Crown House, once frequented by smugglers who left their booty in caves at the end of River Lane. The pub 'crossed the road' to become the Three Crowns. Even when it became open plan and changed its name to the Tudor Rose (with a Sussex cart in front painted in the wrong colours), the pub remained a favourite meeting place for the locals. On Saturday nights it was the rendezvous of the village cricket and football teams after their matches on the Alban Head Playing Field.

The field was bequeathed by the good Captain Head in the 1930s 'for the benefit of the inhabitants of the parish of Coldwaltham and the neighbourhood' – a generous addendum. And because of its beautiful position the field is appreciated by far more people than just the sportsmen who use it. We take strolls here, walk our dogs along the edge of it and into the pinewoods behind. We proudly watch our football and cricket teams getting better and better in a setting which must be hard to beat in terms of scenic peace.

Coldwaltham's pub, evocatively called the

Labouring Man, is still going, and well patronised. One or two of its customers have leaned on its bar daily, for decades!

Many tempting landmarks lure visitors. A short walk down little side lanes reveals beautiful old houses, mostly kept in spanking good order. And

Waltham Brooks Nature Reserve was granted SSSI – Site of Special Scientific Interest – status in 1987. Some of the wildlife it hosts and which can still be seen in the woods are illustrated on the map. They include rabbits, mink, deer, foxes, pheasants and numerous species of wild birds. Then there is Champs Hill, famed for its gardens, especially for rhododendrons, azaleas and heathers that thrive on its sandy soils.

A less attractive but very important landmark is Sandham Hall: unimposing outside, but wonderful things happen inside! A weekly coffee morning is enjoyed by residents of all ages. Some bring their produce to sell. Others just come for coffee and to update news with friends. Many other events take place, including weekly ballroom-dancing, WI meetings, and commercial selling days, which all help the cash flow. Still meeting monthly here is the Wildbrooks Society, formed in 1972 to improve the good appearance and general amenity of the parish, to build up community life through social and cultural activities and to encourage high standards of planning and architecture in new buildings. It's our parish watchdog.

In no more than a cubby-hole in the entrance to Sandham Hall, the village post office is splendidly run two mornings a week by Pauline Streeter. She not only pays out

Champs Hill

pensions and provides stamps and the like, but has a noticeboard where people can advertise their sales and wants free of charge. Pauline knows almost everything that goes on in and around the parish, and so, when in doubt, people always go straight to her!

As more and more cars and heavy lorries thunder along the A29, it is comforting to know that Coldwaltham's community heartbeat can still be heard by those who live here, and love it.

SANDRA SAER

Village cricket on the Alban Head Playing Field

Copthorne

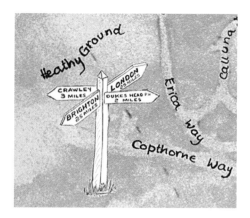

NE MASSIVE OAK TREE. Its roots are deeply embedded into the landscape under a huge green canopy bearing its harvest of acorns. This is the tree that's a map that's an expression of community life – a brilliant conception by the map-makers of Copthorne.

The oak was chosen as the most typical of Sussex trees, by far the most important species in the county's landscape, so prolific that Kipling called it the 'Sussex weed', Dryden crowning it 'the monarch' of the trees. To the people of Copthorne the oak symbolises the strength of community spirit within the village. And it is the tree that creates the map. Roads, footpaths and boundaries form its branches, giving it shape and form.

The tangled and winding roots beneath the tree feature the family names of everyone living in the village – there are close on fourteen hundred names written here – and just as the roots nurture growth so the people themselves make the community, symbolised by the tree. There was always the concern that with so many names more and more roots would dominate the overall picture. They

probably do, but this in itself makes the crucial point the map-makers wanted, that their life here is about a community of people. The essential – and ingeniously structured – message is that people are the life-force of Copthorne. When the map was unveiled in the summer of 2000 excited families gathered around to spot themselves interwoven into the root system.

The acorns take us a stage further into the tree/community analogy: just as the tree brings forth fruit, so the community produces all sorts of activities as a harvest of talent and creativity focused through all the clubs, societies and groups encapsulated within each acorn around the map. Each village organisation was given total freedom to express itself within the acorn format. Produced by artists ranging in age from three years up to 80 plus, each has its own identity and special charm, representing a real shared effort around the village. They are the key to Copthorne's village life.

This – possibly – unique conception behind the making of Copthorne's map – it is certainly unique in West Sussex parish-map terms – is very much the expression of what Valerie Porter writes about in her book *English*

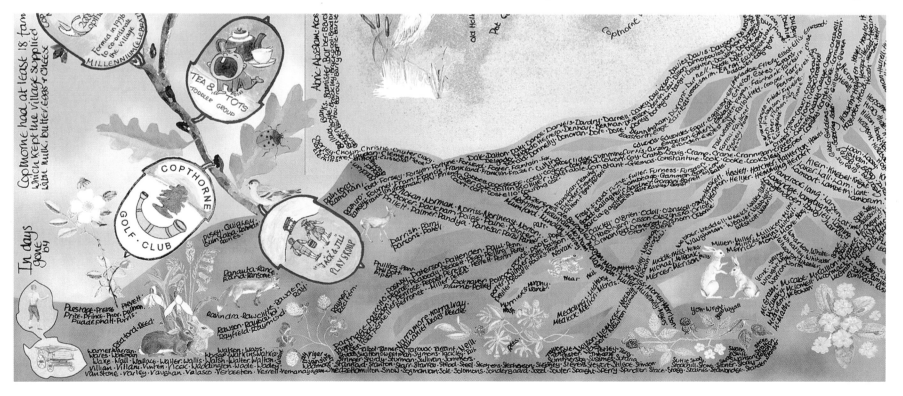

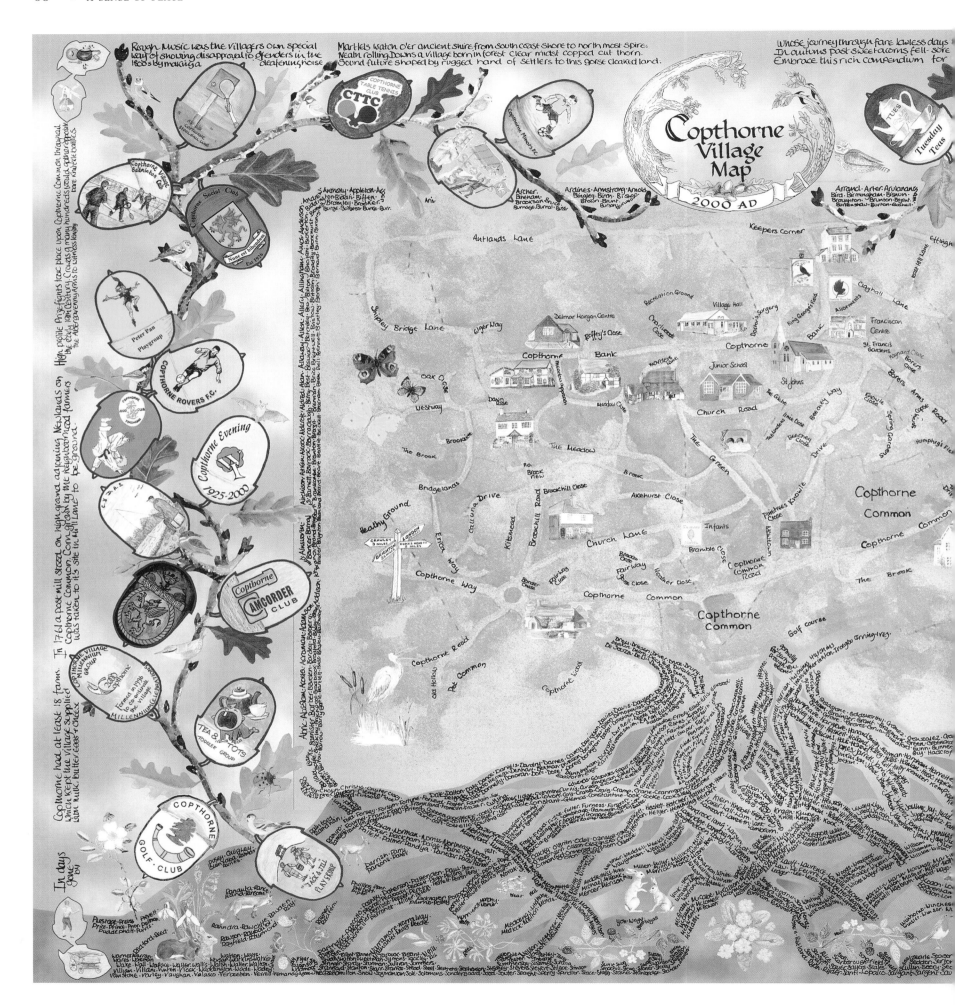

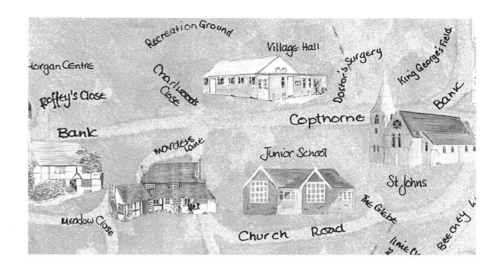

Villagers when she reminds us that 'a village is, essentially, its inhabitants, not its buildings, though the guide-books tend to describe buildings rather than everyday people who keep a village warm'. Hence only a handful of buildings are shown on the map, those that are most prominent and a few of the typical older properties.

What comes through very strongly is not the mass of housing that makes up the modern village, but the greenness representing its historic roots. Copthorne was once an isolated woodland community of scattered housing in one of the remotest parts of Worth Forest. Once seen as one of the wildest, roughest parts of the county, its legends and stories of smugglers, poachers and gypsies are told to this day. Sussex historian Mark Antony Lower wrote that 'The inhabitants were of lawless character, and were sometimes the cause of alarm in the district. A horn was therefore kept called the "Copthorne Horn" for the purpose of summoning the aid of the honest neighbours to quell any outbreak.' Catching the progressive Victorian mood – he was writing in 1870 – he went on to say that 'Thanks ... to advancing civilization, this horn has long been disused'. The horn is incorporated into the acorns for Copthorne Golf Club and the village's Millennium Group.

Copthorne's common land was the regular haunt of dubious roughnecks like the Fancy – the followers of prize-fighting who came to watch some of the greatest bare-fisted contests in the land. At least a dozen fights were staged around here between 1800 and 1823, often billed as world championships, immortalised in literature by Sir Arthur Conan Doyle's *Rodney Stone*,

published in 1896. He tells of thirty thousand 'ring-side parasites and ruffians' flooding into the district before being forced to leave by the law as prize-fighting was illegal. This was why contests took place in remote areas like Copthorne and Crawley Down, often close to county boundaries, for as Conan Doyle's Sussex magistrate says 'my jurisdiction ends at that ditch'. Cross over to Surrey to finish the match and the Sussex police couldn't touch them.

Copthorne has always been very much on the edge, a mix of Surrey and Sussex, its life spilling across the border line. Its historic roots were in Surrey, for in Domesday it was part of Reigate Hundred, its lands later shared between the parishes of Burstow and Horne in Surrey and Worth in East Sussex. Then on local government reorganisation in the 1970s, most of Copthorne became part of West Sussex, its more scattered northern parts – all with Copthorne, West Sussex addresses – remaining in Surrey. But for church purposes the ecclesiastic boundary for the parish – its church is the most northerly in Sussex – takes in this Surrey land, so a small area of what would otherwise be in the diocese of Southwark intrudes within the diocese of Chichester. As Christine Cheesmur of the map group comments, all these overlapping boundaries 'endlessly complicate our lives when it comes to council matters, schooling and everyday things like bus passes and postal addresses'.

It was the boundary issue that really spurred Copthorne people to make the map. They wanted to show what the village meant to them as a community in its own right, to record their existence as a village, as their home – not just a buffer village between local authorities and most certainly not just part of a merged Gatwick conurbation at the mercy of planners, developers and big business.

But Gatwick's proximity is the presence that can't be escaped. Its local focus is the Copthorne Hotel, the huge complex built around Copthorne's oldest farmhouse, linked by shuttlebus and flight departure and arrival screens to the enormous airport just minutes away over the motorway. As part of the London-Gatwick hotel network, this is Copthorne as an international dormitory with a world-wide dimension, its historic name – it simply meant a copped or pollarded thorn tree – now the brand-name for a global network of hotels within the conglomerate Copthorne-Millennium Group.
The Copthorne Anzac Avenue in Auckland, the Copthorne Orchid in Penang and many far-off exotic destinations take a little bit of this corner of Sussex around the world, a long way from the old days when Copthorne was unknown and almost lost in the forest. By distant journeyings far and wide, here is some new meaning to the idea of a sense of place.

KIM LESLIE

Crawley Down

IF YOU DRIVE ALONG the road from Newchapel to Turners Hill, which William Cobbett described as 'by far the pleasantest coach-road from the Wen [his derogatory term for London] to Brighton' you could be pardoned for thinking that Crawley Down consisted of little more than a couple of shops, a village hall, a garage and a church, with a few houses in between. But turn off the road and you will find yourself in a large dormitory village that could easily be mistaken as bland or characterless. Superficially the impression is of houses, and plenty of them there are, for over five and a half thousand people live in them.

Turn east, up Sandy Lane, and a closer look reveals not uniformity, but great variety: a redundant Methodist chapel, the congregation lasting little more than half a century but which has been attractively refurbished as offices; comfortable large houses set back behind thick hedges – one of them the work of James Maclaren, an influential young Scottish Arts and Crafts architect who died tragically young in 1890. He also designed one of the cottages at Grange Farm.

Further on, to the left, the cricket field dates back to 1857, a gift to the village, replacing an earlier one lost when the railway from Three Bridges to East Grinstead was cut through it a few years before. You cannot but notice that Sandy Lane is dead straight, a sign that it was laid across what had once been common land. For therein lies the origin of Crawley Down, until 1848 merely a rectangular stretch of waste alongside the turnpike from Newchapel to Ditchling.

The heart of Crawley Down is the village green with its line of late-Victorian cottages along Bowers Place, built to house workers in the brickyards that lay just behind and which sustained the village economy at the end of the 19th century.

The village has been growing since the 1850s, at times slowly and steadily, more recently with a rush. Study the colour-coded housing on the parish map – note the rash of red for the post-1970 developments – and you

will get a good impression of just how the community has grown over the years. Classifying the housing into periods like this has been a challenge for the map group and makes Crawley Down's map the only one in the project to show its historical development phase by phase.

Down at the bottom of the green, the Royal Oak was originally the station hotel next to the old railway. The line of the old trackbed is now Worth Way, a linear country park, part of the Sustrans cycle network. For a brief period in the 1970s the Royal Oak was renamed the Prizefighters, commemorating the time when Crawley Down saw some of the greatest bare-knuckle matches of the Regency era. Usually drawn there at short notice – for the sport was illegal – huge crowds assembled on the

RAILWAY STATION: the branch line from Three Bridges to East Grinstead opened in 1855, and a station called Grange Road was built five years later. The line closed in 1967 and the station was demolished soon after.

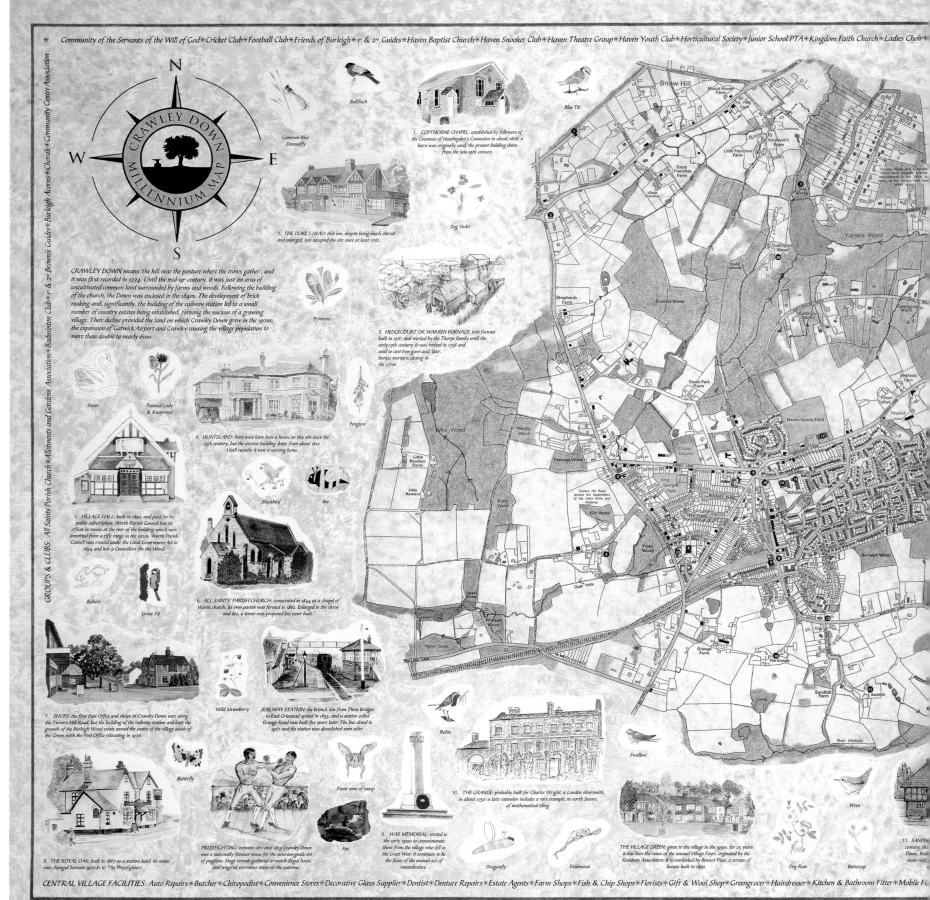

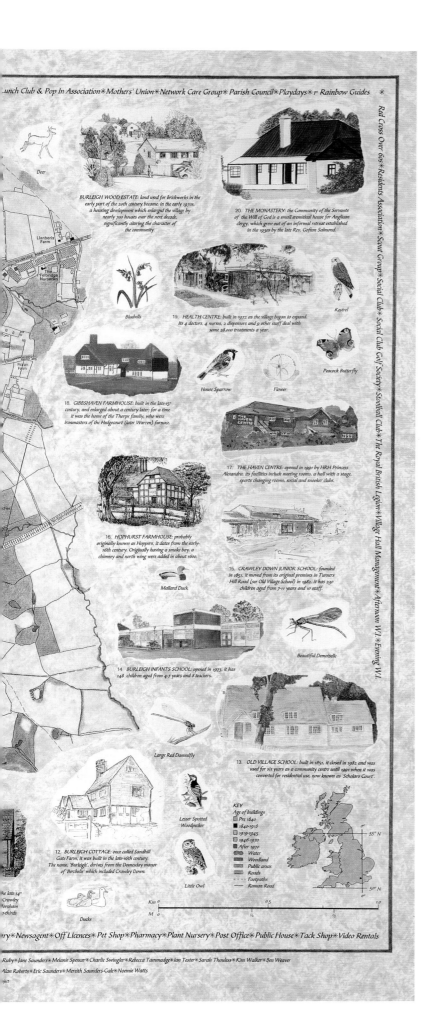

common, one of several wild areas that formerly stretched across to Copthorne. Fortunes were wagered on the outcome of bouts that could last up to seventy punishing rounds. Pugilists like Jack Randall, 'the Nonpareil', and Jack Martin, 'the Master of the Rolls', were the David Beckhams and Jonny Wilkinsons of their day.

For thirty years the green has been the venue for the Village Fayre, a community celebration of stalls, amusements, music and dressing-up held at the beginning of each September. The first was held as a new influx of families had come to live in the village, taking up residence in the houses that were then being put up where the brickworks had been. Burleigh Wood, the name the builders gave the estate of eight hundred or so houses, more than doubled the size of Crawley Down. A health centre, new school and new shops were planned, but feathers were ruffled as newcomers brought in new ideas and the 'old village' looked on, sometimes with resentment, sometimes in amusement. There had been small developments before, but nothing on this scale. Thirty years on and the village has settled down again. The families have grown up and the children then are parents now.

Burleigh Wood Estate

The crowning achievement of the newly-enlarged village has been the Haven Centre. Although there had been promises of a new community hall when Burleigh Wood had been planned, they had come to nothing. The existing village hall, built in 1890, could no longer cope with the demand for jumble sales, Scouts and Guides, badminton and dancing classes. When the old school closed, a group of local people raised money to buy it and convert it into a community centre. And from those small beginnings the plan for a purpose-built centre began to grow. Never before had so many worked to such a purpose. Fund-raising events were organised relentlessly: flower sales, concerts, walks, horse shows. When the British Heart Foundation began its sponsored cycle marathons from London to Brighton – they continue to pass through the village every spring – the Community Centre Association raised funds by providing refreshments for the cyclists. The culmination was a June day in 1991 when HRH Princess Alexandra performed the official opening. Now the centre thrives, providing a home for everything from a social club and football teams to Baptist church services and an office for the local police.

But there was an earlier plan to develop the village. At the very beginning of the last century, Hartley Buckley, who had inherited the Grange from his uncle, set about planning a garden village. A London architect, Edward Weymouth, drew up a scheme for a network of roads and a range of housing, the size and anticipated occupants of which were dictated by the social *mores* of the time. Village amenities and shops were also planned. Building began and a small number of houses were completed along Sunny Avenue and Vicarage Road before the Great War intervened and the project went no further.

'Sunny' is a name that appears time and time again in Crawley Down. As well as Sunny Avenue and its Sunnyside Laundry, now no more, there was a large house called Sunny Hill, together with a lodge and farm named with it. Even the first local-authority housing in the village, built in the late 1930s, is called Sunnymead. What was it that inspired such a twee name? Perhaps it was an advertisement for the benefits of country life, or was it an expression of a utopian ideal of rural arcadia?

The Grange

Crawley Down has its secret places as well. In the woods north of the village is a small monastery, founded in the 1930s. The Community of the Servants of the Will of God is an eremitical house, a largely self-sufficient retreat for a small number of Anglican priests. You will also have to look hard to find the most ancient parts of the village, such as the stream-side clearing down Hophurst Hill where iron was smelted just before the Romans came, the pond where later iron founders cast cannon for the navy at Warren Furnace, and the magnificent medieval Wealden hall house of Sandhill, more recently the home of one of the Led Zeppelin rock group.

This is not a sleepy village to which people retire. Its thriving community, epitomised by its many clubs and organisations, and not least by the cross-section of age groups who contributed to its millennium map, is alive and well and here to stay.

JEREMY HODGKINSON

All Saints' Church

Village Hall

Village shops and pub

Donnington

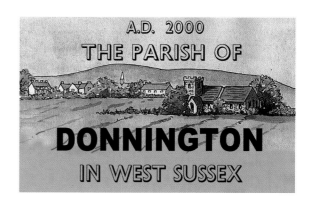

How to portray a parish with two such distinctive parts was the question facing the keen group of thirty map-making volunteers – one part little more than a modern overflow to Chichester, the other the more distant original village out in the countryside. There couldn't be a greater contrast.

St George's Church

'Old' Donnington is just that, a medieval church, the former village school, a cluster of old houses and cottages, hedgerows and fields, all with far-reaching views over the plain towards Chichester Cathedral and the Downs beyond. Intensive high-tech agribusiness, typified by the 'Mini Veg Packer', continues the long tradition of farming these richly-cultivated fields, symbolised by the medieval ploughing illustration from the 14th-century Luttrell Psalter. The field-names hint at some intriguing history.

'New' Donnington is a traffic-jam of a place, focus of major roads from the Manhood, gridlocking into Chichester's bypass that shares its length with the A27 south-coast trunk road. A busy suburb, with shops, a modern pub, street lighting, and plenty of modern housing, this is Stockbridge. Paradoxically its name is ancient, even pre-dating Donnington's 13th-century church; in 10th-century Saxon Sussex its name referred to the wooden bridge that crossed a stream here. That Stockbridge had some status in medieval times is suggested by the fact that it was the open-air meeting place of local government for all the surrounding villages, the 'capital' of what was known as the Hundred of Stockbridge. A hundred was an ancient territorial division. So a modern shifting of the centre of gravity of Donnington towards Stockbridge is merely history coming full circle, especially appropriate as today's local government – in the guise of Donnington Parish Council – now meets in this northernmost part.

Some 95 per cent of people live in less than 10 per cent of the parish, creating a huge imbalance in population density. The map emphasises that urban Donnington – *alias* Stockbridge – keeps a fairly compact shape. Visually this means sharp neat edges to this townscape abutting the fields. And the wide open countryside that covers most of the parish – much of it covenanted with the National Trust – means that there's far more wildlife here than people, pictured in the little watercolours. One scarce insect, a stag beetle, crawls across the map. It's on the national list of endangered species.

Donnington's major attraction for wildlife is the old canal, marking the eastern boundary until turning sharply westwards across the parish, effectively splitting it in two. This was the line of the Chichester Ship Canal, first opened in 1822, that once brought heavy sea-borne freight – mainly coal and timber – right to the city's doorstep. It was famously painted by Turner as he looked north towards the cathedral from the Donnington end. Now cut off from Chichester Harbour by fixed road bridges, a few land-locked boats ply up and down the navigable section, including the *Egremont*. This is a pleasure boat named after Lord Egremont (1761–1837), the local canal promoter who lived at Petworth. A walk that brings the countryside almost into the heart of the city follows the towpath along the edge of Donnington's fields as far as the Basin. On most days fishermen line the bank, for this is an angler's paradise.

Scenes by the canal

Wildlife and walkers similarly haunt Donnington's other old transport relic, the trackbed of the Selsey Tramway that ran from Chichester to Selsey between 1897 and 1935.

Legally called a tramway as a way of saving money on safety measures, but effectively a railway in all but name, it was one of the most remarkable country lines in England. Trains covered the seven and a half miles in forty minutes, making frequent unscheduled stops, on one occasion for the guard to visit a nearby farm to ask if the train was to pick up parcels the following day. Waiting for regular passengers if they hadn't shown up at the station was quite common. Nicknamed 'The Snailway Train', one joke postcard entitled 'From Chichester to Selsey and back in one day (Perhaps)' shows a warning notice: 'Passengers are not to pick the flowers while riding in the train'. There was no station at Donnington, so as the railway crawled through the fields, the locals could jump on and off with no trouble at all.

The only visible reminders now are in the name of the pub/restaurant, the Selsey Tram – its beautifully-painted sign full of nostalgia – and in the footpath that follows part of the original route from opposite the shops. The connection with the parish is still felt to be strong; local people treasure its memory.

The idea that a place has roots both in its past and its local environment can be achieved in all sorts of ways, reinforcing the idea that it's a distinct place, that it's *some*where, not just *any*where. One fairly easy way of doing this is

by naming roads and streets after real local connections rather than just being figments of the imagination. Stockbridge shows how this can be done. Crosbie Close is named after a local 19th-century farmer; Turnpike Close is a reminder that Stockbridge straddled the former 18th-century turnpike – a toll-road connecting Chichester with its port at Dell Quay; Grenville Gardens is on the site of the yard run by well-known local builder, John Grenville Snelling. When a patriotic suggestion to have a Winston Avenue (after Churchill) was thought too controversial by Chichester District Council, Wiston was agreed as a compromise! Local names *can* be a way of expressing local identity.

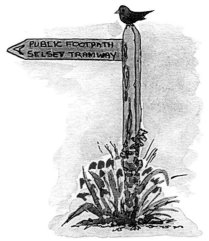

1950s houses

An enormous contribution towards this end has come from the making of this parish map. This is the first map ever produced that graphically illustrates what it is that makes up Donnington as a parish, clearly emphasising what even some people who live in Stockbridge don't realise – that they are part of Donnington rather than Chichester. As local farmer Hugh Brown said at the unveiling, 'It's through the map that the parish of Donnington now means something in its own right, it's no longer just a suburb'.

Stag beetle – an endangered species

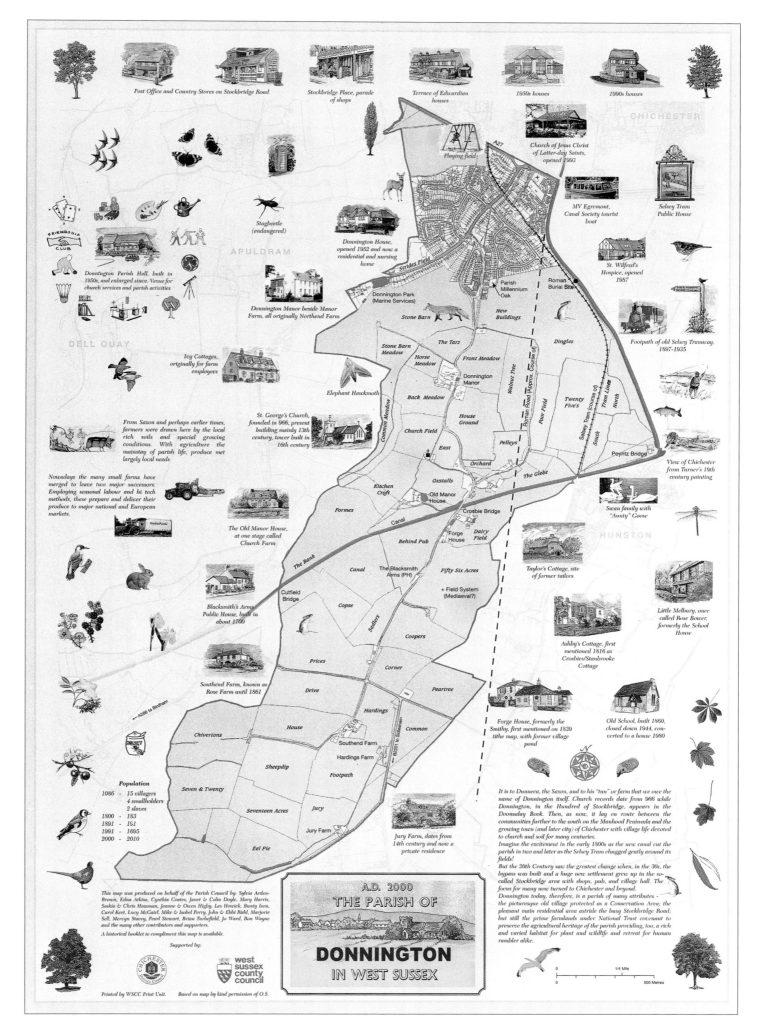

Post Office and Country Stores on Stockbridge Road

Stockbridge Place, parade of shops

Terrace of Edwardian houses

1950s houses

1990s houses

CHICHESTER

Playing field

Church of Jesus Christ of Latter-day Saints, opened 1993

MV Egremont, Canal Society tourist boat

Selsey Tram Public House

St. Wilfred's Hospice, opened 1987

Stagbeetle (endangered)

APULDRAM

Donnington House, opened 1952 and now a residential and nursing home

Strides Field

Parish Millennium Oak

Roman Burial Site

Footpath of old Selsey Tramway, 1897-1935

FRIENDSHIP CLUB

Donnington Parish Hall, built in 1950s, and enlarged since. Venue for church services and parish activities

Donnington Manor beside Manor Farm, all originally Northend Farm

Donnington Park (Marine Services)

Stone Barn

New Buildings

Dingles

DELL QUAY

Ivy Cottages, originally for farm employees

Elephant Hawkmoth

Stone Barn Meadow

The Tarz

Horse Meadow

Front Meadow

Donnington Manor

Walnut Tree

Peer Field

Twenty Five's

Tram Lines

Footpath of old Selsey Tramway, 1897-1935

From Saxon and perhaps earlier times, farmers were drawn here by the local rich soils and special growing conditions. With agriculture the mainstay of parish life, produce met largely local needs.

St. George's Church, founded in 966, present building mainly 13th century, tower built in 16th century

Back Meadow

House Ground

Church Field

East

Pelleys

Selsey Tram (course of) South North

Poyntz Bridge

View of Chichester from Turner's 19th century painting

Nowadays the many small farms have merged to leave two major successors. Employing seasonal labour and hi tech methods, these prepare and deliver their produce to major national and European markets.

The Old Manor House, at one stage called Church Farm

Orchard

Oxstalls

Old Manor House

Crosbie Bridge

The Glebe

Formes

Kitchen Croft

Canal

Behind Pub

Forge House

Dairy Field

Swan family with "Aunty" Goose

HUNSTON

The Bank

Canal

The Blacksmith Arms (PH)

Fifty Six Acres

Taylor's Cottage, site of former tailors

Cutfield Bridge

Copse

+ Field System (Mediaeval?)

Little Melbury, once called Rose Bower, formerly the School House

Blacksmith's Arms Public House, built in about 1700

Sadlers

Coopers

Ashby's Cottage, first mentioned 1816 as Crosbies/Stanbrooke Cottage

Prices

Corner

Peartree

Drive

Hardings

A286 to Birdham

Southend Farm, known as Rose Farm until 1861

House

Southend Farm

Common

Forge House, formerly the Smithy, first mentioned on 1539 tithe map, with former village pond

Old School, built 1860, closed down 1944, converted to a house 1980

Chivertons

Sheepdip

Hardings Farm

Footpath

Population
1086 - 15 villagers
        4 smallholders
        2 slaves
1800 - 183
1891 - 151
1991 - 1695
2000 - 2010

Seven & Twenty

Seventeen Acres

Jury

Eel Pie

Jury Farm

Jury Farm, dates from 14th century and now a private residence

It is to Dunneca, the Saxon, and to his "tun" or farm that we owe the name of Donnington itself. Church records date from 966 while Donnington, in the Hundred of Stockbridge, appears in the Doomsday Book. Then, as now, it lay en route between the communities further to the south on the Manhood Peninsula and the growing town (and later city) of Chichester with village life devoted to church and soil for many centuries.

Imagine the excitement in the early 1800s as the new canal cut the parish in two and later as the Selsey Tram chugged gently around its fields!

But the 20th Century saw the greatest change when, in the 30s, the bypass was built and a huge new settlement grew up in the so-called Stockbridge area with shops, pub, and village hall. The focus for many now turned to Chichester and beyond.

Donnington today, therefore, is a parish of many attributes - the picturesque old village protected as a Conservation Area; the pleasant main residential area astride the busy Stockbridge Road; but still the prime farmlands under National Trust covenant to preserve the agricultural heritage of the parish providing, too, a rich and varied habitat for plant and wildlife and retreat for human rambler alike.

This map was produced on behalf of the Parish Council by: Sylvia Arden-Brown, Edna Atkins, Cynthia Coates, Janet & Colin Doyle, Mary Harris, Saskia & Chris Heasman, Jeanne & Owen Higby, Les Howick, Bunty Ison, Carol Keet, Lucy McGairl, Mike & Isobel Perry, John & Ebbi Ridd, Marjorie Sell, Mervyn Stacey, Pearl Stewart, Brian Turbefield, Jo Ward, Ron Wayne and the many other contributors and supporters.

A historical booklet to compliment this map is available.

Supported by:

CHICHESTER district council

west sussex county council

Printed by WSCC Print Unit.   Based on map by kind permission of O.S.

A.D. 2000
THE PARISH OF
DONNINGTON
IN WEST SUSSEX

When the parish map group was first brought together by John Ridd there was a real feeling that there wasn't too much to put on a map at all – until some brain-storming started. Now with so much to tell, the finished map speaks volumes for Donnington.

What are worth noting are some of its spin-offs:

■ The wildlife advisers followed their initial input for the map by a survey of local plant life around the green at Southfields Close.

Parish Hall

Goldfinch   *Elephant Hawkmoth*   *Hedgehog*

■ Work for the map did much to strengthen community relationships, bringing new faces into parish work, particularly one farmer who is now a valuable member of the parish council.

■ So much information was gathered that a sub-group put together a little history book called *Donnington: A Brief History* to complement the map.

■ Artwork generated for the map was used not only in the book but also in the parish's website – www.donningtonpc.org.uk

■ The map is proving a useful tool for Donnington councillors for planning and environmental issues. Unlike other types of map, it conveys an immediate feel for the many diverse elements that make up the character of the parish.

KIM LESLIE

The Blacksmiths Arms

The Old Manor House

Easebourne

ASEBOURNE – pronounced Ezb'n – takes its name from the little stream called the Es or Ez running beside the village street. It's so small that the name has never been given on local maps, but simply handed down by word of mouth, so the spelling might vary. The parish is at the heart of Cowdray country, nerve centre of the great Cowdray Estate, all seventeen thousand acres of it, its symbols of power and influence past and present gathered within its bounds. Cowdray owns slabs of Midhurst with which it is so commonly associated, but its ancient roots and presence belong to Easebourne.
It is Cowdray's capital.

The estate's centre-piece, the majestic Tudor ruins of Cowdray House, gives focus and meaning to this historic territory. Nearby, its Victorian successor, all turrets, gables and tiles, is home to the present Lord Cowdray whose great-grandfather (1856–1927) laid the family fortune from Mexican oil and building railways, harbours, tunnels and dams the world over, its profits invested in merchant banking, newspapers, publishing and land. These Cowdray lands, bought from the Earl of Egmont in 1909, forge the link with dynastic families rooted in this landscape since the 12th century.

This sense of interconnection between countless generations dead and living – the very essence of aristocracy – ties together land and buildings in a web of ownership badged by 'Cowdray Yellow'. More properly called 'Tivoli Gold', this brash paintwork on tenantry property proclaims proprietorial rights in a riot of vibrant sunshine, a simplistic form of modern heraldry. Around here it's pretty much either loved or loathed in equal measure. All landed estates have their chosen colour, but throughout the whole land there's none with more dash and verve than this statement of possession. It sparks off all sorts of stories, one that when the first rash of yellow lines arrived for marking out no-parking areas, local people simply assumed the estate was adding all the roads to its collection of property! Certainly Cowdray's yellow reinforces the real sense of place and unity across the entire estate run from its Easebourne HQ. You always know when you're on Cowdray land.

The colour is said to have been introduced by the 2nd Viscount, who was more the resident squire in running the estate than his globe-trotting father before him. Early last century it was as Harold Pearson (he became the 2nd Viscount in 1927) that he laid the

By Benbow Pond in Cowdray Park: memorial to the late 3rd Viscount Cowdray

On Benbow Pond

Cowdray Estate Office and the 'Private Byepass Bridge'

THE PARISH OF **EASEBOURNE** IN THE COUNTY OF WEST SUSSEX

IN THE YEAR **2000**

Parish of Fernhurst

To Haslemere

King Edward VII Hospital

THE DUKE OF CUMBERLAND ARMS

Henley

Madam's Farm

King's Drive

Nightjar

Great Common

Parish of Woolbeding

Gruss

Budgenor Lodge

Buddington Farm

Hollist Lane

River Bank Medical Centre

Woolbeding Castle

Maize

Potatoes

A 272

Village Shop and Post Office

To Midhurst

Pound Cottages, Egmont Road

Parish of Midhurst

Birthday House

Cowdray Estate Office

Parish of West Lavington

Causeway Bridge

Parish of Lodsworth

Conifers School

Midhurst Intermediate School

THE HOLLY TREE

Easebourne C.E. Primary School

Loves Farm

Oaters Wood

THE WHITE HORSE

GREENE KING

Queen Elizabeth Oak

Stewards Pond

Lime Bottom

Golf Course

Belvedere Pond and Memorial

Drinking Fountain Easebourne Street

Easebourne Village Institute

Church of St Mary

Millennium Window in the Church

Parish of Graffham

Easebourne Priory

Parish of Heyshott

west sussex county council

This map has been made with support from West Sussex County Council, Chichester District Council and Easebourne Parish Council ©

COWDRAY PARK

Artists: Tina Falovejn, Fiona Gowar, Patricia Luke, Mary Shotter, Jeanette Sutton, Emma Williams, Frank White. Children's school paintings: Easebourne Zoe Edgington, Conifers Sabrina Percy, Midhurst Intermediate School Tom Smith

foundations for Cowdray Park's prestigious position in the world of polo. Since the 1950s his son, the 3rd Viscount (1910–95), made Cowdray into polo's English home as the country's leading club on the international polo circuit. Star players, plus a good sprinkling of top-royalty, have always ensured good crowds, with Gold Cup Finals in July one of the highlights of the British sporting calendar for world-class tournaments. Importantly, Cowdray polo has brought considerable prosperity, an estimated one million pounds rubbing off into the district each season, creating something of a financial bonanza with hotels and cottages fully booked, plenty of employment for stable and hospitality work, with barns and outlying stables repaired and rented by players. It's more than just a game, it's an industry, and even more than just a club, it's an institution. And as with the yellow paint, Cowdray would never be the same without its polo.

Just as the English countryside owes much to its great estates in carrying on traditions of stewardship and care – these days against the unrelenting pursuit of inherited wealth by the taxman – so Cowdray survives as a sign of what much of England was like in the past, lord and tenant united by land.

Three thousand acres bigger than under its previous Egmont owners a hundred years ago,

the estate has ensured that its land and property remain unspoilt, yet economically viable. Farming, forestry and sandstone quarrying exploit the land as in centuries past; its leisure/business potential has been expanded from polo and golf into fishing, shooting, deer-stalking, 4x4 driving, holiday cottages, corporate entertainment, business team-building, wedding receptions and offering the Tudor ruins for television filming. Some five hundred properties, from historic cottages and farmhouses to more modern homes, give a

Cowdray's Tudor kitchen

Causeway bridge over the Rother

substantial stake in the local housing market. All these assets mean that profitability safeguards this precious landscape, accessible not just to those who pay, but for all residents and visitors alike, free to walk, ride and drive through what Disraeli in the 19th century called 'one of the most magnificent demesnes in England'. In its stunning landscapes, little has changed.

Much of what is enjoyed within this natural environment is through its magnificent views to the Downs, its heritage of sandstone and timber buildings so rightly belonging to the landscape, as do its superb trees and all their supporting wildlife. About 36 per cent of Cowdray land is woodland, much of it grown as a crop. The spin-off from modern forestry management is in its guardianship of ancient woodland and historic specimens that make up so much of the character of Cowdray Park, its name significantly derived from a medieval wood called *la Codray* – early French for a hazel copse. Around the gardens of the big house is decorative planting, like the avenue of 19th-century wellingtonias – some of the tallest in the county at over 120 feet – and a rich scattering of rare specimen trees. From opposite the priory church a mile-long avenue of sweet chestnuts strides towards Oaters Wood, home to some of the largest and oldest sessile oaks in the country.

Birthday House for Cowdray Estate workers – opened on 17 June 1965 on the occasion of the 21st birthday of Michael Orlando Weetman Pearson, the present Viscount Cowdray

Cowdray – the Tudor ruins

Cowdray's most distinguished tree is the Queen Elizabeth Oak, named after the Tudor queen who visited in 1591. *The Sussex Tree Book* of 1998 by Owen Johnson – loaded with Cowdray references – delightfully illustrates and describes this old gnarled tree as 'the perfect image of what an ancient oak in an ancient park ought to look like – squat, barrel-chested and clinging cheerfully onto life, with a few blasted limbs and a hollow heart the size of a kitchen and open to the sky, a home to little owls and beetles; almost a Walt Disney tree'.

These trees, like so much on the estate, are the tangible threads lacing these thousands of acres together over time and place. They find unity through their ownership, through the family whose very name, when raised to the peerage, subordinated itself to a piece of land. Cowdray land created Cowdray the family, personal identity absorbing itself into territory. This close identification of land and family running as one – and as a big business – is the key to understanding how such an historic landscape and its people today are maintained so successfully into the 21st century.

KIM LESLIE

Village shop

Easebourne Primary School

Easebourne Priory

Elsted with Treyford cum Didling

THE HAND OF HISTORY has passed very lightly over our three communities. No kings have passed this way, disruptive armies have not battled on our soils, the Saxon parish boundaries still separate us from our neighbours, and only minor roads pass through our villages. We live in a gloriously peaceful part of West Sussex in the shadow of the Downs.

Our predecessors were usually humble folk or yeoman; people who tended the ground around them, usually married somebody from the same parish and, having spent an industrious life tilling the land, were buried where they had been christened. They have been replaced by a new sort of country dweller, those who have chosen to live in beautiful surroundings and either travel many miles to their work or have retired here. One villager told a press reporter that anyone who doesn't retire to Elsted wants his head examined!

In spite of such dramatic social change, our villages present a pretty face to the outside world. The farm workers' cottages have benefited from the enthusiasm and cash new owners have brought with them. Old photographs show peaceful scenes, but not the

deprivation. Much maligned agriculture, having long had official encouragement to chase profits, sometimes damaging the countryside in the process, is now urged to concentrate on landscape management. A vivid example is the scarp slope of the Downs

above 'the Shepherds' Church' at Didling, which having been cleared, presents a face scrubbed of scrub.

Not many parishes, particularly so small, can boast of two churches and the site of two more. Grade-one listed St Andrew's at Didling,

At Didling

a typical small downland church loved by all, was one of three parish churches abandoned in 1849. Fortunately it was re-opened and remains so to this day. Its lonely, isolated setting under the Downs is incomparable. St Paul's at Elsted was also abandoned and then partially restored, but when the nave was damaged by a tree in 1893, only the blocked-up chancel remained in use. Phoenix-like it was again rebuilt in 1951. St Mary's at Treyford was the third to be abandoned, and the removal of the tiles by a rector and his coachman to cover the extension to Elsted village school has meant that it is sadly derelict today.

The reason for this extraordinary mass abandonment? The head-strong patron of the living and owner of the West Dean Estate who refused to pay for the restoration of the older churches, insisting on the building of a single central church, mid-way between Elsted and Treyford. The new church, called St Peter's, was bigger and grander than the others – its 120-feet stone spire a conspicuous landmark for miles around – and was soon being called

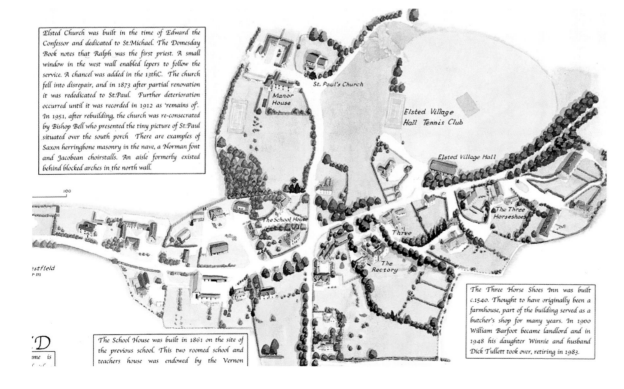

Elsted Church was built in the time of Edward the Confessor and dedicated to St. Michael. The Domesday Book notes that Ralph was the first priest. A small window in the west wall enabled lepers to follow the service. A chancel was added in the 13thC. The church fell into disrepair, and in 1873 after partial renovation it was rededicated to St. Paul. Further deterioration occurred until it was recorded in 1912 as 'remains of'. In 1951, after rebuilding, the church was re-consecrated by Bishop Bell who presented the tiny picture of St. Paul situated over the south porch. There are examples of Saxon herringbone masonry in the nave, a Norman font and Jacobean choirstalls. An aisle formerly existed behind blocked arches in the north wall.

The School House was built in 1861 on the site of the previous school. This two roomed school and teachers house was endowed by the Vernon

The Three Horse Shoes Inn was built c.1540. Thought to have originally been a farmhouse, part of the building served as a butcher's shop for many years. In 1900 William Barfoot became landlord and in 1948 his daughter Winnie and husband Dick Tullett took over, retiring in 1983.

St. Paul's Church

Manor House

Elsted Village Hall Tennis Club

Elsted Village Hall

The Three Horseshoes

Three

The Rectory

The School House

'the cathedral of the Downs'. But it was built out of arrogance, with no regard for local peoples' wishes. Never popular with parishioners dismayed to see their lovely old churches sinking further into decay, and suffering longer walks to church, this building went the way of the others and fell into decay itself. By the 1940s it was in severe structural difficulty and because the cost of repair was four times as great as the cost of rebuilding Elsted's church it was ignominiously blown up by the Royal Engineers in 1951. All that remains of this vain-glorious Victorian white elephant is an atmospheric graveyard, still used today and kept as a wildlife sanctuary by the Treyford Conservation Group.

The South Downs Way between Winchester and Beachy Head runs along the top of the Downs high above the villages, passing close by the Devil's Jumps. This important landscape feature is so called because of the superstition that unusual landscape features were the work of Satan. These seven bell barrows contain the ashes of tribal leaders who lived some three and a half thousand years ago. Other early sites include an Iron Age encampment on Beacon Hill and a Romano-British site at Elsted. Doubtless others are under our feet.

Historically closer to our own day is the site of the Admiralty telegraph station built during the Napoleonic Wars near Beacon Hill. Using a system of opening and closing shutters, messages were passed from hill to hill between Portsmouth and London. News of Nelson's victory at Trafalgar would almost certainly have passed through here. The electric telegraph later rendered these stations redundant and the site was sold. From 1927, Bertrand Russell, the philosopher, lived at Telegraph House, running a somewhat relaxed experimental school that

Telegraph House

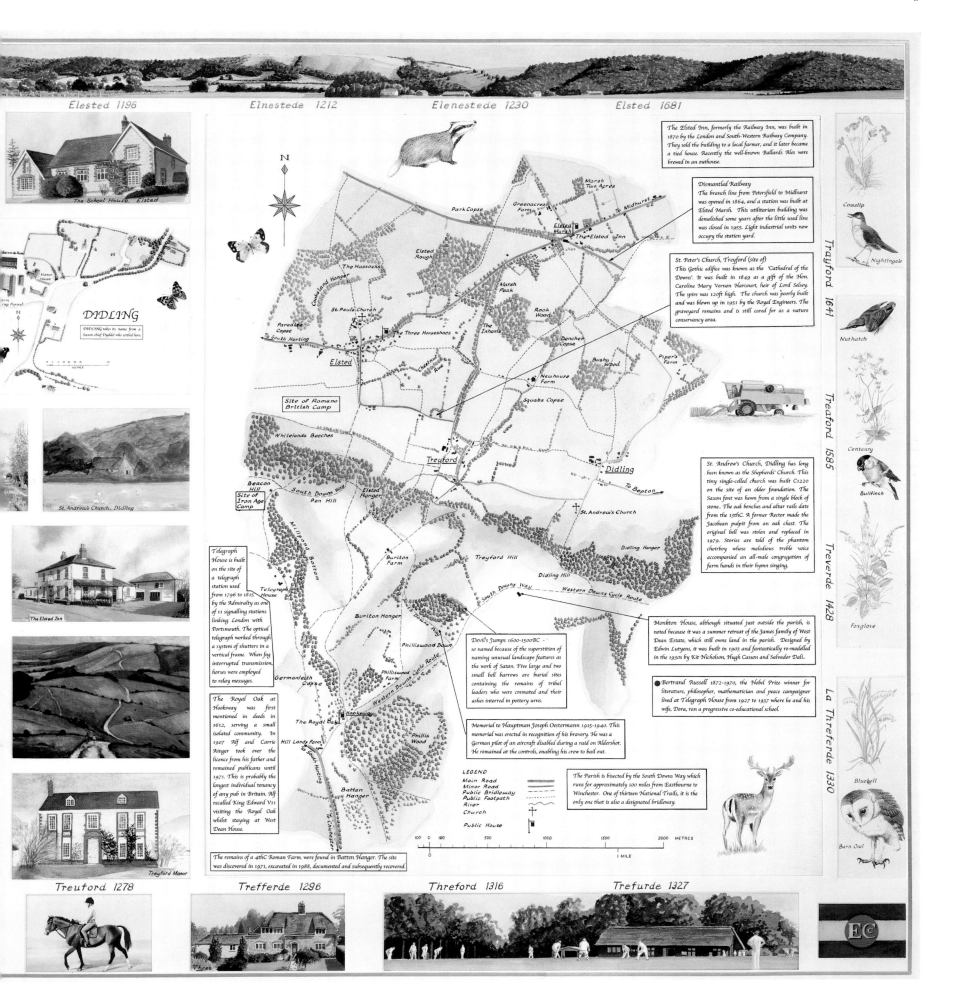

Elsted 1196   Elnestede 1212   Elenestede 1230   Elsted 1681

The School House, Elsted

DIDLING

DIDLING takes its name from a Saxon chief Dyddel who settled here.

St. Andrew's Church, Didling

The Elsted Inn

Treyford Manor

Treuford 1278   Trefferde 1296   Threford 1316   Trefurde 1327

Trayford 1641   Treatford 1585   Treverde 1428   La Threferde 1330

Cowslip
Nightingale
Nuthatch
Centaury
Bullfinch
Foxglove
Bluebell
Barn Owl

The Elsted Inn, formerly the Railway Inn, was built in 1870 by the London and South-Western Railway Company. They sold the building to a local farmer, and it later became a tied house. Recently the well-known Ballards Ales were brewed in an outhouse.

Dismantled Railway
The branch line from Petersfield to Midhurst was opened in 1864, and a station was built at Elsted Marsh. This utilitarian building was demolished some years after the little used line was closed in 1955. Light industrial units now occupy the station yard.

St. Peter's Church, Treyford (site of)
This Gothic edifice was known as the 'Cathedral of the Downs'. It was built in 1849 as a gift of the Hon. Caroline Mary Vernon Harcourt, heir of Lord Selsey. The spire was 120ft high. The church was poorly built and was blown up in 1951 by the Royal Engineers. The graveyard remains and is still cared for as a nature conservancy area.

St. Andrew's Church, Didling has long been known as the Shepherds' Church. This tiny single-celled church was built C1220 on the site of an older foundation. The Saxon font was hewn from a single block of stone. The oak benches and altar rails date from the 13thC. A former Rector made the Jacobean pulpit from an oak chest. The original bell was stolen and replaced in 1979. Stories are told of the phantom choirboy whose melodious treble voice accompanied an all-male congregation of farm hands in their hymn singing.

Telegraph House is built on the site of a telegraph station used from 1796 to 1815 by the Admiralty as one of 11 signalling stations linking London with Portsmouth. The optical telegraph worked through a system of shutters in a vertical frame. When fog interrupted transmission, horses were employed to relay messages.

Monkton House, although situated just outside the parish, is noted because it was a summer retreat of the James family of West Dean Estate, which still owns land in the parish. Designed by Edwin Lutyens, it was built in 1903 and fantastically re-modelled in the 1930s by Kit Nicholson, Hugh Casson and Salvador Dali.

Bertrand Russell 1872-1970, the Nobel Prize winner for literature, philosopher, mathematician and peace campaigner lived at Telegraph House from 1927 to 1937 where he and his wife, Dora, ran a progressive co-educational school.

Devil's Jumps 1600-1500BC -
so named because of the superstition of naming unusual landscape features as the work of Satan. Five large and two small bell barrows are burial sites containing the remains of tribal leaders who were cremated and their ashes interred in pottery urns.

The Royal Oak at Hooksway was first mentioned in deeds in 1612, serving a small isolated community. In 1907 Alf and Carrie Ainger took over the licence from his father and remained publicans until 1971. This is probably the longest individual tenancy of any pub in Britain. Alf recalled King Edward V11 visiting the Royal Oak whilst staying at West Dean House.

Memorial to Hauptman Joseph Oestermann 1915-1940. This memorial was erected in recognition of his bravery. He was a German pilot of an aircraft disabled during a raid on Aldershot. He remained at the controls, enabling his crew to bail out.

The Parish is bisected by the South Downs Way which runs for approximately 100 miles from Eastbourne to Winchester. One of thirteen National Trails, it is the only one that is also a designated bridleway.

The remains of a 4thC Roman Farm were found in Batten Hanger. The site was discovered in 1971, excavated in 1988, documented and subsequently recovered.

LEGEND
Main Road
Minor Road
Public Bridleway
Public Footpath
River
Church
Public House

Map labels: Marsh Two Acres, Park Copse, Greenacres Farm, To Midhurst, Elsted Marsh, The Elsted Inn, The Hassocks, Elsted Rough, Marsh Peak, Rook Wood, The Inhams, Dencher Copse, Bushy Wood, Piper's Farm, Cowsland Hanger, St. Paul's Church, Paradise Copse, To South Harting, The Three Horseshoes, Chestnut Row, Elsted, Newhouse Farm, Squabs Copse, Site of Romano British Camp, Whitelands Beeches, Treyford, Didling, To Bepton, Beacon Hill, Site of Iron Age Camp, South Downs Way, Pen Hill, Elsted Hanger, St. Andrew's Church, Didling Hanger, Millpond Bottom, Treyford Hill, Didling Hill, Buriton Farm, South Downs Way, Western Downs Cycle Route, Buriton Hanger, Philliswood Down, Philliswood Farm, Western Downs Cycle Route, Germanleith Copse, Hooksway, The Royal Oak, Hill Lands Farm, To South Harting, Phillis Wood, Batten Hanger, To Chichester

100 0   500   1000   1500   2000 METRES
0   1 MILE

EC

scandalised local people until it moved away to Essex in 1934. In his autobiography Russell says that the new house, built by his brother Frank, was 'ugly and rather absurd, but the situation was superb'. Making his study in the high tower, he recalled that he had 'never known one with a more beautiful outlook'. Frank also left his mark in the avenue of copper beeches he planted along the drive leading to the house from the Harting-Chilgrove road, still a colourful feature of the landscape today.

Other interesting local residents included Graily Hewitt (1864–1952), the distinguished calligrapher who lived at Brook Cottage, Treyford. Locally he designed the brass war memorial tablet in St Paul's, Elsted, as well as the most unusual and colourful St Christopher waypost that stands outside his old home, bearing the inscription: 'Who carried Christ/ speed thee to-day/ and lift thy heart up/ all the way'. The bearded saint points to both Cocking and Harting along underdown lanes that must surely lift the hearts of all who travel this way. The painter Paul Maze (1887–1979), who has been called 'the last Impressionist', also lived in Treyford, at Mill Cottage. He taught Winston Churchill to paint. Tramping over the Downs, Maze was a familiar figure trundling a baby-carriage stacked with paints, pastels and brushes. Many local people are fortunate to own one of his paintings, and decades later the

scenes he painted are still recognisable. He is buried in the north-east corner of St Peter's graveyard.

For many years drinkers benefited from great continuity at all the local pubs. The Perhams were at the Railway Inn from before the Second World War until the mid '60s. (Their pub was named after the branch-line railway through Elsted that closed in 1955.) But their term of office pales into insignificance compared with the other three hostelries. The Aylwin family ran the ale-house in Didling for over a century before it

The Royal Oak, Hooksway

closed fifty years ago. The Barfoots ran the Three Horse Shoes from 1900 until 1947, when their daughter, Winnie, and her husband, Dick Tullett, took over, remaining licencees until 1983. Of their pub, E.V. Lucas wrote that its site is 'superior to that of many a nobleman's house'. It probably rates as having one of the finest located pub gardens in Sussex. Up in a hollow of the Downs is the Royal Oak at Hooksway, that must hold a

record as Alf and Carrie Ainger came here in 1907, he dying in harness in 1970. The pub had no electricity and was only an ale house – no spirits allowed. Alf and Carrie were legendary in the pub business, well known for their singing the old country songs and the way they refused to modernise. Alf, summoned to the Midhurst magistrates for the renewal of his licence for the umpteenth time, was surprised to hear them ask about the provision of ladies' lavatories. His laconic reply: 'Well, sir, I got nine acres of 'em'. The licence was granted!

At a time of national shortages in the late 1940s, the parish raised an amazing £2,500 to rebuild St Paul's at Elsted. More recently, in 1997, we built a new village hall, replacing a much-loved ex-wartime building made from packing cases used for transporting American aircraft engines across the Atlantic. Fund-raising for the new hall brought our small community together; on average each adult was responsible for raising £200 before any grants were made. We are understandably very proud of our achievement. The new hall is splendid, very popular and viable, so much so that regular well-attended free events are put on for parishioners – it is *their* hall. These events remind us that not only do we live here, but that we are a community.

ANDREW SHAXSON

Cricket under the Downs

Felpham

Alone among the villages surrounding Bognor Regis, Felpham has managed – in spite of all the odds – to preserve a good part of its identity ... what I find most engaging about the place today is the cheerful mixture of the old and the new. They get on well together; and though nobody could claim that there isn't a good deal of hideous stuff here and there ... I would maintain that for the greater part, the decades have made their additions with a surprising degree of tact.

Touring West Sussex for the local newspaper, this is how Sussex poet and writer Ted Walker saw the village some thirty years ago in the early 1970s.

If he came back today he couldn't avoid noticing more traffic, more houses, all the sights and sounds that the world has moved on, but he'd still recognise a lot of delightful corners, the flint walls, the twittens, flint cottages, some thatch, plenty of greenery and a beach of sand and rock-pools that is timeless. An autumn/winter sunset over acres of wet sand turns shafts of fading light into a sea of golden red against the outline of Selsey Bill in the distance. Come here on a clear day and it's possible to see a Channel view from the Seven Sisters in the east to the hills of the Isle of Wight to the west, a sweep of some sixty miles. This is still a magical place to those who know where – and when – to look.

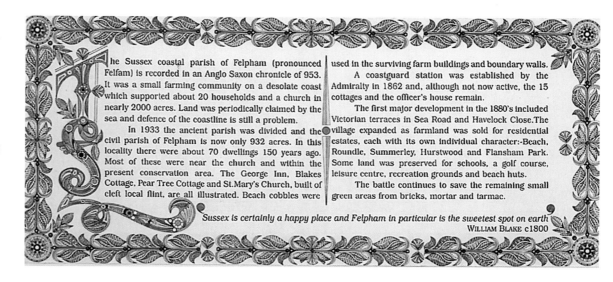

The Sussex coastal parish of Felpham (pronounced Felfam) is recorded in an Anglo Saxon chronicle of 953. It was a small farming community on a desolate coast which supported about 20 households and a church in nearly 2000 acres. Land was periodically claimed by the sea and defence of the coastline is still a problem.

In 1933 the ancient parish was divided and the civil parish of Felpham is now only 932 acres. In this locality there were about 70 dwellings 150 years ago. Most of these were near the church and within the present conservation area. The George Inn, Blakes Cottage, Pear Tree Cottage and St.Mary's Church, built of cleft local flint, are all illustrated. Beach cobbles were used in the surviving farm buildings and boundary walls.

A coastguard station was established by the Admiralty in 1862 and, although not now active, the 15 cottages and the officer's house remain.

The first major development in the 1880's included Victorian terraces in Sea Road and Havelock Close. The village expanded as farmland was sold for residential estates, each with its own individual character:-Beach, Roundle, Summerley, Hurstwood and Flansham Park. Some land was preserved for schools, a golf course, leisure centre, recreation grounds and beach huts.

The battle continues to save the remaining small green areas from bricks, mortar and tarmac.

Sussex is certainly a happy place and Felpham in particular is the sweetest spot on earth
WILLIAM BLAKE c1800

People come here for retirement and for their holidays, perhaps mindful of William Blake, the poet, painter and mystic, who wrote the words of what has become the Women's Institutes' anthem, *Jerusalem*, and who once declared that he was 'Away to sweet Felpham for heaven is there'. And so he came to live here back in 1800. His old thatched and beamed cottage with its blue plaque survives amongst a tangle of little roads right at the core of the old village, now a protected Conservation Area. The Fox pub stands at its centre. The battle to save it from major alterations was the original inspiration for the founding of the Felpham Village Conservation Society. The pub's fine flint exterior survives, embellished with a stylish hooded door canopy like a massive seaside shell, and bearing yet two more of Felpham's blue plaques – commemorating the 18th-century artist George Morland and Blake again, marking his arrest here for sedition.

Like Blake, so many have found their own special bit of heaven here: there are some of the prettiest gardens you can see anywhere, splashes of colour tucked away and full of surprises – the Horticultural and the Allotments and Garden societies are very strong and there is an open-gardens weekend every year; there are dozens of well-regimented beach huts; some weather-stained wooden chalets that started life as railway carriages, most with verandahs and such suggestive names – Merry Moments, Restawhile, Myshanti. Original railway features still lurk behind their home-made façades. It's as though a whole train has disgorged its last passengers and retired by the seaside. At the eastern end of the parish are the tudoresque and art deco houses of the Summerley and Beach marine estates, backed by much more modern developments, from where huge numbers of dogs bounce out as regular as clockwork, all bound for the beach. Felpham is very much an open-air breezy sort of place.

The sea is the great pull for weekend sailors and windsurfers. On good days nets and pots yield their harvest of fish and crabs for the

FELPHAM BEACH

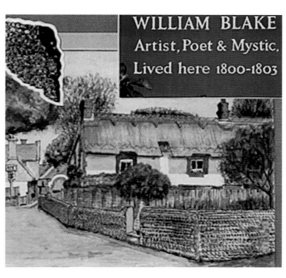

WILLIAM BLAKE
Artist, Poet & Mystic,
Lived here 1800-1803

The Parish of FELPHAM

The Sussex coastal parish of Felpham (pronounced Felfam) is recorded in an Anglo Saxon chronicle of 953. It was a small farming community on a desolate coast which supported about 20 households and a church in nearly 2000 acres. Land was periodically claimed by the sea and defence of the coastline is still a problem.

In 1933 the ancient parish was divided and the civil parish of Felpham is now only 932 acres. In this locality there were about 70 dwellings 150 years ago. Most of these were near the church and within the present conservation area. The George Inn, Blakes Cottage, Pear Tree Cottage and St.Mary's Church, built of cleft local flint, are all illustrated. Beach cobbles were

used in the surviving farm buildings and boundary walls.

A coastguard station was established by the Admiralty in 1802 and, although not now active, the 15 cottages and the officer's house remain.

The first major development in the 1880's included Victorian terraces in Sea Road and Havelock Close.The village expanded as farmland was sold for residential estates, each with its own individual character: Beach, Roundle, Summerley, Hurstwood and Flansham Park. Some land was preserved for schools, a golf course, leisure centre, recreation grounds and beach huts.

The battle continues to save the remaining small green areas from bricks, mortar and tarmac.

Sussex is certainly a happy place and Felpham in particular is the sweetest spot on earth
WILLIAM BLAKE c1800

few local commercial fishermen who very occasionally can be found selling their fresh catch by the boat ramp next to The Lobster Pot café. Most of the Felpham catch is sold by Bognor Pier. At high tide look out for the bobbing flags topping their marker floats. At low tide others are fishing – the seabirds – the solitary heron and little egret coming over from Pagham Harbour, pairs of oystercatchers and excitable dunlin all taking their fill. Out of the breeding season, and just before dusk, flights of cormorants wing their arrowhead formations straight over Felpham on their daily return from Pagham for roosting overnight at South Stoke, near Arundel.

There is so much to see and enjoy here, and this must be the message of the map. So much of Felpham's spirit is captured in this panoramic view of the place.

From its outset in 1998 the parish map group wanted to involve as many village groups and individuals as possible – that's why the original, hanging in St Mary's Centre, is the huge size it is, incorporating the work of so many people and so much local information. The local history group, under Sheila Gould, strongly believed that the map should not just be about Felpham's past, but be as much about life today. They wanted to see a combination of traditional and contemporary features. The map was to be a record of the parish in the year 2000. As they said: 'What we take for granted today will be the history of the future'.

So a careful look shows modern features that one day will disappear – at least in the form shown here – the milk-float, the mobile library, the bus shelter, recycling bins, traffic signs, all the paraphernalia of modern life. And look even more carefully and you'll find the marks of the map's art director who pulled all the many elements together. Eric Bobby's face is on the side of the bus, his wife's name,

Ann, on the bridge of the little fishing boat. Nice little personal touches. Eric's graphic skills are shown to perfection in his line work for the compass point and the title logo. Notice the strip of pebbles defining the beachline.

The centre-piece, the map itself, by artist Colin Clark, is a triumph of detail, claiming to show every house or block of development and even all the letter and phone boxes – notice the old and modern call boxes around the edge. The map emphasises the main open spaces, dominated at the centre by the enormous green block of the King George V Playing Field.

The brief history – boxed at bottom centre – that is such a challenging compression of so many facts – ends with the hope that 'The battle continues to save the remaining small green areas from bricks, mortar and tarmac'. The parish, as elsewhere, fears more infilling and more housing and is acutely aware of

becoming part of a 'greater Bognor', its land-greedy neighbour over the Rife – this meandering strip of water marking the western boundary for much of its length.

Rifes, as drainage channels, are names peculiar to this part of the coastal plain. This rife neatly defines the break between village and town, its survival as an ancient local name an indicator of the persistence of a

traditional past that is such a key to maintaining local identity. It flourishes here – just – and against the odds – because Felpham Parish Council and local people are determined to make this community work and stand apart. This wonderful panorama of the parish at the turn of the millennium celebrates something of this achievement.

KIM LESLIE

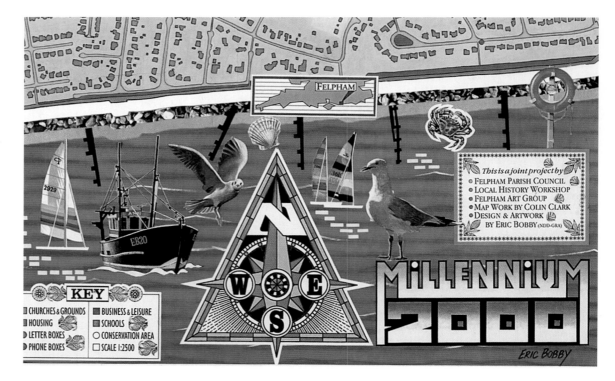

Fernhurst

AN YOU FIND the Fernhurst field mouse about to run across the village? And there are plenty more high-spirited activities going on: winter and summer sports, the annual May Day Revels, Guides and Brownies, six delightfully-drawn characters in familiar pose. The map teems with local wildlife and several military associations are highlighted. One area is still known as Cavalry Quarters, the reputed spot where a troop of Royalist troops lay hidden during the Civil War in the 1640s.

From whichever way the village is approached it's through great waves of well-wooded hills, a reminder that this ancient place started life as a forest clearing. The name is Saxon and is said to mean 'the ferney wooded hill'. So its roots are deep and have left their mark. Significantly fern-leaves decorate the title-piece of the map.

If we wanted to add a suffix – like in Stow-in-the-Wold – it wouldn't be inappropriate to call this place Fernhurst-in-the-Wood. It stands amongst some stunning Sussex scenery, its mixed geology of clays and sandstone producing magnificent oaks, pines and acres of bracken-covered hilltops. E.V. Lucas in that classic of local literature, *Highways and Byways in Sussex*, declared of this countryside in 1904 that 'Sussex has nothing wilder or richer' than this. It's still quite true today and the reason why this is such wonderful walking country. Perhaps that's why our rambling friend at the top of the map looks so happy!

Today the village itself has lost its earlier isolation through good road and rail links, the line at nearby Haslemere in Surrey giving

quick access to London. But away from the main road, much of Fernhurst could be miles from the business of modern life.

The village itself is really in two parts; it is almost as if there were two Fernhursts. The busier is on the main road around the crossroads – called The Cross, where there

used to be a village cross – and on the western side where most people live. Here is the little shopping centre and car park, and across the road is the village hall and the showroom for a sports car dealer that pulls in enthusiasts from miles around. Unusually for a West Sussex village, there is an internet café, part of the Fernhurst Centre.

Then eastwards, along Church Road, with its sandstone walls, past the ancient church and onto the village green, there's a completely different world. As one writer recently reported, this is 'the sort of village green exiled Englanders would die for'. This quintessentially

Village green, looking north

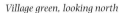

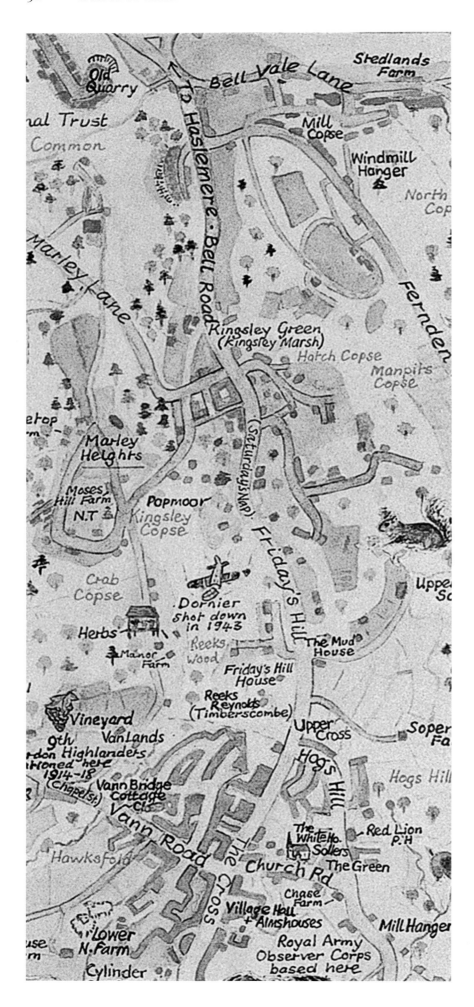

St Margaret's Church

English scene is given as a panorama at the foot of the map. The well-spaced old houses, the church and centuries-old pub around the green are all that make for perfection. No two buildings are alike. Notice the tile-hung walls on some of the houses, typically found in this part of Sussex and adjacent south-west Surrey. Plain tiles were used on many houses, but here linear bands of shaped tiles create an unusual decorative effect. The switchback contours of the stone boundary wall of Sollers also make use of tiles, this time as a capping. The old village school is here, with its tell-tale sign, the school bell, still in place, but silent.

The wall immediately to the west side of the village war memorial includes a stone incised with the letters F and E on either side of a small cross. This is one of the historic boundary stones that once marked the divide between Fernhurst and its neighbouring parish, Easebourne – quite out of place here as this spot has never been on a boundary line. Someone has clearly violated the biblical precept that makes it a sin to move the landmarks of our forefathers!

Fernhurst's limits are still marked by many of its original boundary stones, the subject of a comprehensive survey of its ancient bounds by the Fernhurst Society. Members have been surveying the boundaries and reviving the old custom of beating the bounds. In days gone by it was vital to know where one parish ended and another started. This was for all sorts of

The Village of FERNHURST at the year 2000 A.D.

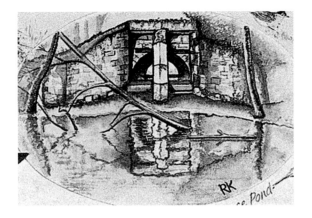

Furnace Pond, a relic of the Wealden iron industry

legal reasons to do with rating property for taxation and welfare purposes when the parish was responsible for much of local government. Fernhurst's boundary was trodden and recorded in immense detail in 1837. The limits described in the original document – preserved in West Sussex Record Office in Chichester – have given the precise route and revealed the surviving stones. They have been photographed and recorded by the society. Fernhurst is the first West Sussex parish to conduct a survey like this, an obvious follow-up to making the parish map where boundaries are so significant.

The Fernhurst Society, under the direction of retired marketing and communications consultant John Tucker, made this delightful map as its first major project. This is a society with an enormous range of activities and must surely rate as one of the most pro-active in the county, binding the village together with enormous energy through projects like its biodiversity studies and oral history recording, both supported by Local Heritage Initiative funding for over £20,000. The society was responsible for the wrought-iron village sign, puts on major exhibitions to display its work, and keeps people in touch through its regular newsletter.

The society is a model of its type and owes much to its first and former chairman, Peter Hudson. Under its wing, the Junior Fernhurst Society caters for children, its emphasis on practical activities centred on wildlife conservation and local history. The society's chairman and studio potter, Julia Roxan, reckons that projects like the parish map have been 'marvellous ways to involve people in local community activities, fostering a real feeling of village identity and togetherness and a great means of membership recruitment'.

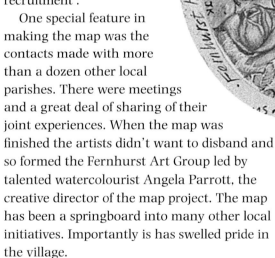

One special feature in making the map was the contacts made with more than a dozen other local parishes. There were meetings and a great deal of sharing of their joint experiences. When the map was finished the artists didn't want to disband and so formed the Fernhurst Art Group led by talented watercolourist Angela Parrott, the creative director of the map project. The map has been a springboard into many other local initiatives. Importantly is has swelled pride in the village.

KIM LESLIE

Some old Fernhurst Village Names: Cooper · Varnes · Wellen · Hollist · Chase · Smithers · Berry · White · Tudor Trussler · Bulbeck · Boxall · Denyer · Bridger · Dudman · Gale · Burt · Hill Kingshott · Enticknap · Glazier · Heather · Gilbert · Lambert · Coombs

Ferring

Visitors come to Ferring for the beach, Highdown Hill and the Conservation Area around the church, but for the people who live or work here, Ferring is primarily a community of just over 4000 people living in the 2200 houses in the southern half of the parish…. There are several important open spaces within the built-up area and many of the houses are on large plots, so that there is a feeling of 'garden estate', as well as the rural character of the village nucleus and the farm cottages in Sea Lane and other pre-20th-century roads…. The northern half of the parish is open country….

Extract from *Ferring Parish Plan 2005 – 2015*

'A community – open spaces – garden estate – rural character of the village nucleus – open country': these are what make Ferring special and such an agreeable place in which to live. With all the benefits of close proximity to Worthing, it rejoices in its independence from its big neighbour. Whenever Ferring counts its blessings, thoughts turn to Goring, its sister village across the fields, gobbled up by a rapaciously-expanding borough since 1929. Whilst Ferring was swamped under the same tide of house-building from the 1930s, it kept apart, kept itself a village. And whatever has happened since, there is still a strong attachment to the idea of a village community.

Its integrity as a village has much to do with physical separation from surrounding neighbours. Except for a bridging-link of

The Ramblers

houses with Worthing alongside Goring Way – across just one-fourteenth of its boundary – Ferring is *totally* surrounded by open space, by fields and seashore. Its distinction is in its setting, the first parish along the coastline west of Brighton where on *both* of its long sides there is a break in housing. Goring Gap to the east, Kingston Gap and Ferring Rife to the west, as well as the downland slopes of Highdown to the north, these are precious acres of countryside tying up Ferring like a neat parcel. And what a sharp contrast

Holly Lodge

between lowland Ferring on the plain and highland Ferring on the Downs, the A259 the crucial boundary cutting across the grain of the parish like a sharp knife. The parish map well emphasises these clear-cut divisions.

Both its setting and separation help explain how Ferring has so successfully held onto much of its old village feeling, a feeling with deep roots. The church guide-book sees the link between past and present: 'in human and material ways we have inherited a large part of an historic village and with it some of the peace and friendliness which blessed the small agricultural community of long ago'.

The parish is of great antiquity, its name going back to the original Saxon settlement well over a thousand years ago. That a place called Ferring was here in 762 is proved by a charter recording its first mention in history. Today its Norman church is surrounded by any number of fine examples of knapped flint

Home Farm Cottage

and cobblestone cottages, some thatched, all lovely and so full of local personality. They line the original village street by the church, a horse and cart lane so narrow in its twist that it has to be one-way for modern traffic. Old Ferring is characterised by another use of flint and cobblestone seen in boundary walls along the old village streets, lanes and twittens, concealing colourful cottage gardens full of roses and old fruit trees. In and around the village, so many that they are a constant delight, are countless evergreen ilex trees (otherwise known as holm oaks), notably seen

Ilex Walk

in the mile-long avenue planted between Ferring and Goring in the 19th century. They all lend a remarkably evergreen feel to the village.

Ferring's old buildings and wildlife are so treasured that they have been made main features on the parish map. The banks of Ferring Rife are a haven for wildlife and are such an important part of the parish's

Ferring Rife

Ferring Playgroup

Cricket has been played in the parish since at least 1797

geography that its course is known here as the Rife Valley. (Rifes are drainage ditches found along the coastal plain.) A great variety of birds, rare moths and dragonflies are lured here and it's also home to sedge warblers, frogs, newts, a colony of marsh orchids and families of water voles.

There is much to protect around the parish. This is where the vigilance of the Ferring Conservation Group is vital, its birth triggered by what was then the most controversial issue to face the village for years when the open space called Little Twitten was threatened with an indoor bowls complex in the late 1980s. Ferring seethed, the group mobilised its troops, and the site was saved, a first victory. Now under its slogan 'Are You With Us?' their four-fold aims keep the environment a high profile issue as they strive to preserve Ferring's beauty and character; cherish its wildlife; keep the open country around the parish; oppose infilling in the village.

Active conservation is balanced by an energetic interest in the past through the Ferring History Group, just one more of the many groups and clubs that bring local people together – over sixty are listed on the parish map. They all do so much to reinforce the sense of village identity, echoing the parish plan in its belief that the quality of community life depends on social and individual relationships.

People certainly seem to be very happy with life here. In the recent parish survey, 99 per cent of those questioned agreed that Ferring was a good place to live (one per cent didn't know!).

The map sums up so much of the good things about the parish, for it's clearly created out of a great deal of love and affection for the

place. One interesting spin-off has been that several of the logos for the various groups were designed especially for the map, as was Michael Parkin's emblem for Ferring at top centre. The village sign on the village green uses the emblem and several groups have since adopted the logos for their own use. Profits from map sales were given to the Conservation Group and History Group as well as to the Jubilee Youth Art Exhibition held in 2002. Wendy Ross, who led the map group, looks back with some satisfaction: 'I think we are all very proud of what we achieved and it's very rewarding to know that it will stand as an enduring record of our village for all time'.

KIM LESLIE

Glass flask, c. AD 400, found on Highdown Hill, now in Worthing Museum

Highdown Hill – once a smugglers' haunt

Ferring Parish Map

Millennium 2000

FERRING

The parish of Ferring lies between the Villages of East Preston and Goring, separated from each by a strategic gap. The Village itself is 2.5 miles long by 0.5 mile wide, stretching from The Downs to the sea. The population recorded in 1901 was 243 whereas this millennium year it exceeds 4,000. Equally, public records show that in 1891 the number of residences numbered 56 whereas today records show 2,308 with 189 businesses. There are 25 Grade II listed buildings in Ferring, some of which are illustrated on this map. The Church is also a Grade I listed building. Highdown Hill is nationally regarded as an important archaeological site, now owned by the National Trust. Finds show late Bronze Age, Iron Age, Roman and South Saxon occupation including a cemetery. Discoveries were made in the 1800s initially by Mr E Henty, an extensive local landowner, and many finds are now in Worthing Museum. During World War II Highdown Hill was used as a radar station.

As we go forward into the new Century and Millennium, we are anxious to preserve the rural character of our Village whilst at the same time moving forward, endeavouring to accommodate the many interests and activities of all ages whilst maintaining the quality of our Village and its environment.

FERRING CP

Holly Lodge (Grade II). Thought to have been built at the same time as other medieval cottages in Church Lane. Has been a Smithy, and Undertakers, a shop and a post office, this being the original centre of the Village. Has been a private residence for many years.

St Andrew's C of E Church (Grade I). A Norman Church, thought to have been built on Saxon foundations in c.1100. Subsequently enlarged and extended following St Richard of Chichester's exile and sanctuary in this area when, in 1245, King Henry III initially refused to accept his appointment. Received the documents of nearby Kingston Chapel in 1626 following its submergence by the sea and seating was provided for the Kingston congregation. Like many Sussex Churches, St Andrew's has its own special quality and charm and is rather unique in its construction of chalk and Sussex marble in some areas. There is no notable spire and only one church bell.

Landalls and Vine Cottages (Grade II). Originally recorded on the Glebe Terrier of 1635 as one property although today they are separately owned.

The Ramblers, Church Lane (Grade II). Recorded on the Court Rolls of 1799. Adjoins Church Lychgate and is partly thatched.

Ferring Village Hall. Originally donated by Mrs Henty, a resident and landowner of Ferring, with her husband Edwin Henty. A further room was subsequently added, named the Griffin Room, all are in almost constant use for numerous Village activities, including the weekly Wednesday WI Market.

Ferring War Memorial – Royal British Legion. Built to commemorate the men from Ferring who lost their lives in World Wars I and II.

Ferring Conservation Group – formed in 1988 and has a membership of around 1,400. Meets monthly in the Village Hall and works actively to preserve the character of Ferring and particularly the open spaces.

Maytree Cottage (Grade II). Mentioned in the Court Rolls of 1632, Maytree Cottage is thought to be one of the earliest cottages in Ferring and adjoins Evergreen Cottage of around the same date, sharing a roof and may originally have been one building. There is evidence of a secret room between the two properties as well as what is thought to be a secret cock pen in the roof, as well as many timber beams of good quality. Today, these are two separate residences.

Ferring Adventure Scouts on an evening trip.

Fledgling Lodge. The Ferring Playgroup for under 5's has been in existence since 1980 and moved to its present site in Sea Lane in 1997. The Playgroup relies on local funding and is a registered charity.

In 1985, a new Abbeyfield House was built for the care of the elderly on the site of the original Ferring Primary School and was named Old School House. A further house was open by this Society in 1986 in Beehive Lane, named Cornwell House after the founder of these homes in Ferring, Mr and Mrs W Cornwell.

Ferring Baptist Church built in 1971

Ferring has been the home of the Mini Cooper since 1970

The Glass Flask discovered on Highdown Hill and thought to have been made in Alexandria in 400 A.D. It is now in Worthing Museum. The Greek inscription reads 'Use me and good health to you'

Ferring C of E Primary School was first established in Ferring street in 1873 with 42 pupils. It was transferred to its present Sea Lane site in 1952 and by the year 2000 had 263 pupils

Ferring Downs WI formed in 1975. One of several active WI Organisations within the Village.

Windmills existed on Highdown Hill from 1378, the most famous one being used to signal to Smugglers in the 18th Century

Ferring Residents' & Owners' Association – originally formed as the Rate Payers' and Owners' Association in 1952 and renamed in 1990. The purpose of this group is to care for and maintain the unadopted roads of Ferring.

Animal Welfare Sally Tanner

Animal Welfare. Fairs run by Sally Tanner since 1984 at St Andrew's Church Hall in support of many needy local and national charities to help animals in distress.

Ilex Walk runs from Ferring to Goring and is an avenue of Ilex oak trees planted by the Lyon family of Goring Hall during the 1800s. This is now a conservation area and held in a Trust.

The river Rife runs through Ferring into the sea. Many alterations were made to its structure and the surrounding area following flooding, and is now an area with interesting plants and birds.

FCC RIDING THERAPY — FCC HORTICULTURE — FCC BROOK LANE

The Stables run by the Ferring Country Centre are co-located with a Horticultural Nursery and has 14 Horses providing Riding Therapy for over 550 riders a month for disabled people. The Nursery covers 18 acres growing plants and vegetables naturally, which are sold from a small Garden Centre. A further enterprise is based at Brook Lane, Ferring where Arts and Crafts are made and sold together with bespoke furniture from a small Coffee and Craft Shop. Disabled workers are involved in all aspects of these projects.

Ferring Amateur Dramatic Society (FADS). Formed in 1931 and produces three plays a year in the Village Hall.

1KM / 1Mile

"Reproduced from the 2000 Superplan Scale 1:10,000 Ordnance Survey Map by Permission of Her Majesty's Stationery Office. © Crown copyright MC 100052920 01/00/2013."

Greystoke Manor, Residential Care Home. Formerly The Square House, built in 1791, later extended and renamed St Maur's, but later became the Greystoke Manor Hotel until 1993 when it was renovated to the present care home.

Home Farm Cottage (Grade II). First recorded in 1535 and mentioned in the Court Rolls of 1652 as a farm house. Two cottages were later indicated but it has been a single residence for many years.

FRIDAY PORTRAIT GROUP

Friday Portrait Group – established for over 30 years.

Cricket has been played in Ferring for over 100 years and since the war, in Little Twitten where a new pavilion was more recently built. The old railway carriage which served as such for many years was passed on to the Bluebell Railway for their use.

Scouts' Table Football. Drawn by one of the players, Matthew L.

Bluebird Café, an all-season seaside café which has been in existence for many years under different names and during World War II was an Army NAAFI.

FERRING TENNIS CLUB

Ferring Tennis Club. Hard courts replaced grass in 1992 and the Tennis Club was formed in 1995.

Bramble Cottage Grade II First Mentioned in the Court Rolls in 1657 this flint and thatched cottage is one of the most illustrated cottages in Ferring

Church Cottage, Church Lane (Grade II). Thought to have been built on the site of a medieval cottage.

Project Supported by

west sussex county council

Ferring District Council   Arun District Council

Published in August, 2000 as part of the West Sussex Millennium Parish Maps Project. We would also like to express our appreciation to Mr. Kim Leslie, the coordinator of the West Sussex Millennium Project for his kind advices, and to the West Sussex County Council Print Unit for their help in compiling this map

ARUN ART SOCIETY

Arun Art Club – established for over 40 years and holds an art exhibition every August in the Ferring Village Hall.

St Andrew's Toddlers Group – formed in 1981 and meets every Tuesday and Friday.

© Contributors Ferring Parish Map Project, Ferring Parish Council

Ferring Flower Club – formed in 1967 and meets monthly throughout the year.

MONDAY KEEP FIT CLASS

Monday Keep Fit Class. A long established group.

Best Kept Village Competition

We ask residents and visitors to help us to keep our village tidy and well cared for KEEP SUSSEX TIDY

Ferring won the award in 1985 for the Best Kept Large Village in West Sussex.

Ferring Horticultural Society

Ferring Horticultural Society, was in existence before World War II and was then re-established in 1957. Has approximately 160 members and holds 3 seasonal flower shows a year.

Rose Cottage (Grade II). Recorded as built in c.1800 and thought to have been, at one time, two cottages and part of Landall's next door. Alterations have been carried out over many years and this is now a separate private residence.

The Ferring Parish Map has been created with as much Village involvement as possible. Artists include Roy Aldam, Roy Rouse, Barbara Doyle, Jean Writer, Joan Evershed, John Cressey, Sally Tanner, Joy Rennard, Janet Wright, Edna Parsons, Ann Hedges, Pauline Smith, D.M. White, Sue Roberson, Rachel Richards, Barbara Davies, Brian Rolf, Gill Kirk, Marcus Vince, Jo Stemmett and Christy and together with other contributors, Advice was received from Mrs. J. Cornwell as well as Michael Parton (who also originated the Village Emblem). David Barber kindly painted and contributed both Land and Sea Birds, and Sandra Martin was responsible for colouring the Map and the Flowers and Butterflies. Jenny Stenner, Age 10, Oliver Barleycorn, Age 9 and Charmain Cooney, Perry Charmington Kathryn Sloane, aged 9 - 10, and Ben Tapenise, age 8 painted the schools and wild life.

The Ferring Parish Map Members for this project have been Wendy Russ, Malcolm Crowle, Michael Tanner, Joyce Cooper and Frank Leeson and Ferring Parish Map.

Mini reproduced by kind permission by Michael Cooper.

The Ferring Glass Flask was reproduced by kind permission of Dr. Sally White of Worthing Museum.

PRINTERS Amherst Direct Mail • Ferring Offset Litho • EMF Publishing **SERVICES** Ferring Parish Council • Brook Lane Caravan Park • Onslow Caravan Park • J Greco – Builder • John Cooper Garages • Yeoman Peugeot • Ferring Library • St Andrew's Parish Magazine • **FARMS HORTICULTURE LAND OWNERS** Castle Goring Farm • A P McIntyre and Son Limited • Chanctonbury Vineyard • County Fayre • Dreamscape Gardens • Ferring Nurseries • Ferring Country Centre • Green Gold Tree Farm • Hillview Nurseries • Hangleton Farm Equestrian Centre • National Trust - Highdown Hill • Northdown Farm • North Barn Free Range Egg Farm • Roundstone Farm • Woodlands Stables •

Fishbourne

Fishbourne's fabric map, hand-painted on linen with embroidery, appliqué and gold work, is one of the West Sussex parish maps probably seen by more people than any of the other maps of the project. This is because it hangs in the Roman Palace, visited by more than eighty thousand people a year. Its vibrant, glowing colours create a wonderful effect, making the map a great ambassador for the project. Cupid riding a dolphin shines out in gold thread, echoing Fishbourne's most recognised mosaic, symbol of the palace.

Fishbourne certainly has a life of its own, but the Romans and what they left behind all those centuries ago continue to have an enormous effect on the locality. The Roman legacy very much affects peoples' views of the present village, inspiring one house developer to come up with Flavian Fields for one of the new estates, and the parish council to name Margary Close after Ivan Margary, through whose generosity the palace site was secured, and Rudkin Place after David Rudkin, the palace director.

Since it was first discovered in 1960, the palace, the largest Roman domestic building north of the Alps, with the largest collection of in-situ mosaics in Britain, and unusually with a Roman-style garden planted on its original plan, has brought fame – and people by the coach load – to Fishbourne. It now occupies a major place not only in the world of archaeology but also as part of the tourist trail of south-eastern England. And they don't come to see the village!

The village itself is bounded by Bosham on the west, the A27 on the north and east, and creeks and marshes of Chichester Harbour on

Saltmill Flats at the end of the creek

the south. These are not all official boundaries, but the A27 proves to be a wall in the minds of people who live near it. The red swathe arching across the map suggests its prominence in local minds. The road, like a motorway, brings a constant hum of noise, day

and night, as a permanent backdrop. It doesn't have any contact with the village because it goes straight past, and to get out of the village on the north and east you have to go over or under it. Officially, Fishbourne continues east to the other side of the A27, into Fishbourne Road East where the Rectory used to be, and in the continuation north up Salthill Road, but in these margins the sense of being actually part of the village retreats behind this modern-day bulwark.

Old Fishbourne is a linear village strung out along the present A259, with the church at the far eastern end. One only has to go back fifty years to find two shops, three pubs, a bakery and a post office. They have all gone except for the cycle shop called Barreg (the name is an amalgamation of the owners' names) and the three pubs. The cycle shop is well-known for providing a never-ending stream of students with a mode of travel to suit them, at any price! Here you can buy anything

to do with pedal power, tricycles, tandems, cycles with trailers or brand new state-of-the-art mountain bikes. It's a cyclists' paradise. The nearby pub, the Black Boy, was a meeting place for smugglers involved in the infamous 18th-century Galley and Chater case when

smugglers beat up a customs official so badly that they killed him. All the smugglers were caught and severe punishment meted out. But that wouldn't have stopped smuggling in the village; like the rest of the coast along here, the creeks and inlets were too useful for bringing in goods unnoticed.

New Fishbourne straggles up Blackboy Lane and Salthill Road, a residential area with every house different from its neighbours. There were shops in Deeside Avenue and Newport Drive, but they too have gone. To the south the sea and its creeks have receded a little, but still provide habitat for a great deal of wildlife. There were once three mills grinding away down here, two of them tide mills, all strategically sited for water-borne traffic. Going down to the foot of Mill Lane and seeing the creek full of reeds today, it doesn't seem possible that only eighty years ago this was a working quay where coal and grain were landed and flour and bricks taken away. The millpond remains, full of ducks and overlooked by Pendrills, a lovely thatched cottage. This is Fishbourne's most picturesque spot.

Pendrills

The map shows a number of houses, old and new. Like most of West Sussex, Fishbourne bears the brunt of a government move to build thousands of new homes in the south-east. Suddenly the old village has gone, as houses spring up, infilling green spaces, sometimes even infilling the infill. The influx of people find that their new home here doesn't have a doctor's surgery, and even the village school is full. The new housing-estate names might reflect the emphasis developers and outsiders

PORCH 74 MOSSE GARDENS

give to the Roman ancestry of the village but they ignore the seventeen hundred years in between, and perhaps sideline the village's true identity.

Some feel that the village is now a dormitory on the edge of Chichester, and that its concerns reflect those of the city. Those who have lived in Fishbourne all their lives worry about housing and facilities, and the changing lifestyles of its residents. They feel that the village has changed out of all recognition. The mood is demonstrated by 'The Log' – a trunk of a fallen tree that lay in a ditch near Deeside Avenue in the 1960s. Children who played on it felt it marked the boundary of *their* village. Adults who remember it saw its removal as somehow the end of the character of the village – at least as they had always known it.

But the making of a video about the village by Shirley Lang in 2000, then the making of the parish map in the same year, and now the publication of a book of old photographs and memories in 2006, show a community spirit that is alive and well. The physical landscape of the village might well be changing, but those traditions and principles in which the community and village are steeped, give

THE FISHBOURNE CLUB

Fishbourne a strong sense of place today.

At the centre of the community is the WI. Since the 1940s they have produced three scrapbooks about Fishbourne life. Now they have made their mark with this outstanding parish map, embroidered in superb detail by a small group of fourteen local residents, led by Margaret Borsberry. It was inspired by embroidery in Durham Cathedral.

From the very early planning of this project it was obvious that if it was to last the test of time then good quality materials had to be used. The map base is made from heavy quality Belgium linen. Every montage has been hand drawn and painted and then permanently fixed, every embroidered piece exquisitely detailed using traditional materials such as silk and cotton and real gold thread. Its colours today are as true as when it was first sewn. At the foot of the map is a fringed and beaded decorative hanging. For display the map is supported by a pole carved with dolphin finials made by Les Eames, a local walking-stick maker. The making of this wonderful map and its stand is a great tribute to the patience and dedication of its highly skilled team that found such an imaginative way to celebrate Fishbourne at the millennium.

CAROLINE ADAMS

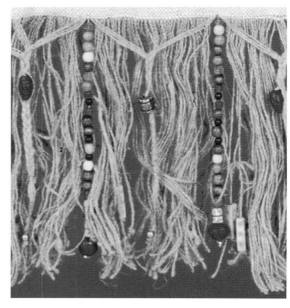

Funtington and West Stoke

YEW TREES, iron beds, radar, pigs and watercress make unlikely partners. In West Sussex they come together uniquely in just one place. Home to Europe's finest yew forest; birthplace of a staggeringly successful business – the Iron Bed Company that started in an old chicken shed, eventually to come third in Virgin Atlantic's top one hundred fastest growing UK companies; radar research centre; once called Pig City UK with Basil Baird's free-range porkers outnumbering local people two to one; and where chalk springs feed the only commercial watercress beds in Sussex – Hairspring Watercress sends huge consignments every week to wholesale markets in Brighton, Bristol and London. We could be nowhere else but in Funtington.

Today's civil parish spreads across four and a bit settlements: there are the two quite separate villages of Funtington and West Stoke, each with its parish church, the two hamlets of East and West Ashling, plus a tiny portion of another called Hambrook intruding on the south-west. Although the separation of all these places is not great in terms of distance, the fields and woodland keep them apart, surrounding each with a very strong sense of space, yet on the people level they are very much united through Funtington Parish Council, the school, and the two churches sharing the same vicar. Distinctly separate, and yet bound together, there is a healthy community dynamic at work across these scattered places.

They are all close to Chichester, but feel remarkably distant and deep in the country. Take the Funtington road out of the city and within minutes it quickly falls into lanes that open up into the heart of a rural landscape. Fork into the West Stoke road and a wide-sweeping panorama opens up to Stoke Clump crowning the lower slope of the Downs. Here is the edge of the Area of Outstanding Natural Beauty where downland slides into the coastal plain. A network of footpaths – marked in red on the map – weaves across this contrasting landscape. Many are very ancient ways: the

route connecting East to West Ashling and then going on to Funtington was a main 'highway' long before the days of metalled roads. Before the days of the motor car these old well-worn tracks gave unity to the parish as villagers made their way from one to another directly across the fields. Now they give accessibility to some of the finest walking country in southern England. Ramblers from near and far make for here – as do botanists, bird watchers and scientists.

They come to Kingley Vale to see its famous grove of yews, hundreds of them, gnarled and twisted, steeped in legend and folklore. Some say they commemorate a great battle against the Vikings, making these ancient trees many centuries old, others call them Druids' trees. E.V. Lucas in *Highways and Byways of Sussex*, reflecting on sombre scenery and dark romance, saw the place as 'grave and silent . . .

*Ancient yew forests line the Downs
in the Northern parts of the Parish*

transformed at dusk into a sinister and fantastic forest'. At other times it's far from silent, home to birds of passage from northern Europe in search of the yews' brilliant scarlet berries. Richard Williamson has seen thousands of fieldfares, blackbirds and song thrushes greedily descend 'like children confronted by bowls of trifle and jelly'. (See his book *The Great Yew Forest: the Natural History of Kingley Vale.*) Richard, son of Henry Williamson of *Tarka the Otter* fame, has been observing daily life here for some forty years. He has the longest-running common bird census in Britain, and one of the longest-running series of fixed-point photographs of vegetation ever made. Claimed by English Nature as the largest remaining Atlantic yew forest in the world, the site was granted special status as one of Britain's first National Nature Reserves.

This outstanding landscape is complemented by fine country houses with commanding settings at the foot of the Downs, or, in the words of one 19th-century observer describing a local property, 'where the hand of art has been most judiciously employed to render the peculiar advantages of nature subservient to domestic comfort'. The little watercolour cameos give a delightful feel for this type of property, a few the homes of famous names. Lord Louis Mountbatten lived at Adsdean with its polo ground in the 1920s and '30s so as to be near Portsmouth dockyard; the man who ran the air war during 1939–45, regarded by Churchill as 'the accepted star of the Air Force', was Chief of Air Staff Peter Portal, the first Viscount Portal of Hungerford, who came to West Ashling House to be near Chichester Harbour for the sailing.

Adsdean

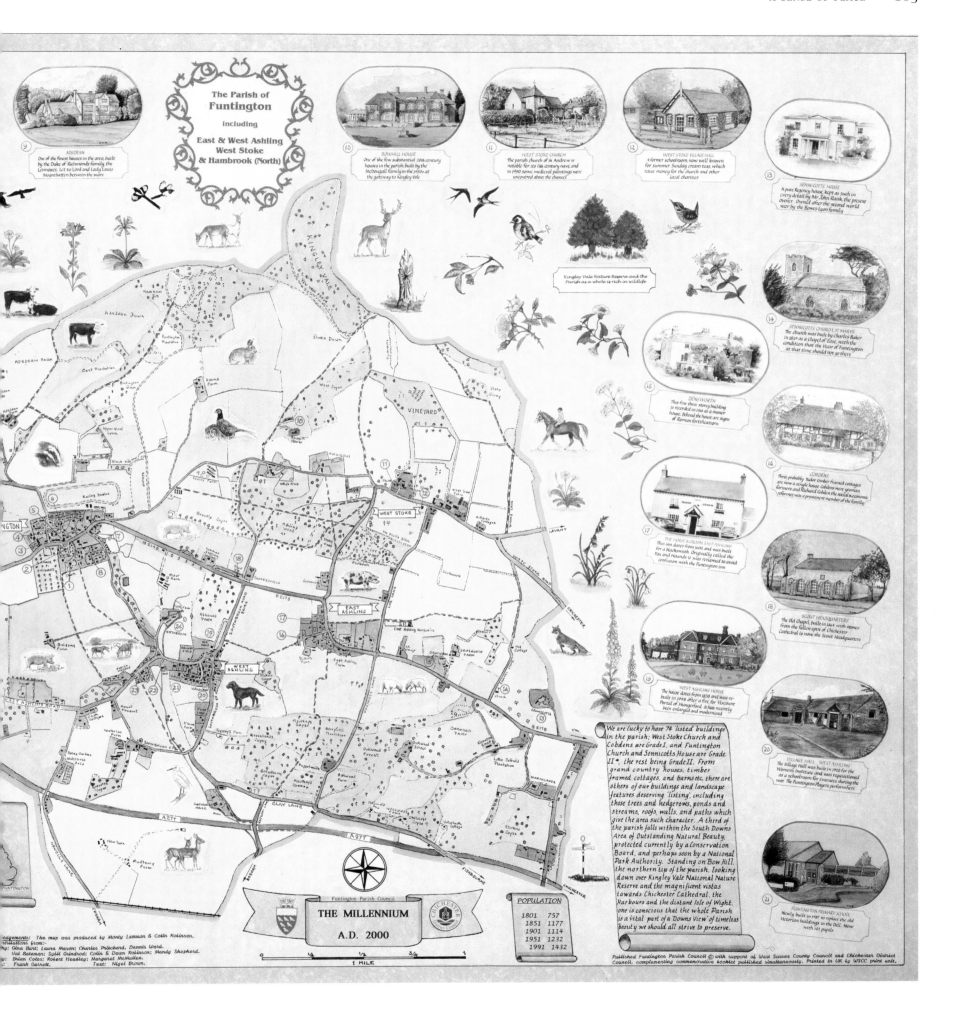

The Parish of
Funtington
including
**East & West Ashling
West Stoke
& Hambrook (North)**

ADSDEAN
One of the finest houses in the area, built by the Duke of Richmond's family, the Lennoxes, let to Lord and Lady Louis Mountbatten between the wars

BOWHILL HOUSE
One of the few substantial 20th century houses in the parish, built by the McDougall family in the 1930s at the gateway to Kingley Vale

WEST STOKE CHURCH
The parish church of St Andrew is notable for its 11th century nave, and in 1990 some medieval paintings were uncovered above the chancel

WEST STOKE VILLAGE HALL
A former schoolroom, now well known for summer Sunday cream teas, which raise money for the church and other local charities

SENNICOTTS HOUSE
A pure Regency house, kept as such in every detail by Mr John Rank, the present owner. Owned after the second world war by the Bowes-Lyon family

KINGLEY VALE

Kingley Vale Nature Reserve and the Parish as a whole is rich in wildlife

SENNICOTTS CHURCH, ST MARYS
The church was built by Charles Baker in 1851 as a chapel of Ease, with the condition that the Vicar of Funtington at that time should not go there

DENSWORTH
This fine three storey building is recorded in 1541 as a manor house. Behind the house are signs of Roman fortifications

COBDENS
These probably Tudor timber framed cottages are now a single house. Cobdens were yeoman farmers and Richard Cobden the social economic reformer was a prominent member of the family

THE HORSE & GROOM, EAST ASHLING
This inn dates from 1600 and was built for a blacksmith. Originally called the Fox and Hounds it was renamed to avoid confusion with the Funtington inn

WEST STOKE

EAST ASHLING

WEST ASHLING

SCOUT HEADQUARTERS
The Old Chapel, built in 1865 with stones from the fallen spire of Chichester Cathedral, is now the Scout Headquarters

WEST ASHLING HOUSE
The house dates from 1838 and was re-built in 1906 after a fire, for Viscount Portal of Hungerford. It has recently been enlarged and modernised

VILLAGE HALL, WEST ASHLING
The Village Hall was built in 1912 for the Women's Institute and was requisitioned as a schoolroom for evacuees during the war. The Funtington Players perform here

We are lucky to have 74 listed buildings in the parish; West Stoke Church and Cobdens are Grade I, and Funtington Church and Sennicotts House are Grade II*, the rest being Grade II. From grand country houses, timber framed cottages, and barns etc, there are others of our buildings and landscape features deserving 'listing', including these trees and hedgerows, ponds and streams, roofs, walls, and paths which give the area such character. A third of the parish falls within the South Downs Area of Outstanding Natural Beauty, protected currently by a Conservation Board, and perhaps soon by a National Park Authority. Standing on Bow Hill, the northern tip of the parish, looking down over Kingley Vale National Nature Reserve and the magnificent vistas towards Chichester Cathedral, the Harbours and the distant Isle of Wight, one is conscious that the whole Parish is a vital part of a Downs View of timeless beauty we should all strive to preserve.

FUNTINGTON PRIMARY SCHOOL
Newly built in 1981 to replace the old Victorian buildings in the Dell. Now with 125 pupils

Funtington Parish Council
**THE MILLENNIUM
A.D. 2000**

POPULATION	
1801	757
1851	1177
1901	1114
1951	1232
1991	1432

0   ¼   ½   ¾   1
1 MILE

Acknowledgements: The map was produced by Monty Lennon & Colin Robinson.
Illustrations from:
...: Gina Bunt; Laura Mason; Charles Pritchard; Dennis Ward.
...: Val Bateman; Sybil Grindrod; Colin & Dawn Robinson; Mandy Shepherd.
...: Brian Cotes; Robert Headley; Margaret McMullen.
...: Frank Garrett.   Text: Nigel Brown.

Published Funtington Parish Council © with support of West Sussex County Council and Chichester District Council, complementing commemorative booklet published simultaneously. Printed in UK by WSCC print unit.

The Edwardian beauty, Lillie Langtry, lived for a time with her second husband, Hugo de Bathe, at Hollandsfield on the edge of West Stoke.

Old sale particulars have waxed lyrical about this elegant type of country property 'pleasantly situate at the foot of the Downs . . . in close proximity to the residences of Noblemen and Gentlemen . . . accommodations for a family of the highest respectability'. One 19th-century writer even went so far as to say

Racehorses training on the Downs

Densworth

that 'The salubrity of the air is so remarkable, that this district may be justly styled the Montpellier of England'. The area attracted families of substance, people of influence and wealth. In more modern times some of these attractive properties have been divided into flats and apartments, West Stoke House is now a hotel and Oakwood a school. The countryside constantly reinvents itself.

From the historic core of the old village of Funtington take the road westwards for sight of a completely different world. A high fence, a guardroom and warnings that all photography is prohibited catch the attention. Behind all the security loom giant reflectors and electronic gadgetry on the site marked on the parish map as DERA – the Defence Evaluation and Research Agency, since 2001 rebranded QinetiQ – QI, ancient Chinese for energy, NET for networking, IQ for intelligence! The site is in the forefront for testing antennae for communication and radar systems for shipping, aircraft and even spacecraft. Despite its hi-tech hardware, there's silence, not a sound to mar the peace and quiet of the nearby village. The greenfield site occupies former RAF Funtington, a Second World War emergency landing field used for D-Day, a neat illustration of how the past that has been obliterated can still dominate the present-day landscape.

KIM LESLIE

Northbrook

St Mary's Church

Goring-by-Sea

A town or village which has lost contact with its history cannot really be a community. In Goring, most of our history has been hidden under the suburban atmosphere of modern development. This book has been an attempt to bring the past to life, telling the story of those who have lived and died here before us . . . this rich inheritance from the past belongs to all of us. Goring is our community, given in trust for us to hand on to the next generation. May God guide our common endeavours as we gain a new sense of belonging and community from Goring's past . . . .

This heart-felt epilogue rounds off the story of how town planners turned a village into a suburb in Frank Fox-Wilson's history, *The Story of Goring and Highdown* (1987). In 1929 it was taken over, its ancient village status transformed into a town – becoming just *part* of a town at that – as land-hungry Worthing crept ever westwards. When the old village forge and cottage were demolished in 1966, the chairman of the Worthing planning committee was reported as saying 'I like old cottages, but I think in this case they are a little out of place'. As Fox-Wilson remarked, 'words fail . . .'.

But for all that has been lost, Goring now *contributes* to Worthing as one of its best

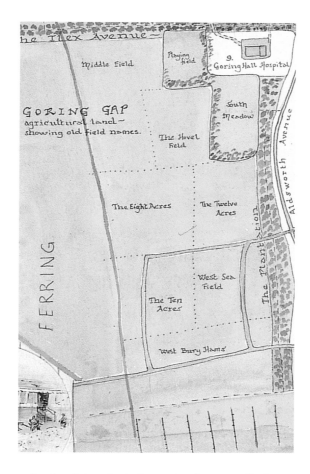

suburbs. It has lost character, but equally has gained another. Old cottages may have gone, along with big gardens and wide-open fields, but there are some good examples of 1930s–40s architecture, a few of the old cottages – notably in Jefferies Lane – still a wealth of trees, and the jewel-in-the-crown – Goring Gap – with its beach, an enormous greensward and uninterrupted views of Highdown Hill to the north. This wide open space, mingling sea and countryside, marking the first major break in coastline development west of Brighton, is jealously guarded by local residents and designated by planners as one of the county's vital 'strategic gaps'. There is a lot to be thankful for here.

Just what it is that delights local people is shown on Goring's parish map. It was put together by the local artists' group called Painting for Fun led by Jane Bond and Vivienne Hooker. As they had never made a map before, Jane said that at first they all

thought the project was way beyond their capabilities. But they bravely decided to have a go, even if the result might have been for no more than their own pleasure, after all they painted for fun. They persevered and here's the result after their year's research, designing, painting and getting copies printed for sale. Profits from sales went to support nearby St Barnabas Hospice, with copies sold to many Goring people and sent all over the country and the world. Altogether it has been judged a great success and certainly brought lots of fun to all the artists involved. As Jane has written in her report, they are so pleased it has been beneficial to the local community as well as giving 'a lasting appreciation for our lovely environment'.

It's an environment with a lot to offer as John Batten, feature writer for the *West Sussex Gazette,* discovered when he dubbed Goring 'salubrious, salty and select . . . mercifully preserved from many of the gimmicks that are part of your popular holiday resort. You don't holiday at Goring – unless you drive there to enjoy a day on the beach – you retire there, or live there in between earning a living elsewhere, so there is no need of . . . bingo halls, coach parks, fish and chip shops and the like.' In other words a beach for a good old-fashioned bucket and spade day at the seaside.

Malthouse Cottages, Jefferies Lane

Another visitor who has publicised Goring came to chronicle his impressions in words and watercolours in the 1990s. Marine artist Peter Collyer set himself the task of recording seaside locations at the thirty-two points of the compass based on bearings taken from the centre of Britain. The Ordnance Survey's point for this is Brown Syke Moss in Lancashire. The last landfall for bearing south-south-east from Brown Syke Moss happens to be Goring-by-Sea. And so he came to paint his atmospheric pictures and pen some very up-beat word pictures. He found it all 'impressively okay':

Spacious and green, Goring is more up-market than the average suburb, there is more individuality and variety, with more architectural integrity . . . . There are some good examples of suntrap houses with their curved glazing and some superb International Style post-New Ways white cubes. Roads, verges and pavements are wide, houses set well back and substantial trees grow everywhere. Modern developers have something to learn from Goring.

With the eyes of an artist he points out that the signs of pre-suburban days can still be found in a few of the old cottages and some grand houses, their grounds having supplied the land for developers from the 1930s.

The grandest of these is Goring Hall, a late Victorian Queen Anne-style mansion, now a private hospital. The Sussex coast was once dotted with mansions like this, each in its own extensive grounds looking towards the sea. Most have long since gone, demolished and built over. Goring Hall is a rare exception.

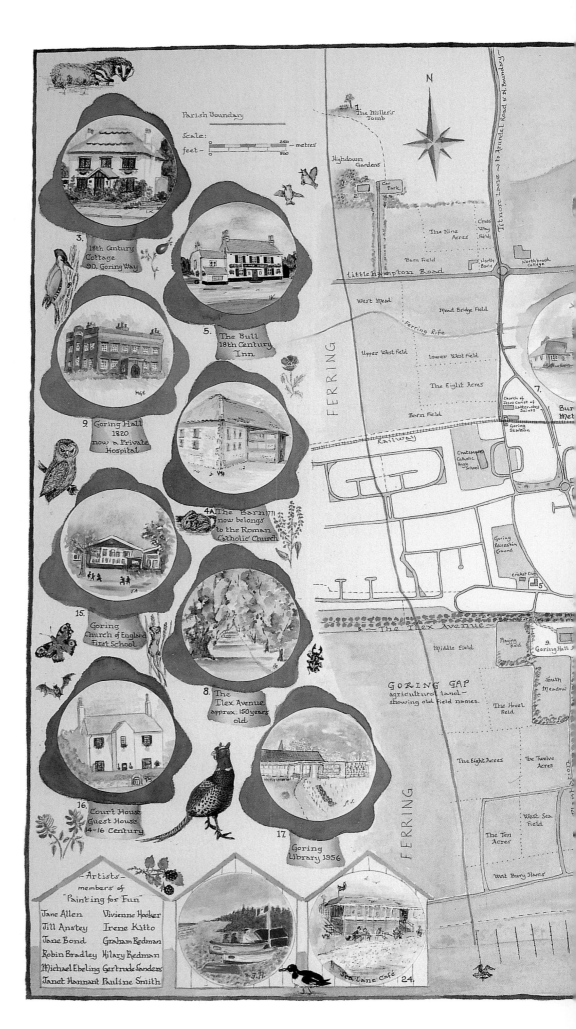

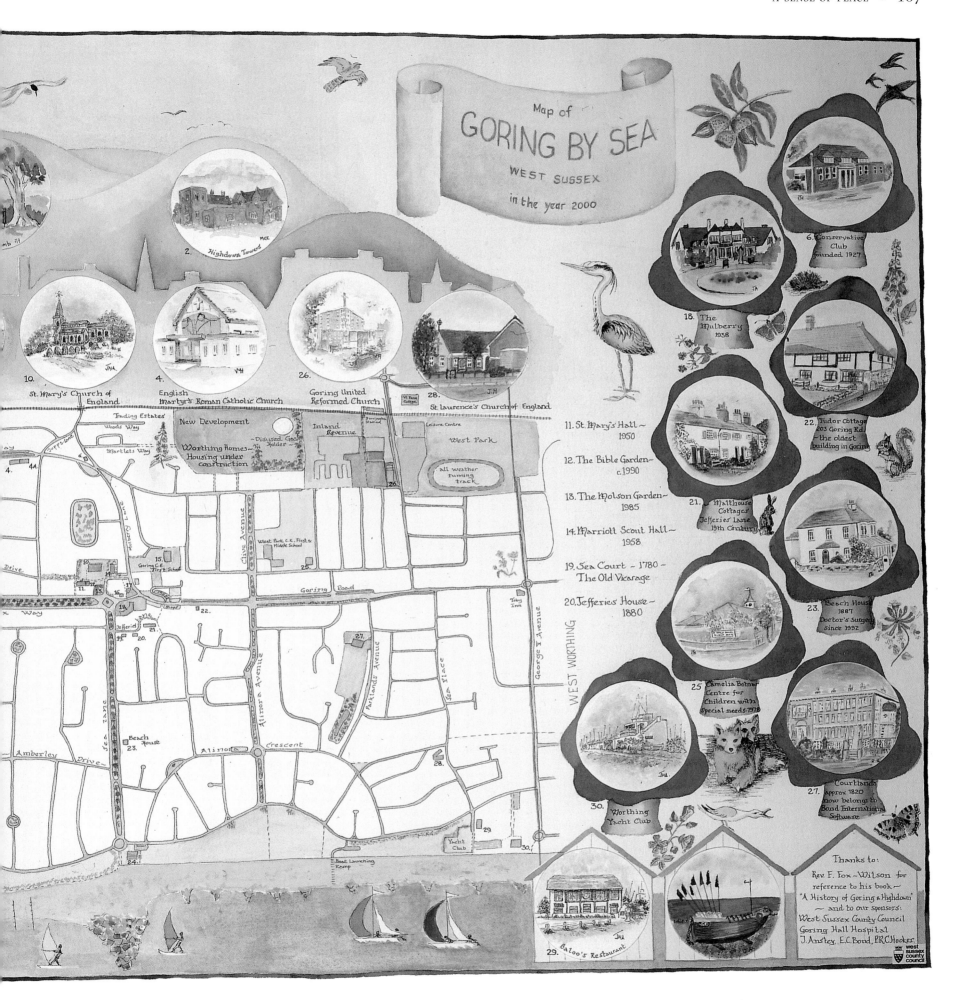

Map of
GORING BY SEA
WEST SUSSEX
in the year 2000

2. Highdown Towers

10. St. Mary's Church of England

4. English Martyr's Roman Catholic Church

26. Goring United Reformed Church

28. St Laurence's Church of England

New Development
Worthing Homes—Housing under construction

Disused Gas Holder

Inland Revenue

West Park

All weather running track

Trading Estates
Woods Way
Jupps Lane
Martlets Way

West Park C.E. First & Middle School

Goring C.E. First School

Goring Road

Toby Inn

Sea Way
Amberley Drive
Beach House 23.
Alinora Avenue
Alinora Crescent
Clive Avenue
Parklands Avenue
Sea Place
George V Avenue
WEST WORTHING

Yacht Club

Boat Launching Ramp

6. Conservative Club founded 1927

18. The Mulberry 1938

22. Tudor Cottage 203 Goring Rd — the oldest building in Goring

21. Malthouse Cottages Jefferies Lane 19th Century

23. Beach House 1887 Doctor's Surgery since 1992

11. St. Mary's Hall — 1950

12. The Bible Garden — c.1990

13. The Molson Garden — 1985

14. Marriott Scout Hall — 1958

19. Sea Court – 1780 – The Old Vicarage

20. Jefferies House – 1880

25. Camelia Botnar Centre for Children with Special needs 1918

27. Courtlands approx 1820 now belongs to Bond International Software

30. Worthing Yacht Club

29. Baloo's Restaurant

Thanks to:
Rev. F. Fox–Wilson for reference to his book — "A History of Goring & Highdown" — and to our sponsors: West Sussex County Council Goring Hall Hospital J. Anstey, E.C.Bond, P.R.C.Hooker.

WEST SUSSEX COUNTY COUNCIL

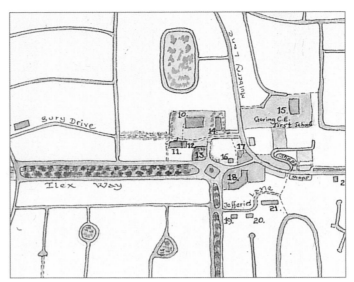

Ilex Avenue on the way to Ferring

Through its grounds runs Goring's much-treasured feature – the magnificent mile-long avenue of evergreen holm oaks (or ilex trees) – forming Ilex Way at one end – with a branch called The Plantation leading down to Goring Gap. The house in its green setting by the sea is a priceless landscape.

Other Goring features are highlighted in the cameo pictures – many in the branches of a holm oak, each numbered for easy location on the map. Every one is special to someone; in total they sum up the real meaning of local life, through its schools, churches, library, sailing club, beachside cafés, the pubs, the seaside *and* countryside. For Goring's ancient parish boundary – now that of Worthing Borough – makes an odd-shaped elongation affectionately known as 'the panhandle', reaching out onto the Downs at Highdown and into a network of downland footpaths. The old mansion up here is now a hotel and restaurant, its noted chalk garden open to the public. The much-visited Miller's Tomb gives views from Beachy Head to Selsey Bill and beyond. Goring's heritage is immensely varied and rich.

KIM LESLIE

Goring Library

Sea Lane Café

Worthing Yacht Club

Graffham, Selham and South Ambersham

THE THREE OF THEM make up the civil parish of Graffham: Selham, a scattering of houses and a tiny Saxon church by the Rother; South Ambersham, once an outlying, detached part of Hampshire, now famous as one of the Cowdray Park polo grounds; and Graffham itself, where most of the community is centred, with its school, two pubs, village hall, shop and church. They share a magnificent tract of West Sussex countryside.

Graffham is isolated, hidden away on a road to nowhere – at least for motorists – as this is one of those rare Sussex cul-de-sac villages where the tarmac stops and nature takes over. The main street is a 'high street' like no other, curling and turning, upping and downing as it climbs towards the church and school under the great hanging woods clinging to the Downs above.

It's from the Downs that the map is viewed northwards across fields and woodland to the Rother Valley, and then beyond to Blackdown in the distance (shown top right), at 919 feet the highest point in Sussex. In just a few miles the underlying geology of this tract of countryside changes dramatically, creating enormous differences in scenery, in wildlife and local building materials. A key is given at the foot of the map, and at the sides two corresponding coloured strips plot the geological succession, helping to explain the reasons for the sharp transition between the chalk and beech trees at one end of the village,

Graffham School

tumbling down to the sandy soils and pines at the other. Graffham enjoys the best of two quite distinct geological worlds. Landscape diversity makes this place somewhere very special.

Surrounded by thick woodland, its isolation is still very tangible today. In coming here there's always a sense of being cut-off and apart from surrounding places, a feeling that has done much to maintain a very strong community life. It was even stronger in the past but it's still a considerable force in the village today.

So, when a parish map was suggested, in true Graffham style there was absolutely no hesitation. Typically, with enormous gusto, Elly Spilberg and her friend, Pru Hart, mobilised a team under Daphne Taylor's chairmanship with an organisation second-to-none in its professionalism – a bulging file now in West Sussex Record Office tells the full story. First they established the group's identity with

its own notepaper; published a regular newsletter; contacted the press; raised money not only from official grants but also special events like a quiz night and ploughman's supper – in total they raised £2,888; they met other groups to share ideas and then got down to the real work of collecting information and then actually making the map. From the start they set out their aims and objectives:

- To produce a parish map to celebrate the millennium

- To involve as many residents as possible

- To record life in the parish in the year 2000

- To make use of, and extend, the village archives

- To encourage participation by members of neighbouring parishes and thereby foster good inter-parish relations

- To draw on, and develop, the many skills in the village

Empire Hall

The work that followed to achieve all these ends was carefully recorded in diary form by Pru Hart. A few edited entries give something of its flavour:

Kim Leslie came and spoke to try and inspire us to create a parish map.

A pressurised week, couldn't work Friday as was discussing the parish map with Elly.

Bell Ringers · Brownies · Church A.M. Investment Club · District Nursing Association · Graffham Garden Group · Good Companions ~ · Guides · Ladies Club · Painting Group

Graffham's name.
It is thought to have derived from the Old English words, the 'graff' element meaning grove and the 'ham' coming to mean home. (The grove was probably a Celtic sacred site at the foot of the Downs.) Therefore it meant "the home by the grove." An alternative gives 'graf' as gravel or ditch. Variations have been Grafham, Gresham and Grofam, used when spelling was a less refined art.

LADYWELL

The earliest evidence of man's presence relates to his hunter-gatherer stage. Flint workings dated at between 8,000 and 5,000 BC have been found on Graffham Common.
Bronze Age barrows remain indicating occupation of the land on the ridge and south-facing slopes of the Downs.
Remains of a possible hill slope fort at Teglease indicate that the area may well have been occupied in the Iron Age.

PETER'S BARN

Early Anglo-Saxon activity was limited to the area between the Downs and the sea. Teglease, including swine pastures, was mentioned in the Anglo-Saxon charter in the 9th granting the land to Bishop Eadbert.
At the time of Edward the Confessor 6 thanes held the manorial land valued at £8. Selham was probably settled before Graffham because of the navigability of the Rother. Selham church is thought to be of Saxon origin.

ST. JAMES SELHAM

The Domesday record of 1086 indicated that the area, including Selham, belonged to Roger de Montgomerie, Earl of Arundel, Lord of the Rape of Chichester and cousin of the Conqueror. Four frenchmen held the land – Robert, Ralph, Rolland & Ernald. Seven villeins + six bordars worked the demesne land. There were 1,200 acres of taxable arable land with a population of 100. Graffham Church was recorded. This was probably small and wooden.

THE PRIORY, SELHAM

In 1150 William de Coisnetto, a descendant of the Ralph mentioned in Domesday was still paying dues on land in Graffham to Lewes Priory. In 1294 Robert de Petworthe, Rector of Graffham, was fined 20 shillings for detaining tythes.
The pottery industry is mentioned in a tax return of 1342. "Rector has easement to the value of XIId from the men who make earthen vessels."

MARSH COTTAGE

The Priory at Selham dates from 1375 and was part of the Priory of Calceto. Three houses shown on the 1597 map survive: Thraves, Ladywell + Stewarts Cottage. Rose Cottage, Tinkers + Waltons Cottage also date from this time.
In 1622 a great wynde broke windows in the church. The first register of 1657 mentions some familiar village names: Baker, Carver, Phelps + Tupper and later Howick, Bridger, Boxall, Challen, Loder, Hilton, Money, West + Whittington appeared.

THRAVES

Church records of 1624 reveal one Flay Nunnery, a potter, attended church in such a drunken state that he spued in our church most beastly before the congregation! Richard Wood, Roger Philps, John Blgnold, Edward Payne and Thomas Munsell were reported "for the night following Christmas Day they rang the church bells very disorderly so that we could not sleep quietly in our beds." The 1641 Protestation Returns were signed by 55 men.

ST. GILES GRAFFHAM

Rector Henry Manning kept records of the occupations and misdemeanors of Graffham families, among them familiar names such as Harriet West, John Boxall, Joseph Todman, Mary Howick, John Pescod and Edmund Albery. The Church of England School was built in 1868, its intake 22. The church was virtually rebuilt as a memorial to Bishop Wilberforce, incorporating the 6th transitional arcades, a 6th West doorway and a font of Saxon design.

THE SCHOOL

The geology of the parish is diverse, and as a result there are a variety of soil types and habitats within it. They stretch from the Upper Chalk of the South Downs through the Folkeston Beds of Graffham and South Ambersham to the overlays of Alluvium by the River Rother. Agriculture here is not intense and much of the land is pasture.
The picture below illustrates three of the habitats identified, Downland, Farmland and Water Meadow.

THE THREE MOLES

A West Sussex parish sheltering in the shadow of the South Downs. Recorded through Domesday to the Millennium and enclosed by contours and trees. Farms and cottages, modern and ancient, grown up along the line of the spring, three public houses, two churches and a chapel along with the school and shop give life and soul to a lively community. Home to three council estates and a bustling recreation ground patrolled by labrador and spaniel, an Empire Hall that has outlived Empire.
A place for hacker and hiker, veteran and farmer, camper and commuter, teacher and student, families old and new.
A well hidden jewel that delights afresh when seen or remembered, Graffham in the crown of the Downs.

These decorative borders were inspired by the 1597 Lavington Estate Map

GRAFFHAM SELHAM & SOUTH AMBERSHAM

During 1999 we asked everyone to tell us their age, sex and place... compared the answers to the... there were 230 households... 537 people (401 in 1891)of whic... In 1999 the parish has a much... with 64% being over 40, only... marked difference is the spl... and females. In 1891 men wer... and women were going away t... 1999 47 M:53F, 1891 36M:44F... no nonagenarians, currently... Mrs T. Bruce Tedd, Mrs E. Loring... In 1891 82% of residents were... by 1999 that had fallen to ze...

The 1597 Map is thought to be...

This West Sussex parish lies on a spring line at the foot of the South Downs. The Roman town of Chichester and the English Channel lie twelve miles to the South, with the market towns of Midhurst and Petworth within six miles to the North.

Above we have portrayed an imaginary view of the villages from up on the South Downs looking north over the River Rother with Blackdown in the north west. On either side of this view we have shewn the underlying geology with a key below.

| ALLUVIUM | VALLEY GRAVEL | MIDDLE CHALK | UPPER GREENSAND | FOLKESTONE BEDS | PETTIC BEDS |
| HILL GRAVEL | UPPER CHALK | LOWER CHALK | GAULT | SANDGATE BEDS | WEALD CLAY |

Hig... whic... Age... Som... reme... Teg...

Committee: Pru Hart (Treasurer), Elly Spilberg (Co-ordinator), Daphne Taylor (Chairman) Fund Raising: Maureen Boulton, Robert Ralph, Teresa Whittington
Contributors: Ed Austin, Ina Bridger, Roger Clarke, John Fellows, Graffham School, Barbara Kemp, Phyll Nicholl, Rosemary Robson, Andrew Shilcock, Mary Taylor ~
Demographic Research: Diane Bellis, Betty Bradley, Paula...
Acknowledgements To: Marion Bowley, Michael Brid...

Tennis Club · Stoolball Club · Sports and Social Club · Line Dancing · Football Club · Cricket Club · Bowls Club · Badminton Club

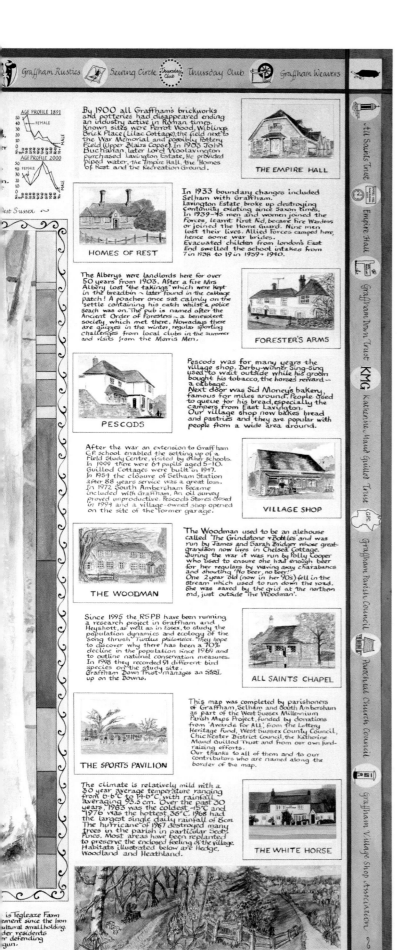

Left panel (illustrated map border)

Graffham Rustics · Sewing Circle · Thursday Club · Graffham Weavers

AGE PROFILE 1891
AGE PROFILE 2000

By 1900 all Graffham's brickworks and potteries had disappeared ending an industry active in Roman times. Known sites were Perrot Wood, Wibling Brick Place, Lilac Cottage, the field next to the War Memorial and possibly Pottery Field (Upper Blacks Copse). In 1903 John Buchanan, later Lord Woolavington, purchased Lavington Estate. He provided piped water, the Empire Hall, the Homes of Rest and the Recreation Ground.

THE EMPIRE HALL

In 1933 boundary changes included Selham with Graffham. Lavington Estate broke up destroying continuity, existing since Saxon times. In 1939–45 men and women joined the Forces, learnt First Aid, became fire Wardens or joined the Home Guard. Nine men lost their lives. Allied Forces camped here, hence some war brides. Evacuated children from London's East End swelled the school intakes from 7 in 1938 to 19 in 1939–1940.

HOMES OF REST

The Alberys were landlords here for over 50 years from 1903. After a fire Mrs Albery lost "the takings" which were kept in the breadbin – later found in the cabbage patch! A poacher once sat calmly on the 'settle' containing his catch whilst a police search was on. The pub is named after the Ancient Order of Foresters – a benevolent society, which met there. Nowadays there are quizzes in the winter, regular sporting challenges from local clubs in the summer and visits from the Morris Men.

FORESTER'S ARMS

Pescods was for many years the village shop. Derby-winner Sing-Sing used to wait outside while his groom bought his tobacco, the horses reward – a cabbage. Next door was Sid Money's bakery, famous for miles around. People used to queue for his bread, especially the campers from East Lavington. Our village shop now bakes bread and pastries and they are popular with people from a wide area around.

PESCODS

After the war an extension to Graffham C.P. school enabled the setting up of a Field Study Centre, visited by other schools. In 1909 there were 64 pupils aged 5–10. Guillod Cottages were built in 1947. In 1954 the closure of Selham Station after 88 years service was a great loss. In 1972 South Ambersham became included with Graffham. An oil survey proved unproductive. Pescods Stores closed in 1994 and a village-owned shop opened on the site of the former garage.

VILLAGE SHOP

The Woodman used to be an alehouse called 'The Grindstone + Bottles' and was run by James and Sarah Bridger whose great-grandson now lives in Chelsea Cottage. During the war it was run by Polly Cooper who used to ensure she had enough beer for her regulars by waving away charabancs and shouting 'No Beer, no beer!' One 2 year old (now in her 90's) fell in the stream which used to run down the road. She was saved by the grid at the northern end, just outside 'the Woodman'.

THE WOODMAN

Since 1995 the RSPB have been running a research project in Graffham and Heyshott, as well as in Essex, to study the population dynamics and ecology of the song thrush *Turdus philomelos*. They hope to discover why there has been a 70% decline in the population since 1969 and to outline national conservation measures. In 1998 they recorded 91 different bird species on the study site. Graffham Down Trust manages an SSSI up on the Downs.

ALL SAINTS CHAPEL

This map was completed by parishioners of Graffham, Selham and South Ambersham as part of the West Sussex Millennium Parish Maps Project, funded by donations from 'Awards for All', from the Lottery Heritage Fund, West Sussex County Council, Chichester District Council, the Katherine Maud Guillod Trust and from our own fundraising efforts. Our thanks to all of them and to our contributors who are named along the border of the map.

THE SPORTS PAVILION

The climate is relatively mild with a 30 year average temperature ranging from 6.6°C to 14.6°C, with rainfall averaging 93.5 cm. Over the past 30 years, 1963 was the coldest -15°C and 1976 was the hottest, 38°C. 1968 had the largest single daily rainfall of 8cm. The hurricane of 1967 destroyed many trees in the parish in particular Scots Pines. Most areas have been replanted to preserve the enclosed feeling of the village. Habitats illustrated below are Hedge, Woodland and Heathland.

THE WHITE HORSE

...is Tegleaze Farm ...ement since the Iron ...ultural smallholding. ...der residents ...defending ...gun.

...len, Shelagh Chapman, Diana Kingsmill, Tim Morton, Diana Williams
...June Challen, Peter Cotton, Stuart leFevre, Kim Leslie, Seaford College, Anny & Mike Spilberg

(side border, top to bottom) All Saints Trust · Empire Hall · Graffham Down Trust · KMG Katherine Maud Guillod Trust · Graffham Parish Council · Parochial Church Council · Graffham Village Shop Association

Right panel (main text)

Since 1995 the RSPB have been running a research project in Graffham and Heyshott, as well as in Essex, to study the population dynamics and ecology of the song thrush *Turdus philomelos*. They hope to discover why there has been a 70% decline in the population since 1969 and to outline national conservation measures. In 1998 they recorded 91 different bird species on the study site. Graffham Down Trust manages an SSSI. up on the Downs.

The climate is relatively mild with a 30 year average temperature ranging from 6.6°C to 14.6°C, with rainfall averaging 93.5 cm. Over the past 30 years, 1963 was the coldest -15°C and 1976 was the hottest, 38°C. 1968 had the largest single daily rainfall of 8cm. The hurricane of 1967 destroyed many trees in the parish in particular Scots Pines. Most areas have been replanted to preserve the enclosed feeling of the village. Habitats illustrated below are Hedge, Woodland and Heathland.

During 1999 we asked everyone in the parish to tell us their age, sex and place of birth. We have compared the answers to the 1891 census. In 1999 there were 230 households (85 in 1891) comprising 537 people (401 in 1891) of which 10 were 2nd homes. In 1999 the parish has a much older population with 64% being over 40, only 31% in 1891. The other marked difference is the split between males and females. In 1891 men were coming in for work and women were going away to be domestics. 1999 47 M:53F, 1891 56M:44F. In 1891 there were no nonagenarians, currently we have three:— Mrs T. Bruce Todd, Mrs E. Loring and Lady M. Bateman. In 1891 82% of residents were born in Sussex, but by 1999 that had fallen to 28%.

Ladywell

The White Horse

Went to the Record Office to collect data on population from the censuses in the last century to compare with this year.

Parish Map Conference at Haywards Heath, an interesting day which sparked off some more ideas and consolidated others. Also useful for networking with other villages and sources of help.

Spent Friday morning getting bits together for tonight's parish map progress exhibition. More people than anticipated came and we had more offers of help. Have nearly completed the funding application, so that will go off this week, and we have set ourselves some targets.

Finalised the village Demographical Survey distribution. [230 households were visited by thirteen researchers seeking contemporary information to compare with the 1891 census.]

The map event at the Foresters went better than anticipated, there were representatives from Fernhurst, Stedham with Iping, Rogate and Heyshott; about twenty of us in all.

The Bring and Buy Sale for the map was a success, raised £302.70. We put together a folder to show progress to date.

Another group member came round and had a look at the pictures and wanted to have a go herself – came back two days later with The White Horse and Ladywell. Collected the paper for the original – would only just fit in the car.

Have sourced a sheet of hardboard large enough to use as a drawing board for the full size (AO) map – most of the kitchen table!

The OS map and aerial photos have arrived – my house is full of map bits – may have to find a home for them upstairs over Christmas.

Received the pictures from the school, and first drafts of the pictures of the different habitats in the village. Our fund-raising efforts were in the paper – the Lottery Heritage Fund had sent them a press release [awarding the group £1,500].

Seem to have had an overdose of the map over the last week. Spent all day preparing boards for the exhibition. We had about sixty people to view the exhibition, mostly positive, some criticism, and also additional information and constructive comment.

Managed to finish the Geology yesterday and started on the inner border. Thursday another long day. The Clubs and Societies part was more involved as we wanted logos rather than initials

for them. Had some fun inventing them. Now just have to get printed and decide how many copies we can sell.

The map was launched at our Village Day . . .

Elly Spilberg, as group co-ordinator, sums it all up: 'It has been a great and useful activity for the village, has given people a taste for their local history and forged friendships which may otherwise have never been made . . . altogether a really worthwhile project'.

KIM LESLIE

Marsh Cottage

Village shop

Harting

THERE ARE MANY WAYS into Sussex, but there is one without equal. The main road from Petersfield to Chichester – more a country lane as it twists across the county boundary – tops a short rise by Torberry Hill to open up a view of stunning grandeur. From here this is more than just one more view of the countryside; it's a picture of a perfect landscape that has long been attracting

artists of distinction. South Harting, neatly huddling around its ancient church under the distinctive green-coppered spire, lies tucked against its backdrop of wooded hills rolling into the distance. Like a great green wave, the South Downs are the very essence of Sussex, the village the gateway to some of the most spectacular countryside in southern England.

But there's more to this parish than just the main village of South Harting. We're in a countryside 'beset with Hartings' – to use H.G. Wells' description – its offshoots all around the compass. There's an East and West, the lost North represented by the isolated valley called Harting Coombe, north of Rogate. It's a big parish (even without Rogate which it once included), still the largest of all in this western fringe of the county, reaching from the top of the Downs right across to the Rother beyond Nyewood, Harting's one-time railway hamlet. Its shape means that its lands extend over four quite distinct geological bands, giving an enormous variety of wildlife habitats within just a few miles.

This is a naturalist's paradise, so much so that in the history of natural history, Harting has yielded up a rich store of knowledge. That great 18th-century parson-naturalist, Gilbert White of Selborne, had considerable lands in Harting from where he collected data on the South Downs for his pioneer fieldwork studies. Later, Harting's most well-known Victorian parson, Henry Gordon, trod in the same footsteps. More than half of his ground-breaking *History of Harting* of 1877 covers his own natural history investigations, giving a baseline from which to measure what has happened to the environment since then. For all sorts of reasons some species have vanished entirely from here, but its varying landscapes still offer great riches to those with eyes to search and see. There are colonies of rare flowers, otherwise scarcely seen elsewhere in Sussex, with over fifty different types of wild orchid. Over one hundred and twenty types of bird – roughly half the Sussex total – have been seen between the chalk Downs and the sandy heathlands to the north.

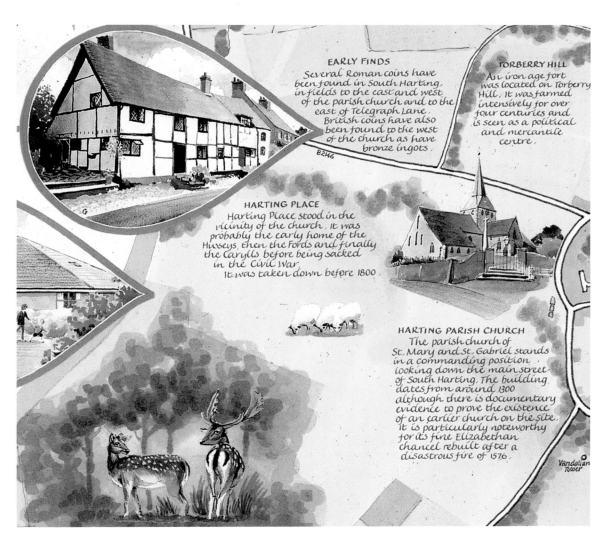

EARLY FINDS
Several Roman coins have been found in South Harting, in fields to the east and west of the parish church and to the east of Telegraph Lane. British coins have also been found to the west of the church as have bronze ingots.

TORBERRY HILL
An iron age fort was located on Torberry Hill. It was farmed intensively for over four centuries and is seen as a political and mercantile centre.

HARTING PLACE
Harting Place stood in the vicinity of the church. It was probably the early home of the Husseys, then the Fords and finally the Carylls before being sacked in the Civil War. It was taken down before 1800.

HARTING PARISH CHURCH
The parish church of St. Mary and St. Gabriel stands in a commanding position looking down the main street of South Harting. The building dates from around 1300 although there is documentary evidence to prove the existence of an earlier church on the site. It is particularly noteworthy for its fine Elizabethan chancel rebuilt after a disastrous fire of 1576.

Vandalian Tower

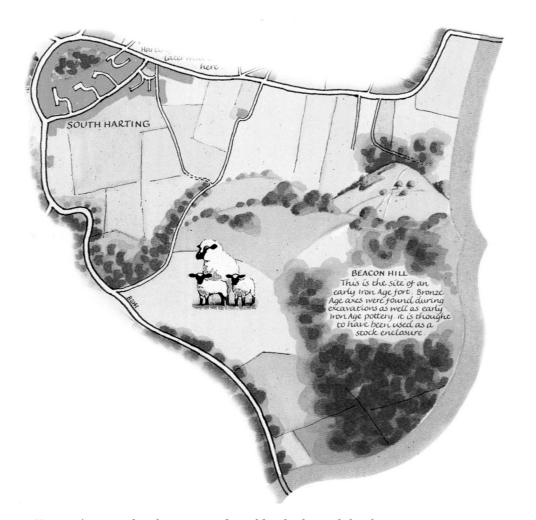

SOUTH HARTING

BEACON HILL
This is the site of an early Iron Age fort. Bronze Age axes were found during excavations as well as early Iron Age pottery. It is thought to have been used as a stock enclosure.

Harting's image has been carried worldwide through books of quite another description from the pen of H.G. Wells. Some of his time as an impressionable teenager was spent here, so that scenes from his young life underpin his earliest novels, their settings and inspiration drawn from the village and its great house, Uppark, high on the hill above. *The Time Machine* (1895) – one of the earliest science fiction books ever written – owes much to Uppark; most of the scientifically-grotesque horror in *The Invisible Man* (1897) takes place in South Harting, confusingly concealed as 'Iping'. In *The Research Magnificent* (1915), Wells' socialist hero, down from London on a walking holiday, learns of Harting's 'little group of artistic people; it is not one of your sleepy villages'. Yes, it's certainly very far from sleepy. Indeed the energy that Wells felt in the village all those years ago has long been at the heart of its success as a community.

No wonder that when the Colonial Office sought the perfect place to star in its 1950s film, *An English Village*, the choice was Harting, giving, as the local paper put it, 'Africans and other races an insight into the community life of

Uppark

HARTING

SOUTH HARTING · EAST HARTING · NYEWOOD · WEST HARTING

The village of South Harting lies on the spring line at the foot of the north facing scarp of the South Downs. It is situated at the junction of the road over the Downs and one running east-west along the foot linking the smaller settlements of East and West Harting. To the north lies the fourth settlement of Nyewood. The parish extends from the ridge of the South Downs northwards down the chalk slope, crossing the succeeding beds of Upper Greensand, clay and Lower Greensand before reaching its northern boundary at the River Rother.
Harting is first mentioned as 'Hertingas' in a Saxon document of 970AD. At the time of Domesday in 1086 Roger Earl of Montgomery held it in lordship with land for 64 ploughs, 128 villagers, 35 smallholders and 20 slaves.

an English village'. The commentary points out that a village is 'something more than a mere collection of dwellings clustered round a church. It's a collection of people who live and work and play together.' The film concentrates on the people of Harting following their 'quiet and traditional course': at school and church, in the pub, meetings of the Young Farmers Club, the WI, the parish council, farming and brickmaking and the annual festivities in the main street. Whilst its subject matter may be dated, its underlying theme about the strength of a community living together survives in many striking ways today.

As a place that lives and plays together, Harting is still a model of its type. The outer dark-green frieze around the map lists an astonishing range of parish groups and activities for such a small place: from an enormous range of sports, to study groups and lectures, churchyard working parties, a group looking after Harting Down, various clubs and societies covering so many interests.

The senior of them all is Harting Old Club, formed in 1800 for the support of members 'in old age, sickness or infirmity' in common with thousands of other friendly societies in pre-welfare-state days. Most of these societies have been wound up long ago, but Harting's survives, keeping up its annual procession, feast-day and other customs alongside the May bank-holiday Harting Festivities. The influential Harting Society keeps a watchful eye on all sorts of conservation and amenity issues, with a publishing record few Sussex parishes can match in its *Harting Papers* on

Harting Festivities

local history and natural history. Their booklets do much to help people understand their common heritage.

Yet more local enterprise is behind the Harting Minibus, one of the first parish-council schemes in the whole country to take over regular scheduled services in the face of the crisis in rural public transport. Since the 1970s the little community bus has proved a lifeline for travel to nearby Petersfield and Chichester, doing an enormous amount to encourage friendliness and a sense of

community. Which is exactly what can also be said about the shop, again saved by the village when faced with closure in the 1990s. Villagers rescued it with a massive cash injection – based on £50 shares – supporting the new owners in meeting the total asking price. As customer Eunice Spicer has said, 'If we lose this shop, it will be a dead village'.

The crucial point is that it's far from being dead, and for all sorts of reasons. Much of its dynamic spirit comes from very strong leadership and public-spirited people who simply love the place for what it is. The very professionally run parish map group led by John Sladden and Bill Hopkins is a case in

point. It's difficult not to be impressed by the service given to Harting over the last few decades by two particular groups: the farmers and men of the land whose roots are here and retired professionals from many walks of life, particularly ex-military men – Admirals, Commanders, Majors, Generals, Captains, Air Commodores and Colonels – their organisational skills honed worldwide, now turned into the parochial arena of this little corner of West Sussex.

One of these retired professionals was the late Don Francombe whose perceptive little book: *Forty Years On: Harting – The story of the post war years* (1988), examines just how its strong identity has survived. Harting's strength is that it has managed to balance the old with the new by adapting itself 'sensibly' (his word) to a world that has changed for ever. Superficially Harting is the perfect picture postcard village; its energetic core beneath its fine looks is what ensures its survival. As Don Francombe fittingly concludes – 'Will a Rip van Winkle forty years on find it the same...? That, surely, rests with us, whose heritage is all the Hartings.'

KIM LESLIE

Passenger trains called at 'Rogate & Harting' station on the Midhurst-Petersfield line

Haywards Heath

A GREAT WILD HEATH that grew into a town, 'The Heath' (as it is affectionately known to locals) is the capital of mid-Sussex commuterland – 'country life within reach of London just minutes away'. Once just a railway appendage to Cuckfield, for years it was awkwardly self-conscious about its status: 'scarcely . . . a town, nor can it condescend to the appellation of a village; it is not even a parish . . . . It might . . . be termed a township – a rising township – after the American States style, and in that capacity is fast becoming a suburb of Brighton' said the local directory for 1879.

Before the line opened in 1841 its prospective station was promoted as more 'for Cuckfield and Lindfield' than anywhere else. Travellers would hardly have heard of this wasteland and its scattered farms, soon to be transformed by the iron-road. Within twenty years the Sussex antiquary Mark Antony Lower was remarking that Haywards Heath, once 'a byword for the wildness of its aspect', was now 'the abode of civilization, many villas and pleasure residences having sprung up almost as by magic'. It was soon to boast a corn exchange, cattle market, reading room, and its own church, St Wilfrid's, said to mark the centre of Sussex. The villas were for those seeking an 'elevated position, healthy locality and beautiful scenery' coming here 'to breathe the pure oxygen that flows from the hills'. One of these Victorian newcomers was Anna Sewell of *Black Beauty* fame who lived at Petlands –

St Wilfrid's Church

now demolished – marked by a blue plaque at Heyworth Primary School.

Haywards Heath has done well in demolishing its history, but pockets full of character can still be found, like Muster Green, the town's first Conservation Area. Its character was said to stem 'from its distinctive appearance, especially when viewed from the western approach to the town, and from its historic connections, which contribute to a sense of permanence in an area of change. . . . The area's pleasing appearance and arcadian character are derived from the setting of substantial houses in large mature gardens, to the north and south of a wedge of tree-lined open space which retains much of the character of a village green.'

The green is steeped in history, the site of a Civil War battle, its name probably coming from the days when the military mustered here. The Dolphin pub, at its western end, is one of the town's earliest houses, and by its eastern end is another equally ancient property, the early 17th-century Boltro Farmhouse.

Muster Green

Just a few yards west of the green are the public grounds of Beech Hurst, for tennis, golf and its model ride-on railway, giving views to the South Downs and its two famous landmarks – the Jack and Jill windmills on the top at Clayton. From here it can be appreciated that the town grew up on a ridge of sandstone with uninterrupted views across the lower claylands of the Weald to the chalk Downs. A similar view can be had from South Road across Victoria Park, an uplifting prospect from the heart of town. Appropriately the highest point along the ridge is called Southdowns Park, once the Sussex Lunatic Asylum, a stunning pile of Victorian coloured brickwork made into modern apartments.

The Dolphin

Beech Hurst

Beech Hurst Railway

001

Oathall Community College

Clair Hall

Population 23,000

Our town derives its name from hayworthe, originally an enclosure for hunting animals and the area was known to Neolithic and Iron Age man, the Romans and Medieval farmers. The town started to grow in the 1840's when the London to Brighton railway was built, passing between Cuckfield and Lindfield. It became a market town and is now a busy residential and commercial area. We have easy access to the South Coast, the beauty of the local countryside and all the variety that London has to offer.

Haywards Heath at the Heart of Mid Sussex

Clair Meadow

Scrase Valley

Peter's Cottage

St Wilfrid's Church

Oathall House

Franklands Village

St Paul's Church

The Priory

Dolphin Leisure Centre

The Orchards

Pennies Cottage

Princess Royal Hospital

Heyworth Primary School

St PAUL'S CATHOLIC COLLEGE

HARLANDS

Northlands Wood School

Sports

Music Art & Drama

Churches

Youth Groups

Schools

Pre School

Went. The artist was Margaret Joss assisted by Jane Reid and Yvonne Wemyss. Designed and printed by Graphic at Haywards Heath. ©Haywards Heath Town Council

Haywards Heath surged forward when the railway was first electrified in the 1930s, the Chamber of Commerce pushing its plum position as *the* place 'where the Southern Railway's modern electric service station acts as a veritable "magic carpet". The electric trains, the most luxurious form of travel, transport its patrons to London in 45 minutes with a service unsurpassed anywhere in the United Kingdom . . . .'

Haywards Heath Station

Since 1931 when the population stood at just over five thousand, the town has grown fivefold and what was once its modern face – symbolised by two art-deco cinemas, the Broadway and the Perrymount – crashed to the ground. Another Haywards Heath emerged from the rubble, the big corporate businesses of office-block Perrymount Road, once full of solid Victorian family homes with good sounding names like Oakfield, Peartree, Elmcroft, San Remo.

But change has brought plenty of good: a wide range of shops, a new shopping precinct, The Orchards, with some lively public art, John Ravera's sculpture called 'Family Outing', Clair Hall, the Dolphin Leisure Centre, the transformation of The Broadway into continental pavement-style eating. There's a lot going for Haywards Heath, and house prices reflect it.

Scrase Valley

*Farmland at
Oathall Community College*

The map is predominantly green. Look hard and you'll find plenty of little houses, but green colours the town, and it's not difficult to see why. Approach from any direction and greenery predominates: at Clair Meadow with its woodland, Muster Green, Beech Hurst and Victoria Park, at Scrase Valley and along so many residential roads. When roads were named, the term 'street', with its more urban connotation, was carefully avoided. If it's not 'Road' it's more likely to be 'Close', Avenue', 'Lane' or 'Way', maybe even 'Copse', 'Bank' or 'Gardens'. The map-makers had a point in making their town green.

It was inspiration from local people, strongly supported by Haywards Heath Town Council, that ensured the town made its mark on the map project. For it is only one of two *large* towns in West Sussex that has so far made a community map (the other is Littlehampton) as towns were generally not keen in getting involved. Put another way, the bigger the place the more are the problems in harnessing a sense of local identity. That in this case it succeeded owed much to Penny Jennings's leadership and project manager Neville Way ensuring that deadlines were met and guides put in place to control a big-town project.

When unveiled by local historian Lilian Rogers it was hailed as the town's first 'democratic map' – the first to be made by the people for the people. Profits from sales of prints went towards restoring the town clock on St Wilfrid's Church tower for the Queen's Golden Jubilee in 2002.

KIM LESLIE

Clair Meadow

Some intensely community-minded people have left their mark. Back in 1929 Haywards Heath took the initiative by forming the first branch of the National Union of Townswomen's Guilds, set up to train women in the art of citizenship. The original 120 women of Haywards Heath sowed the seed that grew into a major national institution.

Thameslink operate from Brighton to Bedford via Haywards Heath

Henfield

THE CAT HOUSE 39

WHAT WAS IT LIKE to live in a West Sussex village at the turn of the new millennium? If a single place had to be chosen to give the answers, Henfield could well be a front-runner in any shortlist. Soon after the map was unveiled the parish council organised a village appraisal, seeking facts, views and personal information from local residents. Taken together, the two documents give an incomparable snapshot of Henfield in 2001. Their strength is in their combination and that they were virtually simultaneous. Then the following year all the data was underpinned by a superbly presented parish history by Alan Barwick, leader of the map team, and Marjorie Carreck, curator of Henfield Museum. Their book takes the story from its origins right up to 2001, supported by a wealth of previously unpublished photographs. All the hard work of artists, historical researchers, parish councillors and officers behind these three initiatives, backed by tremendously supportive villagers, throws a great deal of light on a community working together.

The original map was not only published quarter size as a reproduction print, but has also been put on the internet with enlarged detail and background information. It forms part of the parish council's website at www.henfield.gov.uk which for coverage and clarity of presentation won a Golden Web Award in 2001. The appraisal is also on the website with thirty-nine pages of statistical answers to some seventy-eight questions put to the village.

The questionnaire was large, but Henfield people typically produced the goods with fifteen hundred residents responding out of a total of some five thousand, an extremely high return for a voluntary survey. One of the most telling statistics is that 80 per cent of householders were over the age of 25 – the young were reported as moving out with only 4.3 per cent remaining aged between 18 and 24. The upshot is that one third of the total population are 65 and over.

- 87% said that the quality of the countryside was very important

- 80% thought that Henfield could not take any more housing

- 68% of workers are employed 10 miles or more away

Somewhere behind these figures is the realisation that Henfield is subject to huge forces beyond its bounds, part of a local economy where 'local' means the pull of the city of Brighton and Hove to the south and the Crawley-Gatwick complex to the north. Henfield is right in the middle, attractive as a place to live because it's physically separate and apart. Understand this feeling of being separate and we have the key to understanding much of Henfield's special character. That's why views of the surrounding countryside that close in all around the village – well seen from the Common and South View Terrace (see the panorama at the foot of the map) – are so reassuring to local people.

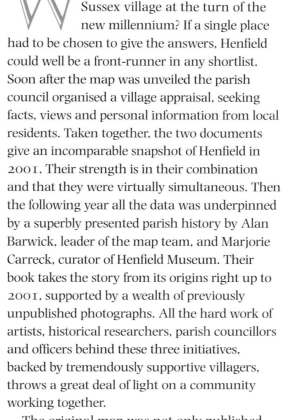

KINGS FIELD PLAYGROUND 37

If the parish map conveys the much-loved character of the place – and there is a very strong sense of place and community – then the appraisal, and all the work that is now going into its follow-up through a closely-monitored action plan, gives the building blocks for its realistic survival, not as a place to be frozen in time, but one fit and able to meet today's social and economic challenges.

The village cannot stand still, the crucial question is *by how much* should it change and how can it deal with the issue raised by the overwhelming majority who say they don't want any more building? Henfield is well qualified to meet the challenge. The crucial issue is the responsiveness and sensitivity of the distant planning authorities to local people trying to protect and enhance their own special patch, *their* homeland.

There are so many layers to its distinct character. One unusual feature is that the parish council was granted its own coat of arms by the College of Arms in 1992. There are said to be only five other villages in the country with this distinction, so the parish occupies a distinguished place in civic heraldry. 'We had the idea of petitioning the College of Arms after seeing impressive coats of arms on signs welcoming drivers to various cities and towns', said former Chairman of Henfield Parish Council, Peter Hudson. 'We thought how good it would be to have something distinctive that would encourage pride in our local heritage.'

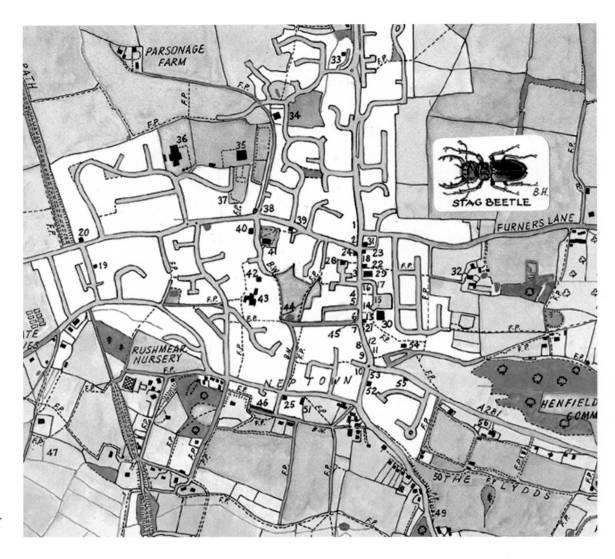

Heritage and local history mean a lot in the village. The coat of arms – designed and painted by local artist Brenda Hobbs – highlights the Anglican and Roman Catholic churches by symbols on the shield, divided by a band with three gold coins representing the Bysshopp family. The most well-known Bysshopp was one Henry, a 17th-century Postmaster-General, famous for introducing the first postmark to show the date when a letter was posted. The bird is the rare golden oriel, commemorating William Borrer, the 19th-century ornithologist who claimed a record sighting of fourteen of them on a local thorn bush. His father, also William (1781–1862), is legendary in the village's history.

Borrer senior lived much of his life in Henfield where he made a remarkable collection of living plants. By 1860 he had assembled 6,600 different species, becoming one of the most famous botanists of his day and a leading authority on lichens. After his death many of his plants were moved to Kew;

ST. PETER'S CHURCH 41

SOUTHERN HAWKER

WILD VIOLET

Flora & Fauna
122 species of birds were recorded in the parish in 2000. Nightingales can still be heard in the parish but numbers are declining. The area is important for its population of Stag Beetles. Henfield Common has an important population of Southern Marsh Orchids. A number of Badger setts exist around the village. Henfield's albino starling was seen for the last time in 2000. Very rare Black Poplar trees have been planted in and around the village.

BADGER

sadly his garden no longer survives, but some of his introduced plants still grow around the village, many specially cared for on 'Borrer Bank' at the top of Barrow Hill. His work is commemorated by the Sussex Wildlife Trust at its headquarters at nearby Woods Mill. The Trust is actively engaged in biodiversity work in the parish, with a special eye on the colony of stag beetles, nationally an endangered species, and the sparsely-distributed southern marsh orchid. Trust officer Mike Russell acted as wildlife adviser to the map group and, as chairman for *Henfield Birdwatch 2000,*

Floods on the Brooks

produced a beautifully printed survey report by over a hundred people. They produced over thirty-five thousand records of their sightings for the whole year, and repeated the survey again in 2005. Another great example of the community in action, their recording has turned out to be one of the biggest community wildlife surveys ever undertaken in the UK.

As museum curator and contributor to the parish map, Marjorie Carreck has been at the centre of Henfield life for a great many years. Asked for her thoughts on what makes the village tick so well, she said that 'Henfield has

always had to stand on its own two feet. Being so far from any large town it had to be self-sufficient, everything had to be done in and around the village. Consequently it's a close-knit community where people have looked after each other and taken an interest in each other's welfare. It's a very friendly place where visitors are always welcomed. In some villages you are not seen as a native until you have lived there for thirty or forty years. That's not the case here. We are an enterprising lot and basically still self-sufficient. Recently we started a farmers' market, and just how many other villages these days can boast of having two bakers and a prize-winning butcher?'

Indeed, just look around the edge of the map to find Alan Barwick's exquisitely-painted signs advertising the full range of village shops. This outstandingly imaginative record of High Street shopping is a feature unique to Henfield's parish map as part of the West Sussex project.

KIM LESLIE

Henfield Hall and Museum

Heyshott

HEYSHOTT IS ONE OF THOSE VILLAGES along the South Downs that doesn't lead to anywhere else. You come in and you get out – unless you live here. It's neither sweet, cute or quaint, just lovely. It's in a rough circle, good for joggers and ladies of the village who like to walk sharply around to benefit their figures.

Apart from houses, the road takes in a bit of common, complete with rabbits, deer and a fox or two, stables for polo ponies, a wonderful fruit and vegetable growing business, a pond, cricket ground, riding stables, the church, village hall, a pub and two farms.

But it is the Downs that have the pull. The car delivery man who came to Manor Farm where I live couldn't get over what a fantastic place he'd come to. Part of the Cowdray Estate, its lands hug the downland slopes, so it has wonderful views. He had often driven on the A286 to Midhurst but never thought of turning off. A young stockbroker in the village regularly takes his family onto the Downs for picnics. When there's a lull at work in his London office he flashes pictures of the hills

onto his computer screen. Apparently everyone asks where he's been on holiday – and they're amazed to know it's West Sussex where he lives and from where he commutes daily.

If only they could all see that downland in spring when it's covered with cowslips, growing so closely together it's impossible not to tread on them. And the scent! Indescribable. Villagers make a point of walking to see them every year. In fact there's an abundance of different wild flowers – orchids in particular – wild creatures like badgers and bats and wild birds, including kites, that you would be hard pushed to find collectively anywhere.

The vicinity supports all these things – a richness which to be truthful all who live here take for quite normal. On the other hand we do know that we are blessed. Our village in its lovely setting is shown in Vivian Palmer's bird's-eye view of the parish.

And sometimes the sheer beauty of a spring morning, when the low cloud wisps around the Downs, stops you in your tracks. Or even on a dull day when the cloud is quite dense.

Mendelssohn's *Hebrides Overture* fits the mood perfectly.

But then, brought by a west wind, the racing-engine sound of a 100 mph Suzuki from along Cocking Causeway reminds us we're in the 21st century and not far from civilisation. Well, Chichester is only twelve miles away, to use the Sussex dialect, 'over

'Under a majestic stretch of the Downs . . . its plan about as easygoing as can be imagined – a long shaggy green . . . which gathers itself into a winding village street . . .' – Ian Nairn in Pevsner's Sussex *(1965)*

them thar 'ills' where the weather can be completely different from ours. We certainly get more rainfall. On the south side farmers produce bumper crops on the extremely fertile Chichester plain whereas we have to endure four distinct soil types: from chalk, upper greensand, gault clay to lower greensand. Badgers love 'em all. Endearing creatures they may look, but they do a lot of damage to both farmland and gardens in the village. Lawns are a speciality.

We have quite a large fallow deer population, too. It's not unusual to see a herd of twenty or so on the downland field where the cowslips and ox-eye daisies grow. They trample the standing corn on the farms, making up their own rights of way to the fury of the farmers. And before the corn there are always gardens. It is breathtaking to see this fawn, sleek beauty, so close up – then you realise that all the rosebuds have been eaten. But as villager John Murray of Upper Cranmore once told me: 'After their first pruning by the deer the roses were terrific second time round!'

It was after John's aunt, Betty Murray, that the Murray Downland Trust was formed. Betty (1909–98) – village stalwart, former principal of Bishop Otter College, Chichester and grand-daughter of lexicographer James Murray, founding editor of the *Oxford English Dictionary* – was a fervent conservationist: woe betide anyone felling a tree, she'd be there, on her bicycle! She would be happy to see that volunteers are looking after the Trust's nature reserve on the Downs. Here the scrub is not allowed to grow – or ragwort – but rare orchids are.

Ramblers are appreciative of Heyshott's unspoilt landscape. Apart from the South Downs Way there are numerous footpaths and bridleways weaving in and around the parish. In the summer it's lovely to see whole families out on their cycles, looking over the hedgerows. Lord Cowdray is a regular sight on his cycle, the heads-down, bottom-up sort, as he rides through the village.

Peter Lovejoy, tenant of the other Cowdray

farm, Leggs, is one of the few remaining 'old' villagers to have been born here. Now in his seventies he remembers the days before television and too many cars, when villagers worked locally and didn't have a lot of money. 'There was comradeship and certainly in wartime the friendship was terrific', he said. 'People are friendly now but they leave the village to work.' He has to smile when asked if he farms organically. 'No, but years ago we were pure organic. We grew six crops in one field, ran a dairy herd, forty ewes, pigs and chickens. Our gardens were full of vegetables

too, not down to grass like you see today.' Richard Comber, tenant at Manor Farm, feels a lot of the wartime spirit still remains.

Each year Richard's farm celebrates traditional farming with an Old-Time Harvesting week-end, 'run', he says, 'by local people who raise a lot of money for charity. In 2005 we raised £6,000.' He added that 'another, perhaps more well-known, event is our huge 5 November village bonfire party attended by literally hundreds of people. The community spirit is alive and well!'

Social activities in the village hall are

another sign of this. Once a month there's a luncheon club for OAPs, the parish council uses it, a play school run on Montessori lines meets here and it is the venue for parties, the harvest supper, wedding receptions and funeral wakes. All this is a wonderful extension to the idea that brought about the village hall in the first place, founded in 1880 as the Heyshott Working Men's Club and Coffee House.

It started with Mrs Jane Fisher Unwin thinking that there should be somewhere for the locals to go other than the pubs – there were two in Heyshott then. A club called the Cobden Club was formed to run the hall and of course it has kept the name of Richard Cobden (1804–65) – Jane's father – alive to this day. Cobden was born at the family farm at Dunford, now Dunford House, Heyshott, run by the YMCA as a conference centre. He was a great champion of the poor, a member of parliament and mainspring of the 19th-century Anti-Corn Law League that was so successful in bringing about cheaper imports of corn and lowering the price of bread. Although widely travelled and a conscientious parliamentarian, Cobden had a great affection for the village, the church and the people.

In Colonel Ronnie Palmers's parish history, to which I am indebted for these facts, Richard Cobden is quoted: 'We are surrounded with pleasant woods, and within a couple of miles of the South Down hills, where we have the finest air and some of the prettiest views in England'.

So, some things don't change, do they?

SUE OGDEN

Highbrook

Almost every single house in Highbrook village features on our parish map – that's how small our community is. The picture makes the houses obvious, but in practice you could drive right through the village and not be at all certain that you'd arrived, though the

village sign with its two 'high brooks' and church spire, together with a sighting of the church itself, would give away our presence. The houses are all different, many of them workers' cottages built by the Clarke family when they owned the land and lived at Brook House. You can see Brook House in the bottom left-hand corner of the map. The signpost in the middle of the front lawn indicates some of

the families who live there now – there are fifteen if you include the lodge, the old coach house and the garden cottage. The house keeps up the Clarke tradition of food, hot punch and Christmas carols under the tree in the hall for the whole village on the Wednesday before Christmas.

It's not just at Christmas that the people of Highbrook come together. The sleepy appearance of the place belies what is a thriving community spirit. Some say the storm of 1987 was a defining moment for us all. The village was without electricity for two weeks, so families emptied their defrosting freezers

and brought food to the two or three homes with solid fuel stoves, and everyone ate together and looked out for each other.

The village hall is the venue for numerous village events, among which feature the harvest supper, an annual feast of shepherd's pies, twenty different kinds of puddings, and home-grown musical entertainment, and the Christmas market, which is *very* high class. Ruby, sadly deceased since the map was painted, and shown in the lane by the telephone box, amusingly holds the hall's oversize key.

New way to play a key?

The village's strong community spirit is not just inward looking. Following the tsunami on Boxing Day 2004, one of our number inspired us all to adopt a village of similar size in Sri Lanka. We clubbed together and bought new fishing boats for the men, sewing machines for the women, and musical instruments for the children. Peter went over twice and personally ensured that the materials, aimed at putting the devastated village back on its feet, were delivered in working order and blessed by the local Buddhist priest.

The map is full of village characters. Can you spot the sports-people? Tennis and croquet combined with judging, badminton, golf and cricket all feature amongst our villagers'

Sport for all . . .

talents. The vicar is at the lychgate, made for the millennium out of local oak by a local joiner. The spire of the church is the highest point of the village and a landmark for miles around, as well as being a welcome resting place for swifts. Inside the tower, beneath the spire, a carillon plays delightfully unexpected tunes every three hours during the day. Visitors will be startled to hear *Men of Harlech* ring out when they least expect it, and many a solemn moment in church has been interrupted as *God save the Queen* suddenly plays in the middle of the sermon. We muffle our laughter. Our own priest is used to it, but visiting priests have a terrible dilemma. The bells are loud: does he carry on regardless, or does he let the bells win? And if so, for how long are they going to play? (as verse two doggedly starts ringing, just very slightly out of tune).

Half the churchyard is kept neat and tidy, and the other half, designated a 'living churchyard', is home to the splendid diversity of wildlife that churchyards permit amongst so much of the countryside rendered sterile by modern farming methods. In the wild part, a young yew tree grows, a sapling from a cutting of an existing yew tree that is more

All are welcome here . . .

than two thousand years old, planted as a living link to the time when Christ walked on earth – a fitting way to celebrate the millennium. We had a huge feast in the village hall as well, of course!

Moving on down the hill from the church you can see the professional couple posing in their garden on their way to work, next to their clearly more relaxed neighbours playing a leisurely game of badminton; there is sheep racing and gardening, horse riding, and if you

If horses can do it . . .

look very carefully to the right of the farmer on his tractor (on the left side of the map) some parrots. Our doughty parrot breeder managed to terrify two weeks' worth of villagers and visitors with her Nazgul scarecrow, made with a real sheep's skull that grinned malevolently from a dark bend in the road shadowed by trees. There were scarecrows in every part of the village at the time, a competition we have held twice now as part of our village open days – more evidence that we don't keep all the fun to ourselves. We don't just breed parrots either. In the bottom

right-hand corner of the map you'll see some standard poodles that have recently been joined by a litter of fourteen labradors.

One great puzzle in the village is the numbering of some of the cottages. We have 113–114 and 127–128 Watney Cottages, but there's no evidence of numbers 1 to 112, nor even of 115 to 126. It seems that the Clarkes numbered their workers' cottages chronologically as they acquired them, rather than geographically, and their cottages are dotted all over the south of England. The 'neighbour' to 113 – number 112 – is, we believe, on the Isle of Wight.

The first large-scale Ordnance Survey map made in 1873–4 shows only three farms and no named village at all in the place where Highbrook now flourishes. Today it's now a haven to not many more than two hundred souls, whose children grow up within a lively community of people who really do seem to care about each other and the environment that nurtures them.

CLAIRE FOSTER and PETER BROWNE

The Highbrook Pollys . . .

Note that Highbrook also forms part of the West Hoathly Parish Map, see pages 259–62

OUTH OF THE CITY of Chichester lies the Manhood Peninsula, a fertile plain bordered by the outer reaches of the Solent and Chichester Harbour in an area some call 'God's Acres'. The weather is fairer this side of the South Downs, with more sun, fewer frosts and plenty of light reflected off the sea.

Hunston lies in the northern part of the peninsula and is a link between the city and agricultural land. Residents like the location as it is not far from Chichester, but is quiet and rural – most of the time. Wildlife abounds – birds inhabit fields and gardens. The calls of

the pheasant and the green woodpecker are often heard, and at night the eerie bay of a fox floats across the fields.

The parish has a water-girt boundary to the north-east. The lakes, formed from old gravel pits, give pleasant walks, bird watching and

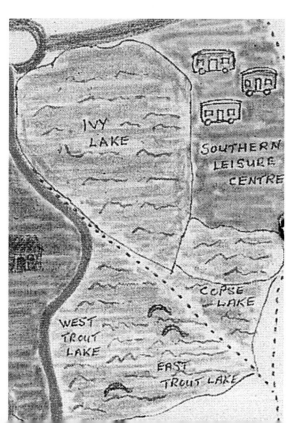

sport for anglers. The western boundary borders the Chichester Ship Canal once connecting the city to the sea, Portsmouth and London. Since its demise and the building of fixed road bridges, this water link with distant parts is no longer possible. But nowadays the Chichester Ship Canal Trust does an excellent job in maintenance and restoration. This is one of Hunston's special places. Peace prevails – with swans, moorhens, ducks and coots making the canal their own special habitat. Anglers spend many happy hours in quiet contemplation of their floats, disturbed only by the occasional passing of the trust's two tourists' boats, the *Egremont* and *Richmond*, or the rowers who can now get

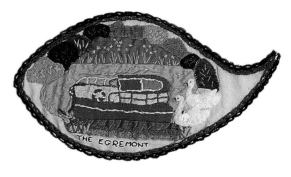

as far as Donnington Bridge. The view looking back from Hunston towards the cathedral was immortalised by Turner in his famous 1820s painting of the canal.

Hunston village itself is somewhat of a ribbon development along both sides of the road to Selsey, reported to be the busiest B-road in the country. Modern-day living has seen a great increase in traffic, including many large lorries and tractors engaged in the commercial cultivation of salad crops on the fertile soils. Once these lands were under shallow seas. Geological upheavals and climatic change pushed up the chalk Downs to the north and water levels receded. Clays and silts were laid down after the Ice Age to make this land a premier growing area. The Romans certainly knew the area – the existence of their road towards the sea has been proved by local archaeologists.

There are some attractive cottages and

houses in the village, including the pub, but sadly much of the housing is the result of piecemeal planning and little thought about the overall attractiveness of the village. Go down Church Lane and find the Manor House, an attractive stone and brick house fronted by the pond. This is another wildlife haven for waterfowl and the occasional heron standing sentinel, ready to stab its prey. Once the grounds rang with the mournful cries of peacocks, but subsequent tenants found that peacocks

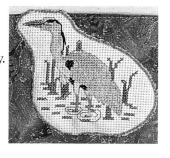

and gardening did not go together. Their place has been taken by life-size wire statues of wild animals – including a giraffe, lions and an elephant – all the inspiration of the artist who currently owns the manor.

The church, dedicated to St Leodegar, is also by the pond. There has been a church here since the early 12th century, although the present one was built in the late 19th century. It is surrounded by a Sussex flint wall with a picturesque lychgate commemorating the

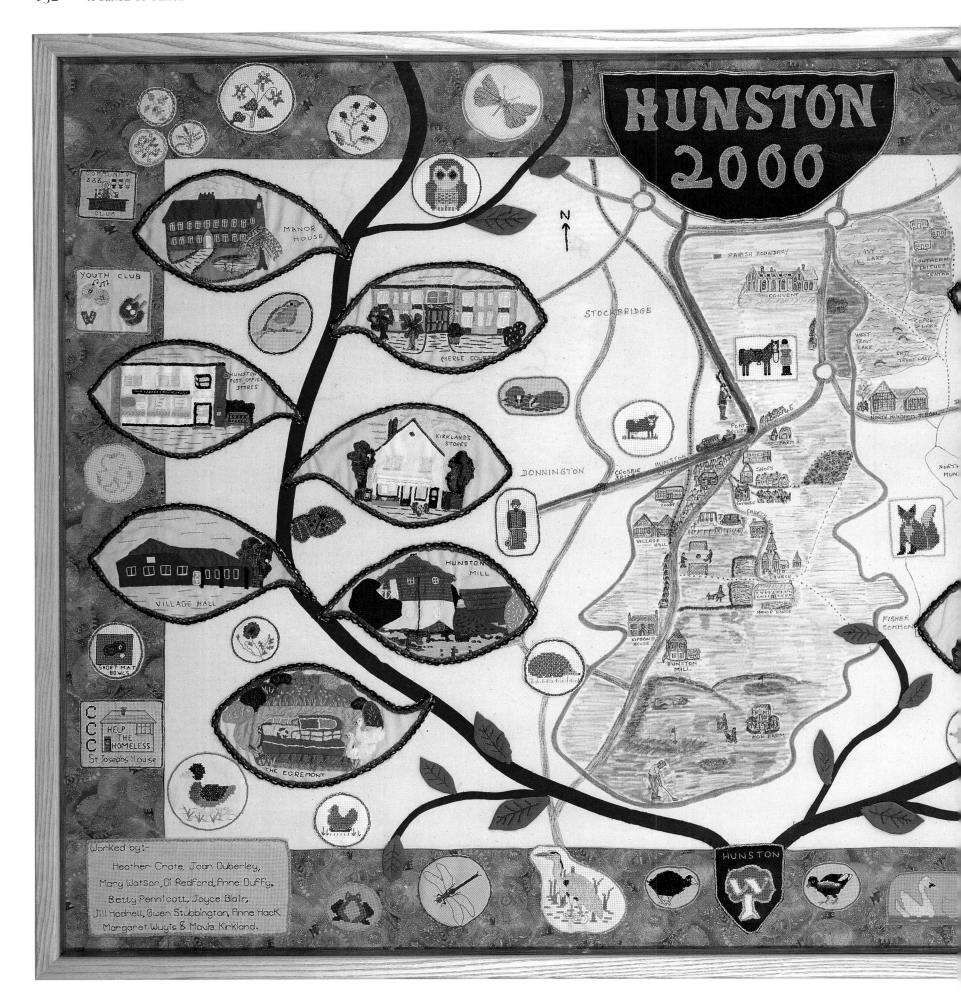

heroes of the Great War. The level of the churchyard was probably raised above the lane to prevent waterlogged graves as the water level is high.

Church Lane is lined with blackberry bushes – laden in autumn with fruit for the industrious to make tasty bramble jelly. Spire Cottage is here, reputed to be built with stone from the cathedral spire that collapsed in 1861.

Hunston lies on the route of the old Selsey Tram, the little country railway that ran across the Manhood. Sadly this is another transport system that fell into disuse many years ago. The track is still clearly marked and is now a footpath. The remains of the station can still be found. Reconstruction of this little line could perhaps ease the commuter-traffic problems through the village.

Hunston's watercourses include the rife that runs along the side of the road before wandering off across the fields to the sea at Pagham Harbour. Once it used to overflow and the area is still designated a flood plain by the Environment Agency. This is probably a blessing as the green areas and playing fields will remain unsuitable for building. Conservation of the local area is important to many people in the village. Hunston Copse is environmentally managed, as is the golf course, while local farmers are growing plants with seed heads attractive to birds.

To the people of Hunston, their village has much to recommend it, though some might wish they could be transported back to the days when the road was a country lane and horses the main means of transport. Its earlier days last century were photographed in a wonderful series of glass lantern slides by a former vicar, the Reverend Edward Outram (1903–83), the subject of a recent limited-edition book to mark the Queen's Golden Jubilee in 2002. The terraces lining the main road existed then, as did the Old Mill, now converted into holiday cottages.

The nuns who lived at the Carmelite convent to the north of the village took no part in village life, but were a closed community, growing vegetables, keeping bees and making communion wafers for local churches. Becoming too elderly to continue, the few who remained moved to other convents in the 1990s. Now the building is a hostel for foreign workers employed in the production of salad crops, a very big business around here.

The parish map shows a rural community with amenities such as two shops, the village hall and the Spotted Cow pub, giving focal points to many of the village activities. So many people rush through on their way to Selsey and the beaches to the south. But those who stop, take time to explore, or have the privilege of living here, experience its special sense of place in today's world.

PAT CARROLL

Hurstpierpoint and Sayers Common

WHAT'S IN A NAME? It has been Herst, the Saxon name in Domesday Book, indicating a wooded hill; Herst Perepunt, first recorded in 1279 as a memorial to the first Norman lords of the manor, the de Pierpoints; Westherst to distinguish it from Herstmonceux to the east. Other variations have been Parpoynthurst, Harstpount, Hurst upon ye point and Hurstperpound. It is now officially Hurstpierpoint, known locally simply as Hurst. It stands on a ridge with wonderful views of both the South Downs and the Weald.

Throughout history it has been an agricultural parish and is still almost completely

LITTLE PARK FARM

surrounded by farms, but practice has changed dramatically over the years. There is now little or no dairy farming because of subsidies. Washbrooks Farm shows an extreme example of this. After the Second World War it employed nearly a hundred and fifty men and women, growing vegetables and flowers for their seeds for sale all over the world, a specialist activity carried on alongside mixed arable and dairy and sheep farming; now two brothers carry out the day-to-day work of the farm, using contractors for seasonal activities such as harvesting and hedging, the remainder of their income being derived from a farm centre open to the public.

Supporting the farming was a wide-ranging retail and commercial centre, including a corn market and a cattle market. Until the latter half of the 20th century the village shops included several bakers, butchers with their own slaughterhouses, greengrocers, a fishmonger and a draper, plus a department store. There are now two butchers, one greengrocer, and a small branch of the Co-op as the only alternative to the supermarkets in Burgess Hill.

Post Office

Farming with horses and many men required blacksmiths and harness and saddlery makers; boots and shoes were made and repaired in the High Street – all now gone, apart from a blacksmith producing decorative ironwork. There are now no banks, the post office and a building society providing the only human faces when financial transactions are needed; cash comes from automatic telling machines. All this while the population has increased from 1,104 in 1801 to over six thousand today.

In parallel with this commercial decline, the tight manorial control of the Norman period eased from the latter half of the 14th century. One remaining legacy from manorial days is the annual St Lawrence Fair, granted its charter in 1313. Danny, the Elizabethan mansion which grew out of a hunting lodge at

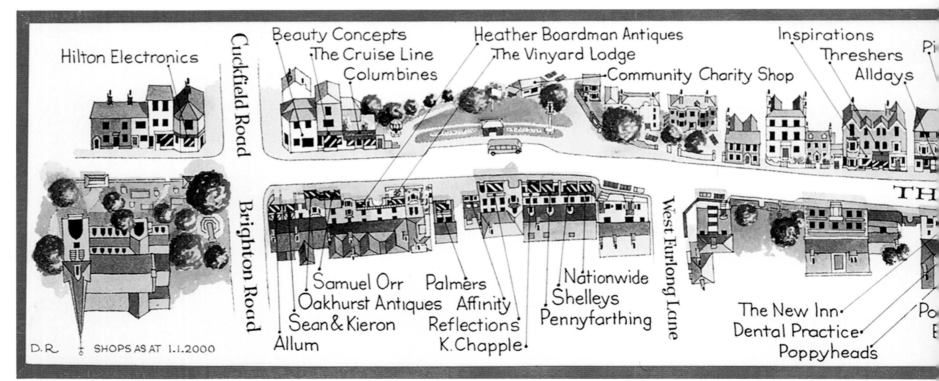

SHOPS AS AT 1.1.2000

ST LAWRENCE FAIR S.S.

HOLY TRINITY CHURCH G.B.

METHODIST, BAPTIST, CATHOLIC CHURCHES B.H

the foot of Wolstonbury Hill, no longer is the centre of a large and flourishing estate, but is divided into very desirable retirement apartments. It was here that the terms of the First World War Armistice were drawn up in advance of the signing on 11 November 1918.

Danny

The other controlling presence was that of the church, here since Saxon times. The parish church was pulled down in the mid-19th century and replaced by a much larger one by Sir Charles Barry who also designed the Houses of Parliament. Regular attendance is now much diminished, but the church is always full at all the major festivals and when the village primary school has its harvest or nativity services. Many non-churchgoers are amongst the first to support any fund-raising for necessary repairs. In addition, Roman Catholic and nonconformist congregations confirm the need that many feel for a spiritual dimension in their lives.

Life in the 18th and 19th centuries has been recorded by a series of local diarists, in particular Thomas Marchant of Little Park and members of the Weekes family of doctors. In the 1860s Alfred Russel Wallace, the explorer and naturalist, wrote *The Malay Archipelago* whilst living at Treeps House in the High Street, his research paralleling that of Darwin. The Darwin-Wallace Society has recently erected a plaque to his memory on the garden wall. Wallace's father-in-law, William Mitten (1819–1906), was the local pharmacist for over fifty years and the acknowledged world authority on mosses. He amassed the largest and most important

Pet Supplies
Murano
Rideaway Cycles
Bentley's
Old Forge Ironmongers
Barry Shell
Hampers
Bole's
Red House Studio
Holly Mews
Hamilton Lodge Interiors
Austen Travel
Harper & Eede
The Poacher
McPhersons Walpole Harding
Evangelical Church
Cool Choice
Feathers

HIGH STREET

Pit Road
South Avenue

Lloyds
Gibsons
The Mint House
The Scriptorium
C.J. McIntosh & Co.
Nelson Seibold
Mishon Mackay
Inside out Trust
Castle & Co
Daniels
Nupur Tandoori
Julian Antiques
Sylvia Florist
Clifford Dann
MPL Cars
etc.
van

collection of mosses held in private hands in his Hurst herbarium. After his death, his research papers, with some fifty thousand specimens, were sold to the New York Botanical Garden where his work is still held in high esteem. His daughter, Flora, became one of the first female pharmacists in the country.

Marchant's diary tells us there was a village school in the early years of the 18th century. Our present primary school started in 1819 in what is now the Players' Theatre, moving to its present site in 1869, now much expanded to cater for over four hundred children. In the

ST. LAWRENCE SCHOOL

1850s one of the early Woodard Foundation public schools – the others are at Ardingly and Lancing – came to Hurst, at first occupying the Mansion House in the High Street before its permanent buildings to the north of the

Hurstpierpoint College, an early Woodard Foundation

village were ready for occupation. For many years a number of small private schools were established, at least in part because of Hurst's reputation for its healthy climate. Shelley's 'soul-mate' and confidante, Elizabeth Hitchener, conducted her own little school in the early 19th century in what is Abberton today, at the east end of the High Street.

Nowadays Hurst is buzzing with organisations, providing a whole range of activities: music, dance and drama; adult education classes; sport, including stoolball as well as football, cricket, tennis, badminton, bowls and gymnastics. A two-week Arts Festival takes place in the early autumn.

Many residents work away from Hurst: in Brighton, Burgess Hill, Crawley or London, the situation of the village between the main London to Brighton road and the railway making this a relatively easy option. A small daily influx comes the other way to work in offices now occupying the erstwhile shops; but from Monday to Friday, Hurst is largely a dormitory, the day-time High Street displaying a high percentage of retired folk, some from sheltered homes, chatting happily to each other. There is a view that you need to allow an hour when going to buy a pint of milk.

We have our own fire station, but there are very infrequent sightings of the police. There are three pubs (down from eight only a few decades ago), two off-licences, a restaurant and a wine bar, and a café with pavement tables; no baker or fishmonger, but a delicatessen; a health centre; a veterinary practice that no longer treats farm animals, and a pet shop; a bookshop, an art gallery and a craft shop; three ladies hairdressers and three beauty salons. However much village life might have changed, the church bells still follow their centuries-old tradition of calling the people to Sunday worship.

IAN NELSON

The All England Showground, Hickstead

THE PARISH OF

HURSTPIERPOINT

&

SAYERS COMMON

PUBLISHED IN 2000 AS PART OF WEST SUSSEX MILLENNIUM MAP PROJECT

new millennium the
STPIERPOINT and
N looks both to its
re. Because it was
in which to live, people
any thousands of
s of new settlers owe
to what it is today.
major communications
axons called the place
and as the Domesday
de PIERREPONT
the Conqueror to add
n to the thriving
ty.

The Parish enjoys a glorious position north of WOLSTONBURY HILL, overlooking the woods of Daneghithe, where a later owner built his spectacular Elizabethan mansion, DANNY HOUSE. This, together with other historic buildings remind us of the rich tradition which has formed our present environment, and in spite of centuries of change, where individual craftsmen and traders became shopkeeper and bankers, horses and wagons gave way to cars and buses, the core of the original Parish still remains. The schools, the library, churches, pubs and clubs, societies and other thriving organisations bind a community determined to extend its life well into the future.

BOWLING CLUB
TOTT FARM B.A.
LLAMA FIELD B.H.
THE TOWER S.P.
TYPICAL SEMI-DETACHED
VALS MAP STUDIO S.E.
ALMSHOUSES OF THE HOLY NAME G.M.B.

THE HIGH STREET

Concepts, The Cruise Line, Columbines, Heather Boardman Antiques, The Vinyard Lodge, Community Charity Shop, Inspirations, Threshers, Alldays, Pierpoint Pet Supplies, Cafe Murano, Rideaway Cycles, Bentley's, Old Forge Ironmongers, Barry Shell, Hampers, Bole's, Red House Studio, Holly Mews, Hamilton Lodge Interiors, Austen Travel, Harper & Eede, The Poacher, McPhersons, Walpole Harding, Evangelical Church, Cool Choice, Feathers

amuel Orr, Palmers, hurst Antiques, & Kieron, Affinity, Reflections, K. Chapple, Nationwide, Shelleys, Pennyfarthing, West Furlong Lane, The New Inn, Dental Practice, Poppyheads, Post Office, Beauty Etc, Swan, Lloyds, Gibsons, Pitt Road, The Mint House, The Scriptorium, Nelson Seibold, C.J. McIntosh & Co., Mishon Mackay, Inside out Trust, Castle & Co, Daniels, Nupur Tandoori, Julian Antiques, Sylvia Florist, Clifford Dann, South Avenue, MPL Cars

ST. LAWRENCE SCHOOL

FUNDED BY HELP THE AGED MILLENNIUM AWARDS – COMMITTEE: *Maxine Tyler, (CHAIRMAN) John Avis, Peter Fry, Paul Hartly,* PLUS ARTISTS: *Geoffrey Bowles, Jan Morley, Derek Rogers* CALLIGRAPHERS: *Valerie Olszewski, Bill Parrott,* ASSISTED BY: *Ben Awcock, Mickie Bennett, Gillian Black, Joan Booker, Evelyn Bowles.*

Michael Cheetham, Joyce Creaton, Kay Cogan, Sally Coleman, Margaret Edwards, Beverley George, Bryony Hill, Mary Faux Jackson, Suzanna Kemp,

Sue Pendred, Susan Skinner, Sylvia Thornhill, Angela Wade, June Ward, Daisy Ware AGED: *Cameron Cresswell-Falvey, Natalie Miller*

Itchenor

Itchenor Park

THE SEA GOVERNS this parish. Although there are copses and farms, hedges, old lanes and little streams, everybody goes down to the shore in their mind. Even the main street eventually finds its way under the tide. Boats have ever been the business. The sea revolving on Itchenor's round shore strikes sparks of light in its endless grind.

By day the glittering sun, by night polaris and the circling stars. Sometimes the north wind hurtles black waves down channel; sou'westers, humped as dolphins, drive them back again. Wherever you are, you feel the hurrying sea and hear its messengers: wigeon from Iceland, brents from Russia, the cry of the wild curlew from Lapland. Shoals of dunlin as silver as sardines travel the tides and the skirl of pipes and whistles endlessly runs as in a nether-world. There are a million ancient mariners in Itchenor.

Half a millennium after the Romans first landed, drowned bells toll the tale of Viking raids. Square sails crossed with the red of English kings sailed past on their flood of war. Centuries more, and the 'black boy', Charles II, as dark as his Italian ancestry, anchored *Fubbs*, the royal yacht. Descendants of the skipper's captain remain in the village to this day. In the late 18th century the 3rd Duke of Richmond constructed his sloop *Goodwood* here, and a 44-cannon, 900-ton warship called *Chichester*, was the biggest launched at Itchenor.

The Duke bought land and made his own little private village for retainers next to his own seaside house and racing stables which he called Itchenor Park. Other notable houses today are the 16th-century Old Rectory, 18th-century Emmets, the 17th-century Sailing Club house, and a remnant of the old Customs House. Coats of arms are still emblazoned here and there. The splendidly simple little church of St Nicholas has a medieval cross remembering its acerbic souls departed – fishermen and boat builders could never afford anything more than prayer.

Itchenor built trading sloops by the score and exported vast amounts of Sussex timber. This little port sent smacks to fish the Channel and inner-Atlantic reaches, even perhaps to Labrador. From medieval times, coal and chalk, wine and wood, bricks and bullocks were brought in and out of the harbour – trade finally ceased in the 1930s. The poet Keats could see the forests of masts by Itchenor's shores when he stayed in Chichester in 1819.

Today the business of boats is for pleasure, run from the Harbour Conservancy's HQ in Itchenor, with the back-up of the Friends. From here Anne de Potier organises waterfowl counts that are the twelfth highest in Britain. Cars clog the

roads today, but there is an escaping ferry for foot travellers away to the Bosham shore. When the summer crowds have gone, and geese clang their wild chorus in the skies again, it is easily possible to imagine Itchenor once more with brown sails in gaff rig, riding the waters connecting this little waterside parish to the wider world beyond.

RICHARD WILLIAMSON

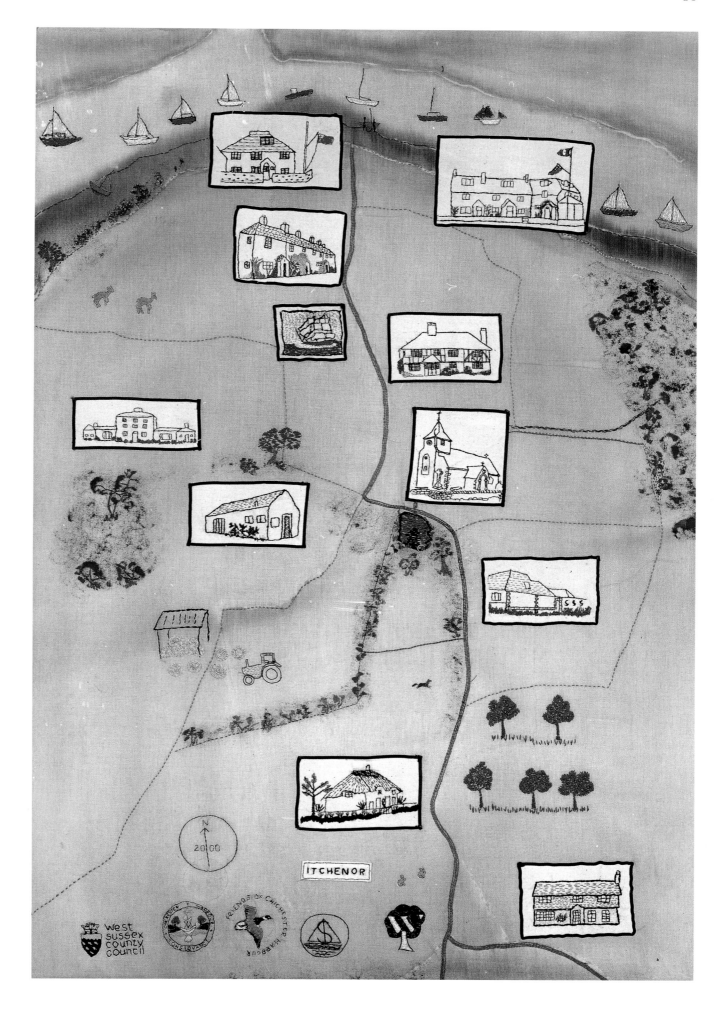

Lavant

IT IS THREE MADE ONE – two villages and a hamlet, each so distinct, yet each as inseparable as a close-knit family, tied by roots deep in the past. The origin of this little family of Lavants tells as much about their setting as about the way in which physical features have shaped our ancient place-names.

Right across Sussex there are very few places with names echoing those of the rivers on which they stand. Famously the Arun has its Arundel, and there are the lesser-known rivers: Es or Ez (Easebourne), Lod (Lodsworth), Lox (Loxwood), Kird (Kirdford), Stor (Storrington), and Chilt (West Chiltington). We can find no more in West Sussex, except here in the Lavant Valley, with not one, but a string of offspring: East Lavant, Mid Lavant, West Lavant.

Sheepwash Bridge

They owe their name to Sussex's most elusive stretch of water, the Lavant Course, more grandly the *river* Lavant, which in turn comes from the local dialect for a small stream – more properly known as a winterbourne –the type of watercourse that only flows seasonally. For months in the summer its bed is dry and parched, but come winter and its saturated reservoir beneath the spongy chalk breaks out in a flood of springs. 'Lavant's out!' was the old cry of reassurance that nature's time-clock was working. 'Have you seen it? The river's running!' still peppers conversation as the first fingers of water trickle through the weeds. Occasionally it never flows at all – 'Is all well with the natural world?' is the usual reaction nowadays. At times it rages

Centurion Way

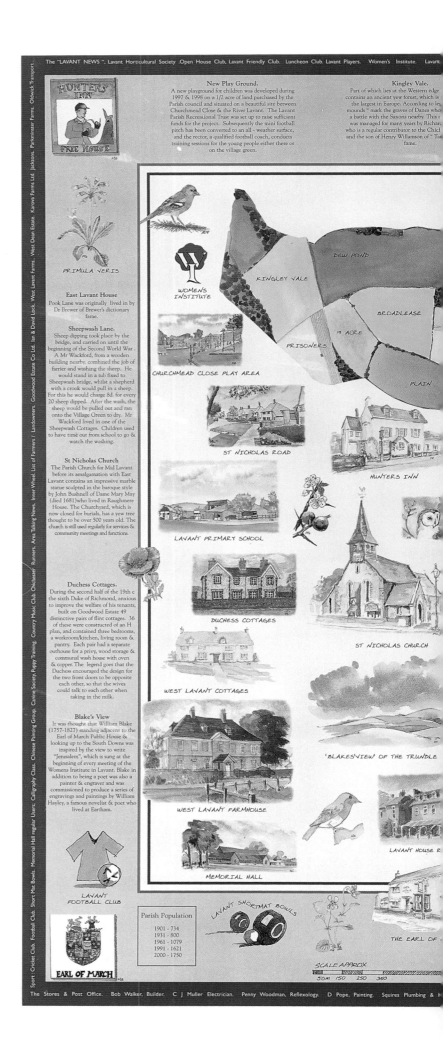

140

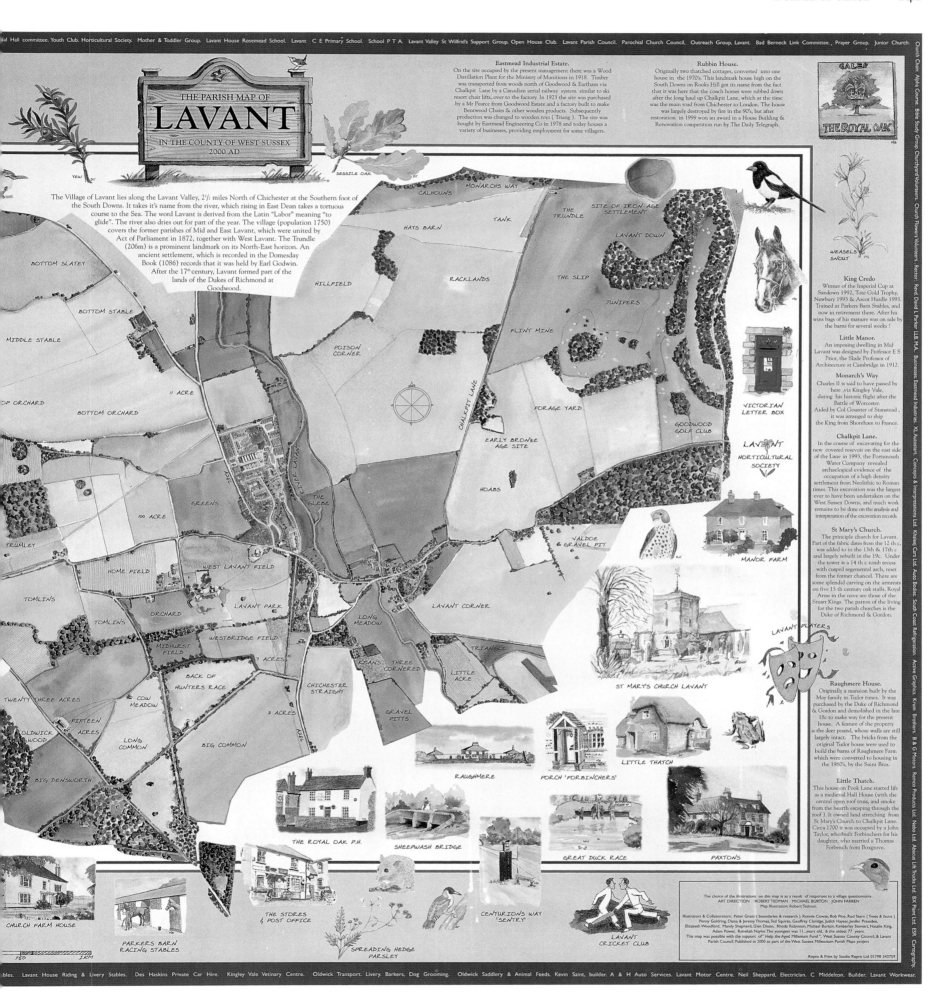

THE PARISH MAP OF
LAVANT
IN THE COUNTY OF WEST SUSSEX
2000 AD

The Village of Lavant lies along the Lavant Valley, 2½ miles North of Chichester at the Southern foot of the South Downs. It takes it's name from the river, which rising in East Dean takes a tortuous course to the Sea. The word Lavant is derived from the Latin "Labor" meaning "to glide". The river also dries out for part of the year. The village (population 1750) covers the former parishes of Mid and East Lavant, which were united by Act of Parliament in 1872, together with West Lavant. The Trundle (206m) is a prominent landmark on its North-East horizon. An ancient settlement, which is recorded in the Domesday Book (1086) records that it was held by Earl Godwin. After the 17th century, Lavant formed part of the lands of the Dukes of Richmond at Goodwood.

Eastmead Industrial Estate.
On the site occupied by the present management there was a Wood Distillation Plant for the Ministry of Munitions in 1918. Timber was transported from woods north of Goodwood & Eartham via Chalkpit Lane by a Canadian aerial railway system similar to ski resort chair lifts, over to the factory. In 1923 the site was purchased by a Mr Pearce from Goodwood Estate and a factory built to make Bentwood Chairs & other wooden products. Subsequently production was changed to wooden toys (Triang). The site was bought by Eastmead Engineering Co in 1978 and today houses a variety of businesses, providing employment for some villagers.

Rubbin House.
Originally two thatched cottages, converted into one house in the 1970's. This landmark house high on the South Downs on Rooks Hill got its name from the fact that it was here that the coach horses were rubbed down after the long haul up Chalkpit Lane, which at the time was the main road from Chichester to London. The house was largely destroyed by fire in the 90's, but after restoration in 1999 won an award in a House Building & Renovation competition run by The Daily Telegraph.

King Credo
Winner of the Imperial Cup at Sandown 1992, Tote Gold Trophy, Newbury 1993 & Ascot Hurdle 1993. Trained at Parkers Barn Stables, and now in retirement there. After his wins bags of his manure was on sale by the barns for several weeks !

Little Manor.
An imposing dwelling in Mid Lavant was designed by Professor E S Prior, the Slade Professor of Architecture at Cambridge in 1912.

Monarch's Way
Charles II is said to have passed by here, via Kingley Vale, during his historic flight after the Battle of Worcester. Aided by Col Gounter of Stanstead, it was arranged to ship the King from Shoreham to France.

Chalkpit Lane.
In the course of excavating for the new covered resevoir on the east side of the Lane in 1993, the Portsmouth Water Company revealed archaelogical evidence of the occupation of a high density settlement from Neolithic to Roman times. This excavation was the largest ever to have been undertaken on the West Sussex Downs, and much work remains to be done on the analysis and interpretation of the excavation records.

St Mary's Church.
The principle church for Lavant. Part of the fabric dates from the 12 th c. was added to in the 13th & 17th c and largely rebuilt in the 19c. Under the tower is a 14 th c tomb recess with cusped segemental arch, reset from the former chancel. There are some splendid carving on the armrests on five 15 th century oak stalls. Royal Arms in the nave are those of the Stuart Kings. The patron of the living for the two parish churches is the Duke of Richmond & Gordon.

Raughmere House.
Originally a mansion built by the May family in Tudor times. It was purchased by the Duke of Richmond & Gordon and demolished in the late 18c to make way for the present house. A feature of the property is the deer pound, whose walls are still largely intact. The bricks from the original Tudor house were used to build the barns of Raughmere Farm which were converted to housing in the 1980's, by the Saint Bros.

Little Thatch.
This house on Pook Lane started life as a medieval Hall House (with the central open roof truss, and smoke from the hearth escaping through the roof). It owned land stretching from St Mary's Church to Chalkpit Lane. Circa 1700 it was occupied by a John Taylor, who built Forbinchers for his daughter, who married a Thomas Forbench from Boxgrove.

The choice of the illustrations on this map is as a result of responses to a village questionnaire.
ART DIRECTION   ROBERT TEDMAN   MICHAEL BURTON   JOHN FARREN
Map Illustration: Robert Tedman.

Illustrators & Collaborators: Peter Grant (boundaries & research). Ronnie Cowan, Bob Pine, Rod Stern (Trees & fauna). Penny Goldring, Diana & Jeremy Thomas, Ted Squires, Geoffrey Claridge, Judith Hayter, Jenifer Presadee, Elizabeth Woodford, Mandy Shepherd, Glen Dixon, Rhoda Robinson, Michael Burton, Kimberley Stewart, Natalie King, Adam Power, Rebekah Naylor.The youngest was 11...years old, & the oldest 77 years.
This map was possible with the support of Help the Aged Millenium Fund, West Sussex County Council, & Lavant Parish Council. Published in 2000 as part of the West Sussex Millennium Parish Maps project.

Repro & Print by Studio Repro Ltd 01798 343759

Map labels: GALES THE ROYAL OAK · CALHOUNS · MONARCHS WAY · SITE OF IRON AGE SETTLEMENT · THE TRUNDLE · HAYS BARN · TANK · LAVANT DOWN · WEASELS SNOUT · BOTTOM SLATEY · HILLFIELD · RACKLANDS · THE SLIP · JUNIPERS · MIDDLE STABLE · BOTTOM STABLE · POISON CORNER · FLINT MINE · 11 ACRE · TOP ORCHARD · BOTTOM ORCHARD · CHALKPIT LANE · FORAGE YARD · GOODWOOD GOLF CLUB · VICTORIAN LETTER BOX · EARLY BRONZE AGE SITE · LAVANT HORTICULTURAL SOCIETY · 100 ACRE · GREENS · RIVER LAVANT · THE GLEBE · HOABS · VALDOE GRAVEL PIT · MANOR FARM · TRUMLEY · HOME FIELD · WEST LAVANT FIELD · TOMLINS · TOMLINS ORCHARD · LAVANT PARK · LONG MEADOW · LAVANT CORNER · ST MARY'S CHURCH LAVANT · LAVANT PLAYERS · MIDHURST FIELD · WESTBRIDGE FIELD · 7 ACRES · TRIANGLE · KEANS THREE CORNERED · LITTLE ACRE · TWENTY THREE ACRES · BACK OF HUNTERS RACE · CHICHESTER STRAIGHT · COW MEADOW · 3 ACRES · GRAVEL PITTS · OLDWICK WOOD · FIFTEEN ACRES · LONG COMMON · BIG COMMON · BIG DENSWORTH · THE ROYAL OAK P.H. · RAUGHMERE · SHEEPWASH BRIDGE · PORCH 'FORBINCHERS' · LITTLE THATCH · GREAT DUCK RACE · PAXTONS · CHURCH FARM HOUSE · PARKERS BARN RACING STABLES · THE STORES & POST OFFICE · SPREADING HEDGE PARSLEY · CENTURIONS WAY 'SENTRY' · LAVANT CRICKET CLUB · YEW · SESSILE OAK · 750 LRM

visionary, poet and artist, often stayed in Lavant, enjoying these views from his friend's house by the top of the village green. From the spot he called 'peerless' and 'blessed', it's not hard to imagine why it is said that his famous lines in praise of the English countryside – in *Jerusalem* – found much of their inspiration here. His few years in Sussex – he lived at Felpham from where he rode out to the Downs – affected him deeply.

Lavant's other precious patch is the block of fields south of the village, called Chichester Straight, 3 Acres and Big Common on either side of the A286, holding back Chichester's advance at Summersdale. This is where the city ends and countryside begins, the vital green space keeping the parish separate and apart. This gap is the dyke that keeps the village from drowning in a sea of joined-up concrete, and is jealously guarded by those who hold Lavant dear.

Walk round Lavant and there are so many contrasts. The old at the extremities – West and East – with more modern Mid sandwiched between, straggling the main road with its light industrial works, housing estates and modern primary school. Overall a good mix of old and new.

in torrents, as it did in 1993–4, causing devastation, nearly drowning Chichester lower down. Small and invisible for much of the time it may be, but the Lavant can never be underestimated in its unpredictability, a salutary reminder that in Sussex dialect its very name means a violent flow of water: 'How it did rain! Tarrible like, right down the street in a lavant'.

As different as they are from one another, the three Lavants are blessed in sharing magnificent views across the wide open spaces of the valley northwards to the Downs, captured in 'Blake's View' of the Trundle on the map. Green sheep pastures, a rash of summer poppies, sheets of yellow rape and the corrugations of newly-ploughed flinty fields clothe the hills in a riot of changing colours. William Blake (1757–1827),

'Blake's View' of the Trundle

Lavant Cricket Club

This is a parish well-known locally for its social scene led by numerous village clubs and organisations, all listed around the edge of the map. A vast range of interests for all ages keeps the village active all year round, through all the seasonal sports, calligraphy and Chinese painting, to caring groups like the Friendly Club and Churchyard Volunteers. This is much more than a picture postcard place, more a 'real' village where things happen, much of it centred on the thriving Memorial Hall, thanks to Tony Bleach who kept the village garage for years and who was awarded the MBE in 1995 for services to the community.

The mix of old and new spreads right across the map, with peeps of ancient and modern side by side, captured in some delightful vignettes. Many of these older properties were once part of the Goodwood Estate belonging to the Dukes of Richmond. They built dozens of 'Duchess Cottages' as a form of model housing for estate workers in the 19th century. Of uniform design, they are a distinguishing mark of villages in this area, a form of Victorian social-need housing from the private purse long before the time of council houses.

The past intrudes everywhere here, a nice touch of this being the names given to all the old fields. Just as we have our own names, so farmers

knew each parcel of their land by a special name, suggesting all sorts of tales and hidden histories. Some are obvious, others less so. There is Top Stable, Triangle and Cow Meadow, but what of Poison Corner, Prisoners and Midhurst Field which is nine miles from Midhurst? They give puzzles to ponder. . . .

In the best tradition of maps this one is loaded with local knowledge and prompts the curious to find out even more. Michael Burton's team of map-makers, led by Robert Tedman and John Farren, tried to involve as many as possible to achieve this result. After sending a detailed questionnaire to every household in the whole parish asking what they wanted to include, a group of over twenty was formed, made up of artists, researchers and those with detailed knowledge of the village. They involved the young people from both schools, the village primary school and independent Lavant House Rosemead, whose pupils contributed the wildlife illustrations of birds, animals, trees and plants.

Duchess Cottages

After just over six months of hard work, the map was finally launched in May 2000, unveiled by Cedric Fletcher, then 93, Lavant's oldest resident. The team found the whole project a most rewarding experience, feeling that 'we learnt a lot about ourselves, made new friends, and involved a good cross-section of the villagers'. Copies were made, and judging by the hundreds of maps sold both here and abroad, they felt that they got it about right, especially in 'achieving the rural feel we were seeking'. They made profits of over £2,000, money which has been ploughed back into refurbishing work for the Memorial Hall where the original now hangs.

KIM LESLIE

Lavant Football Club

EARL OF MARCH

Stores and Post Office

Parkers Barn Racing Stables

Lindfield

6 LINDFIELD HAS ENTIRELY its own personality of a large, house-proud village with its half-mile long High Street on which everything is concentrated. It is without any doubt the finest village street in East Sussex.' Notwithstanding that West Sussex won this much-prized place as its own in 1974, Pevsner's heady claim – written before boundary reorganisation – holds good whichever side it's in.

John Batten in the *West Sussex Gazette* described it as 'a treasure-trove of architectural wonders, of character, charm and all things bright and beautiful'. Eulogies pour from books about Sussex: 'one of the most picturesque villages in England'; 'truly the archetypal Sussex village'; 'we doubt if a more perfect or favourable specimen of an English village can be found in all England than Lindfield'. Visitors are ecstatic, residents well satisfied with their lot in this mid-Sussex gem.

Its showpiece status rests on four great blessings – its vast Common, village pond, magnificent High Street and the fact that it hasn't been swallowed up by the town on its doorstep. Haywards Heath keeps its distance – just. Lindfield survives with its own very special identity. Villagers jealously guard its independence. A few years ago they successfully won their fight with Royal Mail after officialdom eliminated 'Lindfield' as the official address. Villagers insisted that the village is a place in its own right and not a mere neighbourhood appendage to the town. (The Lindfield Postal Address Action Committee's website is an eye-opener on bureaucratic intransigence versus fiercesome fury that stirs when this village is agitated.) But its dependence on the Heath is considerable, both for major services and proximity to the railway line. Work in London – just forty-five minutes away – yet live in a commuter's paradise is the estate agent's boast.

Approaching from the north, we cross a bridge over the Ouse with a tale to tell about how good local things are lost. It used to be called by its ancient name – Midwyn Bridge – meaning the middle winding river. Then government surveyors came along in the 1870s, and without any local knowledge, blandly renamed it Lindfield Bridge which might as well be used for any other bridge around the parish. Ignorant insensitivity like

King Edward Hall and the Pond

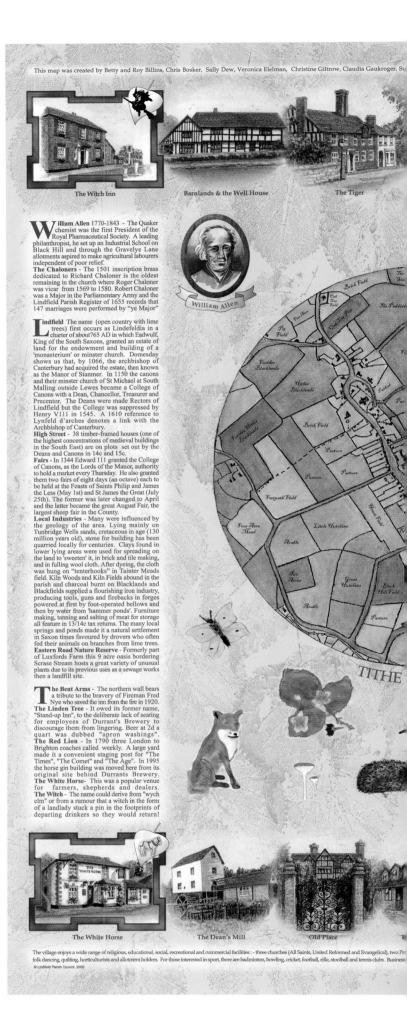

Thatched Cottage

wins in The Best Kept Village in All Sussex, a feat unequalled by any other contestant.

So approaching from the north and over the mis-named bridge and then up Town Hill, and what a sudden change there is from countryside to village – and what a sight! Around the edge of the churchyard is one of the most spectacular groupings of timber-framed buildings to be seen anywhere. Then past the church the High Street gently drops down through more stunning homes of timber, brick and stone, running between green limes and red-brick pavements down to the pond, with glimpses of the Common beyond. There is one of the highest concentrations of listed buildings in these few yards than in any other Sussex village.

Humphrey's Bakery

this wipes out so much local history and local meaning. Multiplied many times over, this is exactly how places lose contact with their past, although this is far from the case in Lindfield where strenuous efforts have been made by the parish council and the local preservation society to preserve and enhance its character.

Each year since 1993 the *Lindfield Parish Directory and Year Book* (brainchild of Gwyn Mansfield who also co-ordinated the parish map) has been published by the parish council, pulling together a vast amount of information about the village in diary form. It makes a major contribution towards this exceptionally active community. No other West Sussex village produces anything remotely comparable to this high quality gazetteer-cum-journal. Lindfield rides on a very professional wave.

The first few issues of the preservation society's journal didn't deal with constitutions, rules and meetings but got down to the basics that really matter. From the start they concerned themselves with the ingredients that create what they described as 'the collective impression conveyed by the village's natural and man-made features. These include trees, verges, ponds, paving, road surfaces, signs, lamp standards and lighting, shrubs, fencing and the roofs, windows, walls, chimneys and surrounds of our buildings . . . . It is obvious that what property-owners and tenants do with their property can affect the character of the village.' With such guardians this village is in impeccably good order. No wonder that it has achieved three successive

The old-time fair on the Common

From Haywards Heath much of the approach is through ribbon development along West Common, but it's pleasant enough with so much greenery alongside, then up Black Hill and suddenly the road opens into some delightful houses on the one side and on the other the sweep of the Common, famed for cricket since 1733, stoolball (very much a Sussex game), the summer fairground and one-time home to huge sheep fairs as well as the site for the great annual bonfire party. Stop near the cricket pavilion and across the house-tops distant views open up across trees towards Ashdown Forest; this is a place encompassed on most sides by woodland from which the parish was originally carved. Lindfield means an open clearing with linden (or lime) trees. The map rests against a background of linden leaves.

The parish map captures so many buildings, typical views and happenings that could be nowhere else but Lindfield. Centre stage is the village sign, its post, for the purposes of the map, combining the varied historic spellings of the village name, plus its website address. On either side are what makes the parish map unique in the West Sussex project – two medallion-style maps, one based on the 1844 tithe map emphasising the original linear shape of the village and the old field names, the other an aerial perspective of 2000, revealing its more modern growth east and west of the main street. Blocks of text to left and right encapsulate historical and up-to-date information. It's a good example of the

Bonfire Night

way parish maps convey the feel for a place so succinctly. One sheet of paper, so feelingly created, summing up what would otherwise take volumes of text. Through a parish map a place is so readily understood.

The map was unveiled in King Edward Hall by local MP Nicholas Soames at a celebration 'of all that's good, worthwhile and traditional', according to the local press. Reproductions, both poster and postcard size were sold, eventually resulting in a total profit of nearly £2,000, money that was used to provide a foetal heart detector and framed print for the village medical centre. Framed prints were also donated to the Lindfield Ward at the Princess Royal Hospital in Haywards Heath and to local schools, and another used as a prize to generate funds for the Queen's Golden Jubilee. The parish council sent a map to its namesake, Lindfield, now a suburb of Sydney, Australia, founded by a 19th-century emigrant from here. Prints of the map were turned into jigsaw puzzles and even inlaid into coffee tables.

Producing the little cameos inevitably meant a careful scrutiny of what was to be painted for the map. In the case of the village war memorial a closer inspection suggested the need for cleaning and restoration which was put in hand by the parish council, an unexpected side effect in making the map.

Its successful production and widespread sales meant that confidence soared amongst the map group – their names are listed along the top of the map. Then under the leadership of Margaret Nicolle and project leader Richard Bryant, the map group went on to produce a colour brochure for visitors (so far with more than 10,000 distributed); they also established the Lindfield History Project Group, organised a Lindfield Weekend featuring 'Times Past and Present' and more recently a major exhibition on Lindfield in the Second World War. In these ways community map-making opens up much wider territory.

KIM LESLIE

All Saints' Church

New Lindfield Primary School

Old Lindfield Primary School – now converted into homes

PROGRESS — LITTLEHAMPTON TOWN COUNCIL

Red Clover

Ringed Plover

Biting Stonecrop

Oystercatcher

Sea-Kale

Black-headed Gull

Lady's Bedstraw

Song Thrush

LITTLEHAMPTON LOCAL SOCIETY

Cormorant

Bee Orchid

House Sparrow

Beach Crescent, The Green

Hawthorn

Cottages, Arundel Road

South Terrace

The Black Ditch

Pier Road. Award-winning Floyd's Cottages

Flintstone Community Centre, East Street

Tomato Growing Nurseries, Toddington

Millennium Clock.

Cottages, Beaconsfield Road, Wick

Victoria Terrace, Bayford Road

Library and Information Centre

Body Shop HQ

Winterton Lodge, Goda Road

Old Farmhouse, Toddington Lane

Leila Cottage, Wick Street

Cottages, Church Street

Floyd's Corner, Surrey Street. Award-winning restoration.

Shopping Precinct, High Street

Windmill Theatre and Harbour Park

Chennevières-Sur-Marne Garden and Civic Centre, Maltravers Road

Manor House, Church Street, (Town Council Offices and Museum)

Bait Diggers

Cottages, Church Street

Sand Dunes, West Beach

Littlehampton, West Sussex, lies at the mouth of the River Arun, between Brighton and Portsmouth. It has a population of about 27,000 (2001 census). There are six schools, a cottage hospital, sixteen public houses, various Council offices, a modern Museum, a Library and Information Centre, and a pedestrianised precinct in the High Street.

The modern railway station provides access along the South Coast and to London, while the road network leads to connections with all parts of the country, and to Motorways M23 and M25.

Littlehampton is twinned with Chennevières-sur-Marne and Durmersheim.

LITTLEHAMPTON

Regatta: Zap Cats

Regatta

Shipping on R. Arun

River Scene

Jubilee Fireworks

River Arun

"The Black Shed", Boat House

Mewsbrook Park and Sportsdrom

ARUN DISTRICT COUNCIL

148

Littlehampton

THREE SEPARATE CENTRES eventually grew into the Littlehampton we know today – a port, village and seaside resort, centres that eventually merged to make the pleasant town shown on the parish map. For Ian Nairn, the Rustington architectural historian (writing in Pevsner's *Buildings of England* series), Littlehampton was 'exasperatingly disjointed ... the final result ... a rather bewildering mixture of Old Hastings and Bournemouth', a view recognising the fact that these scattered centres are still identifiable amongst the town's later development. The fact that a harbour of medieval date has formed an integral part of Littlehampton's growth gives the town some similarity with Hastings and Brighton, setting it apart from Sussex resorts of more straightforward origin such as Bognor, Eastbourne or Worthing. It is also significant that of the three Sussex ports, Newhaven, Shoreham and Littlehampton, this is the only town that has successfully incorporated a resort into its development.

Littlehampton harbour has a special attraction because of its position at the mouth of the fast-flowing river Arun – one of the swiftest in the country. The lower reaches, used

in medieval times to ship Caen stone up-river for the building of Arundel Castle, made it the Port of Arundel, a status underlining the strong link between these two places. The Dukes of Norfolk, whose seat is at Arundel, owned much of Littlehampton until the early 1930s. Shipbuilding and regular coastal trade existed by around 1800, and for some twenty years in the late 19th century Littlehampton operated cross-Channel services to France and the Channel Isles. Notice the name of the public house near the footbridge over the river – the Steam Packet, the only visible evidence today of this once important continental link.

Sea Bindweed

Blue Tit

Lesser Hawkbit

Swift

Yellow Horned Poppy

Littlehampton Churches Together

Mute Swan

Mallow

Ockendens (1802-2002)

Lob's Wood, Fitzalan Road

Pedestrian Precinct

Marina Gardens, Irvine Road

Golf Club House, West Bank

Brookfield Park

Oyster Pond, The Green

R. Arun Shipyard

Littlehampton Bonfire Society, 50th Anniversary

Littlehampton Swimming and Sports Centre

Norfolk Road Bowling Green

'The Sportsman', Littlehampton Sports Club

Maltravers Bowling Green

War Memorial (by Lutyens)

The Arcade, High Street

Road Train

East Beach

The Old Quay House, Fisherman's Quay

Swimming Centre, Mewsbrook

Boatyards, River Arun

East Bank development

The Friends' Meeting House, Church Street, 350th Anniversary of the Quakers

Littlehampton Marina

View across the Arun

WEST SUSSEX

west sussex county council

This 2002 Jubilee Map of Littlehampton Civil Parish was produced by Littlehampton Local History Society as part of the West Sussex Parish Maps project. We were supported by financial contributions from Littlehampton Town Council, Arun District Council and West Sussex County Council, and gratefully acknowledge active support from the staff of Littlehampton Museum and of West Sussex Record Office. The original may be seen in the Manor House.

Reproduced from Ordnance Survey mapping on behalf of The Controller of Her Majesty's Stationery Office © Crown Copyright.Licence No. MC 100038356. Printed by Selsey Press Ltd.

149

The river bank forms a most attractive waterfront – a favourite promenade with always so much to see, boats riding the waters, squadrons of swans, the Downs in the far distance and on breezy days the singing of the wind through the rigging of yachts and craft at anchor. Looking towards the river mouth we see the Pier (more a jetty than a traditional pier), the harbour lights and, across the river, West Beach and its dunes. Apart from the

Littlehampton – famous for its lifeboats

Sand Dunes, West Beach

river, the greatest natural advantage the town still enjoys is this unspoilt and undeveloped countryside so close to the town – one of the few surviving examples of natural seaboard along the entire Sussex coastline. Moving down Arun Parade and into Pier Road we pass the rebuilt Nelson Inn and the site of old Mussel Row, now a line of small shops tempting the visitor with fish and chips, novelties, ice cream and postcards.

Further up Pier Road and beyond were the once busy wharves for timber and coal, recently vanished under the East Bank Riverside Development of housing, Youth Hostel and Look & Sea! Visitor Centre with its viewing tower. One great bonus of this regeneration scheme is its new riverside walkway. Strangely in the midst of this development, close to the stylish new lifeboat station, stands the old Britannia Inn, once the focus of Fishermen's Quay, abandoned and in decay, crying out for restoration!

Up by these reaches are the boatyards that have made Littlehampton renowned, with names like Harveys for ocean-going vessels in the 19th century, Hillyards in the 20th for wooden yachts whose most well-known customer was Arthur Ransome of *Swallows and Amazons* fame – they built his last boat,

the sloop *Lottie Blossom* here in 1952 – and William Osborne, whose Arun Class lifeboats are on station all around the country.

Turning down Beach Road from High Street we come to a large open space, Caffyns Field, presenting a pleasant village green effect set in a leafy, wide Victorian-Edwardian development. Striking south-east and skirting the delightful Lobs Wood in Fitzalan Road – a triangle of natural woodland carefully left to its own devices – the seafront is reached, separated from the sandy shoreline by the Green that lends a spacious landscape quality to this marine location.

At the east end of this front was Beach Town, called this until about 1900. It was the original Littlehampton resort where the Earl of Berkeley built his marine residence in 1790 (demolished in 1948) and where a short line of Regency-style houses was put up some ten years later. Beach Town was the real start of Littlehampton as a resort, still retaining some of its original atmosphere. It took almost a century for South Terrace to extend from this eastern end to the rebuilt Nelson Inn by the river, and in the process presents a striking account of changing architectural styles through the 19th century. The completion of South Terrace effectively brought the three centres together at around the time when Littlehampton became an urban district council in 1893.

Today Littlehampton retains a high reputation for family holidays, very much as a traditional bucket-and-spade resort with miles of sandy beach. From the late Victorian period the resort claimed to be a 'children's paradise' with the essential credentials of safe sands, donkeys, discreet concert parties and ice cream.

One of those who came as a child early last century was the cartoonist and writer Osbert Lancaster (1908–86). He embedded the town's name in English literature with his *Littlehampton Saga*. His trilogy, *The Saracen's Head*, *Drayneflete Revealed* and *The Littlehampton Bequest* satirised social fads and foibles through the Littlehampton family, so called because he liked both the ring of the name and the feel of the place with what he called its 'homely charm'. This is the only West Sussex town made famous by a book title that has become a classic of its genre.

With obvious nostalgia, Osbert Lancaster considered what he called this 'unbutlined Littlehampton' representing 'the English seaside at its best'. He meant the town before the arrival of Billy Butlin's Windmill

The Old Quay House

Amusement Park by the river mouth in 1931, an event that caused deep foreboding, some fearing a tripper take-over – one commentator even anticipating the advent of a 'Whoopee City'! But such was not Littlehampton's fate and Butlin's, now transformed into Harbour Park, continues to enliven the holiday scene, although its crowds and car parking impinge on the traditional atmosphere of the Green. Thankfully much of this wide open space survives, despite the relentless creep of so many intrusions and the replacement of the Beach Hotel by the overbearing Beach Crescent. It's still the biggest seaside green in any Sussex resort – and hopefully will remain so.

Littlehampton's ancient village centre is still recognisable at the east end of High Street where the rebuilt St Mary's Church and

The Arcade, High Street

Millennium Clock

Manor House

Manor House, with the gothic-style school (1835), now the Friends' Meeting House, and 18th-century cottages, are grouped around the site of the former village pond and pump. The High Street is now pedestrianised and remains the busy centre of the town's commercial activity with the main focus at its junction with Surrey Street. At this point an attractive weather-boarded clock tower has been erected to mark the millennium. Surrey Street developed as a link with the harbourside, once associated with mariners and ship-builders and their houses, some still surviving and partly integrated with the new East Bank redevelopment. Floyds Corner, at the end of a terrace of late Georgian mellow red-brick houses, narrowly escaped demolition some years ago, and an award-winning line of matching Floyds Cottages added. Happily this has been successfully blended with the new buildings along the East Bank.

Turning back along High Street we make for the museum which occupies part of the Manor House. Lately enlarged and modernised inside, it presents and promotes the town's history, the ideal rendezvous for all interested in local history and the story that makes Littlehampton what it is today.

ROBERT ELLERAY

Lodsworth

ASK ANYONE ABOUT West Sussex rivers and they'll name Adur, Arun and Rother, maybe even the fugitive Lavant, but what of the little Lod that tumbles its short way from a hillside near Haslemere down to the Rother at Lodsbridge? 'The Land of Lod' – title of a recent book by John Rickman – is an intimate, secluded tract of countryside, thick with woodland, full of dells and ancient millponds held together by this tiny secret river whose 'capital', Lodsworth, has good claim to be one of the loveliest and best kept villages in England.

When a visiting Victorian in 1877 can write of the village as yet 'another of the nooks and corners of England which looks as if it might have been untouched for hundreds of years' and then a century later we find the opening lines of Lodsworth's parish history of 1995 describing the sunken lane suddenly opening into the little street looking just like a 'a time capsule', then we know we are somewhere very special. Its joint authors, Martyn Hepworth and A.E. Marshall, set the atmosphere: 'Seventeenth and eighteenth-century houses of outstanding beauty line the streets and, just around the next corner, stands a village inn of great antiquity facing a very small triangular green. The sense of the past is so all-pervading that it would occasion little surprise if a man wearing knee-breeches and a tricorne hat walked out of the inn and called for his horse.'

It would take a very special map to convey the qualities of this extraordinarily well-preserved and peaceful place, and this is

WOODMANCOTE

exactly what we have from the sensitive hand of local artist John Fellows. Its soft and delicate feeling of calm, its warm muted colouring and elegant text knitting the overall composition together, mirror so finely all that makes Lodsworth such an outstanding village.

It's not surprising that John, who paints around the world, followed in the footsteps of others of his calling by making Lodsworth his home. Charles Sims RA, RWS (1873–1928), Keeper of the Royal Academy, whose work is in the Tate Gallery, lived at Woodmancote, the very same home of the more famous Ernest Shepard (1879–1976) who gave the world some of the best-loved characters in children's literature. Whilst Winnie-the-Pooh, Eeyore, Piglet, Ratty and Toad were the creation of A.A. Milne and Kenneth Grahame, it was Shepard's pictures that brought them to life as an essential part of childhood for millions around the world.

In Lodsworth today, Shepard is still remembered with great affection, his memory kept alive by the use of his original 1962 design for the parish magazine's cover, his house marked by a blue plaque. Down in the churchyard extension at the bottom of Church Lane, appropriately close to the river, his grave is carved with two of his much-loved riverbank creatures from *Wind in the Willows*, with Mole, Toad in a boat and a willow tree entwined with an artist's palette in its branches. (Churchyard explorers will find Lodsworth's *Titanic* grave a few steps away in the S.W. corner.)

Down in this riverside part of the village is one of the keys to Lodsworth's earlier importance, for it was a place of medieval pilgrimage. St Peter's Well, its waters once renowned as a cure for bad eyes, drew pilgrims to the village, and so it has been suggested that St Peter's Church was built specifically for holy travellers journeying to this isolated health-giving place in the forest.

If Lodsworth today, still with a feeling of isolation, suggests a certain aloofness from more humdrum worlds kept at a distance, then there is ample precedent for its superiority: the 'Liberty of Lodsworth' made this a special independent territory. For here the bishops of London, who owned the manor, were outside English law. The original 12th-century charter confirmed that the bishops' lands at Lodsworth were exempt from any authority of the Sheriff of Sussex, the Chamberlain of the King's

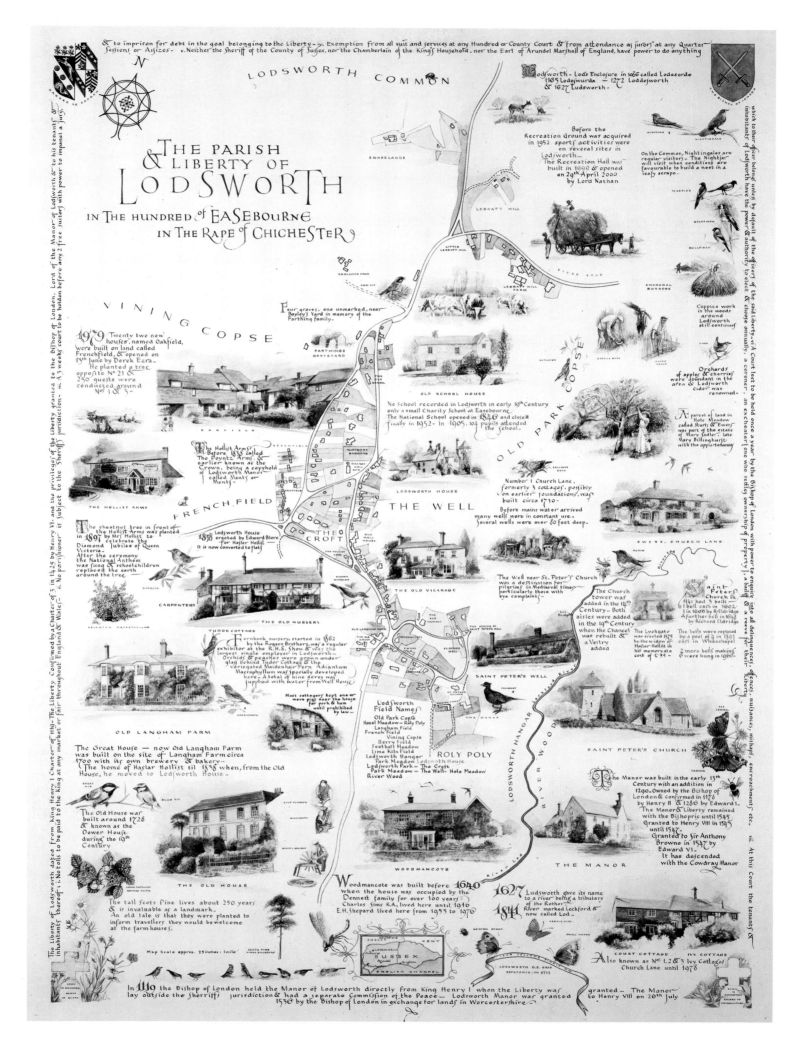

153

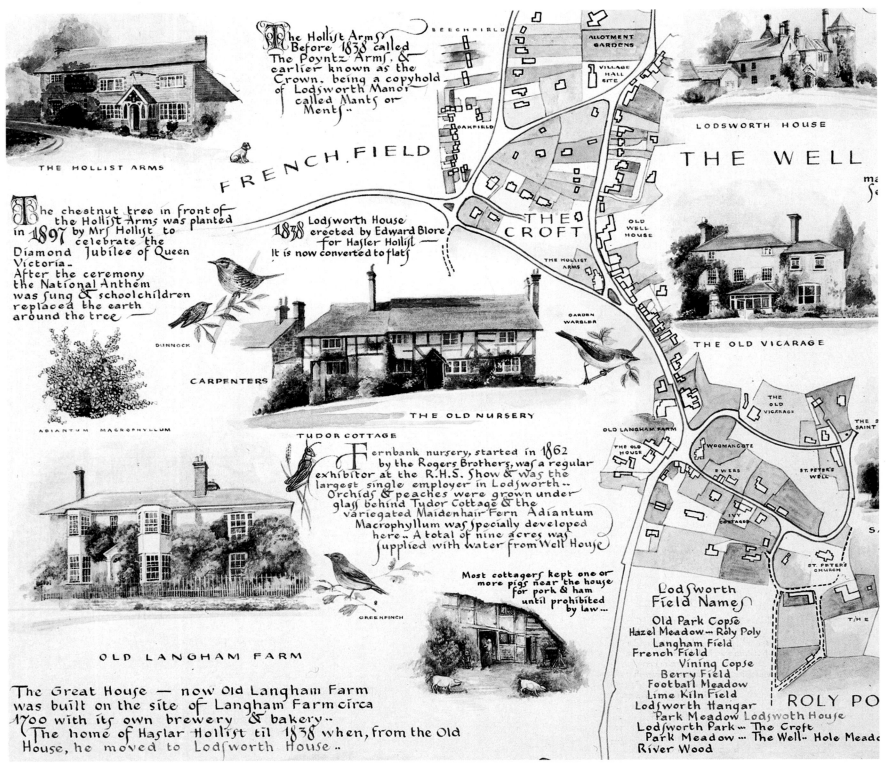

THE HOLLIST ARMS

The Hollist Arms. Before 1838 called The Poyntz Arms, & earlier known as the Crown, being a copyhold of Lodsworth Manor called Mants or Ments "

BEECHFIELD

ALLOTMENT GARDENS

VILLAGE HALL SITE

OAKFIELD

FRENCH FIELD

LODSWORTH HOUSE

THE WELL

THE CROFT

OLD WELL HOUSE

THE HOLLIST ARMS

The chestnut tree in front of the Hollist Arms was planted in 1897 by Mrs Hollist to celebrate the Diamond Jubilee of Queen Victoria. After the ceremony the National Anthem was sung & schoolchildren replaced the earth around the tree

1838 Lodsworth House erected by Edward Blore for Hasler Hollist It is now converted to flats

DUNNOCK

GARDEN WARBLER

CARPENTERS

THE OLD VICARAGE

THE OLD NURSERY

THE OLD VICARAGE

ADIANTUM MACROPHYLLUM

TUDOR COTTAGE

OLD LANGHAM FARM

THE OLD HOUSE

WOONANGCOTE

SEWERS

ST. PETER'S WELL

Fernbank nursery, started in 1862 by the Rogers Brothers, was a regular exhibitor at the R.H.S. Show & was the largest single employer in Lodsworth. Orchids & peaches were grown under glass behind Tudor Cottage & the variegated Maidenhair Fern Adiantum Macrophyllum was specially developed here. A total of nine acres was supplied with water from Well House

IVY COTTAGES

GREENFINCH

Most cottagers kept one or more pigs near the house for pork & ham until prohibited by law...

ST. PETER'S CHURCH

Lodsworth Field Names
Old Park Copse
Hazel Meadow ~ Roly Poly
Langham Field
French Field
Vining Copse
Berry Field
Football Meadow
Lime Kiln Field
Lodsworth Hangar
Park Meadow Lodsworth House
Lodsworth Park ~ The Croft
Park Meadow ~ The Well ~ Hole Mead...
River Wood

ROLY PO

OLD LANGHAM FARM

The Great House — now Old Langham Farm was built on the site of Langham Farm circa 1700 with its own brewery & bakery. The home of Haslar Hollist til 1838 when, from the Old House, he moved to Lodsworth House.

Household and the Earl Marshal of England. Villagers were even free to sell their goods in any market or fair throughout the country without paying any tolls. The bishops themselves looked after local justice, holding their own courts and exercising their own powers of imprisonment and execution. Capital offenders were hanged at Gallows Hill, on the parish boundary with Graffham.

Both court and prison were in the 13th-century Manor House, the oldest house in the village just south of the church, its massive stone walls, three feet thick, concealing its ancient dungeon and first-floor courtroom. So many of Lodsworth's buildings are of this same warm-coloured sandstone, for this is the stone-belt of Sussex roughly demarcated by the A272 that strides across the county, stone

THE MANOR

SAINT PETER'S CHURCH

'EWERS, CHURCH LANE'

to the north, clay, flint and chalk to the south. Up here in the rising ground of the higher Weald, the whole character of the county changes from further south, with deep hollow lanes, sandy soils and rocky outcrops from which building-stone has been dug for centuries. We see this stone used around here in houses, barns, churches, bridges and walls, giving unity and connection with the landscape 'in some of the loveliest and best kept countryside in England', according to Ian Nairn in Pevsner's *Sussex*.

Lodsworth's historians, Hepworth and Marshall, remark on the demise of the old inward-looking village, once with shops, plenty of local employment and social life. Whilst these old days have long gone, they claim that the money and time found in today's village 'were actually to the village's advantage'. They come up with a theory about the *extent* of change: that 'the more beautiful the village, the greater . . . the change. . . .

If people had paid a large sum of money for their property, they were likely to look after it and maintain it well. . . . Similarly, it was entirely to the village's advantage to be occupied by a large number of people who were not working and who could therefore devote themselves to village activities.' Add all the working commuters, plus home-workers with their computers, and the evidence 'seems to indicate that people who choose to come to live in a beautiful village devote considerable energy towards preserving its natural beauty; throw themselves enthusiastically into local events and are generous with their time and money . . . a village may well change . . . but far from dying it is often given a new lease of life. . . . It is a fine and worthy heritage which it is the destiny and privilege of the present Lodsworthians to cherish and preserve.' It is this heritage that John Fellows' map captures so exquisitely.

KIM LESLIE

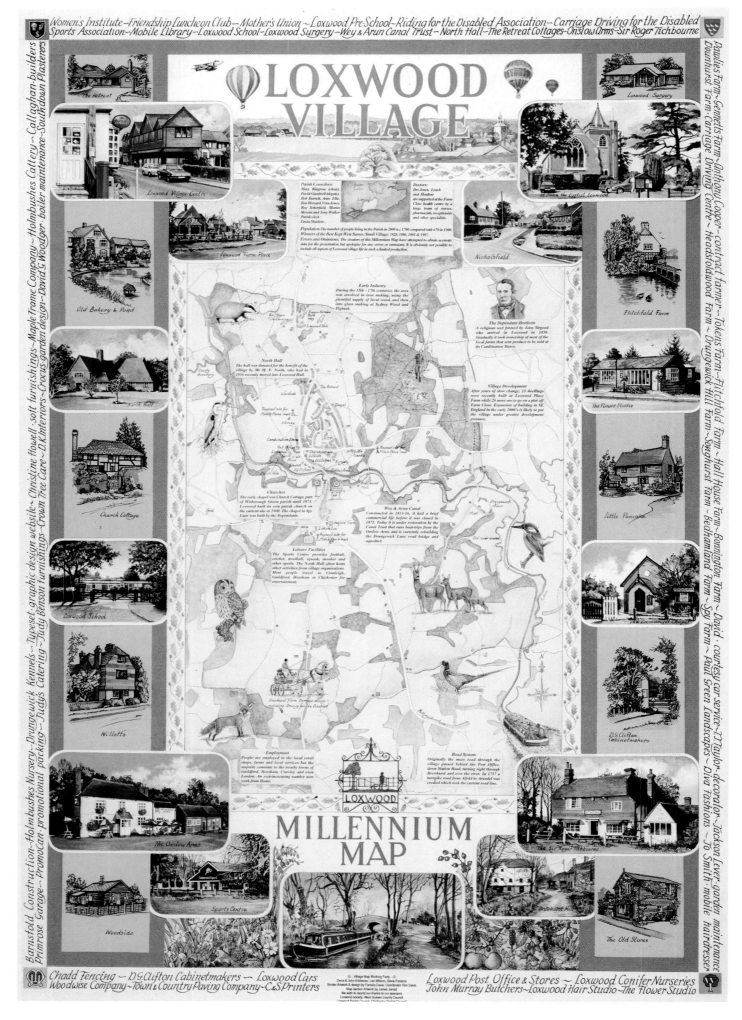

Loxwood

oxwood! Where's that then? Fourteen miles south of Guildford and ten miles east of Haslemere, both in Surrey – ten miles west of Horsham and six miles north of Billingshurst in West Sussex. You roll into it as you drop down over the Surrey-Sussex border and find you pay your council tax to Chichester, some twenty-five miles away; we are on the very edge of the council's territory. But in church matters, Loxwood has been united with Alfold in Surrey since 1978 and so comes within the diocese of Guildford. If you want to inspect the parish records dating from 1873 you will have to go to Surrey's archives in Woking. To add to the confusion, for its much earlier history you will have to untangle its records from those for Wisborough Green in West Sussex Record Office in Chichester, as Loxwood was once part of this much larger parish.

In many ways this scene says much about the parish. A place in which people live very happily, yet in which they can have difficulty in finding an identity. We are very much a borderline community, on the edge. And as well as being drawn between two counties, this difficulty may also be because the place has no real centre. Where perhaps in a typical village there would be a church, a few shops and a community hall around a green, in Loxwood these are spread out along a mile and a half of main road.

Yet Loxwood has many fine attributes and surprises. Its setting is its chief bonus, tucked deep in the countryside surrounded by fields and woodland – a 'forgotten border village' says a recent author, echoing E.V. Lucas a century ago who commented about its position 'on the edge of a little-known tract of country, untroubled by railways'. 'Leafy, with pleasant tile-hung cottages', added Ian Nairn, the architectural historian, when he came to write about its buildings.

Travelling through the parish you sense a delightful informality of structure. Even in the village where there are only small housing estates with regular lines, most houses are

well hidden behind hedges and trees. Many of the roads and lanes have no footpaths and at night, away from the modern estates with their street lights, the night sky is a joy to behold on a clear evening.

Crossing from Surrey, the little hamlet of Alfold Bars marks the entrance to West Sussex and the beginning of Loxwood parish. Its name signifies the geographical proximity to its mother-village of Alfold in Surrey; the 'Bars' element in its name could suggest a frontier-line or boundary (it's nothing to do with being a toll-gate as some people think). This is an area with a split identity, where Surrey falls into Sussex. A collection of late-19th century houses line the road, there is a shop and an old listed building, once a pub, the Sir Roger Tichbourne, closed since the map was made a few years ago. It was given this name – which was always curiously mis-spelt – to commemorate the celebrated trial of the notorious 'Tichborne Claimant' who impersonated Sir Roger to claim the family fortune in the 1870s. His case was championed by Guildford Onslow whose family were major landowners in Loxwood. The impersonator, a man called Arthur Orton, got fourteen years hard labour for perjury!

Then off the main road from Alfold Bars is Pigbush Lane, just one of the fascinating old names scattered across the parish – we also have Spy Lane and Merryhills Lane that

The Onslow Arms

The Sir Roger Tichbourne

Little Pancake

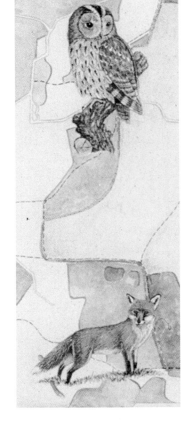

Connie Bayley, in her book of Loxwood reminiscences, says means 'ancient, dancing hills once used for a meeting place'. In looking at local names, maybe the most curious for a cottage is Little Pancake. There's one name with a false promise: hopeful travellers might think that Station Road would end up at a railway. But at its end – it's very short – it simply changes name and winds on for another four miles to Rudgwick, where the line has been closed for years.

The big house at Alfold Bars is Loxwood Hall. With associated outhouses and infill it provides a delightful mix of properties. One of its owners, Mark Frederick North, was a great local benefactor who gave the money to build North Hall in 1936. A good example of a pre-war village hall, it gives amenities for some of the local clubs and organisations listed around the border of the map as well as a site for visiting caravan clubs and the annual village fête.

Travelling on southwards we enjoy a tree-lined road, in summer a tunnel of oaks and horse chestnuts leading into the main village of Loxwood, a compact triangle of properties developed over the last five hundred years, although the majority have been built since the Second World War.

The sense of the original village is felt in the area around the post office, shopping parade and duck pond, then east down Station Road and south down the High Street. Most of the buildings are private dwellings, but many have traces of their more commercial past as inns, garages and other shops. Continuing south we cross the canal and the little river Lox (a headstream of the Arun) by the village pub, the Onslow Arms, and then climb Vicarage Hill, passing the late Victorian church of St John the Baptist. We reach Flitchfold Farm and its duck pond at the top of the hill where the road west to Ifold and Plaistow leads to the village recreation ground and sports centre.

The history of Loxwood does not appear in big volumes and little of it is obvious in the village. On the outer fringes is the once

St John the Baptist Loxwood.

North Hall

Loxwood Village Centre

Brewhurst Mill

fortified and moated Drungewick Manor going back to the 13th century, Loxwood's oldest building, once belonging to the bishops of Chichester, and much later the Onslow family. Loxwood has a good tally of old buildings well scattered around the parish, with forty-nine of them listed as being of special architectural or historic interest, including barns, cottages, farmhouses, and a watermill called Brewhurst. The mid-19th century saw the coming of the Dependant Brethren (or Cokelers) to this part of

The Dependant Brethren
A religious sect formed by John Sirgood who arrived in Loxwood in 1850.

north Sussex. They lived in several nearby villages, but their main centre was Loxwood where they ran their own departmental stores – the Combination Stores. Their place of worship in Spy Lane is still in use today, but by a different religious persuasion.

The most obvious link with a bygone age is the Wey and Arun Canal. Many local buildings have canal connections with names to suit such as Canal Villa and The Wharf, whilst the Onslow Arms was the original canalside ale house. The restoration of the canal, a slow process that started in the 1970s, has the ultimate intention of re-joining the rivers Wey and Arun, thereby

linking three thousand miles of inland waterways with the English Channel. Even today in its unfinished state, the canal restoration brings history alive, giving the village a significant link to its past. People come from far and wide to see the work, have a ride on one of the boats and enjoy the pub and countryside around.

The canal is also a convenient link into the countryside for the people of Loxwood. It is like a long, thin park where they walk their dogs or amble on a weekend afternoon, catching sight of a darting kingfisher, stately heron or moorhen with its young chicks. Footpaths and bridleways reach out from all corners of the parish into a substantial network of cross-country routes. Locals with an interest in walking can leave home with their boots on!

Although there are small businesses in Loxwood and an ever-increasing number of people work from home, most commute to Guildford, Horsham, Crawley and elsewhere. They have chosen to live here because it gives them peace and privacy. Their wish is that the careful stewardship of Loxwood over past generations may continue for many years to come.

LEN MILSOM

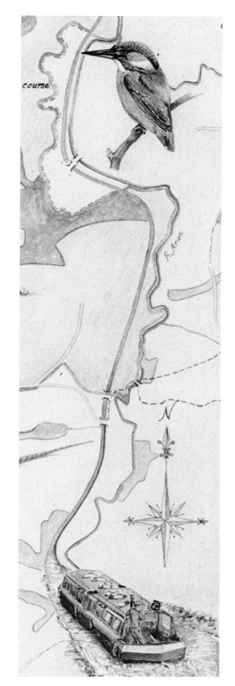

On the restored canal

Lurgashall

This statue of Tennyson sitting in the garden of Aldworth, was unveiled by his great grandson, Mark Lord Tennyson, on 23rd August 1997. The sculptor was Antonio Arena

THE OLD VILLAGE SCHOOL still looks out across the green, the bell still clinging to its upper wall, but those who once heard its call and filled its rooms with chatter and life are moving a little slower these days. The chalk was put away and desks closed for the last time shortly before the harvest of 1951, since when the young of Lurgashall have travelled elsewhere to spend their schooldays. Most of those who bustled their way in during the building's 107-year working life, spending some eight or so years in its fold, left to support and maintain a way of life that is now held only in sepia photographs and the recollections of an older generation.

The Old School

But Lurgashall still echoes that earlier age when the thirteen- and fourteen-year olds left school to labour on the farms, in the woods and in the houses of the rich. Those grand dwellings still stand, with the grandest holding the most commanding positions. The most notable of these, and not by chance with the most splendid views, is what was the summer home of Alfred, Lord Tennyson, Aldworth House, built between 1868–70. Tennyson lived at Freshwater on the Isle of Wight, but the hordes of summer tourists, who treated him as an object of curiosity, made his life there intolerable. He found both the peace and seclusion he sought some seven hundred feet up on the eastern slopes of Blackdown. On a ledge in Black Horse Copse he built his stone retreat.

Blackdown – the highest spot in Sussex, rising to 919 feet south of Aldworth – has beauty in all weathers. It can fold itself in cloud and disappear from all below, or in sunshine it can be an eye across miles of rolling wooded Sussex countryside to the line of the South Downs. Through a break in these, near Chanctonbury Ring, can be followed the view Tennyson enjoyed from the terrace of his home from where he saw

> *Green Sussex fading into blue*
> *With one gray glimpse of sea.*

Tennyson loved Aldworth, where he died in 1892, and from where he started his last journey to his burial in Westminster Abbey.

A little over two hundred years before Tennyson created his sanctuary, William Yaldwyn built Blackdown House. Tucked into a fold on Blackdown's southern slopes, it has height, natural protection, views and a strength one would expect from such a staunch supporter of Cromwell in the Civil War. By the end of the 19th century the property was in the possession of the Phillipson-Stow family and Lady Florence

Blackdown House

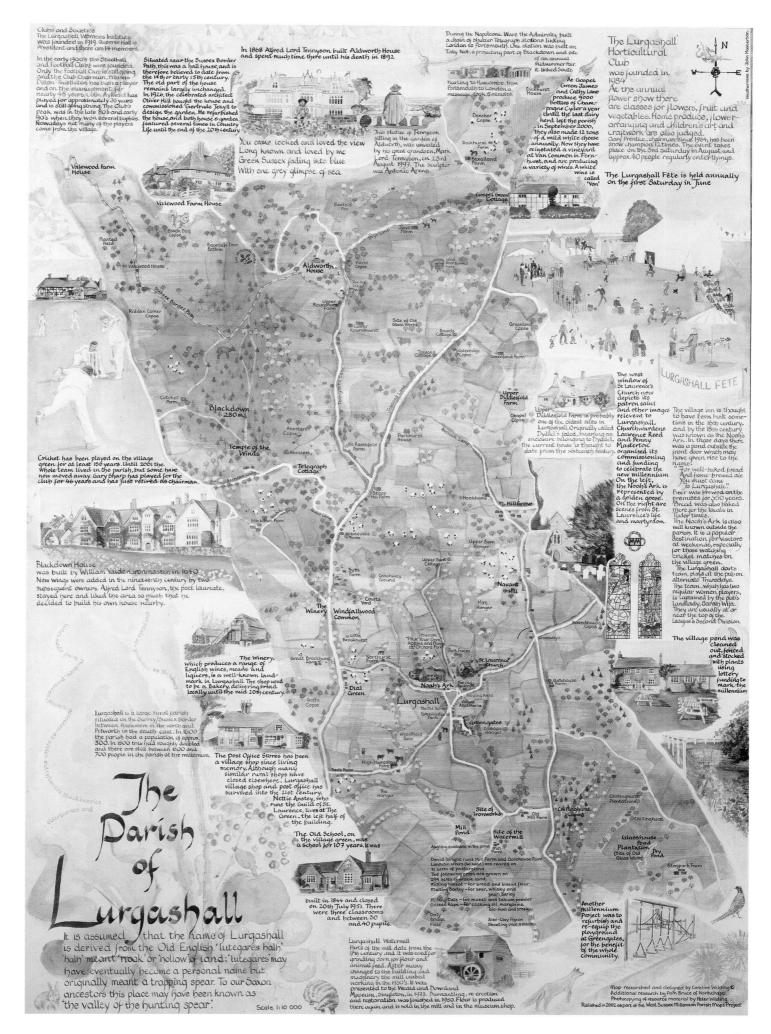

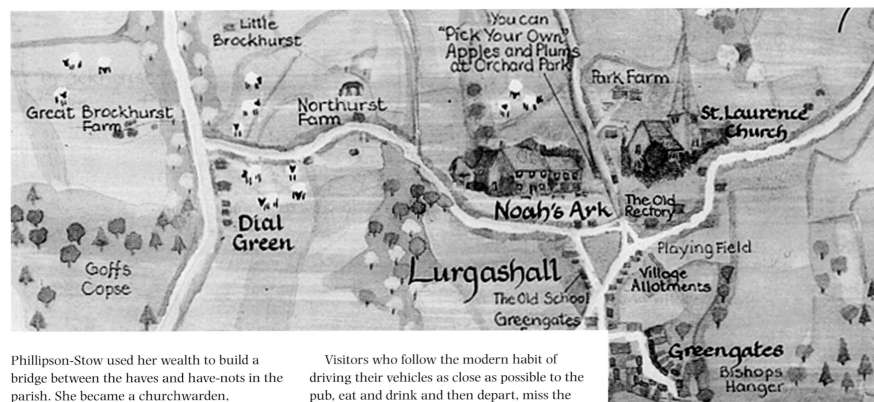

Phillipson-Stow used her wealth to build a bridge between the haves and have-nots in the parish. She became a churchwarden, benefactor of the village school and was instrumental in the creation of the village hall.

Money and high ground joined forces again in the early 20th century when a former brewery building was converted into a splendid home on the raised western end of the green in the heart of the village. Today the Malt House, a comfortable union of mock-Tudor and mellow brick, has a slightly aloof appearance, part of the village, but looking down upon it. The scenes the house surveys have changed but little over the past hundred years. True, the cows from Greengate Farm, at the south-west corner of the village green, have all gone, as have all the other dairy herds in the parish. They are no longer tethered to graze the green – today's manicured sward would give them little reward. But winter's snow still transforms it to a favourite Christmas-card scene, complete with the Noah's Ark pub and black and white cottages, the candles on the majestic chestnut swaying in a breeze to celebrate spring, and the sound of bat on ball and polite applause blending with summer sunshine to proclaim *this* is England.

Visitors who follow the modern habit of driving their vehicles as close as possible to the pub, eat and drink and then depart, miss the real feel of the parish. For this they must travel along green cathedrals of trees to the hamlets of Roundhurst or Hillgrove, or further afield to Valewood. Of course they have been prettied, with properties 'improved', but they are all hilly, still retain an unhurried air and throw reminders of the past with house names such as the Old Forge and Wheelwrights. The richest rewards go to those who travel on foot. Lurgashall has many miles of lovely footpaths offering huge variety, from hills with distant views to gentler walks across the southern fields.

If green is the most peaceful of colours, then Lurgashall must be the most peaceful of parishes – everywhere it's so green, so prominent in Caroline Wilding's beautiful artwork for the parish map. Green of course except for the Mill Pond fed by the Lod. The river wriggles its way into the south-west corner of the parish at Lickfold. For most of the year it is quiet, lazily running through the water meadows below High Hampstead Farm, through mysterious reeds and into the murky Mill Pond. But winter rains can change its mood in a few hours. The water rises in the

Lurgashall Mill

narrow channel, the road at Lickfold becomes impassable and the pond ejects its unwanted burden through sluice-gate and weir. The 17th-century mill the water once drove fell into disuse in the 1930s, but happily found a new lease of life at the Weald and Downland Open Air Museum at Singleton. Fully working again, it once more produces Lurgashall Stoneground Flour.

The church of St Laurence and the Noah's Ark pub are neighbours on the north-east corner of the green. They eye each other through the trees, and in the churchyard between them lie generations of sleeping parishioners. The pub is the commercial newcomer, not arriving there until 1537. But in the eyes of most visitors, its mellow brick, harmonious scale and views across the green combine to epitomise Lurgashall. Sitting at a table outside and watching the cricket, the time-weathered buildings blending into the green background, the customer has bought far more than food and drink.

The church is very much the senior resident. Saxon in origin, it has survived the centuries, seeing huge social and economic changes as well as wars. A reminder of those from the parish who gave their lives in the two world wars of last century stands in the churchyard, with thirty-one names inscribed, many from old-established local families. Many would have worshipped here, perhaps sung in the choir, passed under the great yew tree, and spent their days in the village school. Though nearly all lie in 'some corner of a foreign field' it's easy to imagine that when they lived in Lurgashall they had their 'hearts at peace, under an English heaven'.

MIKE OAKLAND

St Laurence's millennium window with its allusions to local life: the Noah's Ark (symbolised by the golden goose – a medieval motif), cricket, watermill, church and medieval glass-making

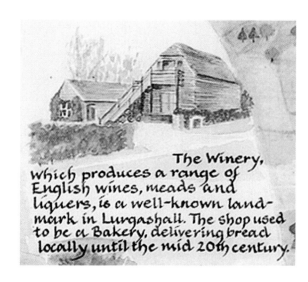

The Winery, which produces a range of English wines, meads and liquers, is a well-known land-mark in Lurgashall. The shop used to be a Bakery, delivering bread locally until the mid 20th century.

Lyminster

ORE THAN A thousand years ago the Saxons called it Lullyngminster, then over time its name kept on changing and changing. In all, nine different ways of spelling Lyminster fill the frieze around the map. When most people spoke rather more than they wrote there was nothing particularly unusual about this. Names gradually evolved from mouth to mouth, from century to century, and were just as local people pronounced them. So, like a game of place-name Chinese whispers, modern forms of village and town names were forged out of a very long oral tradition.

But by the Victorian period names became fixed and cast in stone, just as we know them today, the effects of officialdom from Ordnance Survey map-makers, the Post Office and the railways – all demanding uniformity.

Lyminster was a peculiar case. What had been Limister for at least two and a half centuries was mysteriously transformed sometime in the late 17th century into Leominster – and then given the stamp of authority by the Ordnance Survey's adoption of this corrupted spelling. Confusion reigned, especially with misdirected letters: was it Leominster in Herefordshire or Leominster in Sussex? When the Postmaster-General set up a telegraph station in the parish in the 1880s it was decided to revert to what was called its 'ancient name' – ordering it to be 'Lyminster' in future. So it has remained officially ever since.

That Lyminster wasn't too concerned about modern ways comes out in the saga of the telephone. In 1888 the South of England Telephone Company wanted to link Arundel with Littlehampton by erecting poles and wires all along the main road. The locals were up in arms: it would interfere with watercourses, would be unsightly and in any case there was 'no special desire of any inhabitant to have the telephone'. They were quite happy as they were. The application for a wayleave was rejected outright.

Lyminster is full of hidden tales and hidden places for anyone who will take the time to stop and explore. The map leads us a good way through the parish.

Following the boundary around the map shows up the importance of water in defining the parish limits: to the north and west by the Arun, partly along its old abandoned course, and then making its southern edge by the Black Ditch. The Six Bells, the parish's local, is firmly in Wick, and Arundel Station belongs to Lyminster. The railway was forced to build its station here rather than closer to Arundel Castle as townsfolk argued that the proposed railroad would be to the annoyance of the Duke of Norfolk. It was of much more consequence to the town to have a duke than a railway. So as a long-term consequence

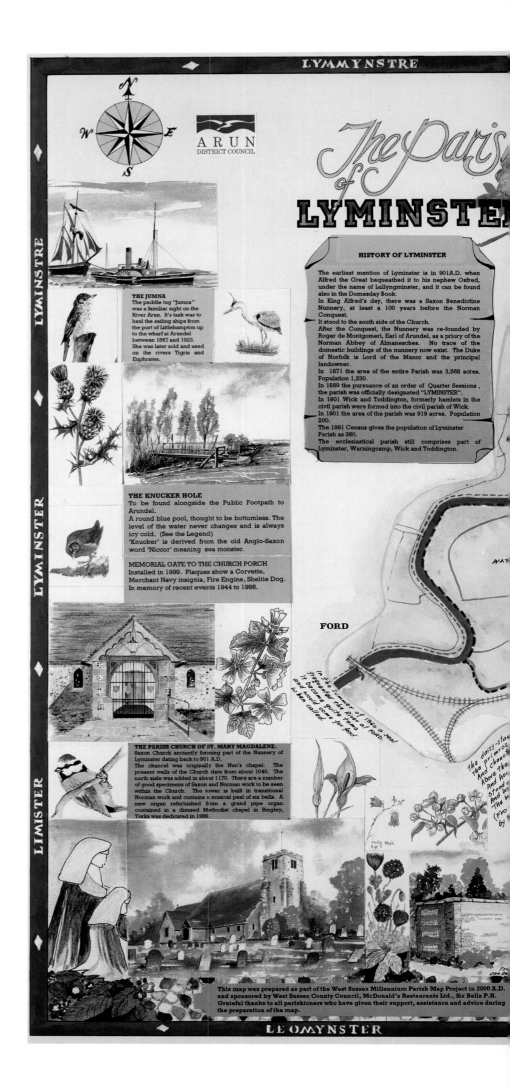

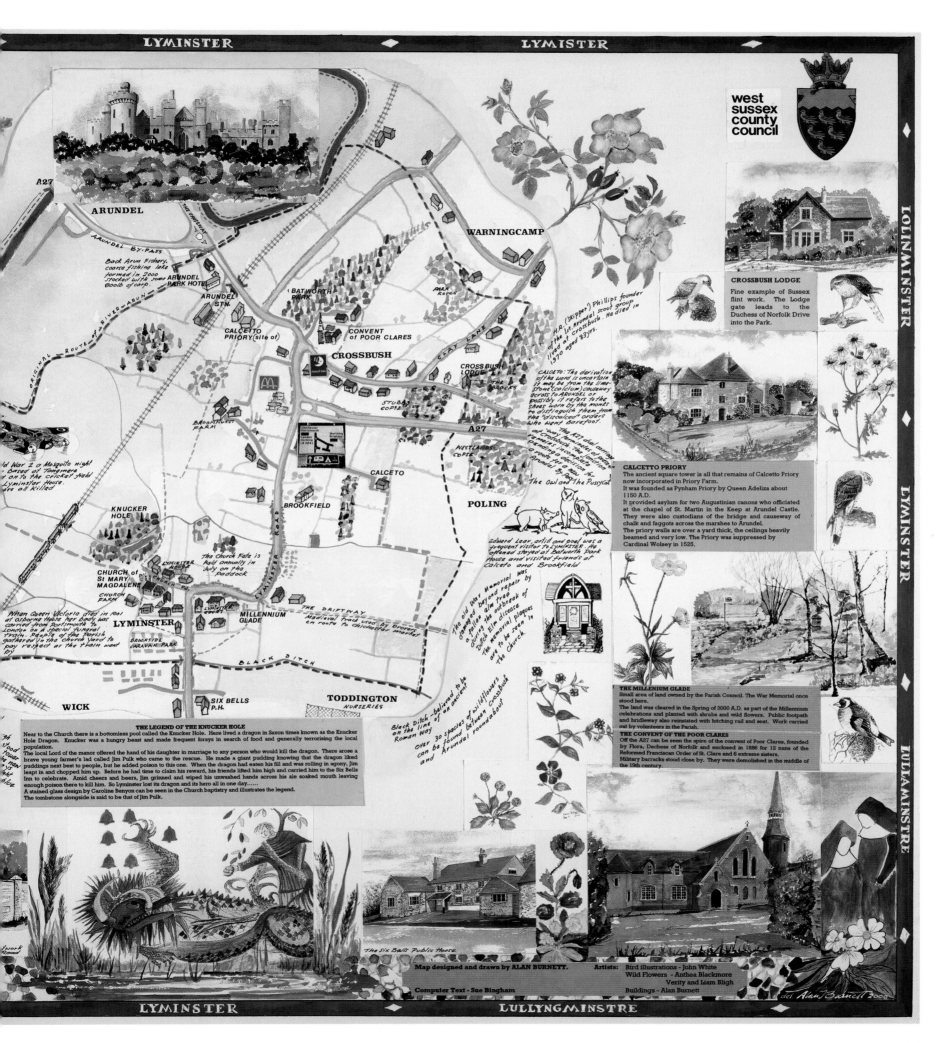

LOLINMINSTER
LYMINSTER
LULLAMINSTRE

west sussex county council

ARUNDEL

A27

ARUNDEL BY-PASS

Back Arun Fishery, coarse fishing lake formed in 2000 stocked with some Boobb of carp

ARUNDEL PARK HOTEL

ARUNDEL STN.

CALCETTO PRIORY (site of)

WARNINGCAMP

BATWORTH PARK

PARK ROUGH

CONVENT of Poor Clares

CROSSBUSH

CLAY LANE

H.R. (Skipper) Phillips founder of the 1st Arundel scout group lived at Crossbush. He died in 1970 aged 83yrs.

CROSS BUSH LODGE

THE BROOKS

STUBBS COPSE

A27

NESTLANDS COPSE

CALCETO: The derivation of the word is uncertain it may be from the lime-stone (calcium) causeway across to Arundel or possibly it refers to the shoes worn by the monks to distinguish them from the "discalced" orders who went barefoot.

The A27 dual carriage at Crossbush. Plans of 1992 remains incomplete, pending a decision to extend to a new road south of Arundel By-pass.

The Owl and the Pussycat

BROADHURST FARM

World War 2 a Mosquito night fighter Based at Tangmere crashed on the cricket field by Lyminster House. The men were all killed

KNUCKER HOLE

BROOKFIELD

CALCETO

POLING

Edward Lear, artist and poet was a frequent visitor to Lyminster. He often stayed at Batworth Park House and visited friends at Calceto and Brookfield

LYMINSTER HOUSE

The Church Fate is held annually in July on the Paddock

CHURCH of St MARY MAGDALENE

CHURCH FARM

When Queen Victoria died in 1901 at Osborne House her body was carried from Portsmouth to London on a special funeral train. People of the Parish gathered in the church yard to pay respect as the train went by

LYMINSTER

LYMINSTER COURT

MILLENNIUM GLADE

THE DRIFTWAY Medieval track used by drovers en route to Chichester market

This old War Memorial was damaged beyond repair by a fallen Elm tree during the outbreak of Dutch Elm disease The memorial plaques are to be seen in the Church

BROOKSIDE CARAVAN PARK

BLACK DITCH

WICK

SIX BELLS P.H.

TODDINGTON NURSERIES

Black Ditch - believed to be on the line of an ancient Roman Way

Over 30 species of wildflowers can be found between Crossbush and Arundel roundabout

CROSSBUSH LODGE
Fine example of Sussex flint work. The Lodge gate leads to the Duchess of Norfolk Drive into the Park.

CALCETTO PRIORY
The ancient square tower is all that remains of Calcetto Priory now incorporated in Priory Farm.
It was founded as Pynham Priory by Queen Adeliza about 1150 A.D.
It provided asylum for two Augustinian canons who officiated at the chapel of St. Martin in the Keep at Arundel Castle. They were also custodians of the bridge and causeway of chalk and faggots across the marshes to Arundel.
The priory walls are over a yard thick, the ceilings heavily beamed and very low. The Priory was suppressed by Cardinal Wolsey in 1525.

THE MILLENIUM GLADE
Small area of land owned by the Parish Council. The War Memorial once stood here.
The land was cleared in the Spring of 2000 A.D. as part of the Millennium celebrations and planted with shrubs and wild flowers. Public footpath and bridleway also reinstated with hitching rail and seat. Work carried out by volunteers in the Parish.

THE CONVENT OF THE POOR CLARES
Off the A27 can be seen the spire of the convent of Poor Clares, founded by Flora, Duchess of Norfolk and enclosed in 1886 for 12 nuns of the Reformed Franciscan Order of St. Clare and 6 extreme sisters. Military barracks stood close by. They were demolished in the middle of the 19th century.

THE LEGEND OF THE KNUCKER HOLE
Near to the Church there is a bottomless pool called the Knucker Hole. Here lived a dragon in Saxon times known as the Knucker Hole Dragon. Knucker was a hungry beast and made frequent forays in search of food and generally terrorising the local population.
The local Lord of the manor offered the hand of his daughter in marriage to any person who would kill the dragon. There arose a brave young farmer's lad called Jim Pulk who came to the rescue. He made a giant pudding knowing that the dragon liked puddings next best to people, but he added poison to this one. When the dragon had eaten his fill and was rolling in agony, Jim leapt in and chopped him up. Before he had time to claim his reward, his friends lifted him high and carried him to the Six Bells Inn to celebrate. Amid cheers and beers, Jim grinned and wiped his unwashed hands across his ale soaked mouth leaving enough poison there to kill him. So Lyminster lost its dragon and its hero all in one day......
A stained glass design by Caroline Benyon can be seen in the Church baptistry and illustrates the legend.
The tombstone alongside is said to be that of Jim Pulk.

The Six Bells Public House

Map designed and drawn by ALAN BURNETT.

Computer Text - Sue Bingham

Artists: Bird illustrations - John White
Wild Flowers - Anthea Blackmore
Verity and Liam Bligh
Buildings - Alan Burnett

del Alan J Burnett 2000

many Arundel people have a longish walk to reach their trains over the river in Lyminster parish.

The surrounding water keeps the old village fairly compact, preventing it spreading and growing too much. This is not big-building territory. It's a very low-lying countryside, the meadows to the west and south interlaced by a labyrinth of man-made drainage ditches and dykes feeding the Arun. They are Lyminster's defence, like a moat, keeping the northward spread of Littlehampton from engulfing it as it had done at nearby Toddington. The Black Ditch and its tributary dykes are crucial in maintaining Lyminster's identity.

And it's water that has brought fame to the place with its colourful legend of the fiery water dragon that lived in the pool called the Knucker Hole.

Lyminster is just one of two Sussex places that have famously harboured a legendary dragon – the other is St Leonards Forest, near Horsham, where there lived a 'strange and monstrous serpent or dragon' that slaughtered men and cattle. Similarly Knucker was a hungry beast that made alarming forays in search of food, terrorising the neighbourhood. A farmer's boy, Jim Pulk, finally came to the

rescue. He made a giant pudding, knowing that the dragon liked puddings next best to people, but to this one he added poison. When the dragon had eaten his fill and was rolling in agony, Jim leapt in and chopped him up. Amid cheers and beers, Jim grinned. Wiping his unwashed hands from the pudding across his ale-soaked mouth he spread enough poison to kill himself. So Lyminster lost its dragon and its hero all in one day.

Jim's tombstone in the church is said to be the medieval stone slab with the worn design of a cross superimposed on a herring-bone pattern. Near the slab the legend is shown in stained glass. To find the Knucker Hole from the church take the footpath northwards to the round blue pool, always icy-cold, said to be bottomless. Whilst archaeologists and skin-divers have reached its bottom at well over a hundred feet – and we know that in Sussex dialect Knucker holes, always said to be bottomless, are found elsewhere in the flatlands along the coast – it makes a good story. Knucker is supposed to be derived from 'nicor', Saxon for a water serpent or sea monster. Whatever the truth, the Lyminster legend certainly connects with ancient folklore. And Knucker's fame has spread far

The Owl and The Pussy Cat

Edward Lear, artist and poet was a frequent visitor to LYMINSTER. He often stayed at Batworth Park House and visited friends at Calceto and Brookfield

and wide. Copies of the Lyminster map with its dragon are sent for sale to the Dragon Museum at Llandrindod Wells in Wales.

Look for some more homely creatures, the Owl, the Pussy Cat and Piggy-Wig with a ring at the end of its nose, tell-tale signs that nonsense writer Edward Lear came this way. He visited relatives and friends, coming to stay in several houses in the parish around 1830, just at the time he started to work on his famous parrot paintings.

Looking around the map, there's plenty about the past to see around here, but the map-makers acknowledge the present in a parish so affected by the motor car. Cars mean road signs and services, so notice the little

Knucker, the water dragon

Lynchmere

What a wonderful place, so peaceful in this troubled world.

A magical spot for a church to be.

Thank you for keeping the church open. I found comfort in a time of need and was touched by the wording on the glass door – 'For now we see through a glass, darkly; but then face to face' – very helpful.

These are some of the recent comments in the visitors' book of our ancient parish church of St Peter, Lynchmere, that has stood here for a thousand years. Through the glass south door we see the countryside unfold down the valley of the Sussex Weald and far beyond to the South Downs; Wlenca the Saxon had his settlement by the mere just below. So why is the church, unusually for Sussex, built on the top of a hill? We think it was because it was also a place of refuge; on either side of the Saxon door in the west wall there are still signs of the slots where oak beams could be pulled across and the people could feel impregnable.

The Black Canons of Shulbrede with their distinctive tall square hats walked up through the woods from the Augustinian priory to read the office for the people until they were dissolved in the 1530s. The last prior, George Waldern – beautifully commemorated in stained glass in the church –

became curate of St Peter's (until the middle of the 19th century Lynchmere was technically known as a perpetual curacy united with Fernhurst). Successive generations have continued to add to the church, the last only fifty years ago, but old and new complement each other, each with its own little bit of history contributing to make the church a hallowed place. In recent years pageants enacting the village's history have taken place in the churchyard.

Shulbrede Priory

St Peter's lies at the end of the village green with its old oaks; we like to think that they were planted when King John gave a licence to Shulbrede in about 1210 to hold a fair on the Feast of the Holy Cross – 23 September. Round the green are stone-lined banks, quite likely built as an enclosure for the fair. The oaks shaded the fair and those who, with their bullocks, sought rest and refreshment after their difficult journey through the mud and darkness of the Weald. If you pace it out you will find that the length of the green is 220 yards – one furlong. This possibly means that it was also used for archery practice; Henry VIII forbade archery ranges to be of a distance less than this.

Medieval wall-painting of animals announcing the birth of Jesus

The backbone of Lynchmere is a sandstone ridge running east to west.

Stanley Farm – Origins date back to 1248

There was a scattered community of small farms with meadows in the valleys and sheep grazing on the sides of the ridge. Peewits laid their eggs in the furrows of the ploughed fields, larks soared into the skies and the song of the nightingales filled the night air. Now sheep no longer graze and coppices of sweet chestnut have replaced many of the open fields. As one walks through the dappled green canopies, woodsmen are making clearings, and here carpets of bluebells fill the air with their scent; on the damper parts, snowdrops and primroses grow.

Spanish Chestnut Coppicing

Over the years some of the ridge has been cultivated, but most is common land. Here some of the villagers exercised their rights of common. They were allowed to have a certain number of animals, to gather wood or peat and use the heather for roofing and bracken for animals' bedding. The farms had grazing rights, but they have lapsed over the years. This lowland heath has become one of the most threatened areas of this countryside and, since 1800, much of its unique habitat has been lost and our commons invaded by birch, fir and bracken.

Springs bubble out in Lynchmere Marsh to the south of the church. They form the

headwaters of the Lod and used to be the only water supply for the farm workers in their little cottages, with gardens full of vegetables and a pig in its sty at the bottom. It is hard to imagine that for two hundred years the peaceful valley was the site of a roaring iron furnace at North Park, one of the largest in the Weald, only ceasing in the mid-18th century.

To the north of the ridge the ground drops away to the valley of the Wey. The tiny river, more a stream here, forms both the parish and county boundaries and once provided power for a series of mills for flour, paper, and at Pophole, another ironworks. Along its way the stream was also harnessed to feed tumble bays in the water meadows. These fed the carriers: little canals that enabled the meadows to be flooded so that two and sometimes three crops of hay could be produced in the year. The millers' houses were strung along the river. Down here this was a rural scene with only a small community around Shottermill Ponds, with Springhead Farm and a wheelwright's shop.

There have been more changes to the village in the last hundred years than in the previous nine hundred. This scattered community of small farms and mills was transformed when John Grover, realising the potential for building around Hindhead – Surrey's highest village dubbed 'Little Switzerland' for its views and health-giving air – took over, modernised and extended the little brickworks at Hammer in 1898. He brought his workers from High Brooms brickworks near Tunbridge Wells, built them houses and their own nonconformist church. Land and

Three Counties Church – Built as the 'Free Church' by John Grover for the Kentish brick workers in 1902.

Camelsdale School – opened in 1904, the first school built by West Sussex County Council

materials were cheap, so Hammer and Camelsdale grew rapidly. For the next forty years the valley was dominated by the tall chimney of the brick kiln, the lives of the people regulated by the brickworks' whistle that woke them up and summoned them to work. The works shut in 1938, the busy yards where bricks were fashioned and the kiln where they were baked, replaced by houses, whilst the enormous quarry from where the clay was dug, is now a quiet recreation ground with a children's play area and graded walks for the elderly and their dogs.

Since 1996, following negotiations with the Cowdray Estate, our commons are now owned and being restored by the Lynchmere Society, so they are safe for ever. Traditional heathland wildlife is coming back, the whirr of the nightjar can be heard and Dartford warblers have taken up residence in the gorse. Dragonflies find the restored ponds in Danley Bottom are just what is needed. The society has a hundred conservation volunteers who have now been joined by some amiable Shetland cattle who munch their way through grass and tender shoots of birch.

With its incomparable walks and views, Lynchmere is still as beautiful as ever. It is a friendly place with a thriving community spirit. The Lynchmereans' pantomime has been going for nearly sixty years, involving over one hundred children and helpers and playing to packed houses. At Lynchmere's heart, the ancient parish church – home to the parish map – still provides the focus and a place of peace and calm to all who live here.

MICHAEL TIBBS

Tiny villages – many hardly more than hamlets – dot these western Downs, reached by winding dead-end lanes going nowhere but deep into the hills. Little out-of-the-way places – some no more than a church, a farm and some cottages – they seem to belong to other times rather than the 21st century. Such is Madehurst, tucked into wooded downland near Arundel, known to very few but those who live here. But even the church guide, written in the 1980s, acknowledges that it's barely known by those who live in the area. Go just a few miles from the village and ask the way here and the chances are that you'll be directed to Midhurst instead. Maybe that's a great comfort to residents, for they like it as it is, a very small and private place.

Not many people live here at all. At the last count, in 2001, there were just 105, the lowest ever recorded since the census first began two hundred years ago: at the first count in 1801 it stood at 133. By 1861 the population of just over two hundred was double what it is today, since when it has been falling to its all-time low today. So Madehurst bucks the trend of big population increases found in other parts of Sussex where ever-upward figures are well above the national average. It's a very special place, quiet and remote, where remarkably only one new house – Woodruff – has been built in the last fifty or so years.

Such small numbers mean that Madehurst's parish map can show every house and cottage in the parish, featured in the forty little watercolours around the border. A great many

are built in the local flint found freely across the downland; that's the significance of the handful of black and white flint-stones in the bottom left-hand corner of the map. This is the reason why places like this are always so visually satisfying: because the buildings are made from local materials that seem to grow from the very ground of which they are such a part. Blending naturally with the flint-strewn chalky landscape they are in complete harmony with their surroundings. They respect not only the environment, for being widespread and scattered, they respect their neighbours, not crowding each other, being set well apart in their seclusion. Local people like their space.

These scattered homes are dwarfed by their magnificent setting, best appreciated from Madehurst's heights up at Canada, the jokey Victorian place-name used for far-off remote places like this. Up here at some six hundred feet, we stand on Madehurst's northern boundary, a sweep of hillside falling into the valley to Great Bottom below. Hanging thick with woods, the backdrop the distant horizon where sea and sky meet beyond the coastal

The WI Hut

The Old Vicarage

Black Barn Farm

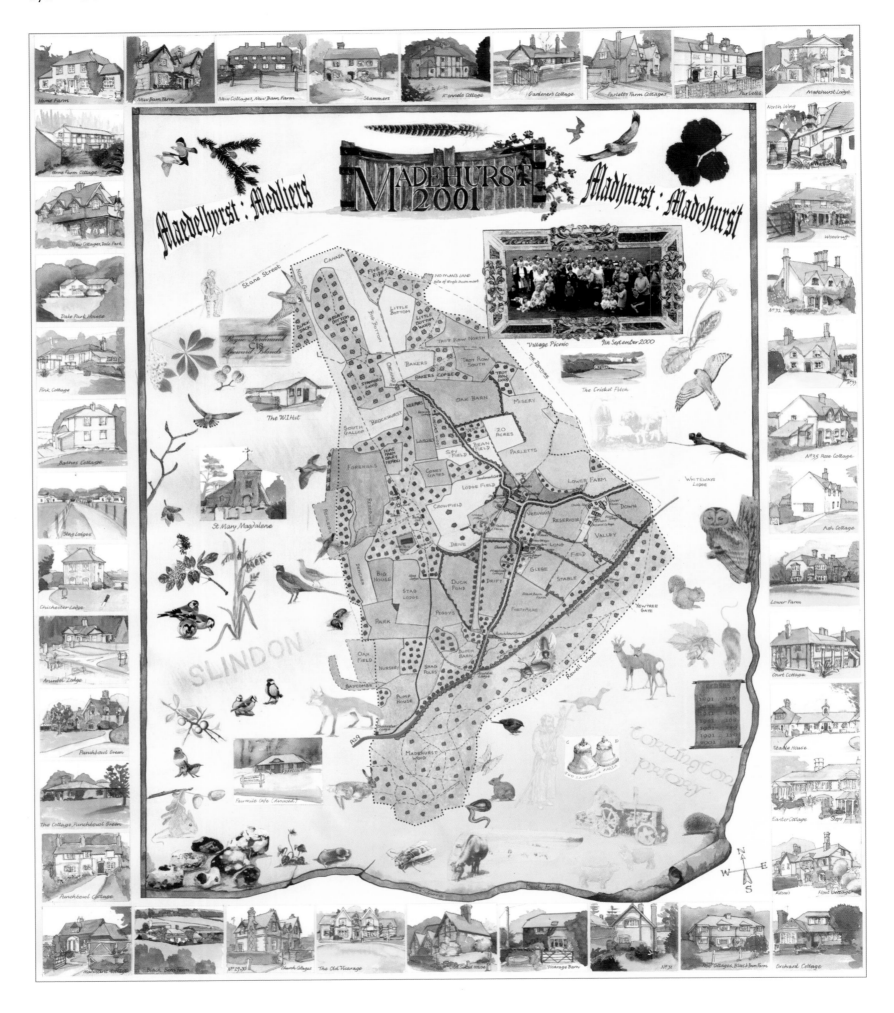

plain, this is a spot echoing Tennyson's own breath-taking view seen from another place, but so apt for here – of 'Green Sussex fading into blue/ With one gray glimpse of sea'.

Hilaire Belloc, that arch-protagonist of all things good in Sussex, walked and rode on these very same hills – he lived as a boy and young man in neighbouring Slindon. He was in touch with the magic of these lonely out-of-the-way places amongst the hills – what he called 'strongholds of silence and of desertion . . . where the passage of strangers is rare and unperceived'. Creative people have long been drawn into these solitary parts where landscapes rather than people take centre stage. Follow the lane past Stammers, once home to science-fiction novelist Edmund Cooper (1926–82) and it will soon be appreciated that

Stammers

he too came here for writer's solitude, beyond the casual reach of ordinary men. Cooper actually turned Madehurst into a literary device, as a symbolic place of escape from the world's troubles. The unnamed, isolated cottage to where the reclusive Dr Roland Badel fled to grow his own vegetables and read 19th-century novels as he 'he tried to abolish the twentieth century' from his life was inspired by Stammers in *Prisoner of Fire* (1974) and was the refuge – at a place he called Misery – for those fleeing from the devastation of Arundel in *The Cloud Walker* (1973).

Field-names, still familiar to those with roots deep in this countryside, conjure up so many intriguing pictures. Misery is a real place-name – not fictional – so called because of all the back-breaking work needed to clear the flints, a relentless, never-ending, labour. Remove them and yet more always turn up.

Stone is the harvest of the fields, where men, women and children once earned precious pennies in 'stone-picking', clearing these flinty slopes for the plough. Then there is No Man's Land, that isolated box-shaped spot of land right on the parish boundary shared with neighbouring Bignor, the name commonly given centuries ago to strategic sites where parishes line-up together. On Madehurst's lower ground, in the crook of lanes just north of the church, we find exotically-named Vesuvius, more mundanely just a high point of Lower Farm. There's been a farmer here with a rich sense of escapist humour for his everyday surroundings.

Another Madehurst curiosity linking the far-outside world to this tiny Sussex place takes us back to eighteenth-century lifestyles, a time when it was fashionable for wealthy English households to employ black servants, many of them saved from slavery in the sugar plantations. A little window into this faraway world is the church memorial dated 1789 to Roque Ferdinand 'Native of the Island of Bona Vista' in the West Indies: 'This Stone is erected as a Token of Regard and in Commemoration of his Worth'. For fifty-two years he faithfully served Sir George Thomas, former Governor of the Leeward Islands and his family, with 'unremitted Zeal Affection and Honesty', dying in service at their Dale Park home.

Dale Park has always been the 'big house' of Madehurst, set in parkland to the west of the

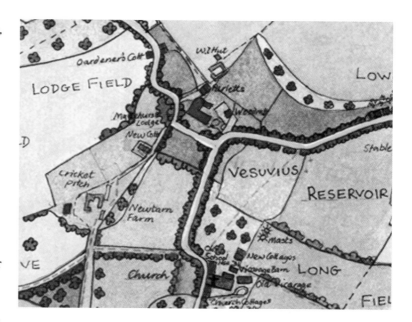

Chichester Lodge

village. The original 18th-century Italian-style house has gone, replaced by a smaller modern house, but still enjoying what was once described by Sussex historian Thomas Walker Horsfield in 1835 as its 'commanding eminence, having an extensive sea-view, and delightful prospects of the rich vale and city of Chichester. The dells and declivities of the Downs included in the Park have been judiciously planted, so as to render it a scene of unusual beauty and variety.'

'Prospects', 'dells and declivities', 'unusual beauty' – these are still very much the essence of Madehurst today. Indeed much of what has been written about the place in the past might well have been written in our own time. Even out-dated maps can still be reliably used as the passage of time has been kind to this little place; a place that in consequence is looked on with much feeling by those who quietly live here in tune with its countryside, shown in such detail in their parish map, made to mark the millennium. Mandy Faulkner walked its ways and studied old maps to set out its framework, then Annie Simson took over for all its artistic work and background historical text, capturing just how villagers see this very special place they call home.

KIM LESLIE

Midhurst

SOME PEOPLE call it 'Midhurst', carefully aspirating the second syllable; to others it is 'M'd'ust', a pronunciation nearer to the medieval. Two sides of the same coin? Not really. There are two Midhursts within the same community: the urban and the village: what you see and what has to be searched for.

To understand the place, look at its basic plan. This is a reverse capital letter P. From Easebourne cross the narrow Rother bridge on the northern boundary and ahead of you is the ribbon development of the main street. Take the first turning on the left and you enter another world. This is the Old Town, the bowl of the reversed P, within which the straight line of shops changes to a network of ancient lanes. Two Midhursts, different in every way, yet only a stroll apart.

Parish Church and Red Lion Street

The Old Town was the original settlement where the market developed, perhaps in Saxon times, but certainly after the 1066 Conquest. In the 16th century everything changed when the lord of the manor built the great mansion of Cowdray down by the river. He entertained the Tudor monarchs here: Henry VIII came, as did his son, Edward VI, and his daughter, Elizabeth I. Local merchants wanted to be near the action; they abandoned their shops on the top of the hill and moved down onto the previously unoccupied lower slopes. The result was today's North Street – all that many travellers see of Midhurst.

Here everything is bustle. The visitor finds a car park, post office and tourist information centre. Residents' everyday needs are met by modest supermarkets, the usual variety of multiple stores, the inevitable charity shops and by places of refreshment. There is a comfortable small town atmosphere. Note the number of chattering groups of local people; this must be an index of a town's vitality, and friendly Midhurst scores high. The magazine *Country Life* named it as the second best place to live in England – after Alnwick in Northumberland.

PoLo

In the summer life hots up with the coming of the polo season. The orange of the Veuve Clicquot sponsorship mingles with the Cowdray yellow livery. Expensive restaurants echo to half-a-dozen languages, private helicopters buzz like midges; the Royals and the Internationals take their pleasure here.

Cowdray Ruins

Huge horse-carriers add to the confusion in North Street, and those whom Shakespeare called 'golden lads and girls' cruise past in their 4 x 4s. But not all of them are immaculate urban tractors, many are coated in honest Sussex mud. The jet set and the county set meet here and are symbiotic.

Tourists with time to spare may lift their eyes above the shop-fronts and notice the late Victorian and Edwardian decorative architecture. Seeing the blue and white plaques commemorating H.G. Wells' associations here in the 1880s – there are three plaques to be discovered – they may congratulate themselves on recognising the era when the town developed. But they would be wrong. North Street is a paradox. Look more carefully, the buildings are not what they seem. The sides of many of the houses reveal Tudor timbering and plaster infill. Another glance will show 18th-century Georgian re-fronting, perhaps with 20th-century modernisation. Peel back the layers to see their origins.

North Street is home to the bane of Midhurst – the traffic. To car drivers, anxious to get to Goodwood races or the Festival of Speed, the town can be a nightmare, sometimes gridlocked by one carelessly parked vehicle. Demand here, as in countless other places, is for a bypass, despite fears of

Browne

Poyntz

Pearson

Lords of Cowdray

174

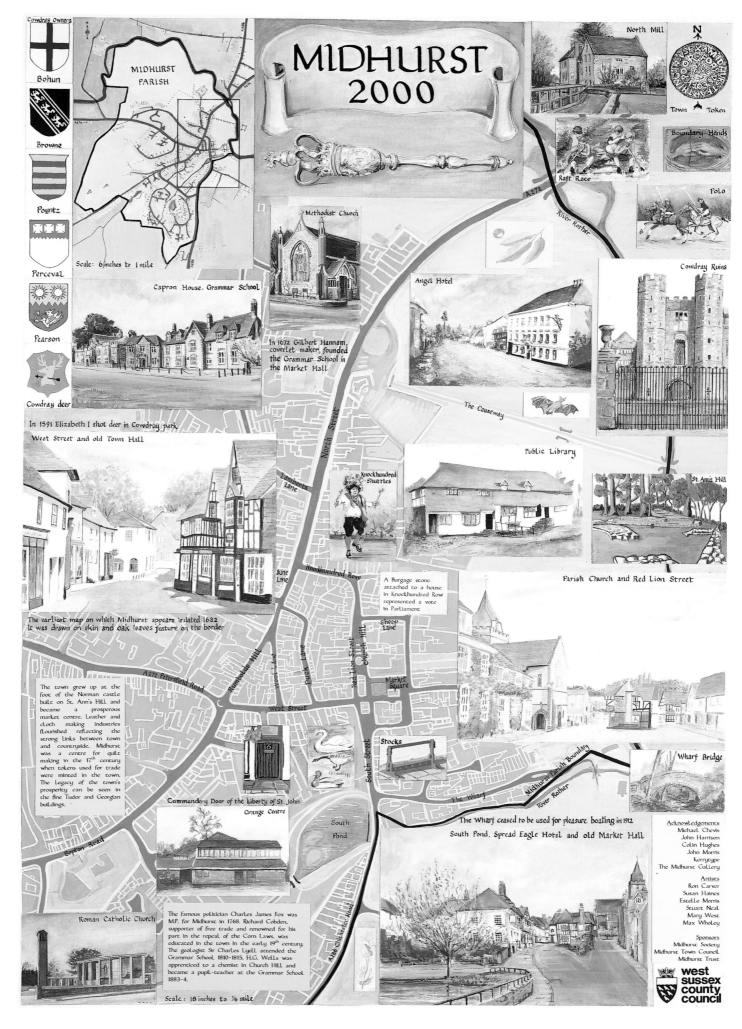

urban sprawl and loss of the green belt. Ironically, Midhurst owes its existence to the crossroads which now bedevil it, where once the track north from Chichester (now the A286) met the east-west route (the A272) to the Saxon capital at Winchester. This was a strategic intersection defended by the castle whose foundations can be seen on nearby St Ann's Hill.

We lose most of the traffic when we turn the corner into the Old Town. Nearly every building here has been listed by English Heritage and even the name of the approach road tells of its antiquity. Knockhundred Row leads to the 'cnoc' (or hill) where the hundred court for the local area met from early

South Pond, Spread Eagle Hotel and old Market Hall

West Street and old Town Hall

medieval times. At the summit of the hill is the library, like none other in Sussex, formed from five 16th-century cottages, their exterior all tiles and timber framing and inside, a glorious beamed roof.

We sense immediately that this, unlike North Street, is a community with homes and businesses side by side. Like all good villages – and the Old Town is a village – there is a social mix. A million pound Georgian house may be next to an ancient cottage that is still the home of a working family whose forebears have lived in Midhurst since time immemorial. Sometimes, however, when they have moved to somewhere more modern and convenient, the old property becomes the bijou treasure of retired incomers

who love the tiny rooms more than did those who brought up their children there.

In the narrow lanes, laid out as a now-forgotten grid a millennium ago, buildings of all ages jostle each other for space. This is a house detective's paradise where wattle and daub, crown posts and smoke hoods can be found – if you look for them. At eight o'clock every evening the curfew bell – now computer-controlled – rings out from the parish church as its predecessor did in Norman days.

The shops are mostly privately owned and sell goods of an individuality that is increasingly rare. Their proprietors know customers' names and needs. The elderly can buy one carrot and be courteously thanked for their custom. The pace of life is slow. People sprawl leisurely outside the pubs or under the sun-umbrellas on the cobbles outside the 16th-century market house. The peace is only destroyed when a brewer's lorry reverses fussily, trying to reach an inn that has been selling ale ever since the Knights Hospitallers collected money here to pay for the Crusades.

Those who speed through the town miss its secrets. It is a place to savour, to amble through and explore. Amid today's traffic, if you listen carefully, you may hear the ghostly voices in the medieval market or perhaps sense the bustle of a cavalcade going to feast at Cowdray.

BRIDGET HOWARD

Knockhundred Shuttles

Milland

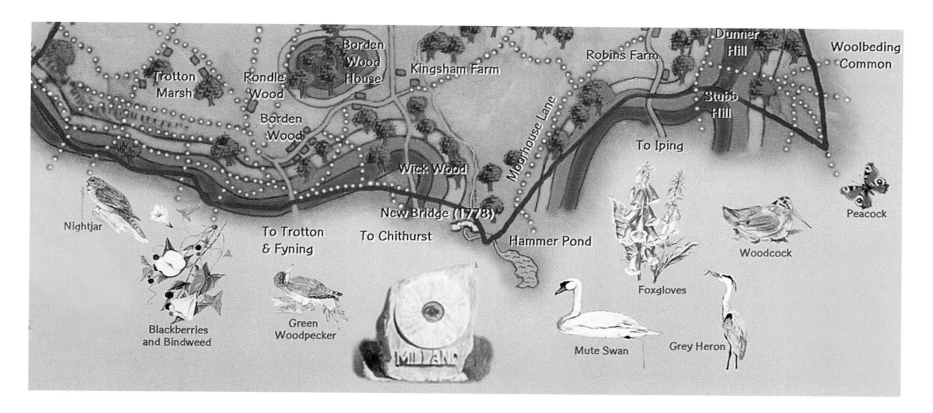

Nightjar

Blackberries and Bindweed

Green Woodpecker

To Trotton & Fyning

To Chithurst

New Bridge (1778)

MILLAND

Hammer Pond

Mute Swan

Foxgloves

Grey Heron

Woodcock

Peacock

Trotton Marsh

Rondle Wood

Borden Wood House

Borden Wood

Kingsham Farm

Wick Wood

Moorhouse Lane

Robins Farm

Dunner Hill

Stubb Hill

To Iping

Woolbeding Common

DROPPING DOWN from the crest of the hanger that carries the Old Portsmouth Road on its spine, you know with a great sense of relief that you are coming home to Milland. As the narrow lane squeezes southwards between the two pillars that guarded the old Milland Estate, and before it twists down the steep, deep hill, there is a glorious glimpse of the sweeping valley spread out below, perhaps with a soft mist rising from the brooks and ponds stitched into the patchwork of meadows, cornfields and abundant woodland. There are many secret places here and you need to walk or ride to find them. What you see from the road is not the real Milland.

Had you visited here for the first time only half a century ago you would have found nothing in the way of a village down on the broad, sunny valley floor – just a few scattered stone cottages, widely separated, independent and self-sufficient, and random farms. Today, the village now known as 'Milland' is perhaps divorced from the place's history and sense of its old self, but it has a vivid life of its own.

The flat valley, caught in the embrace of a horseshoe of distant wooded ridges, was always damp from the waters that spring forth all along the sandy hangers and trickle down to the claylands, gathering in pools, ponds and marshes. They channel into the arterial Hammer Stream that cuts southwards through a chink in the southern greensand hills to run into the old iron-working Hammer Pond and thence into the Rother. Many local place-names end in 'marsh', though today the

The Entrance Piers
(Milland Place)

area is more one of properly drained and fertile farmland than bog.

Wander away from the modern crossroads development and its comfortable housing estates with its 'roadhouse' Rising Sun pub, rebuilt in the 1930s when there was an unfounded rumour that the A3 trunk road would be re-routed through the valley. Wander up the little byways and follow them beyond tarmac, tracing the old routes along sandy hollow ways and muddy tracks through the woods, and you will find the real Milland and its history. You will never find an old *village* of Milland – there has never been one – but you will find a couple of hidden hamlets with handfuls of cottages: the delightful Wardley Green next to the village school known as Hollycombe (it was built by the owners of the huge Hollycombe Estate who used to own much of the valley); in the south-west corner of the parish is the tiny Borden 'village' street that used to look to the Borden Wood Estate for its employment and welfare, and to Chithurst for its church.

But you still have not found 'old' Milland.

For that you need to climb back up the northern hangers and puff your way up the seventy-six steps set into the hillside above Maysleith Farm. At the top you are in for a surprise. In a lovely, leafy setting there is the large Victorian church of St Luke's, Milland; ignore it and step into the ancient Tuxlith Chapel that St Luke's was built to supersede but which still survives in its arrogant shadow. Tuxlith, once known as Milland Chapel, is Saxon in origin and its graves are mere corrugations and hummocks in the grass, unmarked by headstones and far too ancient for anyone to know who lies buried here. Pause awhile in this peaceful, numinous place, so close to the highway, but so remote in spirit. Flora Thompson – of *Lark Rise to Candleford* fame – who lived for a short spell in Liphook, described its setting lyrically in 1925, wandering up the 'one long green lane which does duty for a street there; a street where violet banks and primrose copses intersperse and outnumber the houses, and the sound of the traffic is never loud enough to drown the singing of the birds'.

Of course she was writing long before the growth of settlement around Milland crossroads: for Flora, Milland was the few old stone cottages still scattered along the higher part of Milland Lane near Maysleith. She described the view from the top of the steps: '... stretched below is a

Steps To Tuxlith Chapel

wide expanse of the most lovingly praised county in England; green meadow and sparkling stream, wood and lane and distant hillside all melting together into the dim blue distance where the seaward hills cut the skyline'. And like many other writers, she was dismissive of the Victorian church, but fell in love with the old chapel. Her final words were: 'After dreaming for a time within it would not be surprising to find a Sedan Chair in waiting in the outer sunshine'.

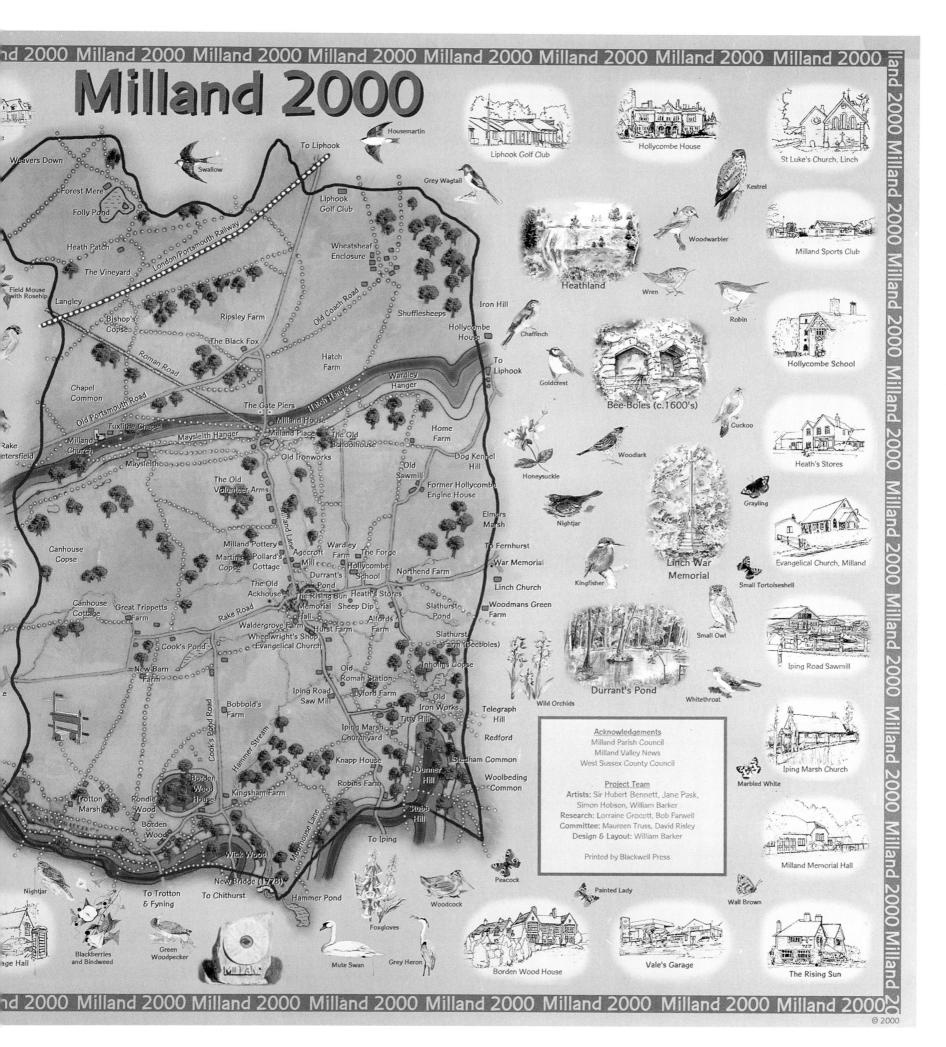

Milland 2000

Weavers Down
Forest Mere
Folly Pond
Heath Patch
The Vineyard
Langley
Field Mouse with Rosehip
Bishop's Copse
The Black Fox
Ripsley Farm
Chapel Common
Old Portsmouth Road
Rake Petersfield
Tuxlithe Chapel
Milland Church
Maysleith Hanger
Maysleith
Canhouse Copse
The Old Volunteer Arms
Canhouse Cottage
Great Trippetts Farm
Milland Pottery
Martins Copse
Pollard's Cottage
The Old Ackhouse
Cook's Pond
New Barn Farm
Cook's Pond Road
Bobbold's Farm
Trotton Marsh
Rondle Wood
Borden Wood House
Kingsham Farm
Borden Wood
Wick Wood
New Bridge (1778)
To Trotton & Fyning
To Chithurst
Hammer Pond

To Liphook
Swallow
Housemartin
Grey Wagtail
Liphook Golf Club
London/Portsmouth Railway
Wheatsheaf Enclosure
Old Coach Road
Iron Hill
Shufflesheeps
Hollycombe House
Chaffinch
Hatch Farm
Wardley Hanger
The Gate Piers
Milland House
Milland Place
The Old Schoolhouse
Old Ironworks
Old Sawmill
Home Farm
Dog Kennel Hill
Former Hollycombe Engine House
Elmers Marsh
Agecroft Mill
Wardley Farm
The Forge
Hollycombe School
Northend Farm
Durrant's Pond
The Rising Sun
Memorial Hall
Heath's Stores
Sheep Dip
Alfords Farm
Slathurst Pond
Slathurst Farm (Becboles)
To Fernhurst
War Memorial
Linch Church
Woodmans Green Farm
Waldergrove Farm
Wheelwright's Shop
Evangelical Church
Hurst Farm
Old Roman Station
Lyford Farm
Inholms Copse
Iping Road Saw Mill
Iping Marsh Churchyard
Old Iron Works
Titty Hill
Telegraph Hill
Redford
Knapp House
Robins Farm
Dunner Hill
Stedham Common
Woolbeding Common
Hammer Stream
Stubb Hill
Moorhouse Lane
To Iping
Milland Lane
Rake Road
Goldcrest
To Liphook
Honeysuckle
Wild Orchids
Woodcock
Foxgloves
Mute Swan
Grey Heron
Green Woodpecker
Blackberries and Bindweed
Nightjar
age Hall

Liphook Golf Club

Hollycombe House

St Luke's Church, Linch

Kestrel

Woodwarbler

Milland Sports Club

Heathland

Wren

Robin

Hollycombe School

Chaffinch

Goldcrest

Bee-Boles (c.1600's)

Cuckoo

Heath's Stores

Woodlark

Grayling

Nightjar

Linch War Memorial

Evangelical Church, Milland

Kingfisher

Small Tortoiseshell

Durrant's Pond

Small Owl

Whitethroat

Iping Road Sawmill

Marbled White

Iping Marsh Church

Peacock

Painted Lady

Wall Brown

Milland Memorial Hall

Woodcock

Borden Wood House

Vale's Garage

The Rising Sun

Acknowledgements
Milland Parish Council
Milland Valley News
West Sussex County Council

Project Team
Artists: Sir Hubert Bennett, Jane Pask,
Simon Hobson, William Barker
Research: Lorraine Grocott, Bob Farwell
Committee: Maureen Truss, David Risley
Design & Layout: William Barker

Printed by Blackwell Press

© 2000

179

Yet she did not know one of the chapel's biggest secrets. Very close by, undiscovered and even unsuspected until the 1940s, is a long-lost Roman road that was the spine of Milland, running right through the modern village from south to north and very probably the reason for the chapel's existence.

From Chichester, the Romans needed to link with Silchester, near Reading, and their road began at the city's North Gate. Their first landmark was Linch Down, the second highest point on the South Downs, from the summit of which they could set their sights on Dunner Hill, now in the parish of Milland and another of its secret places. Thence they could point the road up to the Maysleith hanger and across Tuxlith's extensive and heathery Chapel Common towards Weavers Down and beyond. There is a feeling about Tuxlith of cultures more ancient than the Romans, and many a worked flint has been discovered in the area of Maysleith at the foot of those seventy-six steps – an area linked by the streams to the Iron-Age hillcamp at Hammerwood.

Unlike its historic neighbouring parishes, Milland only became a civil parish in its own right in 1972, when it was carved out of the 'outlier' northern sections of the river parishes of Iping, Trotton, Chithurst and Stedham. It sprawls over nine square miles, more or less centred on the pub crossroads but embracing such diverse 'settlements' as Wheatsheaf Enclosure, Ripsley Park, Forest Mere with its famous Champneys health resort, Liphook Equine Hospital and Liphook Golf Club – all within Milland's northern boundaries and yet all tagged with Liphook, Hampshire addresses – and stretching southwards to include remote places like Titty Hill, Queen's Corner, Iping Marsh, Trotton Hollow and Rondle Wood. Yet even with such a short local government history and such a new 'village', Milland has a powerful sense of community and vigour, with numerous clubs and local groups, its school, two pubs (the other is the Black Fox on the old Portsmouth coaching road) and its village hall. It holds a mammoth Milland Rural Fair

Bee-Boles (c.1600s)

every other year, when the population of the place quadruples, and runs a vibrant *Milland News* local paper in full colour that does so much to bring the valley together.

Yet there is no shop now in Milland – the old one at Wardley Green closed in the 1980s – nor is there a church in 'new' Milland; the parishioners look to the hilltop Victorian church and Tuxlith, or the little church at Linch across the parish border. Many of the villagers used to love the Church of the Good

Shepherd, otherwise known as Knapp Church at Iping Marsh, but this was demolished in the early 1980s and now there is only a peaceful churchyard there, surrounded by pasture and woodland and right on the Roman road.

Milland's story is not one of famous people; it is of ordinary folk who lived here and who worked in the fields and in the woods, people who gossiped and bickered and wandered and remembered. You can feel their presence, all those people from the past lingering, not wanting to leave their valley. My valley.

VAL PORTER

Kestrel

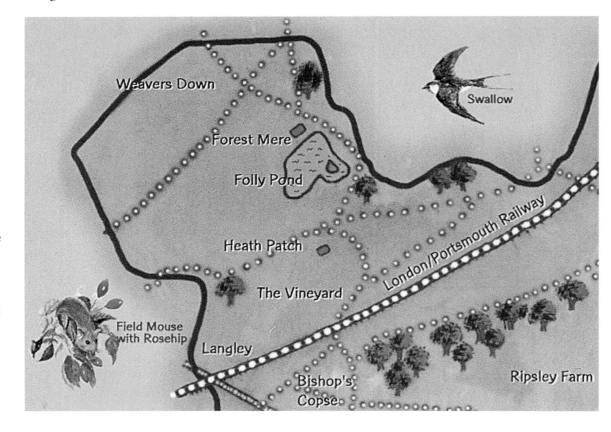

Northchapel

WHEN YOU DRIVE over the county boundary at the top of Cripplecrutch Hill and begin the descent from Surrey into West Sussex there is a subtle sense of change in the landscape as the view begins to widen. You have arrived in the parish of Northchapel. Framing the horizon to the west lies Blackdown – 'dark sentinel of the western Weald' and the highest hill in Sussex – whilst to the east open farmland stretches towards distant woods. Another mile or so further on and the road winds up past Frith Wood, over Valentines Hill and down into Northchapel village.

The Toll House is a notable landmark at the northern end of the village. Built with local brick in Georgian times it is arguably the most

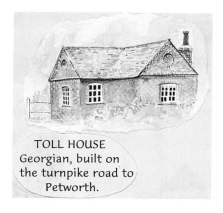

TOLL HOUSE
Georgian, built on the turnpike road to Petworth.

distinguished purpose-built toll house in the county. In the pavement outside there are still cobblestones, a tangible reminder of where the turnpike gate stopped travellers on the road to and from Petworth and beyond. The Northchapel table of tolls showing the price demanded for passing vehicles and animals is now on display at the Weald and Downland Open Air Museum at Singleton.

Northchapel, as its name suggests, was once a chapelry in the north of Petworth parish. The church was built as a chapel-of-ease, probably around the 14th century, saving parishioners the long, and no doubt often muddy,

walk to services at St Mary's, Petworth. It was not until the end of the 17th century that Northchapel became a separate parish in its own right. The present church is the result of Victorian rebuilding, and lies tucked behind houses in the centre of the village. The civil parish covers about three and a half thousand acres, with the southern boundary lying some two miles south of the village, where the wall encompassing Petworth Park begins.

Like many other villages in this part of the Weald, Northchapel evolved from a small wooded settlement, with echoes of its history

SUSSEX OAK
17th century

lying all around in the local landscape and buildings. There is a village green which used to be common land used by villagers for grazing stock and is now a valued recreation ground. Northchapel supports a thriving

ST MICHAEL AND ALL ANGELS
Victorian, rebuilt on site of medieval chapelry. Restored in 1998/9, with five new millennium bells.

sports club, and football matches are a regular event throughout much of the year, whilst on a summer's evening you may catch an all-women's team playing stoolball, a game with particular Sussex associations. In fact stoolball is thought to have originated among woodland communities, the 'stool' being the local term for a tree stump used as a wicket.

Some years ago Northchapel also supported a cricket team – indeed the village has a long cricketing tradition. The legendary 18th-century cricketer, Noah Mann (1756–89), lived here and played with the famous Hambledon Cricket Club that beat an all-England team in 1777. Noah Mann was reputed to be an amazing left-handed player and one of the fastest runners of his day. Cricketing author John Nyren, writing in 1833, explains that he used to run over to Hambledon – a distance of well over twenty miles – to practise. Sadly, Noah Mann met an untimely death by falling into the fire at the Half Moon inn after an evening's drinking.

The Half Moon dates from the 17th century and is typically clad with Sussex bricks and tiles, like many timber-framed houses in the parish. At that time Northchapel lay at the hub of the Wealden iron industry. You can still find traces of the hammer ponds at Mitchell Park Farm to the east of the village and the site of the ironworks in Frith Wood is a regular visit for walkers, especially in springtime when

THE HALF MOON INN
Early 17th century

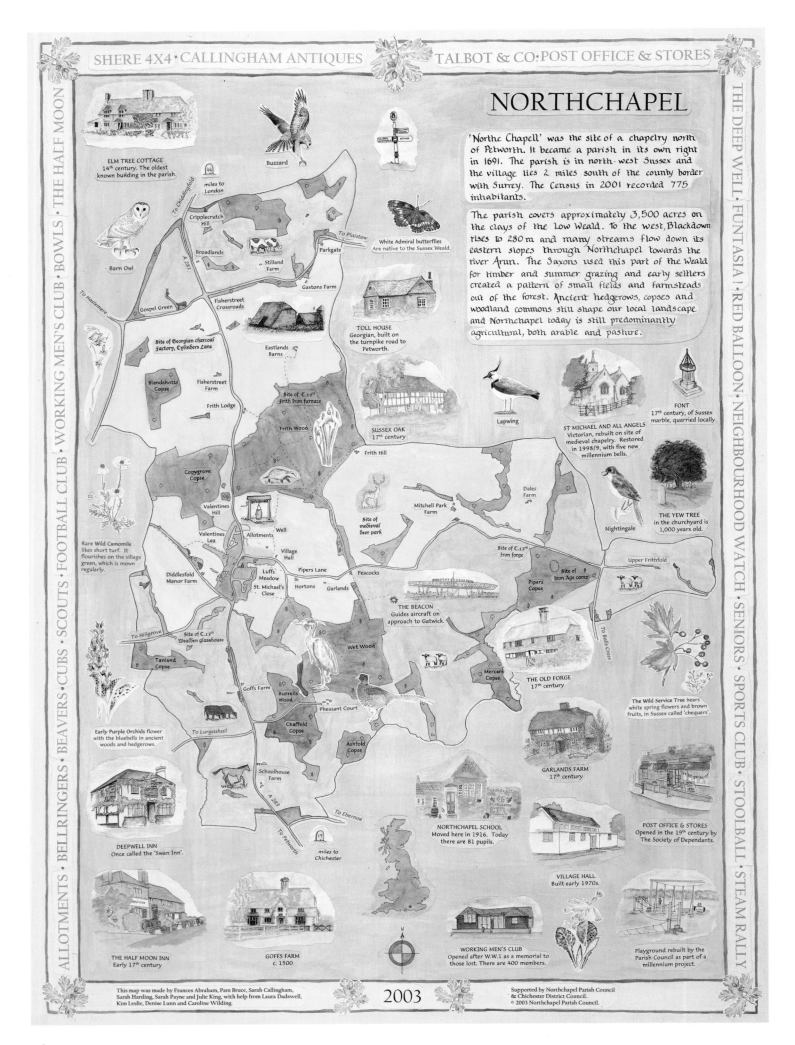

the site of the old furnace is carpeted in snowdrops. The local terrain and plentiful woodland also supported Wealden glass-making centred on Chiddingfold in Surrey during the medieval period that later spread south over the county border into Sussex. Glass kilns were small affairs and thus easily destroyed; quite unexpectedly, in 2000, the remains of an Elizabethan kiln were found in woodland to the south of the village.

When we began thinking about making a parish map we were keen to convey a sense of our heritage, together with the thriving, diverse community of today. Initially we sent questionnaires to every household asking people what they would like to see on the map, inviting any contributions. In the event the team of map-makers all turned out to be women, four of whom were mums with young families. Northchapel has a flourishing primary school and we wanted to include a

NORTHCHAPEL SCHOOL
Moved here in 1916.

POST OFFICE & STORES

contribution from the next generation. So an art competition was organised and the winning picture of the school, by Laura Dadswell aged ten, was selected.

Other key community buildings, such as the church, village hall, working men's club and shop are all depicted in cameos on the map, together with the names of all the organisations around the edge. The village is fortunate to retain a shop and post office when so many have disappeared in rural communities.

There is an interesting story attached to Northchapel Stores. It goes back to the 19th century when a fundamentalist sect, the Society of Dependants, or Cokelers as they were known locally, ran a chain of shops in Northchapel and surrounding villages. Their founder, John Sirgood, a London shoemaker, came south to spread the gospel and drew converts from the local farming communities. By the late 1800s the Dependants had not

only established chapels – the chapel in the village was built in 1871 and is now a private house – they had also ventured into commerce and built their own 'Combination Stores' – 'combination' meaning both spiritual unity and practical social and economic co-operation. They had a strict religious code – worldly pleasures such as dancing, drinking and even marriage were frowned upon – and although numbers began to decline by the early 1900s their businesses continued to flourish, with Northchapel Combination Stores remaining under Dependant control until the 1950s.

Over past years there has been a certain amount of infill-building in the village; traffic on the main road has inevitably increased, and yet Northchapel remains an essentially rural parish. The results of our questionnaire confirmed that the peace and beauty of our landscape are highly valued. The map highlights the woods and farmland, with detailed cameos of plants and wildlife, beautifully painted by local artist Julie King. We wanted to illustrate some of the more unusual species native to this part of the Weald, for example the wild camomile that thrives on the mown grass of the village green. As with other map teams we faced the inevitable constraints of time and space, but once we had begun work the map was completed in about six months. The framed original now hangs in Northchapel Village Hall.

PAM BRUCE

North Mundham

A CLUSTER OF deep gravel-pit lakes – Vinnetrow plus nine more – fills its northern end, tidal saltmarsh and mud scour its southern extremity on Pagham Harbour. Meandering rifes called Pagham and Bremere mark its two sides to east and west, each fed by an intricate web of gutters – the old local name for drainage ditches. This is Mundham's watery necklace, the bounds of a landscape for the most part not much higher than sea level. Old parish-names pay witness to the water that has fashioned these flatlands.

There is Vinnetrow with its original Old English meaning of 'tree of the fen dwellers'; Bremere signifies 'broom-covered marshland'; then there is Marsh Farm, Marshgate and Waterhouse Barn; Brookside is a sanitised euphemism for an older Watery Lane. North Mundham – by which we mean three villages, North and South, and Runcton, with the two hamlets of Fisher and Bowley and two and a half thousand acres of rich cropland – is well watered like a miniature fenland, prone to flooding in the south. The incoming tide is held back by Pagham Wall.

Southwards from North Mundham and Runcton, the houses left behind, the lanes narrow into a lonely windswept landscape. There is a great sense of space and openness, a place to catch the feel of the Manhood Peninsula with its rich alluvial farmland, wind-distorted trees alongside winding lanes disappearing into fields and mud. It's a moody,

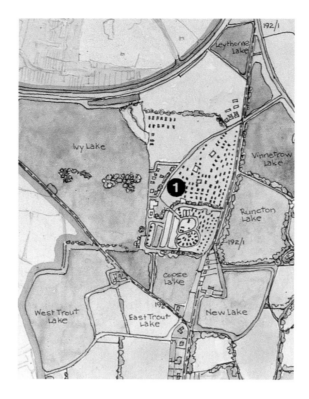

isolated countryside opening into a nature reserve of international importance for its birdlife, where there is still a strong sense of wilderness under the vast open skies.

These skies bring record-breaking hours of sunshine with a winter light factor highly favourable to glasshouse crops. Once Worthing led the country for fruit, flowers and salad crops, but its terminal decline in and around the town last century saw the industry gradually shift westwards along the coastal plain. Mundham and Runcton eventually became a major focus for the UK horticultural industry. The parish has produced some staggering statistics:

- Hazelwood VHB was recently growing 130 million tomatoes a year, 8 per cent of UK production under one of the largest concentrations of glass in the country – 34 acres – including one 25-acre glasshouse, reputedly the largest in the country. Now – as Humber VHB – tomatoes have been reduced in favour of herbs for Tesco and Marks & Spencer – over 9 million pots and punnets a year.

- Madestein UK produces 6 million lettuces and 10 million bedding plants each year for the major supermarket chains, operating the largest fully-automated propagation plant in the country.

- Donaldson's Flowers is the largest UK-owned cut-flower producer, growing an average of 10 million chrysanthemum stems throughout the year. Approximately one-third is supplied to Sainsbury's supermarkets.

- Natures Way Foods operating from its high-tech packing centre at Chichester Food Park at Runcton – operated jointly with its HQ at Selsey – is the leading lettuce distributor in the UK. The company draws on 4,000 acres of land around Chichester and 1,000 acres in Spain, producing 14 billion salad leaves a year for the supermarket trade, mainly for Tesco.

This vast tonnage of food and flowers from Mundham and Runcton – there are over a dozen producers, big and small, in the parish – means heavy traffic with huge refrigerated lorries bound for country-wide supermarkets as well as the continental ferry ports. A massive road-freight operation is carried on from here, much relieved by the Food Park having direct access onto the A259 away from the villages.

The other local attraction for a completely different type of traffic is Lakeside Holiday Village centred on the former gravel pits. Part

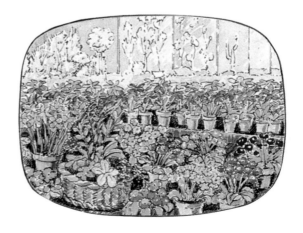

THE MILLENNIUM MAP AD 2000
OF THE CIVIL PARISH OF NORTH MUNDHAM

·THIS MAP SHOWS THE PARISH AT THE START OF THE TWENTY FIRST CENTURY·MOST PARISHIONERS HOPE THAT ITS RURAL CHARM AND PEACEFUL BEAUTY WILL BE RETAINED FOR FUTURE GENERATIONS TO ENJOY·

1. Lakeside Village Caravan Park. fishing, birdwatching and watersports.

2. North Mundham Farm. Early farm cottages progressively expanded to Victorian farm house.

3. St. Stephens Church. Part 13 ct. with major restoration in 1883. The centre of village life during the last millennium.

4. Ostlers' Cottage. Victorian stable converted in 1900.

5. Fletcher House. Original N. Mundham Vicarage. Retirement flats since 1983.

6. Post Office Stores. Post Office since 1903. Now incorporates thriving general store.

The Mundham Map Committee is grateful to the West Sussex County Council and the Chichester District Council as well as to numerous parishioners who have given their support, assistance and advice during the preparation of this map.

Map designed and drawn by Arnold E. Hooton Des RCA

Scale   Public footpath

7. Vinnetrow Farmhouse. 13th century origins with 19th century facade.

8. Walnut Tree Inn. Canalside 'pub' before this section of the Chichester to Arundel canal was filled in.

9. Runcton Nursery. Now growing 8% of Britted kingdom tomato production

10. Runcton Mill. Georgian millhouse on the site of medieval mill.

11. Manor Nursery. Garden centre and contract flower grower.

12. Pagham Harbour Nature Reserve. A top birdwatching area of the south.

13. Runcton Garth and Old Hundred. Converted 17th century farm cottages.

14. Bowley Farm. 17th century facade. The land linked to Thomas a Becket.

15. S. Mundham House. 17 th. front is almost perfect marriage of plainness and ornament.

The parish of 1136 people lies south east of Chichester in the county of West Sussex and is seven kilometres north to south and less than three east to west. Most of the population live in North Mundham and Runcton as it is mainly open farm land to the south. Many of the old farm cottages and barns now house retired people and weekend residents. The high winter light of the area is favourable to the horticultural industry growing tomato salad and flower crops. One greenhouse is the largest in the country at Runcton. Redundant farm buildings house small industrial enterprises and old gravel workings provide lakes for a leisure park, fishing and birdlife.

We are fortunate that further residential and industrial expansion is constrained by planning policy. It is the aim to perpetuate strategic gaps between Chichester and Bognor Regis to preserve the rural character and peace of the area.

CHICHESTER District Council

Lakeside Village. Caravan Park fishing, birdwatching and water sports.

Ostlers' Cottage. Victorian stable converted in 1952.

Runcton Mill. Georgian millhouse on the site of mediaeval mill.

of a chain of leisure parks across south-eastern England, the Runcton site offers caravanning, camping and chalet accommodation amongst its complex of ten large lakes. Stocked for trout and coarse fishing, they also offer windsurfing, water ski-ing and plenty of good bird watching. Being so close to Chichester, the sea and Downs, the village is a major local attraction for this type of outdoor holiday. Although close to the nearby mega-business of lettuce and tomatoes, Lakeside at Runcton seems a world apart. As they advertise it: 'Once across the causeway you enter a world of relaxation. . .'.

Side by side with all this big business there is yet another world – for the local people who have made Mundham's villages and hamlets their home, the world of school, village hall, church and shop. Down the lanes and in its older parts there are links with a history traceable to its first appearance as a place-name. North Mundham in 685 was called 'northra mundan ham' with South Mundham relegated to its position as simply the 'other mundan ham'. Runcton's first mention is much later, in the Domesday Book of 1086, where it is called 'Rochintone'. In 1162 part of Mundham was given to the monks of La Lucerne Abbey in Normandy, a French link revived in the 1980s that has brought regular exchange trips with the villagers of La Lucerne d'Outremer near Avranches.

The historic core of the parish centres around St Stephen's church in North Mundham, originally dating from the 13th century. Nearby are some most attractive properties like Ostlers Cottage, a converted Victorian stable still with the beam that used to haul up fodder for the horses below. Brick-built Pigeon House Farmhouse, with its oak-framed porch, is said to date back at least six hundred years. Its rebuilt and thatched circular pigeon house was once a living larder for the birds eaten in winter. Scattered around the whole parish are a great many picturesque old cottages, and some most substantial farmhouses. There is South Mundham House with its Dutch gables and lovely brickwork, stone-built Bowley Farm House with its Thomas à Becket associations, probably as old as the church, and the

Bowley Farm. 17th century façade, the land linked to Thomas à Becket.

18th-century Runcton Mill, once a corn mill, converted to a private house by the Fry family (of Fry's Chocolate fame).

Fittingly, with so much interest here – neglected by some guide-books that omit it altogether – the millennium celebrations in 2000 were taken as the opportunity to spell out exactly what it is that makes North Mundham the place we know today. John Hole led the team to produce Arnold Hooton's impressive map – significantly the six tomatoes he has featured to symbolise horticulture stand out so well. Profits from map sales, added to lavish sponsorship from the major local glasshouse businesses, then made possible an outstandingly-presented parish history. With text written by John around colour pictures by professional landscape photographer Iain McGowan, North Mundham celebrated itself at the millennium in some style.

KIM LESLIE

Pagham

The Parish Church of St Thomas

Pagham was technically a 'peculiar' – a parish situated within one diocese but under the jurisdiction of another, in this case the Archbishop of Canterbury. Caedwalla, King of Wessex, gifted it to Bishop Wilfrid in the 7th century who transferred it to Theodore, Archbishop of Canterbury, whose successors remain the patrons of the living. It is one of a number of such anachronisms within the diocese of Chichester.

Despite a history stretching back as far as the Bronze Age, and with a significant Saxon presence, Pagham has, until relatively recently, minded its own business in the lee of St Thomas à Becket's Church marooned at the extremity of the parish. Its situation was ex-centric in the parish of Pagham which is a shadow of its former self. It originally extended as far as the Aldingbourne Rife, but lost a substantial acreage when Bognor (in 1871) and Aldwick (in 1934) were carved out of it to become separate parishes.

Pagham's farmland shown on the map emphasises its traditional rural character. Mixed husbandry, typical of a self-contained community, has been replaced by more commercially-orientated farming, initially by cereals and more recently by market gardening and glasshouses. Residential development associated with the expansion of Bognor Regis, has advanced to the edge of the green belt which is being tightened to resist repetitive challenges to its integrity.

The schematic representation of the built-up area on the map conveys an impression of uniformity, but in reality it obscures a wide diversity of buildings, ancient and modern. Recent developments are interspersed with footprints from the past. Becket's Barn is the residue of the rectory (or palace) that accommodated an archbishop and his retinue. Nyetimber comprises an anthology of local building materials – flint and sandstone cottages, brick and eyebrow thatch raised above Pagham Rife which winds its way inland via Lagness and Merston to Oving. Barton Manor, incorporating a medieval chapel, originated as part of the lord of the manor's landholding. The windmill survives as the centre-piece of a retirement complex.

A large proportion of the residential development was taken up by King's Beach Estate, beyond which a

THE CIVIL PARISH OF

PAGHAM

The name Pagham dates
from Saxon times
and means the ham
or settlement of Pacca

Originally it centred
around the church and
harbour area. By the
13th Century, it had become
the 9th largest port and
the 4th wealthiest parish in the
kingdom. A series of storms and
consequent silting up of the
harbour mouth ruined this
prosperity and by the beginning
of the 14th Century Pagham
was omitted from the list of
harbours.

Pagham was a rural
community until the
mid 20th Century when
holiday-makers, who had
come to the seaside
began to settle
here and it
is now one
of the
many
suburbs along
the south coast

PROMOTED AND PRINTED BY
THE BOGNOR OBSERVER

graveyard of redundant railway carriages commandeered a prime position overlooking the sea. A wilderness of pebbles persuaded a motley collection of cyclists, campers and day-trippers to sample the good-life enjoyed by their wealthier counterparts by squatting on the shingle ridge. L'Estrange, The Limit, The Outpost, The Shack are stark reminders of the isolation and remoteness at the end of the line. Ramshackle structures, unmade roads, the absence of services, were components in this primitive and unconventional arcadia. It was a classic example of 'plotland culture' – a pioneering adventure by people on borderline incomes colonising marginal land, practising their libertarian ideals and celebrating their place in the sun.

Officialdom vowed to obliterate the utopian vision. In the face of determined and articulate opposition it failed and astutely performed a u-turn, adopting a policy of co-operation rather than confrontation – 'if you can't beat them – join them'. Owners were encouraged to 'improve' or rebuild and move up-market. The settlers responded positively, thereby inadvertently destroying the raffishly picturesque and betraying the principles of the founders. The colony was planted, went forth and multiplied, despite having been built on a foundation of shifting sands and seeds broadcast on rocky ground, but nonconformity eventually succumbed to bureaucracy – a modern parable.

Church Farm has assumed many guises. Initially it served the purpose its name suggests, but after the Second World War

catered for a new crop – caravans – meeting the demand for a new and popular form of holiday. More recently it has again adapted to changing fashions by re-inventing itself as a holiday village, housing visitors in over one thousand on-site static caravans.

The Bear, the Lion and the Lamb resonate with tales of smuggling and characters such as Sir Alexander Shawe, the litigious 16th-century vicar who assaulted parishioners and kept 'two queans which would seem to be naughty women'. Some modern symbolism can be found in these three historic Pagham inns: the Bear for parish resistance to predators nibbling away at its boundary, the Lion as a show of strength and dignity in the face of adversity, the Lamb for ultimate weakness and vulnerability against the demise of its agricultural heritage perpetrated by those without any affinity for its ancestry.

Pagham Harbour is an exaggeration, but not a misnomer. Once it was the ninth most important port, and fourth wealthiest parish, in the kingdom, exchanging cargoes of corn and wool for coal and wine until a combination of silting, storms and larger vessels killed the trade. At high tide it resembles what the Victorian ornithologist, A.E. Knox, termed 'a great salt lake', with Sidlesham and its former tide mill perched on the edge of the saltings 'like a little Dutch village' above its polder.

The receding tide exposes mud flats that are dissected by tongues of slithering water. The nationally-renowned Pagham Nature Reserve acts as a lay-by and service station for the birds of passage and itinerant wildfowl collecting a free take-away. In the severe winter of 1838–9, Knox observed 'as many as twenty male sparrowhawks hanging on the skirts of a miscellaneous army of little birds . . . harassing their outposts like a hostile party of Cossacks'. Bird watchers travel long distances to see such sights and take pleasure from the abundance or rarity of transient travellers. The harbour has recently been plumbed into an overflow scheme from the Lavant so that a tap can be

turned on for it to receive surplus water in the event of a threat of flooding to Chichester.

In 1929 when King George V was recuperating from a serious illness at Craigweil House – which was then in the parish of Pagham – Queen Mary attended St Thomas à Becket's Church for Sunday worship. Sir Arthur du Cros donated the magnificent rose window to commemorate the visit and the King's recovery. The feel-good factor and reflected glory rubbed off on the parish and persists to the present as it goes about its business with a swagger accentuated by this regal connection.

A king, queen, princes, princesses and paupers, saints and sinners are all woven into Paghams's tapestry of time. Pagham is 'peculiar' not just technically in its parochial allegiance to Canterbury, but because within its fabric is embedded the odd, strange and unusual, reflecting its coastal location, amalgamating land and maritime influences. As an inlet and an outlet, part suburban and part rural, Pagham preserves a healthy balance between being submerged by external factors and keeping its head firmly above water.

SPENCER THOMAS

Parham

6 HOW DO YOU ADEQUATELY convey a "sense of place" when you live in such a spectacularly beautiful countryside as this?' This was the challenging question put to the people of Parham by Glenys Rowe, mastermind behind the parish map. 'Tucked into the east side of the Arun Valley and its Wildbrooks and set against the backdrop of the South Downs as our constant marker, we know that we live in one of the most special areas of West Sussex', said Glenys. 'We asked why people liked living here – "it's unspoilt" they said; "unchanging"; "for its peace and quiet"; "its clear light and air"; "the sky at night"; "the wide open spaces". "I just love the whole place" replied Mrs Christian Hardie – and she lived here for over ninety years.'

They echo the feelings of the famous, some of the literary giants of the early 20th century who came to stay with the publisher Wilfrid Meynell and his poet wife, Alice, at Humphrey's Homestead at Greatham. As much as a home, this was a literary colony where great writers of the day gathered for lazy summer days of charades, croquet and cricket. People like First World War poet Edward Thomas; philosopher Bertrand Russell; novelist D.H. Lawrence who spent several months here in 1915 completing his suppressed earthy book *The Rainbow*; his friend was children's writer and poet Eleanor Farjeon, famed for her hymn *Morning Has Broken*, who knew every inch of this countryside which she tramped with Lawrence. He wrote of its therapeutic effects on his soul, but had to correct himself. It wasn't '*rather* beautiful' but '*very* beautiful' [my italics]. As he told another friend of his days here 'I am very fond of Sussex – it is so full of sky and wind and weather'.

Lawrence soaked up Greatham's atmosphere. Its owl-haunted wilderness of bracken and heathland became the landscape for the tensions he wrote about in *England, My England* where 'savage England lingers' in these 'snake-infested places near the foot of the south downs. The spirit of place lingering on primeval, as when the Saxons came, so long ago.'

Eleanor stayed in a little Rackham cottage, 'a left-over from another time, simple, old and rambling. . . . Coming out of the woods you discovered it like a secret, in a dip below a rough slope crowded with flowers . . . in the distance the saddle of Rackham Down. I can remember no other such enchantment of scent and colour as . . . this dell between the woods.' Early one morning she walked with Lawrence to the top of the Downs 'in one of those white Sussex mists which muffle the

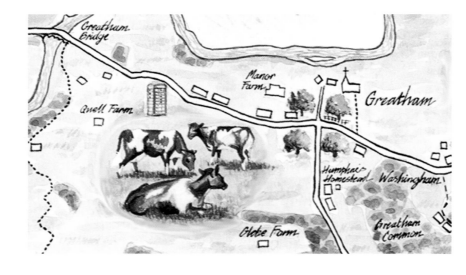

meadows before sunrise, lying breast-high on the earth. . . . The low-lying sun began to melt the mists as we climbed, unpacking the world from its lamb's-wool.' Expressed so beautifully, this was their world of ninety years ago. If they came back today to these same woods, open spaces and downland, they would find little that has changed. And that's why people like it so much today. To them it's heaven.

Thankfully, in times of great change elsewhere, Parham remains rural with great walking and horse-riding country and an abundance of diverse wildlife. At Wiggonholt, the RSPB operates its major Sussex nature reserve through controlled flooding of the Pulborough Brooks, attracting thousands of ducks, geese, swans and waders in the winter.

The civil parish covers not only Parham, but also the ancient ecclesiastical parishes of Greatham and Wiggonholt, plus the hamlet of Rackham, extending from near Pulborough in the north right up to the crest of the Downs and beyond in a quirky finger of land intruding into Burpham in the south. Extensive it may be in acreage, but in terms of population there were only just over two hundred at the last census in 2001. They are listed by their names (and ages if under eighteen) first by place and then by individual property. This is the only West Sussex parish map to include this type of personal information.

Parham House has long been at the centre of many peoples' lives – it has given unity to the surrounding estate and parish as its capital dwelling – so it's highly appropriate that James and Lady Emma Barnard and their two children, Benjamin (then three) and Arthur (then one), take central place in the top margin of the map. Parham, 'the big house'

Parham House

of the parish, is not only one of the great country houses of Sussex, it is one of the finest Elizabethan mansions in England. Simon Jenkins gives it his maximum rating of five stars, putting it into his top-twenty houses in the country (in *England's Thousand Best Houses*). Parham has so many distinctions – to name but two: its collection of historic needlework is said to be 'the finest private collection of embroidery in the country'; another collection relates to the explorer-naturalist Sir Joseph Banks who sailed around the world with Captain Cook in the 18th century. The kangaroo painting he commissioned from Stubbs – shown in the Green Room – is the first western portrait of this hitherto unknown marsupial ever seen in Europe. Parham is a treasure-house of history brought together by generations of owners who have made this their home, now made open to the public in the summer months.

To the north of the house is the four-acre walled garden that includes a 1920s Wendy House. The great lawns to the south of the

Parham House Gardens

house open across the deer park to the little church of St Peter, the only remnant of the old village swept away in the 18th century – their new homes were built at Rackham outside the park. The church then became more of a private chapel than a parish church, complete with private pew with its own fireplace. One rector always knew when his sermon was over-running when the squire started to shovel coal onto the fire!

Two more gems of church architecture are in the parish, the tiny one-roomed, bell-turreted, churches at Greatham and

*Greatham Church
12th Century*

Wiggonholt Church – 13th Century

Wiggonholt, so simple and unspoilt. Arthur Mee tells the story that on visiting the first he remembers being warned 'not to mistake it for a haystack!' as it was so small amongst the fields. Stand by Wiggonholt church and there's the feeling that not too much could have ever happened here, but in the first half of the 18th century it was a mecca for one of the great church scandals of the time – clandestine

marriages where the vicar turned a blind-eye on whom he was joining together. In 1724 when there were only seven families living in the parish, there were seventeen weddings, couples coming from miles away to hide their secrets and no doubt bigamous relationships, aided and abetted by a compliant parson. Up to 1753, when the law was tightened up, hundreds of strangers flocked to Wiggonholt for their mischievous unions.

Rackham, where nearly half the parish lives, may not have a church, but plays its part in bringing the four communities together in the old Victorian school, now used as a village hall. Its setting, by a wide clearing in the shelter of a sandstone cliff topped by ferns, bracken and pines, makes it an idyllic place, and is where the annual Rackham Fête and Flower Show is held. Not only local people, but visitors from afar, swarm here, drawn, says resident John Davison, 'by the magic of a country fair that has remained unchanged since it was first started in 1946 to celebrate the return of peace; in the eyes of fancy it could represent a tradition going back a century or more. Thomas Hardy would have recognised it instantly.'

John feels that 'this extraordinary event epitomises the peculiar charm of this place. We see it in the easy mix of all classes and all ages, a celebration of country skills in showing flowers and vegetables, baking, jams, drawing and painting in an unconscious enjoyment of this exquisite rural setting, and over all a sense of history and the continuity of ordinary lives lived in a similar way and in a largely unchanged environment for centuries.' So many Parham people share these same thoughts for this lovely place, beautifully summed up in this affectionate portrait of their parish.

KIM LESLIE

Petworth

PERHAPS MORE than with most towns, an impression of Petworth will depend on initial assumptions. Approach Petworth as a feudal dinosaur and it will seem so. Come from Heathrow or Gatwick travelling west and see it as the quintessential small English provincial town. It will oblige. Such impressions can be fickle. Here's E.V. Lucas writing in 1904: ' I should not like to make Petworth my home, but as a place of pilgrimage, and a stronghold of architectural taste, it is almost unique'. 'Stronghold of architectural taste'? That has occasionally been challenged. A visitor in 1824 complained that the housing had been 'constructed in every age since the invention

of the art, except the civilized ones'. Even Lucas himself was prepared to trim. By 1915 he was renting a house at Tillington, a mile up the road, and seeking a permit from Lord Leconfield to enter his lordship's private park.

Perhaps it all depends on something as indefinable as smell. Here's an evacuee returning after an interval of some forty years. 'It was a wet day that seemed to hold in the very smell of Petworth. Perhaps it was the rain on the plants that grow in the mossy walls, but it was almost as if I had never left. No other place smells like Petworth and as soon as I was here again I knew that smell.' And the lady had come all the way from New Zealand.

'A wet day'? 'Wetworth' is how the troops billeted here in the autumn of 1914 had rechristened the town by the time they left in 1915. Actually it doesn't rain here any more than it does anywhere else. Perhaps it's that Petworth in the rain loses some of its character? Quite the reverse. Here's a visitor in 1935: 'I think most towns look dismal in the rain. Petworth is not like that. It has a quiet appeal in its narrow winding streets and in its market place which is always present'. Would the ceaseless flow of traffic affect this judgement now? Perhaps only the outsider can say.

Petworth can be reticent. I've known people who have come regularly to Petworth for decades and yet are transported by a first view of the Shimmings Valley. 'We never knew it was there.' Well, Petworth's not going to tell you. It doesn't have to try too hard. Antique shops? In historical terms an essentially

193

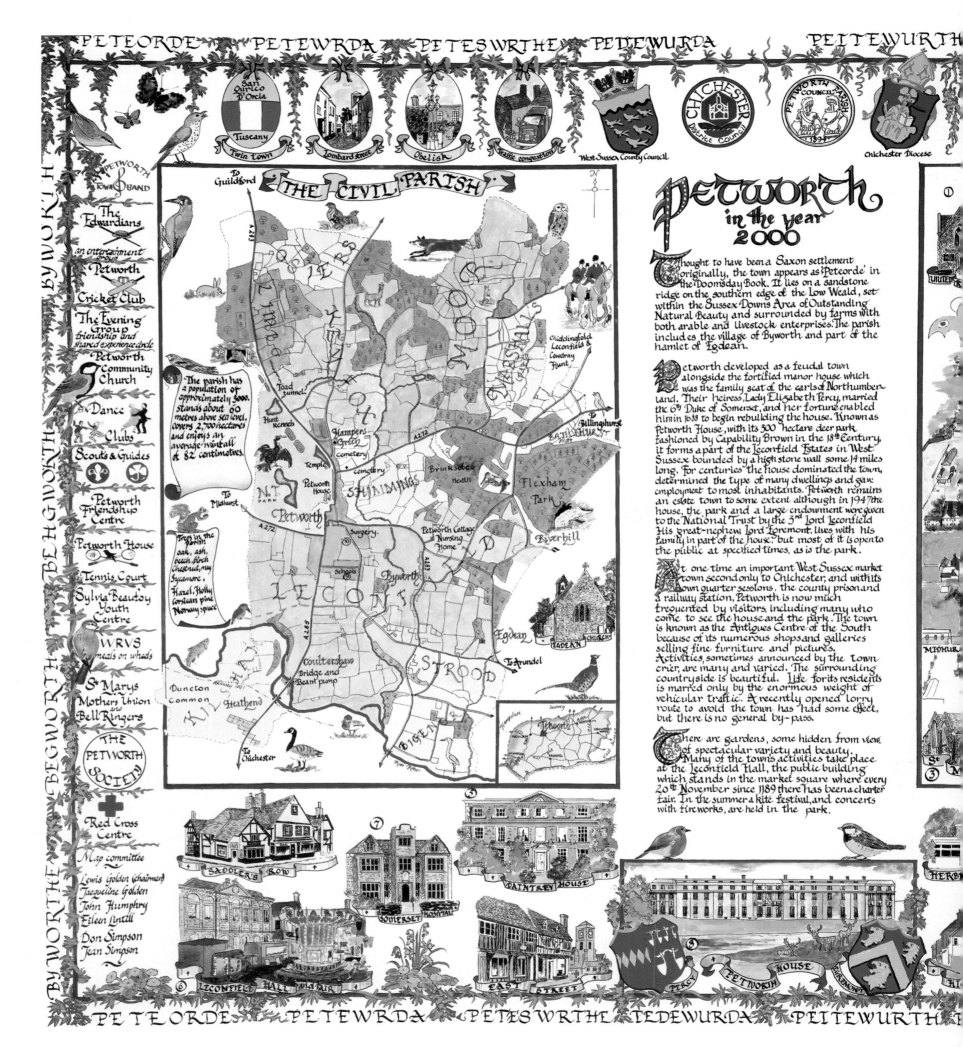

Tuscany
Twin Town

Lombard Street

Obelisk

Traffic congestion

West Sussex County Council

CHICHESTER DISTRICT COUNCIL

PETWORTH PARISH COUNCIL 1894

Chichester Diocese

THE CIVIL PARISH

Petworth Town Band

The Edwardians
an entertainment group

Petworth Cricket Club

The Evening Group
friendship and shared experience circle

Petworth Community Church

Dance

Clubs

Scouts & Guides

Petworth Friendship Centre

Petworth House

Tennis Court

Sylvia Beaufoy Youth Centre

WRVS
meals on wheels

St Marys Mothers Union *and* Bell Ringers

THE PETWORTH SOCIETY

Red Cross Centre

Map committee

Lewis Golden (chairman)
Jacqueline Golden
John Humphry
Eileen Lintill
Don Simpson
Jean Simpson

The parish has a population of approximately 3000, stands about 60 metres above sea level, covers 2,700 hectares and enjoys an average rainfall of 82 centimetres.

Trees in the Parish oak, ash, beech, birch, chestnut, may, sycamore, hazel, holly, corsican pine, norway spruce.

To Guildford

To Midhurst

To Chichester

N.T. PARK

Petworth House

Petworth

Surgery

Schools

Toad tunnel

Hunt Kennels

Hampers Green

Cemetery

Temple

Brinksole Heath

Shimmings

Byworth

Flexham Park

Riverhill

Petworth Cottage Nursing Home

Egdean

EGDEAN CHURCH

Coultershaw Bridge and Beam Pump

Duncton Common

Heathend

KILSHAM

STROOD

BIGNOR

To Billingshurst

To Arundel

PETWORTH
in the year 2000

Thought to have been a Saxon settlement originally, the town appears as 'Peteorde' in the Doomsday Book. It lies on a sandstone ridge on the southern edge of the Low Weald, set within the Sussex Downs Area of Outstanding Natural Beauty and surrounded by farms with both arable and livestock enterprises. The parish includes the village of Byworth and part of the hamlet of Egdean.

Petworth developed as a feudal town alongside the fortified manor house which was the family seat of the earls of Northumberland. Their heiress, Lady Elizabeth Percy, married the 6th Duke of Somerset, and her fortune enabled him in 1688 to begin rebuilding the house. Known as Petworth House, with its 300 hectare deer park fashioned by Capability Brown in the 18th Century, it forms a part of the Leconfield Estates in West Sussex bounded by a high stone wall some 14 miles long. For centuries the house dominated the town, determined the type of many dwellings and gave employment to most inhabitants. Petworth remains an estate town to some extent although in 1947 the house, the park and a large endowment were given to the National Trust by the 3rd Lord Leconfield. His great-nephew, Lord Egremont, lives with his family in part of the house, but most of it is open to the public at specified times, as is the park.

At one time an important West Sussex market town second only to Chichester, and with its own quarter sessions, the county prison and a railway station, Petworth is now much frequented by visitors, including many who come to see the house and the park. The town is known as the Antiques Centre of the South because of its numerous shops and galleries selling fine furniture and pictures. Activities, sometimes announced by the town crier, are many and varied. The surrounding countryside is beautiful. Life for its residents is marred only by the enormous weight of vehicular traffic. A recently opened lorry route to avoid the town has had some effect, but there is no general by-pass.

There are gardens, some hidden from view, of spectacular variety and beauty. Many of the town's activities take place at the Leconfield Hall, the public building which stands in the market square where every 20th November since 1189 there has been a charter fair. In the summer a kite festival, and concerts with fireworks, are held in the park.

SADDLER'S ROW

SOMERSET HOSPITAL

DAINTREY HOUSE

LECONFIELD HALL AND BUR

EAST STREET

PERCY · PETWORTH HOUSE · EGREMONT

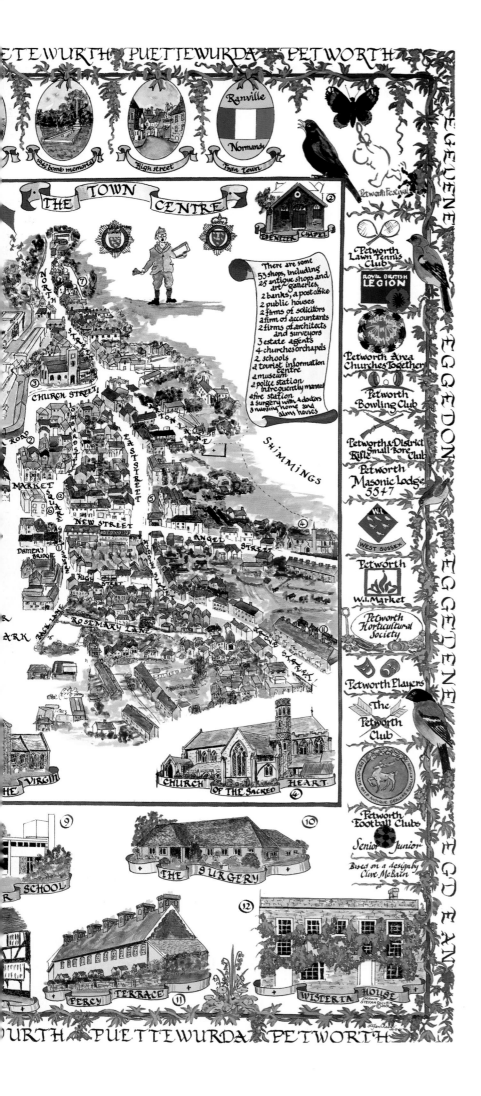

There are some 53 shops, including 25 antique shops and art galleries, 2 banks, a post office, 2 public houses, 2 firms of solicitors, a firm of accountants, 2 firms of architects and surveyors, 3 estate agents, 4 churches or chapels, 2 schools, a tourist information centre, a museum, a police station (infrequently manned), a fire station, a surgery with 6 doctors, 3 nursing home and alms houses.

modern phenomenon. Permanent? Only Petworth itself is permanent. Is there already a hint of change, a movement towards the boutique style? Some lament the proliferation of antique shops, but they do give the streets a buzz and they do bring in visitors.

There's the great house, of course. A hundred years ago, Lucas, in a famous simile, likened Petworth to Pompeii 'with Vesuvius emitting glory far above'. Fair comment then, perhaps, but in these egalitarian times, like Vesuvius itself, somewhat over the top. Petworth House is a National Trust flagship, but the Leconfield Estate remains a flourishing concern. Like the light brown paint that is its livery colour, it can afford to be a little understated. On a smaller scale the popular Cottage Museum in the High Street offers a snapshot of that Edwardian context Lucas suggested.

Not everyone approaches Petworth from outside. Petworth people can view their town with a quizzical eye. Not for them to let the imagination wander. Antique shops? An alien enclave, economic salvation or a bit of both? The jury is out but in any case who are the jury? Property prices are high, Petworth, in the jargon of the estate agents, is 'desirable'. Antique dealers, teachers and others may be castigated for living out of the town, but not everyone can afford a property in Petworth. It's not a problem peculiar to Petworth. Expectation for some can be severely limited. There is a price to pay for Petworth being Petworth and the need for a continuing conscience.

Certainly Petworth can no longer glory in the old self-sufficiency. Petworth shops once catered for Petworth people and a sizeable agricultural hinterland. No more. The old family businesses are only a fading memory now. At Olders you could smell the coffee, buy butter or cheese from bulk and sugar in those conical made-up blue bags. Petworth can lament the loss of the old shops but it cannot call back a day that is past.

And shall we forget the inconsequential? Why does a bust of William of Orange adorn the north front of the Leconfield Hall, capacious, central and listed? No one

knows. One morning in June 1870, at the unsocial hour of three o'clock, 'a large flock of jackdaws settled in the market-place, and so great was the screeching and noise they made, that several persons were awoke out of sleep. After strutting about and fighting in the market-place for some time, they winged their way to some other locality.' So the *West Sussex Gazette* on the Jackdaws' Parliament. I am reliably informed that King William did not bat an eyelid.

Petworth has had its sadnesses too. The casual visitor may come and go without knowing of the heavy loss of life when the North Street boys' school was bombed on Michaelmas Day 1942. The landmark steeple

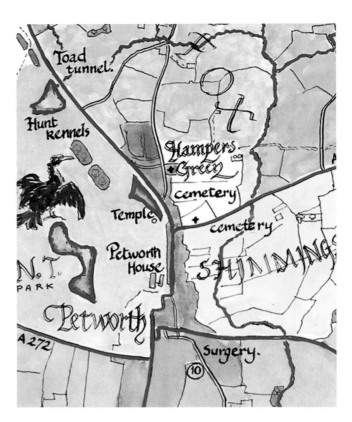

of St Mary's was taken down in 1947. For some the decapitation still throbs. In the Leconfield Hall you will find the maple-leaf flag of Canada. Once that very flag flew from the Peace Tower on Parliament Buildings in Ottawa. It's a gift from the Toronto Scottish Regiment, so early on the tragic scene in 1942, and the reminder of a shared sorrow.

The map encapsulates a moment in a long history. Even five years on there will be changes. Some organisations will have succumbed, others no doubt have come into being. It doesn't matter. Petworth, like anywhere else, must balance change and permanence. Look at the ridged medieval field system, still visible on the slopes of the Shimmings Valley. Take your time, get the light right and see the fields come alive. But, as a Saxon foundation, Petworth was old even before those hills were terraced. Or there's the November fair. In 1273 Edward I tried to hustle Eleanor de Perci into applying for a charter. She refused. The right was prescriptive, age-old. No man could remember its beginnings. Edward's justices-in-eyre took the foundation back to Richard I's accession in 1189, but everyone knew the fair was older than that. Or you might like to look to find dates and names from Petworth's fearsome House of Correction, demolished in 1881. They're etched into bricks re-used to build a wall. Silent testimony to solitary confinement, the rule of silence, the treadwheel, hard labour, 'hasty pudding' and the rest. Petworth, as I've said, can be reticent: you'll need to seek out the wall yourself.

Petworth changes and will change. The estate bell no longer summons men to work, nor do men line up to be paid by heads of department like Mr Wilcox or Mr Allison. Petworth doesn't throw itself at you, but persevere and you'll find a depth you won't readily find elsewhere. 'Almost unique'? Not quite, Mr Lucas, Petworth *is* unique.

PETER JERROME

6 'REMOTE' AND 'ON THE EDGE of a little-known tract of country, untroubled by railways, the most unfamiliar village in which is perhaps Plaistow.' The writer was E.V. Lucas, seeker after little unhurried places for his *Highways and Byways in Sussex*, published in 1904. Memorably he then went on to say that 'Plaistow is on the road to nowhere and has not its equal for quietude in England'.

Twenty-five years later, S.P.B. Mais followed his footsteps in discovering little out-of-the-way places for his own book, simply called *Sussex*. 'I can testify to Plaistow's quietness' he wrote, 'for a friend of mine has recently engaged a housemaid from that village, who at the age of twenty had never seen a train.' (Mais, always digging out unusual characters – he was one of the BBC's first roving reporters for the wireless – loved chancing on stories like this to demonstrate the idiosyncrasies found deep in the countryside.)

So what has changed since Lucas and Mais strayed off the beaten track and discovered Plaistow? (And if you want to find it, ask for 'Plastow', sounding like the first part of 'plasticine' as if there's no 'i' in the name.)

That unstoppable trio of modern life have made their relentless impact – more people, more houses, plenty of cars. Work, leisure and travel have been revolutionised.

But go back a few centuries and then it was Plaistow's poor roads, muddy and full of holes, that were hot topics of conversation. They were so bad that in the 18th century the Archbishop of Canterbury even gave permission for

Kirdford's curate, who served Plaistow, to make the journey there for Sunday worship 'only once in a month or six weeks'. Thus Plaistow was marginalised as an inconvenient neighbour. And even one hundred years ago it took the local carrier two days to get to Guildford and back – now the same return journey, with even a little business in town added on, can be done in just about two hours. Mobility has had dramatic effects on the parish. How else could Ifold – Plaistow's largest concentration of population – have grown to what it is today without the car as a lifeline?

And yet, despite all its growth and change and the liberating effect of the car, there remains a strong feeling of Plaistow's isolation: that it's sealed off by woodland from the rest of the world. 'That's why its enclosure by wooded countryside around its boundaries features on

our parish map', says Maureen Tully who got the whole map-making project going. 'We wanted to show that green is dominant, just as it was in the past.'

And as in the past, it keeps up its sense of independence. It has a shop (with another at Ifold), church, pub and school (serving Kirdford as well), a village hall, a multi-sports facility, sports field and recreation ground. 'All in all it's an ideal village' says Maureen again, 'happily not troubled by too much traffic, well away from main roads and railway lines. Hopefully our map conveys a good feeling for our village atmosphere, with plenty going on, but in the peace and quiet of the countryside.'

Into this countryside of seventy years ago intruded two eccentric developments with enormous consequences for Plaistow: Ifold and Durfold Wood.

They gave this Sussex/Surrey borderland a quite new and distinct identity, echoing the more well-known anarchic world of shacks and shanties going up all along the Sussex coastline; places like Peacehaven, Shoreham Beach and Pagham 'more reminiscent of the American frontier than a traditionally well-ordered English landscape', say Dennis Hardy and Colin Ward in their *Arcadia for All: The Legacy of a Makeshift Landscape* (1984).

They put Ifold's makeshift landscape of the 1930s as the most easterly of a string of inland 'plotlands' that erupted in a line going west from here over half-a-dozen sites as far as exotically-named Palestine in Hampshire.

These isolated places were settled by 'plotlanders' – people who wanted to escape the towns for a little plot in the country they could call their own – their own little arcadia – with plenty of fresh air, peace and quiet and, above all, a sense of freedom. With loose planning laws these new plotlands flourished, their home-made houses, many no more than sheds, were scattered unevenly in plots of varying shape and size along unmade roads with little in the way of services.

Connie Bayley and her family were amongst the earliest Ifold settlers in the mid-'30s after reading an advertisement in the London papers for cheap land out in the country. The old Ifold Estate was being broken up and the mansion demolished. Woodland plots – 75 feet by 200 feet – costing £15 each, opened up a whole new way of life for ordinary working people. (With wages about £3 a week, this only represented five weeks' work.) At first here just at weekends, they lived in a shed they called Myosotis – a neighbour's was Oikesis, very suggestive of their individualistic way of life. There was no main drainage, no electricity, water came from local springs, the roads rough and potholed. But those who came really wanted to be here and were very happy with their new homes.

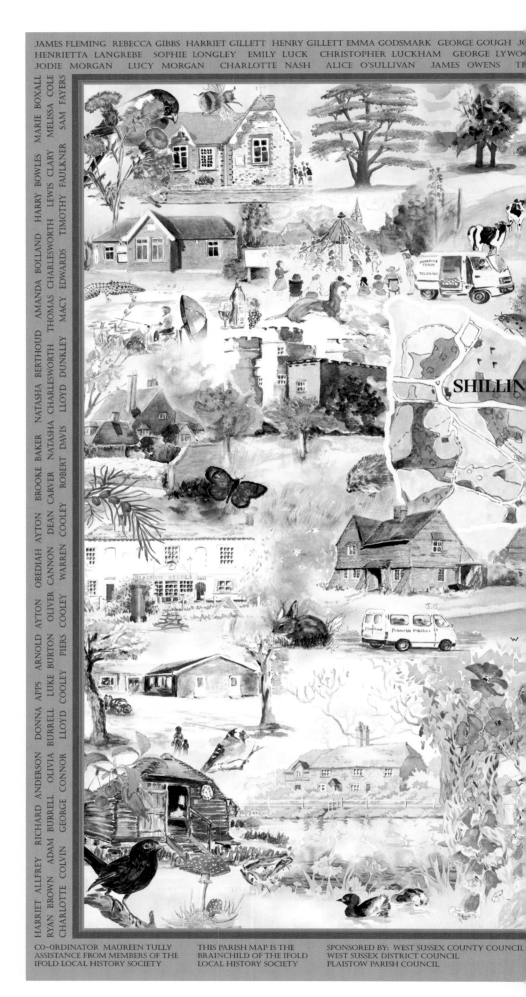

JAMES FLEMING REBECCA GIBBS HARRIET GILLETT HENRY GILLETT EMMA GODSMARK GEORGE GOUGH JO
HENRIETTA LANGREBE SOPHIE LONGLEY EMILY LUCK CHRISTOPHER LUCKHAM GEORGE LYWO
JODIE MORGAN LUCY MORGAN CHARLOTTE NASH ALICE O'SULLIVAN JAMES OWENS TH

SHILLIN

CO-ORDINATOR MAUREEN TULLY
ASSISTANCE FROM MEMBERS OF THE
IFOLD LOCAL HISTORY SOCIETY

THIS PARISH MAP IS THE
BRAINCHILD OF THE IFOLD
LOCAL HISTORY SOCIETY

SPONSORED BY: WEST SUSSEX COUNTY COUNCIL
WEST SUSSEX DISTRICT COUNCIL
PLAISTOW PARISH COUNCIL

OCK CLEMENTINE HARDCASTLE GEORGIA HARDCASTLE STEPHANIE HILLMAN CHARLEY HILLS ELISE HOUNSLOW CHLOE JOHN JOSEPH JOHN THEA JOHN PHILIPPA KIRKHAM STEPHANIE KIRKHAM
ACK JAMESMACKINNON LAURA MACKINNON LUKE MACRAE MATTHEW MASSETT EDWARD MCCORD LAURA MCCORD MATILDA MEANOCK AARON MORGAN GEMMA MORGAN
NSTHOMAS PATIENT THOMAS PAYNE SOPHIE PEACOCK WILLIAM PEGLEY BENJAMIN PHILLIPS SOPHIE PLUMB THOMAS REDFORD JACOB REYNOLDS JOSHUA REYNOLDS

DURFOLD WOOD

IFOLD

PLAISTOW

CLARY RICHARDSON EMILY SAGE HENRY SAGE GREGORY SMART JESSICA SMART MELANIE SMITH MEGAN SPALDING HENRY STEPHENSON SHOLTO VAN DEN BOGAERDE EMMA VARIDAL GEORGE WARD HOLLY WHITE OSCAR WIGART HELENE WOOD . CHILDREN OF PLAISTOW COUNTY INFANTS SCHOOL SUMMER TERM 1999 HEADMISTRESS MISS B. CLAUSON. PLAISTOW COUNTRY INFANTS SCHOOL WAS GIVEN TO THE VILLAGE IN 1869 BY JOHN NAPPER OF IFOLD HOUSE . ARTISTS:- JANET AUSTIN ANN BROOKS JO GOULDER PEGGY HARMAN GWEN MILCHAMP WENDY RAFLEY STELLA RIBBENS EILEEN RIGHT

west sussex county council

Y IFOLD LOCAL HISTORY
COMMEMORATE THE
2000

PLAISTOW PARISH

POPULATION OF THE
PARISH CENSUS IN 1991
WAS 1774

WINTERTON HALL GIVEN
TO THE VILLAGE BY EARL
WINTERTON IN 1908.

THE PRESENT HOLY TRINITY
CHURCH WAS BUILT IN 1810
IFOLD HOUSE BUILT IN 1812
DEMOLISHED 1936

PLAISTOW COUNTY INFANTS
SCHOOL WAS GIVEN TO THE
VILLAGE IN 1869 BY JOHN NAPPER
OF IFOLD HOUSE.

SHILLINGLEE HOUSE ONCE THE HOME
OF EARL WINTERTON WAS BURNED DOWN
DURING THE 2ND WORLD WAR WHEN
OCCUPIED BY CANADIAN SERVICEMEN.

The old granary

Connie's memories weren't of problems but of the sheer joy of being out here in the country. 'The grass verges were alight with wild flowers. Scent of the honeysuckle pervaded the air. The scolding of the blackbirds, the humming of the bumble bees were unforgettable. Crisp fresh air made us so alive!' Asked why she had come here in the first place, she replied: 'I wanted to find myself'.

The dreams of these original plotlanders were shattered when Petworth Rural District Council imposed stringent planning regulations in the mid-1950s, leading to the removal of their little shanty homes. A sad exodus of pioneers followed, land changed hands, the shacks and shanties pulled down and new development, mainly bungalows, created the basis of today's community in the woods. Still reflecting something unusual about themselves, with wayward names like Roundthebend, and Costa Porsche, these homes, hidden in the woods, perpetuate the original character of ancient Ifold as a 'fold' or clearing in the forest. There's the feeling of leafy suburbia, but without a nearby town centre and its amenities – it is actually a

Scout Hut

'suburb' of several towns some miles distant where many work, like Horsham, Guildford, Crawley and Gatwick. But despite the modern appearance of these homes, their original eccentric roots can still be detected amongst its residents, proud and happy to be here.

Ifold's growth impacted on Plaistow so much that it was one of the main reasons that Plaistow was made into a new civil parish by separating it off from Kirdford. Long before the creation of civil parishes at the end of the 19th century, when there were just ecclesiastical parishes, Kirdford, with its church, was the parent parish, Plaistow a mere chapel-of-ease appendage. In 1851 there were seven times more people in Kirdford than in Plaistow. But like the cuckoo in the nest, by the 2001 census, Plaistow's population of 1,856 stood at just more than double that of Kirdford's 912, with more than half this Plaistow total belonging to Ifold, ample demonstration of Ifold's local significance in the wider community.

Plaistow's countryside is full of surprises with wonderful views across to the Surrey hills and the South Downs; fields with emus, llamas

Plaistow Stores

and Highland cattle; the opportunity to find one of Sussex's least-known rivers, the Kird, starting its life in the grounds of Shillinglee with its Deer Tower and China Bridge; remains of medieval glass-making and ironworks, and the old canal – now being restored – along paths, green lanes and sunken roads, past names like Nell Ball, Barbary and Quennells, each with a tale to tell. Remote this intriguing countryside may be – 'on the road to nowhere' – but that's its appeal.

KIM LESLIE

Poling

It all started with four ladies sipping coffee, then we formed a millennium committee and the village set up the Poling 2000 Action Group. But what shall we do to celebrate the millennium? I bumped into Pauline Halls who was producing the Arundel Parish Map and she introduced me to Kim Leslie of West Sussex County Council who came and spoke to an enthusiastic audience in the ballroom at Manor Farm. We decided to make the Poling map.

Valerie Shepherd remembers vividly how it got underway, all the research, walking, talking – 'my husband Norman even hired a Cessna for aerial photography paid for by a couple of residents'. Getting to know 'every tree, lump, bump and dimple' in the parish, Poling's Action Group captured its landscape in beautiful detail with a map covered with interest from end to end. Yet apart from locals, how many people really know anything about this place

as they thunder along the A27 through its northern reaches? Poling's great fortune is that the old village still hugs a little country lane going nowhere but brooks and marshland. And who could say that the following, published in 1919, wasn't written for today? – its essence now still much as it was then:

It may be doubted if one in a thousand of the inhabitants of Sussex could say whereabouts in the county Poling is situated, or is, indeed, aware of its existence. It does not lie on a main road, and even the bye-roads on which the straggling village is centred form a cul de sac. . . .

Poling Street runs north and south from the high road, till it joins a narrow road going east and west, and the village is dotted about the junction of these two roads. This east to west road is practically impassable in winter though it leads directly to Lyminster, and must anciently

have been of some importance: and on the eastern side it dwindles to little more than a farm track on its way to Angmering. Besides these, there is another uncertain track or causeway over the marsh, which crosses the 'rife' on its way to . . . Littlehampton: but a stranger trying to find his way from that pleasant sea-side resort to coy and retiring Poling, will, in nine cases out of ten, get bogged, or find himself cut off by the 'rife'. The remoteness of Poling is still a fact to be reckoned with. . . .

A very noticeable characteristic is the deeply sunk level of the lanes . . . which . . . marks an old inhabited country. This peculiarity is very noticeable in the north-to-south road. . . . The situation and surroundings of the church are most attractive and quaint. There is no road directly up to it, but it is approached by paths and stiles, and appears to be half in somebody's back garden and half in somebody else's farmyard.

Farmland, narrow lanes, flint walls, cottages and some new homes and a few barns, old and traditionally built; Poling survives as a rare glimpse of what Sussex coastal plain villages used to be like before the builders flooded their

fields in concrete, a precious place still in tune with its setting. Just across the fields, land-hungry Rustington and Angmering show what might have been Poling's fate but for the watery barrier that has kept it long isolated – the marshland of the Black Ditch marking the parish boundary on both its southern and eastern sides. Feeding the Arun, the Ditch has been vital in preserving Poling – like neighbouring Lyminster – as a place apart.

Christopher Robin

The Black Ditch springs from the low chalklands north of the A27 around Hammerpot, making its first bold appearance as the Decoy Ponds on Poling's boundary. This place has become the stuff of literary legends, for here that most famous bear in the world found half his name when A.A. Milne's family spent happy days at Decoy Cottage in the early 1920s. Christopher Robin befriended the swan on the old Decoy Pond, calling him Pooh 'because, if you call him and he doesn't come (which is a thing swans are good at), then you can pretend that you were just saying "Pooh!" to show how little you wanted him'.

Then 'when we said good-bye, we took the name with us, as we didn't think the swan would want it any more'. So whilst Edward Bear became Winnie after a famous black bear in London Zoo, he was Pooh after a Poling swan!

In just a few steps across the Poling fields the gap closes between children's fantasy and starkly-contrasting echoes of war once played out in the skies above. Poling's radar station was a major landscape feature for years during and after the Second World War, still vividly remembered by those who have spent so much of their lives around here. From these fields seven huge lattice-work towers probed the skies for approaching enemy aircraft, part of a great chain of radar stations along the southern and eastern British coastline, the first operational defensive radar system in the world. Today Radar Cottages, the receiver block, water tower, pillbox and its blast wall tell of Poling's vital link in Britain's wartime defence. A tribute 'Radar Remembered' hangs in the church under the RAF flag.

Poor box in the church

Communication Centre

But these days are long gone, the towers long demolished. Poling's at peace with its woods and fields, conveyed in all the fine detail and beautiful colouring of the parish map. Villagers, including young children, painted the vignettes such as the plants, birds, animals, insects and houses, all assembled by Valerie Shepherd around her four seasons corner pieces and seeds-of-time cartouche – a dandelion seed head – incorporating various spellings of Poling's name over the centuries. The names of all those living in Poling in the year 2000 are recorded in the blue border, this and all the other text scripted by David Turgoose in his beautiful architectural hand.

The original map now hangs in the little church down by the farmyard, an appropriate place as the church already brings together so much communal history of this tiny parish. In the churchyard, commemorated in the language of Uganda, rests Sir Harry Johnston (1858–1927), British administrator in Africa, explorer, author and painter, discoverer of a large number of African flora and fauna, notably the okapi, scientifically named after him *okapi johnstoni*. He retired to St John's Priory in the village in 1906 from where he pleaded for local public opinion to 'eschew ugliness', stop 'the needless destruction of landscape and objects of historical interest . . . save the wild flowers from extermination' and that 'Sussex must be saved from the speculative builder'. He would be happy that Poling still stands apart amongst the fields.

KIM LESLIE

7. BACON HALL

Glebe Field.

JA.

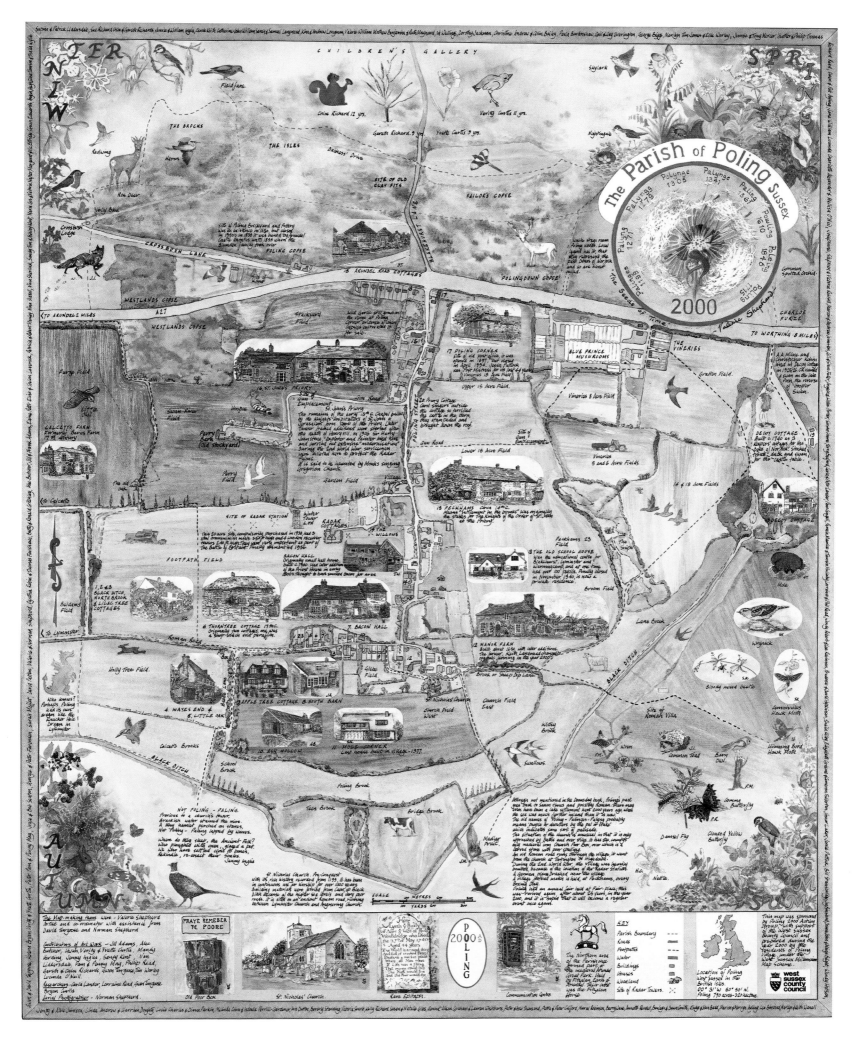

The Parish of Poling Sussex

2000

The Seeds of Time

203

Pulborough

THE INLAND WATERS of Sussex have long been renowned for their rich bounty of fish and fowl: the Arun, its longest stretch and principal river of the county, traditionally providing three of the Seven Good Things of Sussex for the lover of fine and tasty foods: Arundel Mullet, Amberley Trout and Pulborough Eel. Once so valuable, they were within the jurisdiction of the water-bailiff, 'the ancient officer on ye high streame' responsible for the preservation of all the 'swanns, fowle and fish' with oversight of all tackle and nets used to 'entrap or deceave'. His list of notable fish, written down in the early 17th century, included 'the winding Eels and Griggs' (i.e. young eels or elvers). By customary use, eel-men were forbidden to use pritchers (eel spears) along the Arun's banks. Times have changed, new controls are in force, but Pulborough waters still give good fishing and plenty of good slippery eels – one local dish suggests stewed eel eaten with fine bread and butter and parsley sauce.

Pulborough is quite inseparable from its waters, its setting captured in the naming of modern developments. Arun Prospect, River View, Swan View, Wildbrooks Close, Little Rivermead are the ties people want with the watery countryside on their doorstep. Every local history, every guide-book, weaves its

fortunes with those of the Arun and its tributary the Rother that come together here. The castle at Park Mound was sited to defend the junction of these two rivers. Standing high on its sandstone ridge, Pulborough commands the river crossing from Chichester to London by the great Roman highway, Stane Street – not for nothing has it been dubbed our local 'Gibraltar' for its role in guarding all passing traffic. The older picturesque bridge is now bypassed by a more modern replacement (of 1936 and aesthetically most pleasing in stone), but Pulborough itself has not been so favoured, so the route laid down by the Romans some two thousand years ago still pours its heavy burden of traffic through the narrow crossroads down by the river.

But once there was traffic of a quite different type, in the barges and other craft that came to Pulborough's river banks to its one-time wharves and small dock. Excursionists, picnickers and fishermen have been attracted here ever since the Victorians opened up the local countryside when the railway came to Pulborough in 1859. Punts and skiffs for hire did good business for those coming for pleasure and sport.

Pulborough's modern development is abruptly halted by the brooklands. Its long southern edge is no straggly border but a neat and tidy line following the river and its wetlands, geography still clearly dictating Pulborough's shape along its banks. Extensive flooding has not been unknown in the lower reaches of the village, across the meadows and over the main road southwards. Centuries-old cottages were built around the Arun Valley on little plateaux above high water-mark, one local resident saying that it has not been

uncommon in the past for flooded homes to be condemned unsafe: 'We had to put duckboards along all the passages downstairs and walk along to our bedrooms in wellingtons'. Given unusually high rainfall, Pulborough can easily be cut off from its southerly neighbours across the low-lying causeway to Hardham, although, as an indication of the serious risk to property, active steps like raising the road and deepening the river have reduced the chances.

In his *Highways and Byways of Sussex* first published a century ago, E.V. Lucas put it more picturesquely: 'Pulborough has no invader now but the floods, which every winter transform the green waste at her feet into a silver sea, of which Pulborough is the northern shore and Amberley the southern . . . . The village stands high and dry above the water level, extended in long line quite like a seaside town.' And just like being at the seaside – although miles inland – Pulborough's waterside is tidal right up to here and even beyond.

The view southwards emphasises its superb position. When Winifred Cousins wrote of her long life in the village spanning most of last century, it was the view over the brooklands that prompted her feeling that 'there are so many wonderful things in this world of ours which are simple and free and there is so much

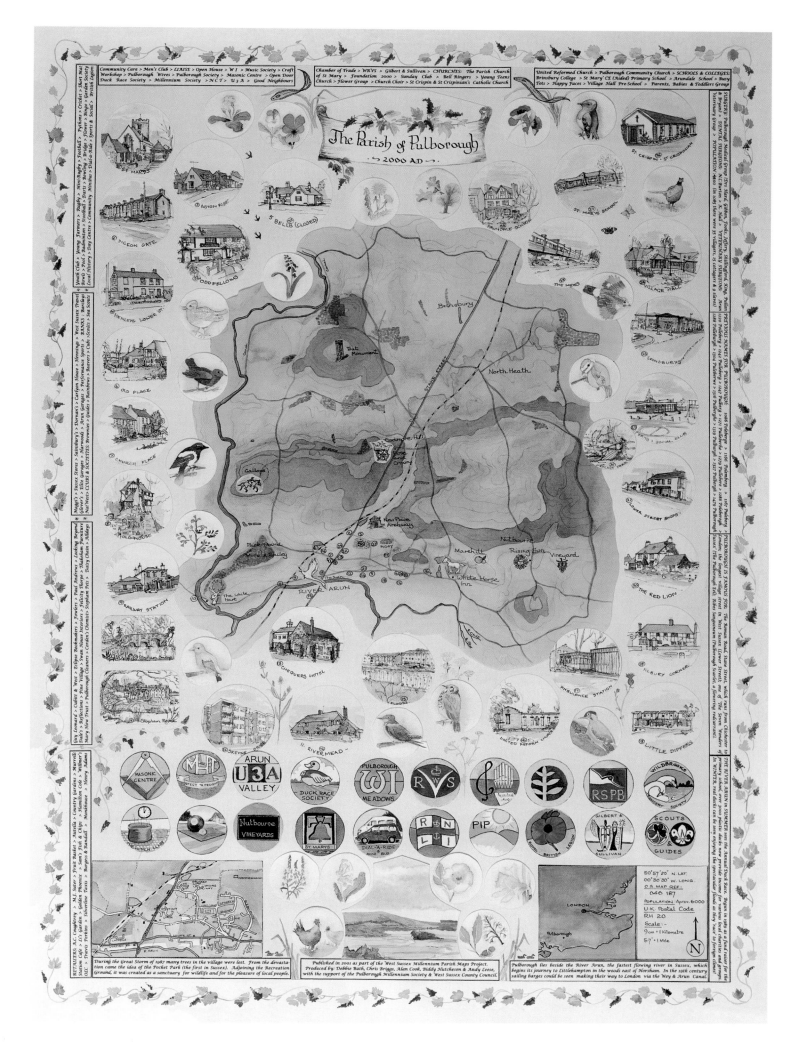

beauty all around'. She had the happy gift of finding so much pleasure in Pulborough's ordinary and everyday surroundings, revelling in the adventures to all the little secret places in the parish she had found: Forty Steps, Frog's Hole, Black Gate, Steppy Lane, The Hollow, The Rocks, Blue Doors. Winifred questioned whether Pulborough's newer residents had ever heard of these names.

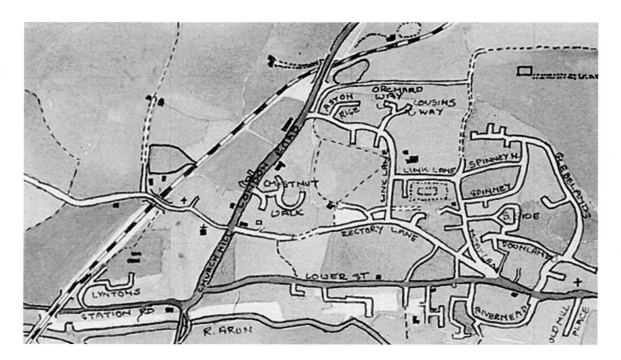

And as eels once brought fame to Pulborough's name, so do birds today, Pulborough Brooks being home to the RSPB's major Sussex nature reserve, a nationally significant wetland, bringing thousands of visitors, avian and human, through the seasons. It has been good for the birds, good for tourism and good for education. Its grassy meadows, dyked and ditched, watered by controlled flooding in winter, transform into an open-air classroom for wetland studies through its visitor and education centre. Pulborough's influence has been enormous in countryside education.

More Pulborough wildlife is given prominence on the parish map – the outer frieze is decorated with sprays of a deep red flowering currant known as Pulborough Scarlet. First discovered and brought on by Jim Knight of Cheal's Nursery in the 1930s, it still flourishes around the parish, kept going around Pulborough's gardens by local stalwarts like Biddy Hutcheson who ensured its inclusion on the map when she led the map team. (How many other plants can claim to be named after Sussex towns and villages?)

If its waterside and rural environment is one major focus, then others are to be found in its built environment. Upper Street, around the church, is the old village centre that grew up alongside an ancient east-west ridgeway, its course followed by Church Place and Rectory Lane. This is the historic core of old Pulborough. Then down through the sandstone cutting called Church Hill lies Lower Street. Here shops and services are strung out along one of Sussex's longest and narrowest high streets. Change is now being felt here as two new major supermarkets in London Road create yet another focus as retail competition shifts northwards.

Pulborough's noteworthy residential expansion has been immediately to the south of Lower Street on the old meadows and gardens of older properties. This is the concentration of flats and apartments piled high above the Arun's flood plain, setting the tone for urban living by the riverside. Seen from the brooks to the south they give Pulborough a long bulky edge, like a townscape dropped into the countryside. One part village, one part town – or as Ian Nairn puts it in Pevsner's guide 'a puzzling place, undecided whether to be village, town, or suburb'. Whatever it is, its age-old functions persist today. It's still a traffic funnel and principal centre for the upper Arun Valley that gives Pulborough its outstanding setting in the countryside displayed across the parish map.

KIM LESLIE

Rogate

ROGATE, LIKE REIGATE, was the medieval roe-deer gate or pass into the protected forest. Those deer were under forest law: enclosed, valuable, hunted only by kings and nobles. Before this it is not difficult to imagine Celts and Romans in the dense, dark forest of Rogate's Anderida. This is where the great sand-reared oaks were to be found for the iron furnaces and bloomeries. There will be slag piles near the ponds, but below those will be the flint arrow heads and skin scrapers, knives and axes of the boar- and bison-hunters who lived safely on the nearby chalk hills of Harting to the south, to which Rogate was joined at Domesday. There is a furnace pond near Hill Brow, and the dark and coiling Rother, stained sometimes and foaming as beer, had its water-driven mills.

Habin Bridge

Today Rogate still has its commons and coombes, its marshes and meadows, a people's parish of little enterprises. It has a hobbit history, a dense matrix of smallholders and farmers: fifty-four of them just before the Civil War, the largest owning only 120 acres, with twenty cottagers all keeping pigs and geese, hens and sheep.

The Tudor houses had rotted to their stumps; stone was the new saviour of the fairly prosperous and so the houses have remained through the ensuing four or five centuries. The blacksmith, the baker, the tailor and the bucket-maker beat or sewed their ways to a living in this hillocky damp relic of the ancient seabed.

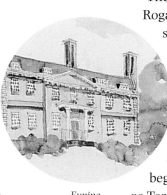
Fyning

People even of later centuries probably never saw the sea, though they may have gawped at the blue-serged sailors of Nelson's navy on their way to Portsmouth and Southampton with cracks of the day from the city of London. They would have walked to Petersfield fair and market place, a rare treat and a distance. They would have tickled for trout in their tawny river and knew where to butt-fork for sea trout running home from the Atlantic by way of Littlehampton.

The Rother is still the jewel of the parish, and Habin Bridge one of its crowns, for there are several of like character. They are robust with round arches and cutwaters like the bows of ocean ships, and have carried the community for five hundred years. Variously spelt Habin, Haben, once even Hawbedyne, its name anciently tangled in the thickets of thorn enclosures, the medieval haga or hawthorn. It was monks who originally built the local bridges just as they tamed the Rother's waters with Rogate's two corn mills, at Habin and Durford. The abbey at Durford, on the extreme edge of the parish, almost in Hampshire, was home to Premonstratensian canons; those white-clad, austere Augustinian off-shoots from France, whose fortunes dominated Rogate's life until dissolved by the fanaticism of Henry VIII in 1537. The abbey stones rose again into Durford ('deer ford') Farm, until they were knocked down once more in 1784 by Lord Stawell to help build his manor.

There are a few fine houses hidden in the Rogate hills. Fyning is Georgian and stuccoed with seven bays. The name runs on north and south from these sandy hills to Fyning Common, and Fyning Moor, and means simply marshy place. The hamlet of Terwick, a model of modern proper planning integrated sensibly into the character of these hills, has another plain beginning for its name: its earliest reference as Tortewyck embodying the Old English word 'tord' – vulgarised into 'turd' – was just a dung heap. Its metamorphosis into modern 'Terwick' hides the truth and sweetens the pill! The Red House in Rogate was latterly of interest to students of ecology when it was used by King's College, London, as a field station to study the ecosystems of Sussex.

The parish does indeed have its rich share of wildlife, with kingfishers and grey wagtails breeding along the Rother; buzzards and sparrow hawks among forty species in the woods and a rare colony of woodlarks breeding among skylarks on the Site of Special Scientific Interest on Chapel Common's western meadow.

The collection of ponds and small lakes between Harting Combe and Canhouse Lane are rich in dragonflies; grass snakes abound together with newts, toads and frogs. There are white admiral butterflies with other high-forest species like the silver-washed fritillary in the woodland glades, and silver-studded blues breed on the heather and gorse of the commons. The parish has perhaps four hundred species of wild flowers that include lesser gorse, spotted orchid, southern marsh orchid, bird's foot and marsh violet.

Rogate's riches have been captured by pen and pictures in a book to treasure: *Walking with Fancy*, published by Country Life in 1943. Through the genius of naturalist E.L. Grant Watson and wood engravings by Charles Tunnicliffe, one of the greatest 20th-century

Wenham

illustrators of nature, we feast on the landscape of Wenham, Watson's Rotherside home to the west of the village. In words and pictures they take us around the farm, through its meadows and marshland, its orchards, animals and wildlife, with its old farm buildings that 'have quite forgotten themselves in the landscape. They have been there so long that they are part of it . . . and have found harmony with the rhythm of the changing seasons, and in their conservative manner seem almost to have achieved the eternal.'

The small roads of the parish cross and wander like its changing history, but at one point the most modern meets with the most ancient. On the very edge of the parish the Portsmouth-London railway touches the Roman road; two single-minded ideals in a hurry – as straight as possible was the only answer.

At the centre of the village the church of St Bartholomew is as changed as the parish history with bits of Norman and Plantagenet culture clinging onto the mainly much

wealthier Victoriana. The church has a splendid Noterman organ almost a century old, rebuilt in 1922, and properly boasts the three-hour peal of bells of 5,040 changes in 1905. One of its out-of-tune bells was recast to commemorate the Reverend Canon Arthur Simpson, the Sussex parson from Fittleworth who was the first to understand and describe the science of modern bell-tuning. From the 1890s all UK bell foundries adopted 'Simpson-tuning'.

Nowadays the locals have become travellers again to the cities, but on return are blessed by the peace their hobbit ancestors knew too well. Today they learn dancing and foreign languages, trip abroad and join local clubs to meet their friends. Rogate village itself on the A272 is its centre, its church, general store and White Horse pub at the heart of this historic, hilly and very happy parish.

RICHARD WILLIAMSON

St Bartholomew's Church at the centre of the village

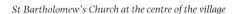
Mouse-time dramatics

PARISH OF ROGATE ~ 2000 AD.

Selsey

SELSEY'S A PLACE APART, a little bit of Sussex that has slithered out to sea. It's literally the end of the road; at Selsey Bill we are at the most southerly point of Sussex. 'Bill', just as in Portland Bill, probably comes from its meaning a pointed bit of land looking something like a bird's beak or bill.

It marks the very tip of the distinctive low-lying countryside south of Chichester known as the Manhood Peninsula, thrusting the county southwards into the Channel. The London, Brighton and South Coast Railway once advertised this 'healthy rural village', highlighting its location '3 miles into the sea'.

Selsey has always been much affected by water. In distant days this little place was once all at sea, literally an island – the Isle of Seals.

A seal basks on its rock at the top of the map. By the early 18th century the area was known as Selsey Peninsula – 'nearly an island'. The sea was on all three of its sides, cut off from surrounding villages by what was then a much more extensive Pagham Harbour that almost reached the shoreline west of Selsey. Even a fairly recent guide to Selsey insists that it is still technically an island because the Broad Rife, linking the head of Pagham Harbour to the sea towards Bracklesham Bay, completes the water boundary around the parish.

This liquid landscape of rife-lands and marsh has always cut off Selsey from easy contact with villages on the western side of the Manhood. The drive to Bracklesham, just three miles away as the seagull flies, becomes a circuitous journey of more than twice the distance around the edge of the marshes. Nature still wins. People still talk of the 1998 tornado, floods and the threat of the sea claiming Selsey as an island once more. On stormy days it's a very elemental place.

Stand on the south-westerly tip of Sussex in heavy weather and be humbled by the might of the elements. Face stinging, eyes squeezed to slits and deafened by the noise of the tireless muscle of the sea grinding billions of pebbles, you feel an exultation tinged with fear such as Selsey folk have felt for centuries.

This was how Alan Stanley in the *West Sussex Gazette* captured the feel of the place one dark winter's day.

Look for the ferryboat with its two passengers being rowed over the water. This spot on the main road, still known as the Ferry, has always marked the one major route onto the island. Even today many Selsey residents have a distinct 'island mentality' so that when they cross the bridge at the old ferry-point they think of themselves as back home. This is a real boundary, reinforcing the idea that the parish is a separate place, somewhere very special. Despite modern developments this 'specialness' isn't at all difficult to find. Clues pepper the map.

It's part of a very historic and holy landscape. The first invading Saxons – Sussex means the kingdom of the South Saxons – made their first landfall at a spot on the former shoreline now under the waves off Selsey. St Wilfrid came this way to spread Christianity in the late 7th century and here built his monastic cathedral at the place we know in Selsey as Church Norton, the predecessor of Chichester Cathedral. The Venerable Bede tells Wilfrid's story at Selsey in one of the nation's earliest history books, his *History of the English Church and People*, finished in 731. Selsey's roots are deep in English history. Go to the war memorial by the parish church and you'll see fragments of Saxon interlaced carvings, Selsey's earliest artwork that is over a thousand years old.

Until the seaside was 'discovered' for holidays, the old village of Selsey was an isolated farming and fishing village. In more recent days much of its farmland has been swamped with housing and enormous summer caravan parks covering the old fields, but at the northern end of the parish a new type of intensive farming has grown up. As the map tells us 'salad crops are produced on a large scale'. It is on a *very* large scale, the company called Natures Way processing and packaging millions of lettuce a year for the national supermarket trade. High light levels are crucial for this type of horticulture. The company reports that on the beachline there is 110 per cent of light through reflection from the water's surface; for every mile inland there is a loss of one per cent; that is why the lettuce fields hug the coastal plain.

St Wilfrid's Chapel, Church Norton

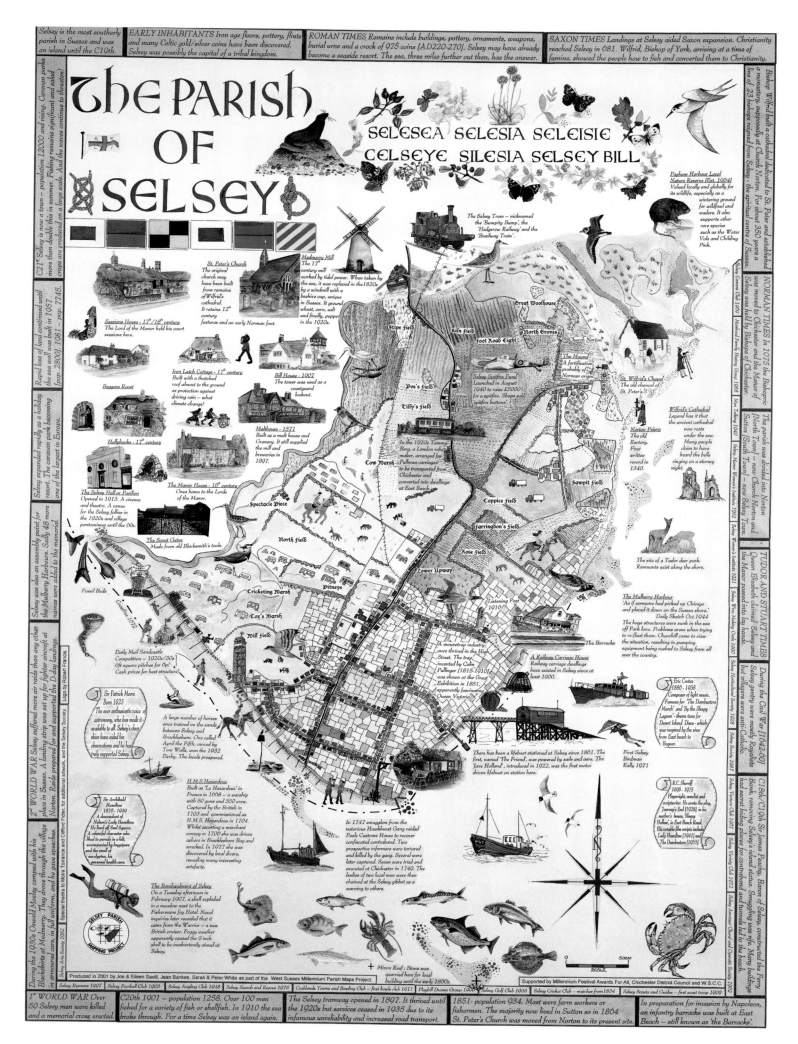

Mixon Reef : Stone was quarried here for local building until the early 1800s.

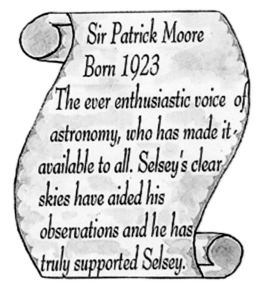

Sir Patrick Moore Born 1923 The ever enthusiastic voice of astronomy, who has made it available to all. Selsey's clear skies have aided his observations and he has truly supported Selsey.

The local fishing industry remains significant; the fishing fleet operates from East Beach and when not at sea can be seen drawn up on the shingle or anchored in the shallows. Selsey's seaward interests are symbolised with great ingenuity, the map-makers giving the place its alternative spelling in maritime semaphore flags. Six colourful flags spell out SELSEY in international sailors' code.

Selsey people have done much to bring fame to the place. Colin Pullinger once made the village the mousetrap capital of the country. His humane traps – quite different from the modern spring-loaded back-breaker – were sold all over the country and beyond, even in America. Selsey traps were exhibited at the Great Exhibition in 1851 and were still being advertised by the Army and Navy Stores in the 1920s.

R.C. Sherriff, the playwright, came here and wrote his First World War tragedy, *Journey's End*. Composer Eric Coates, of *Dambusters March* fame, came as well, and it was from East Beach looking towards Bognor – marked by a blue plaque on Selsey's Heritage Trail – that he was inspired to write *By the Sleepy Lagoon*, theme tune for the BBC's

Desert Island Discs. Strange to think that this suggestion of a tropical paradise was inspired from just here! Catch it on a calm, sunny and clear day and the sweep of the coastline backed by the Downs beyond is still an English paradise. Years later, taking advantage of its clear and unpolluted skies, Selsey's most famous resident, Sir Patrick Moore, settled here with his observatory in the garden. His notepaper ensures we know where he lives: at latitude 50° 43'49.25" N and longitude 00° 41'41.25" W. He loves the place, giving his time and talents unstintingly to local good causes.

The greatest curiosity on the map must be the Listening Post in Beach Road. The device, a sound or acoustic mirror for detecting the approach of German Zeppelins, dating from 1916, was later built into a house, now a listed building. The sound signal was reflected by the dish, via a stethescope, to a microphone. Eventually made obsolete by radar in the 1930s, Selsey's Listening Post is a rare survival of early technology.

So answers weren't hard to find when the map group went public, asking local people 'what makes Selsey so special?' Three years and many hundreds of hours later they came

up with the answers when they presented the finished map to the parish, 'immortalising', as the local paper reported, 'Selsey's past and present'.

Fifteen hundred copies were printed for sale through local outlets and the RNLI lifeboat shop. Good sales meant that profits could be put into several other local community projects, such as buying plants for the Medical Centre's wildlife garden and helping fund Selsey's new Wildlife Project Officer, whose role is to implement Selsey Action for Wildlife.

In tandem with the parish map, the team has been working on wildlife surveys, mapping vegetation for identifying local habitats for its Biodiversity Action Plan, and feeding information into the Sussex Wildlife Trust's hedgerow survey. Currently members are working on the East Beach pond project, improving access and developing its educational potential. Investigating local history is yet another strength in creating the Selsey Heritage Trail around a series of blue plaques. The original team, still keeping its original title – Selsey Parish Map Group – continues to thrive, so much so that their energetic leader, Joe Savill, recently reported their achievements on Radio 4.

KIM LESLIE

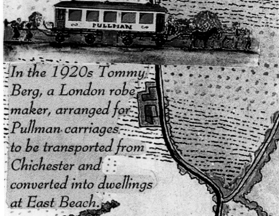

In the 1920s Tommy Berg, a London robe maker, arranged for Pullman carriages to be transported from Chichester and converted into dwellings at East Beach.

The Selsey Tram – nicknamed the 'Bumpity Bump', the 'Hedgerow Railway' and the 'Snailway Train'.

Shipley

THE POST AND RAIL FENCE marking the map's wavy border is much more than decoration, it symbolises the idea of separation from surrounding lands, that Shipley's lands are distinct and different from others. It's an imaginative, emotional fence all about territory, a protective barrier of real meaning to all those who care and feel guardianship over their own little bit of Sussex.

But there is another meaning to the fence, all about Shipley's place in history. The fence conveys the notion of enclosure: historically Shipley's roots lie in its origins as a clearance in the forest for sheep farming. The Saxons cut their pioneer settlements out of the forested Weald, marking out their lands by natural and man-made boundaries, guarding their precious animals behind the security of

fencing in their folds or fenced enclosures.

Farmland dominates the map in its chequerboard pattern of little fields. Farms have always been small here, for historically these wet, sticky and unyielding clay soils of the Weald have given tough farming with severe limitations on the amount one family could cultivate. So in this one parish alone there are a huge number of farming properties – sixty are listed in the top margin of the map. Some come with delightful names like Saucelands, Butterstocks, Rascals and Dragons.

Look carefully to find sheep and cattle grazing, crops growing and harvested as agriculture still plays a significant part in the life of the parish. Exactly by how much is spelt out in the right-hand margin of the map, recording acreages at the turn of the millennium given over to such crops as wheat, linseed, oats, barley, beans, flax, oil seed rape and peas. Beef cattle and sheep are bred, but the decline has been in dairy cattle. Whereas fifty years ago there were as many as twenty-seven milking herds, just two survived when the map was made and even these were destined to finish by the end of 2000.

The village is a peaceful place with a great feeling of remoteness and isolation. Its approach roads add to this sense of feeling distant and withdrawn, reinforcing the idea that this is an off-the-beaten-track type of place. Winding and turning through fields and woodland, they are typical of Wealden ways where most east-west routes along these flat claylands have made travel arduous and difficult. There are so many right-angled bends where metalled roads continue their alignment into unmade green paths and bridleways, sure sign of an ancient settled landscape. The path cutting through the village forming Kingsbridge Lane is part of a much longer route from the Surrey border right down to Washington and the hill country beyond. Up in the far north of the parish, at Crookhorn Farm, the same path cuts a giant swathe some forty feet wide through the woods, the clue that it was once a drove road for herding beasts, wide enough for

The map was compiled by: Barry Robinson · Mandy Robinson · Jane Grinling · Graham Peacock · Bob Philips · Peter Sanderson · With thanks to the Artists: Jane Grinling · Claire Searle · Ann Clarke · Deanna Hilder · John Redman · Ann Green · Sarah Delaney · Pat Lawrence · And to those who helped in many other ways: Zar Roggendorff · Joy Redman · Kim Leslie · Charles Burrell · Harlot Anniss · David Bucks · Phyllis Humphrey · Mike Gibson · Brian Lee ·

Farms · Baker's Farm · Hooklands Farm · Oaklands Farm · Church Farm South · Blanks Farm · Perryland Farm · Brookhouse Farm · Bextons Place Farm · Hammer Farm · Hazelbrook Farm · Smoke House Farm · Pound Farm · Falconers Farm · Hampshires Farm · Seacalands Farm · Jenden's Farm · Church Farm North · Knights Farm · Bridgehill Farm · Patman's Farm · Hillside Farm · St Julians · Ponthill Farm · Thornhill Farm · Goringlee · Bailey's Farm · Hoe's Farm · Oakleigh Farm · Rainbow Farm · Slaughterbridge Farm · Shepard's Farm · Placeland Farm · Gattisland Farm · Dragons Farm · Emms Farm ·

Purveyor's Farm · Brick Kiln Farm · Copyhold Farm · Trawler's Farm · Chivers Farm · Pollardshill Farm · Bouges Farm · St Johns Farm · Courtland's Farm · Birchwood Farm · Crookhorn Farm · Landfill Farm · Durrants Farm · Madgeland Farm · Floodgate Farm · Greenstreet Farm · Butterstocks Farm · Hill House Farm · Lodge Farm · Rascals Farm · Malden Farm · Dummers Farm · Juniper Farm · Barnhouse Farm · Oakwood Farm ·

The map was compiled as part of the West Sussex Millennium Parish Maps Project and is designed to depict the parish and its activities in the year 2000. We are grateful for the support of Horsham District Council, West Sussex County Council, Shipley Parish Council, Mike Bettle Print Partnership Limited.

PARISH OF SHIPLEY

A.D. 2000

WEST SUSSEX

The Old Butchers Shop

New Buildings

Bextons

Shipley Church of England Primary School

Red Lane

Greenstreet Farm

Whiteheart Cottages

The George & Dragon

Polo at Knepp Castle

Bee Hives Knepp Castle

Hoe's Farm

The Crosley & Horsham Hunt at Knepp Castle

Gate to Allotments

Scout Hut

A Traveller stops at Butterstocks

Polo at Butterstocks

William Penn Primary School

Dorrance Manor

Church Farm South

The Selsey Arms

Barnhouse Farm

Seacalands

St Julians

The Countryman Inn

Knepp Lake

The Parish Church of St Mary The Virgin
Priest in Charge: Reverend Don Pope
Mrs Marfe Pope

Shipley Signpost

Knepp Castle Ruin

Andrew Hall

Ned Church Causeway

Bales of Straw

A fearsome dragon once lived in this part of St Leonard's Forest, causing such devastation that St Leonard himself was forced to get rid of it. After a terrible battle (or so legend goes) the dragon was slain, and wherever St Leonard's blood had been spilled patches of lilly-of-the-valley appeared. On a less fanciful note, there was an ordinary family of Dragons, natives of Raffey, living nearby in the parish of Cowfold in 1296, so this place name could have originated with them.

This village, noted for its association with the poet and historian Hilaire Belloc, stands at what early settlers in the area referred to as Scáspa Léage, (at tha) sheep clearing', a cleared patch of woodland where sheep were kept. It appeared in the Domesday Book as Sepelei, having been recorded as Scapeleia 13 years earlier in 1073, subsequently developing to Shepeley by the beginning of the Tudor period.

Coolham was known as Coolham Green in the 19C and had its own cricket and football teams. There were several shops and businesses including a Butchers, Saddlers, Wheelwright, Forge, Cobblers, a large Village Store including Bakery and Post Office and a smaller Grocery and Sweet Shop, Telephone Exchange, and from 1920 a garage with motor car sales and hire service. The village centre until the 1940's was known as the Square.

214

grazing on the hoof. It was part of a network of ancient greenways linking up the isolated communities of the forest with those at the foot of the Downs.

One newly-appointed school head refused to take up the post in the 1940s when she realised just how isolated it was, but this is precisely why so many others have enjoyed Shipley so much, like writer and poet Hilaire Belloc (1870–1953) who made it his home for nearly half-a-century. The story is told that in the 1930s he made a stand for peace and silence by stopping one of the teachers passing his house on a motor cycle. 'If you must go to your school by this road', he thundered, 'get off that wretched thing, switch off the engine and walk past my house. If you want to ride it, go the long way round.' Faced by this man of some considerable bulk – and influence – the young teacher adopted the second suggestion! Peace in the village was restored.

Belloc bought the big house and a few acres at the centre of the village – Kingsland – where he lived for nearly fifty years until his death in 1953. It gave him ownership of Sussex soil and was his own little bit of heaven on earth. His son-in-law, Reginald Jebb, wrote that Shipley brought him 'peace of mind and a sense of permanence that no other place could bring him in like measure'. Here he wrote dozens and dozens of books, historical, biographical, political, religious, topographical, novels and verse – he was like a one-man publishing industry – their introductions and prefaces addressed from 'Kingsland, Shipley' circling the world . In this way he advertised the village like no other and after his death pilgrims in search of the Bellocian spirit continue to find their way here to see the house – at least its exterior, for it's not open to the public – and the great windmill he once owned, restored by West Sussex County Council to his memory.

Belloc put his genius to work in extolling the

Number 1 Church Causeway

county in prose and verse. Certainly no Sussex anthology is complete without lines from his pen. When J.B. Priestley wanted to celebrate the magic of the English landscape in *Our Nation's Heritage* in 1939 he chose for its introductory essay Belloc's 'The Mowing of a Field' set in a remote Sussex downland valley. Belloc was always drawn to remote spots – hence the attraction of secluded, silent Shipley with its panorama of the South Downs to the south.

Similarly another famous name came to Shipley for its calm and peace. Although never living here, the composer John Ireland (1879–1962) frequently made the journey from his home at nearby Washington just to sit in the church porch and gaze over the Adur water meadows towards the outline of the Downs. To him these were musical landscapes, for he turned these hills into music in his *Downland Suite, Legend* and *Equinox*. Interviewed a few years before his death he said that 'much of my music has been inspired by the beauty of Sussex and its ancient past'. So strongly attached to the idea of place and its power over his work, he wanted to be buried within sight of Chanctonbury Ring. At his own wish he was laid to rest in Shipley churchyard, although tree-growth since his death now hides the downland view he loved so much. We have already mentioned the

Belloc's mill, known variously as King's Mill, Vincent's Mill – or even 'Mrs Shipley' – is one of the youngest Sussex windmills, built in 1879

school's head who quickly departed because she couldn't stand Shipley's isolation.

But eventually the school managers found Margaret Kent from a tiny Welsh village who was just right for this very out of the way place. So much did she fall for Shipley that she settled down to spend the last years of her career – from 1945 to 1954 – teaching at the village school. Well-known for her children's books about animals, nature and the countryside, with pictures by well-known book illustrators like Eileen Soper and Honor Appleton, Margaret Kent carried on her writing at Shipley whenever she could, her own creativity nurtured by this new Sussex home. Her book *Nursery Rhyme Nature Stories* is dedicated 'For the Children of Shipley School Sussex'. *Scamp: A Dog's Story*, published in 1968 after her retirement from teaching, tells of village life through the story of her own pet dog. Shipley names are disguised, but it is firmly set in the village she knew and loved so well.

Hilaire Belloc, John Ireland and Margaret Kent are but three figureheads to whom Shipley has given so much happiness, their feelings still echoed by those living here today. 'We are so lucky to retain our rural feel where we have so many activities, so much wildlife and simple pleasures that can be found in the true countryside all of which we have tried to express through our map' said Mandy and Barry Robinson who led the map group. There is a feeling of well-being and contentment, that life here, deep in the countryside – and within the refuge of the fence – is the best place to be.

KIM LESLIE

Sidlesham

With all the sensitivity of his craft, Sussex poet and writer Ted Walker found the very essence of Sussex around here. No one has captured better the feeling for Sidlesham: that it is special because it is ordinary and unspectacular, where good things are subtle and elusive. His was a very special way of looking at places, a deeply perceptive view of landscape and scenery where the ordinary and everyday are invested with deep meaning:

This is not the sort of place to attract the attention of those purple-prose authors of guide-books on Sussex. It isn't a village of obvious, staggering beauty set in dramatic countryside; indeed, a superficial glance reveals little more than a straggle of nondescript building half-way between Chichester and Selsey.

I find it more characteristic of the true spirit of this county than any number of self-conscious show-places whose cosmetic charms clamour for the attention of travelogue writers.

Sidlesham is without a formal plan; there's no single village centre, but rather a scattering of far-flung hamlets and isolated farms, each little unit possessing its own individual personality. The parish church stands more or less at the geographical centre of the village, yet it is by no means (for all its size) the kind of landmark which – even in this flat, open landscape – serves as a hub around which the other communities revolve. This wayward development is engagingly typical of Sussex.

The B2145, much of it distressingly ribbon-developed, in fact by-passes what is best in the village; Sidlesham is to be found along the lanes and tracks leading away from this busy road, and it is these by-ways and their loops which create such

cohesion as exists between the various components of the village.

They lead us into countryside of intense, if elusive, beauty. Most writers on the topography of Sussex dwell upon the delights of downland and the gently rolling Weald and choose to ignore the more subtle attractions of the coastal plain. Around Sidlesham you find this at its very best.

St Mary's Church

The skies are huge and scoured; the Downs are a constantly-changing and hauntingly mysterious backdrop which, according to the light conditions obtaining, seem to swell or shrink and which vary in colour through every gradation of green and blue; the land is rich, meticulously farmed, riddled with little streams whose banks support more wild flowers than you will ever see elsewhere in the county; tall

Down a Sidlesham lane

trees full of rooks and hedges and isolated shrubs are shaped by the wind off the sea. Cottages and farm buildings look vulnerable, not soft and cosy.

Turn off the main road by the Anchor, and at once you enter, along Church Lane, an atmosphere you'd scarcely suspect could exist so close to all that busy traffic. From the pub to the church there are six or seven old cottages and one new house (which blends perfectly with them) that, in the space of a hundred yards, create an unforgettable effect. No single cottage claims more attention than the rest; but the combination of them all, and the superb gardens which bind them together, produce an infinite variety of shape, line and texture. . . .

Mill Lane brings us to the collection of superb cottages and the Crab and Lobster

Sidlesham's quayside on Pagham Harbour

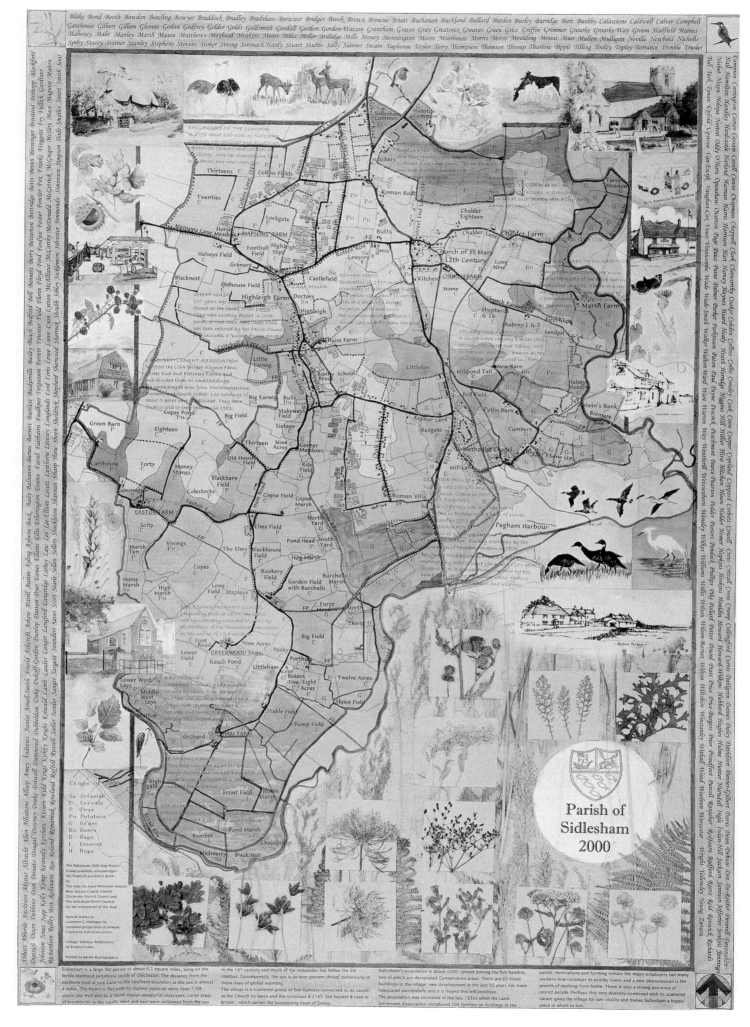

Parish of Sidlesham 2000

217

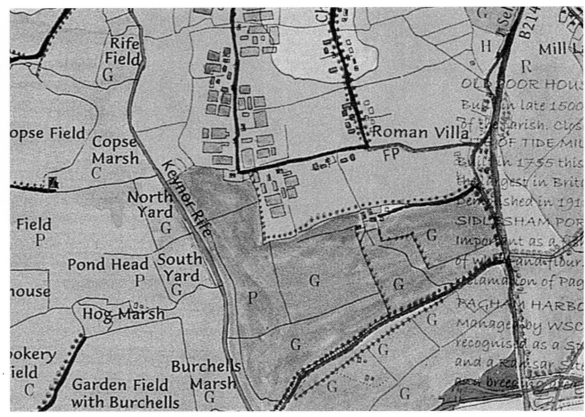

near the waterside. . . . Such is the nature of this all but landlocked harbour that this part of Sidlesham will keep its unspoilt character. . . . It's perfect as it is, the lonely mudflats and the tongues of weed and sandbanks entirely given back to nature.

Sidlesham's spell has worked on many people. Round-the-world yachtsman Robin Knox-Johnston was asked which part of Britain he thought about when on the high seas. He chose here, with its 'briny smell of the marshes, the sense of unspoilt wilderness'. Sidlesham 'was never far from my mind; it represented all that is beautiful in England'.

Come to Sidlesham's quayside on Pagham Harbour on a summer's evening as dusk falls. Then wait the turn of the tide as it pours back on its relentless journey over the mud-covered creeks. Curlew and duck echo over the rising waters. It is then that Sidlesham offers up its most magical, mystical experience.

Nature, wildlife and crops appropriately dominate Sidlesham's parish map, put together

as a WI-led initiative under Joyce Fairbairn, its many elements blended together by architect David Scott. The wildlife that makes this map unique amongst the West Sussex collection is in the decoration added to the original map. Real dried flowers and plants gathered around the harbour have been made into a collage by Brigitte Crafer, skilfully reproduced through the computer by naturalist and wildlife photographer Lawrence Holloway.

Each distinctive colour represents a different farm-holding. Old field-names give every parcel of land its own special personality – Horse Marsh, Nine Acres and Sluice Field might be obvious in telling their stories, but

what of Big Earwig, Money Stones and Blacknest? Look carefully to find the letter coding showing the local crops grown around the parish in the year 2000. Fields of rape and linseed, plus acres of 'Setaside' around Ham and Rotten Row testify to the impact of the European Common Agricultural Policy. There's a field of hops, fields for a herd of prize-winning Holstein cattle – and two ostriches!

Ask about life in Sidlesham and it's not long before stories about the Land Settlement Association – the LSA – come to the surface, a most successful experiment in social engineering, according to the most recently produced local history of the village. In the 1930s unemployed families from Northumberland, County Durham and South Wales settled on smallholdings, each with a greenhouse, piggery, poultry-house and family home under a distinctive pitched roof. These uniform-style houses are a sure sign that this is LSA country. Although the enterprise wound up in 1983, its folklore is still very much alive. But smallholders still make a most important contribution to this thriving village with its many scattered parts: Ham, Highleigh, Keynor, Chalder, Fletchers, Easton, the Common, the Mill – a big parish with a deep sense of its place on the Manhood.

KIM LESLIE

Singleton

How many parishes encompass a world-famous racecourse, the country's leading centre for vernacular architecture, one of the UK's top-ten onshore oilfields, England's oldest Women's Institute, a sometimes invisible river and the only hilltop north of the Alps dedicated to a saint of healing? Singleton has the lot.

Set in glorious countryside in the heart of the South Downs, this is a picture postcard village with a plus factor – the plus of some remarkable people in their very different endeavours.

Village Pond

What better example than the Singleton children whose sole initiative launched the Richmond Playground opened in 2003. It was *their* idea. Astonishingly, as a kick-start, they raised a total of £6,500. They made their presentation to the parish council, wrote letters, appealed for money, held discos, washed cars and odd-jobbed to raise the cash. It was at their request that it was named after the Duke of Richmond, who is always so supportive of local enterprise. Shortly afterwards the access footpath to the playground was upgraded, giving a path to the church as well, picnic tables have been added, and summer barn dances organised for fund-raising to cover ongoing maintenance. The children's original initiative has had some really beneficial knock-on effects for village life.

In the 1960s a visionary – retired lecturer Roy Armstrong – arrived to make his indelible mark on Singleton. He came seeking the impossible: a large plot of land – for nothing – on which to rebuild old houses – to be obtained for nothing – transported here by volunteer labour in one of the riskiest insurance categories – demolition (but more politely called dismantling). Singleton's Weald and Downland Open Air Museum was started against almost impossible odds.

Weald and Downland Open Air Museum

Armed with nothing but the £11.17 shillings and twopence (£11.86) that Roy handed to Kim Leslie as the museum's first treasurer, plus his own dogged determination, West Dean Estate miraculously granted a peppercorn lease. Fortuitously, Singleton resident Geoffrey Godber was Clerk of West Sussex County Council. He abhorred small thinking of small men and leant heavily on Roy's opposition – the rest is history. Under the late Chris Zeuner's directorship this museum of historic buildings from all over south-eastern England has won many awards, brought thousands to the parish and put Singleton firmly on the tourist/educational trail.

Town Lane, part of the old coach road from Chichester to London, leads from the village towards the museum and racecourse, dividing the West Dean Estate from the Goodwood

Goodwood Racecourse

Estate of the Dukes of Richmond. It was the 3rd Duke who in 1801 started the original racecourse on the hill above Singleton. Scenically one of the finest courses in the land, the July meeting – known as Glorious Goodwood – is a summer highlight of the British sporting calendar.

Overlooking the racecourse from an even loftier hill is Singleton's crowning summit – the Trundle – topped by the earthworks of an Iron-Age fort bristling with telecommunication masts and dishes, giving outstanding views across the Downs and coastal plain to Chichester Harbour and the Isle of Wight.

Within the prehistoric fort there was once a chapel dedicated to St Roche – locals pronounce it to rhyme with the fish – hence the Trundle's alternative name of St Roche's Hill. Roche the saint (1296–1327), born in Montpellier in France, was the

The Trundle

healer of plaque victims. In France, Italy and Spain there are numerous churches and statues dedicated to his memory. Singleton's hilltop name is unique in this country. Annually on St Roche's Day, 16 August, a pilgrimage and service of healing is held on the top of the hill.

Singleton

The village name is Saxon. 'Single' is derived from 'sengel' and means a burnt clearing and 'ton' means a settlement. So Singleton was originally a settlement in a burnt clearing.

The Domesday Book shows the population of Singleton in 1086 as 89 villagers, 58 smallholders and 20 slaves. In 1801 Singleton (with Charlton) was 445, 1901 was 513 and 2001 was 459.

 Wayside

The Old Rectory

Singleton X Wellsite

Rose Cottages

Levin Down

Budd's Hill Cottage

The Forge

Bankside

Little Yarne

Cobblers Row

Singleton Tea Rooms

The Old Post Office

Corner Cottage

Singleton C.E. School

Cricket Club

Village Pond

The Surgery

Kingsham Cottage

Duchess Cottages

Myrtle Cottage

War Memorial

Village Hall

Manor Farm

W.I. Jubilee Tree

St Francis Cottage

Parish Church of the Blessed Virgin Mary

The Leys

Little Garth

Grove House

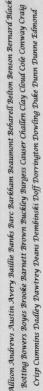

Weald & Downland Open Air Museum

The Fox & Hounds

The Trundle

Goodwood Racecourse

SINGLETON SONG
© M Morris/M Pollock

Singleton, it's the heart of the valley,
Singleton, it's a very good place.
Singleton, on the Lavant River,
Friendly caring people have a smile on their face.

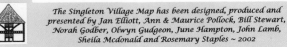
The Singleton Village Map has been designed, produced and presented by Jan Elliott, Ann & Maurice Pollock, Bill Stewart, Norah Godber, Olwyn Gudgeon, June Hampton, John Lamb, Sheila Mcdonald and Rosemary Staples ~ 2002

west sussex county council

We gratefully acknowledge financial support from West Sussex County Council and Singleton Parish Council

Allison Andrews Austin Avery Baillie Banks Barc Barkham Beaumont Beharell Belton Benson Bernard Black Botting Bowers Boyes Brooke Barnett Brown Buckley Burgess Causer Challen Clay Cloud Cole Conway Craig Crisp Cummins Dadley Dawtrey Deans Dembinski Doff Dorrington Dowling Duke Dunn Dunne Edmond

Elliott Farmer Fleming Fox Freeman Fulford Gattrell Geddes George Goacher Godber Green Groom Gudgeon Hall Halsey Hamilton Hampton Hanson Heath Hillier Holán Hope Houlding Howard Husbley Hutchison John Kaminski Kenzie Kettink Kingsbury Knight Lamb Lawrence Layman Lock Long Low Maber

Macdonald Madgwick Mahony Mancini Mather Mcdonald Mcgarrity Merry Miller Mills Mitchell Morris Muir Mulhern Norrell Oldham Oliver Osborne Page Palmer Pearman Penny Perry Pesterfield Pinnington Pollock Prior Reed Reeves Richards Richardson Ridley Ringwood Runeckles Saint Salmon Satterthwaite

Saunders Scott Seratier Sheeran Shepherd Simmonds Simpson Snow Spanton Spence Staples Stay Stewart Stretton Sutton Symonds Thompson Thorold Toft Treacher Tritton Tucker Turner Vandersteen Vine Wakefield Ward Watt Weld White Whitmarsh Wilcox Wilder Williams Wilson Winterflood Woods Wright Young

The Domesday Book shows the population of Singleton in 1086 as 89 villagers, 58 smallholders and 20 slaves. In 1801 Singleton (with Charlton) was 445, 1901 was 513 and 2001 was 459.

The Leys

'Jam and Jerusalem' – those twin symbols of the Women's Institute – have great significance for Singleton. It was at Charlton, in Singleton's little hamlet to the east of the village, that the first WI in England held its inaugural meeting in December 1915, a direct consequence of wartime stringencies. A month before, Singleton Parish Council and the War Agricultural Committee had a lecture

on improving food supplies and home economics addressed 'particularly to the Guardians of the household'. Local women immediately rose to the challenge with home-grown produce and home-made clothes and bandages for the troops in the trenches. The essence of this down-to-earth village movement, pioneered in England at Singleton, is that it is deeply rooted in the countryside.

The countryside looms large in local lives. The downland is a strong presence, pressing

Manor Farm

Singleton between its slopes along the river valley. The Lavant, dry and waterless for most of the year, is a powerful force of great meaning, the annual Easter Duck Race symbol of spring-time rebirth. Occasionally it's been known to sweep down the valley in floods, but sometimes not even giving the expected trickle, cue for all sorts of grim stories of environmental catastrophe. Sometimes lost

Levin Down

and invisible, the Lavant is viewed with great respect. And above this wet/dry valley is Levin Down, rich in flowers and butterflies, now a Sussex Wildlife Trust Nature Reserve and Site of Special Scientific Interest. It's strange to think that within a mile is 'Wellsite Singleton X', Singleton's most secret place buried deep in woodland. Out of thirty onshore UK oil sites,

Singleton's ranking is seventh in tonnage production. This is heavy industry with a light touch.

That this countryside is held dear emerges strongly from Singleton's Parish Appraisal made in 2001. For the majority, life is good

Cricket Club

precisely because of its environment and situation. People like Singleton as their home because of the immediacy of the countryside. The surrounding hills give a great feeling of enclosure and separation, producing the village's very own distinctive feel.

That there is a great sense of affection for the place comes over strongly from Singleton's website; it's full of news, diary dates, of church, school and club events, places to stay, walks, local services and local history. Those lucky enough to live here are putting so much back into community life. And from the parish council's *Newsletter* on the same website we learn of yet another Singleton first: their Clerk, Jenny Martin, is the first in the county to pass the Certificate in Local Council Administration with Distinction – a distinction that shows in the way things are run with such a first-rate information service from this high-achieving and notable parish – see www.singletonvillage.com

KIM LESLIE

Slinfold

SLINFOLD LIES to the west of Horsham in the heart of the Low Weald. The parish is effectively divided into four segments: firstly by the Roman Stane Street from Chichester to London running south-west/north-east and secondly by the route of the old railway line from Guildford to Horsham which runs south-east/north-west and now forms part of the long distance Downs Link bridleway – perfect for walking, riding or cycling. In fact Slinfold boasts an enormous number of footpaths, covering some thirty-six miles around the parish in all.

After the building of the church in the 1300s, Slinfold village began to develop gradually on the church's south side. But some of the former common land remained as open farmland which is why, even today, fields come right into the heart of the village, a much-cherished feature 'framing' many views to and from the village centre. Since Roman times Slinfold has been on busy trading routes, but in the early 19th century two roads – now the A264 and the A281 – were turnpiked, effectively bypassing the village, with the result that a relatively peaceful atmosphere remains.

For centuries the people of Slinfold were engaged in agriculture and the exploitation of the woodland, but now relatively few people in the village are in either. Many of the farmhouses have been divorced from their land, and some former farmland is now given over to leisure pursuits such as golf and clay-pigeon shooting. Slinfold still has large tracts of ancient woodland, old coppiced woods and species-rich hedgerows where bluebells, wood anemones, wild garlic and primroses abound. A recent survey north of the village identified seventy-two different varieties of small animals, including deer.

The centre of Slinfold is a Conservation Area, preserving the character of the architecture. The church, pub, school, village hall and houses of different dates, styles and materials all blend together into one harmonious whole – Ian Nairn in Pevsner's *Buildings of England*

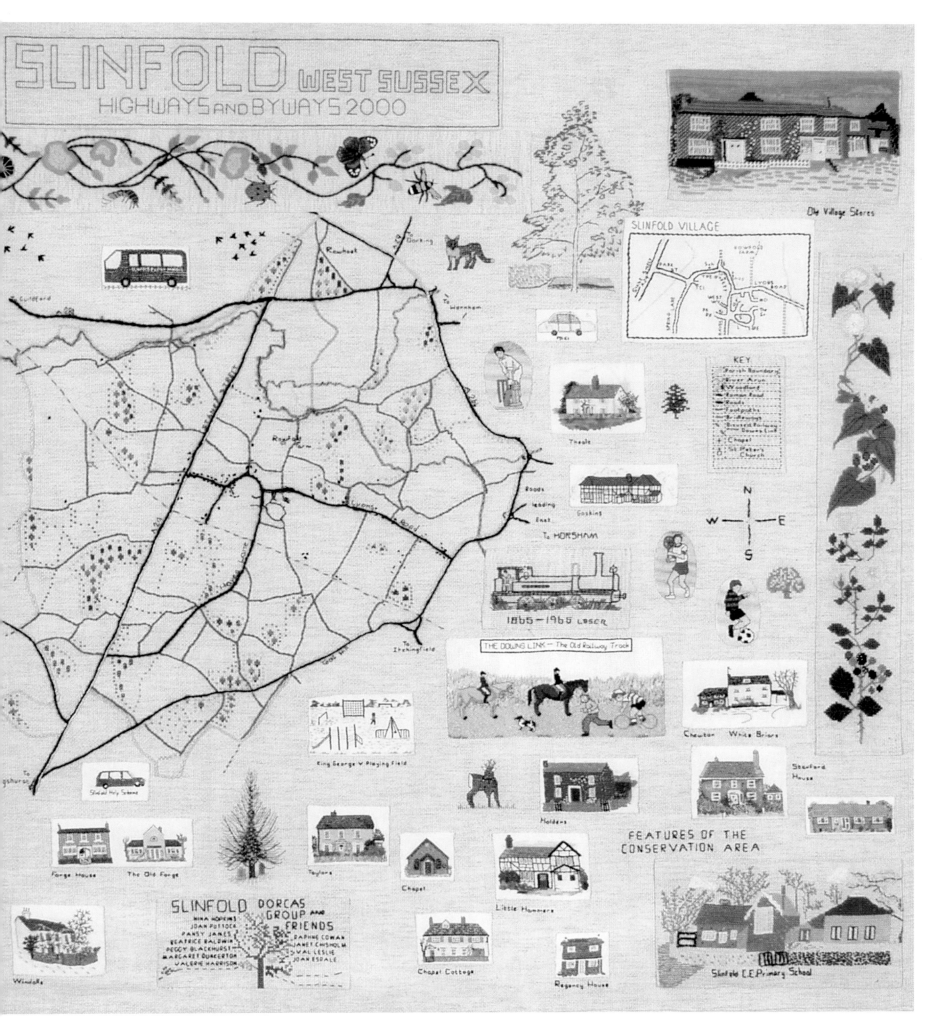

SLINFOLD WEST SUSSEX
HIGHWAYS AND BYWAYS 2000

Old Village Stores

SLINFOLD VILLAGE

KEY

Theale

Goshins

To HORSHAM

1865 — 1965 LBSCR

THE DOWNS LINK — The Old Railway Track

Chewton   White Briars

Stanford House

King George V Playing Field

Holdens

FEATURES OF THE
CONSERVATION AREA

Forge House   The Old Forge

Taylors

Chapel

Little Hammers

SLINFOLD DORCAS GROUP and FRIENDS
NINA HOPKINS
JOAN PUTTOCK
PANSY JAMES
BEATRICE BALDWIN
PEGGY BLACKHURST
MARGARET DUNCERTON
VALERIE HARRISON
DAPHNE COWAN
JANET CHISHOLM
VAL LESLIE
JOAN ESDALE

Windflo

Chapel Cottage

Regency House

Slinfold C.E. Primary School

223

calls it 'mellow' and 'leafy' and is highly complimentary at the way the village is 'beautifully cared for. Caring has not impaired the character as it sometimes does: the old cottages are preserved but not made artificially

Old Village Stores

quaint, a new estate on the road west of the village has been admirably landscaped, and the best individual house in the centre [called Brickwood, 1959] is in fact modern.' With Slinfold as the example, Nairn concluded that 'Sussex is a better place to see this happy marriage of old and new than anywhere else in England' – praise indeed!

But Slinfold is much more than its picturesque centre. There are areas of more affordable housing, social housing and new developments of three-, four- and five-bedroomed houses, all of which bring variety and life to the village and have helped to secure the future of the school, pub and shop.

But it is the people of Slinfold that make it so special. There is an abundance of well-supported activities and clubs for everyone, from toddlers to senior villagers. For those of a

sporting nature there is a thriving Cricket Club – playing since at least 1775 – an active Tennis Club with a junior section, and a football team. There is short-mat bowls for seniors and juniors, table tennis and bridge clubs. Other interests are variously catered for

by the Concert Band, History Group, Art Group, a Thursday Club (for more senior villagers), the Horticultural Society, Hand-Bell Ringers and an Open House Group that meets for a speaker and coffee. Rural and village life can be difficult for the younger generation, but despite its small size, Slinfold has a Youth Club, Brownies, Rainbows, Beavers, Cubs and a Toddlers Group.

It was another of Slinfold's active groups, the Dorcas Group and friends, led by Janet Chisholm, that celebrated the millennium with their embroidered parish map, one of the few in West Sussex made this way. At the same time the Slinfold Society published a millennium history written by Diana Chatwin called *Slinfold Street: The Development of a Village in the Sussex Weald*. Taken together, the book and map give an unrivalled picture of this lovely parish at this most significant moment.

The Dorcas Group is made up of ladies who enjoy embroidering and like to share ideas and have a chat. It was decided to make the message of the map quite simple, developing its theme around Slinfold's 'Highways and Byways'.

The materials used included a coarse oatmeal canvas for the background, sewn boldly in chain, tent and cross stitch using fine embroidery wools. The numerous smaller illustrations with their intricate details were sewn onto a softer cream canvas using stranded 'silks', often with only one or two strands in the needle. When finished, three weeks had then to be allowed for stretching and framing to avoid distortion before glazing. The map was then hung in the newly-extended village hall. Its position here has meant that its size could be generous enough to show quite distinctly our great wealth of paths and bridleways and for the illustrations

Slinfold CE Primary School

of buildings to be sewn large enough to be clearly recognisable. The group is justly very pleased at the way the map gives such a detailed and informative picture about the parish in such a decorative style.

Slinfold's active social life, along with the fact that all the components so vital to a healthy village – shop, school, church and village hall – are still functioning at its heart, help sustain a real sense of community. In 2002, when it looked as if we might lose our shop, the village clubbed together and bought it. This is typical of the response to a problem, people come forward and offer their time and expertise to solve it. The Help Scheme has been serving the village for twenty-five years now, providing a monthly get-together, but primarily organising lifts for

those who cannot use public transport and have no-one to take them to essential appointments such as the doctor or hospital. It is a free service, but donations are welcome. It is very rare for the Help Scheme to have to say 'no' to anyone as there are fifty registered drivers on the books, all volunteers. Then we have a Mini-bus Club that raised the money to buy a replacement bus for the village. It is this spirit that makes Slinfold so special.

JANET VALENTINE

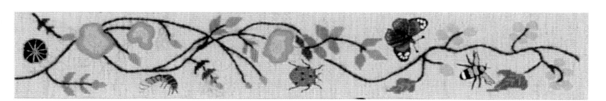

South Stoke

ACROSS THE STONE BRIDGE at the end of Arundel's lime-tree avenue lies the parish of South Stoke and its little hamlet of Offham. Local places that many think belong to Arundel – Swanbourne Lake, the Wildfowl and Wetlands Centre and the Black Rabbit – are actually in our parish. This southerly area of the parish is Arundel's playground. So the story of South Stoke is very much bound up with the history of Arundel, the majority of the land here being part of the Norfolk Estate.

On high days and holidays and whenever the sun shines, this area draws visitors. It was the site of mills mentioned in Domesday as part of Roger de Montgomery's Offham holdings. It was also the subject of John Constable's last great oil painting – *Arundel Mill and Castle* – shown at the Royal Academy following his death in 1837. He wrote:

I long to be amongst your willows again, in your walks and hangers . . . . The trees hang from excessive steeps and precipices . . . I never saw such beauty in natural landscape before . . . . The meadows are lovely, so is the delightfull river . . . but the trees above all.

It's the same today with the steep hangers of beech trees reflected in the water, parts of the lake dark and mysterious, parts a wonderful turquoise. The whole area teems with wildlife, local and exotic birds, dragonflies, bats, water rats and voles as well as rowers, walkers and strollers.

In 1643, during the Civil War, the parliamentarians drained Swanbourne in order to stop the castle's water supply. In recent years there have been problems in maintaining the water level. The dredging of 2001 helped, but lack of rainfall and ever

The Black Rabbit Inn

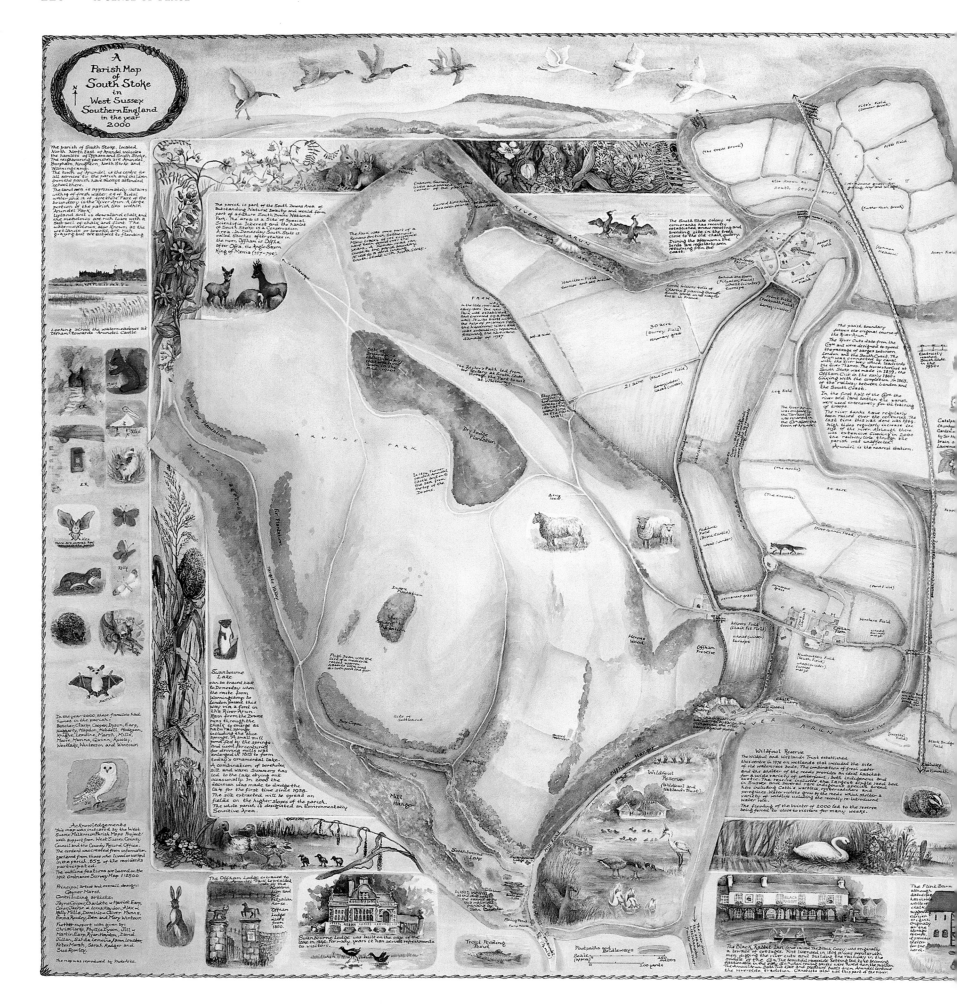

increasing demand for water means that the lake needs to continue being cherished. From the lake, tracks lead to the trig point on top of the Downs. The extraordinary views extend south to the coast with the spread of the Arun Valley to the east and northwards towards the Weald. From here Turner created one of his loveliest panoramas, the 1824 watercolour *Arundel Castle, on the River Arun*.

Across from the lake, the Wildfowl and Wetlands Trust's reserve is home to ducks, geese and swans from around the world. They scuttle across the road into the ditches. Some are migrants but there are also many native birds, including peregrine falcons, sparrow hawks, wagtails and

kingfishers. Small boats nudge through the reed beds and thatched look-out huts give wonderful viewing. Geese fly in formation up the river, and along the valley swans come into land with a great flapping of their wings.

Offham Hanger's steep sides are crammed with beech and chestnut, hazel and ferns. Pheasants and rabbits, moorhens and coots, foxes and bats cross from the steep banks to the gentler haven of the reeds, willows and lush grasses of the water meadows.

At the Black Rabbit the world sits with beer and soaks up the view. Years ago pleasure boats could be hired, ferryboats stopped by and barges were loaded with chalk from the quarries behind the pub. This marks the end of the tourist beat and the part of the parish known to the world. Only keen walkers, ramblers and lovers of the countryside continue further. Offham Cut is a dark green tunnel with steep banks of chalk and fern. The light at the end is the light of downland farming country.

In the summer cattle and sheep graze the slopes and the water meadows, known locally as the brooks. In winter they are windswept and waterlogged – or flooded – whilst the Arun is tidal and currents strong. The mists rising from the river and brooks create a mysterious world floating in the clouds.

The year-round activity of the farmland and never-ending variety of the birds accentuate the seasons. In April the cuckoo signifies the warming of the soil and the end of cold mists. Swallows arrive. Each year there are several nesting pairs of swans at the side of the brooks, content in the quiet of the valley. The shallow brooks are regularly cleared; frequent cutting prevents them from reverting to reeds. The quality of the sward helps the yield of hay and silage. Careful husbandry results in a haven for nesting birds, especially lapwings. If the grass is cut before 20 June it is said that the lapwings will be wiped out. Their population is increasing, a wonderful site on a summer's day. The marsh marigolds, yellow irises, marsh orchids and teasels are thriving.

The Arun smells of the sea as it sweeps through the water meadows. Gone are the days when this was the main transport link between London and Portsmouth. Coal, gold bullion, chalk, seaweed and oak timbers used to be transported by barge. The coming of the railway in 1863 and subsequent introduction of two cuts in the river – at Offham and South Stoke – changed the course of the river and the way it was used. On a late February afternoon, with mists rising and light fading, the trains passing through the valley float in and out of a magical world. The old river beds are dark and misty in winter, green, shady and enchanting in summer. Some parts are isolated and lonely, a haven for water plants, creatures and birds. This damp, mysterious world is vividly depicted in Michael de Larrabeiti's *Foxes' Oven*, fiction inspired by this curiously-named little spot between Offham and South Stoke.

Now the seasons are changing. For the past few winters there have only been a few nights of frost. Milder, wet, stormy weather has brought flooding in winter and spring with water shortages in summer and autumn.

The parish population has also changed, halving over the past thousand years. In 1806 Arundel Park was extended and a new boundary wall enclosed much of the existing common land. Parishioners lost grazing rights on the rich pasture which led to hardship. Farm mechanization and out-sourcing have meant that most of those living in the parish work elsewhere. Few houses have been built in the past century whilst several marked on old maps have not been replaced. Happily this has not undermined the sense of commitment to the environment of those who love this place.

Glimpses of the quiet green valley show the river looping through it. There are sheep, cows and all manner of birds; tractors working and gulls following; bales, maize, ditches and muddy paths; the Downs and hanging woods above; primroses, campion and wild garlic; cormorants on the beech trees – this is their dormitory, they fish in the sea at Bognor and Pagham, sleeping here at night.

South Stoke clusters around St Leonard's Church, the focus of village life since the 11th century. Candles light its simple interior and the wire gate on the porch provides protection from the sheep grazing in the churchyard. The neighbourly spirit is alive and well thanks to the close relationship between church, farm and the community. *Folly Farm* (published in 1954) – about country life, the environment, 'progress' and other wide-ranging issues of the time – was written by Cyril Joad, the philosopher (1891–1953), under the influence of staying on the farm at South Stoke. It was the dream farm of his imagination where he wrote many of his books. His life was celebrated recently by the Joad Society's *Festival of Thought* in the farm's Chapel Barn.

The barn is the setting for much social activity and merry-making and was the departure point for the second day of the beating-the-bounds walk and boat ride for the parish map. As the parish came together to reaffirm boundaries and common rights and bless the crops at Rogation, the words of the 17th-century parson-poet George Herbert were so very apt: 'a Blessing of God for the fruits of the field ... Justice in the preservation of bounds; Charity in loving, walking and neighbourly accompanying one another...'.

GAYNOR MARSH

Staplefield

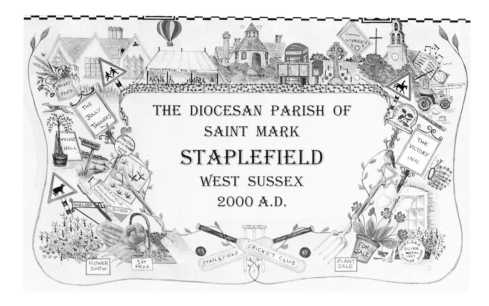

THE DIOCESAN PARISH OF
SAINT MARK
STAPLEFIELD
WEST SUSSEX
2000 A.D.

IMAGINE A VILLAGE without a traditional 'High Street'. The houses here cluster round the edges of one of the two commons that make up Staplefield. It looks more like a hamlet than a village, but there is a parish church, St Mark's, albeit Victorian rather than a cosily-settled Norman edifice. Car drivers have been known to blink on their way through the village and miss it altogether. Somewhat hazily they may well ask 'Is that the place with the pretty pub where they play cricket?'. There are many Sussex villages, I'm sure, answering to this description, but somehow we'll answer 'yes' and be certain we're all speaking of the same place so that travellers and residents alike are reassured it's Staplefield.

Staplefield only came of age in 1848 when it became a parish in its own right, carved out of Cuckfield. Originally it was more just a green – or common land – around which cottages were built as waste-edge settlement. Its new parochial status echoed the expansion taking place in the first half of the 19th century

– hence the need also for a church built in 1847 and a village school in 1849 – reflecting the flurry in putting up 'tied' cottages for the growing number of workers employed on the farms and larger houses then being built.

The Ouse, that has just begun its journey to the sea at distant Newhaven, gently meanders through the parish to the south of the village. Unless of course it's at a time of flood, and then the age-old problem of travelling in Sussex makes itself apparent. Beautiful woodland, a mixture of native broad-leaved trees with the predominant mighty oaks, tops the high ridges and gently descends to the lush river valley below.

Farming lingers on, precariously in these times. The cows, on their way to the milking parlour, no longer cause a rush-hour hold-up beneath the busy A23 where heavy traffic, oblivious to the more gentle pursuits

proceeding beneath, roars its way between London and Brighton.

The countryside once resounded to the workings of a thriving timber industry that, in turn, fuelled the heavy ironworks and more malodorous tanning trade – we have the Jolly Tanners pub as a constant reminder of past times. But these rural industries have all gone, with the landscape now quiet and pastoral;

     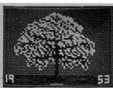 

229

Jill "The Artist"

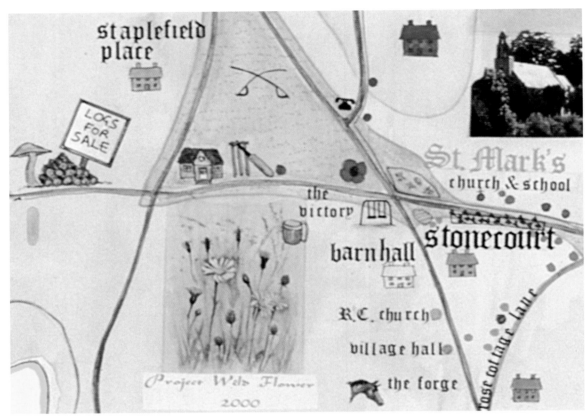

ironically it's much more of a rural idyll than centuries ago. Sit by our other old pub across the green, the Victory, and watch village cricket or morris dancers performing their age-old rituals, and you'll agree that this must be the most perfect village picture.

It's wonderful to be here on summer days with the sun shining and trees in full leaf. But what of the early spring days when the mist clings so closely to the valley floor that you feel you could put your hand up and your arm would disappear into the clouds? Such natural phenomena take us into an entirely different, secretive, world of our own. These misty mornings with coppice merging from brown to hazy, almost green, are ours for the pure pleasure of witnessing winter giving way to a burgeoning spring. And in Staplefield these natural wonders are all around us, everyday.

For the visitor wishing to be either an interested spectator or willing bit player, strike north from Brighton or south from Crawley towards the end of May. Leave the hustle and rush of the monster road – one of the busiest in Sussex – and head down one of the lanes and you could find yourself in the midst of the busiest day in Staplefield's calendar. For on the larger of the two commons will be a traditional village occupation – the annual fête, going here by the name of 'The Fun Day'. Everyone and anyone is able to pause and pass the time,

enjoy refreshment from one of the two pubs, listen to a brass band and just 'people watch'. The church bells mark the passage of time, their chimes gently wafting across the festivities. This annual event on the big common gives many visitors their one abiding memory of the village, a good slice of an older England at play.

The Jolly Tanners

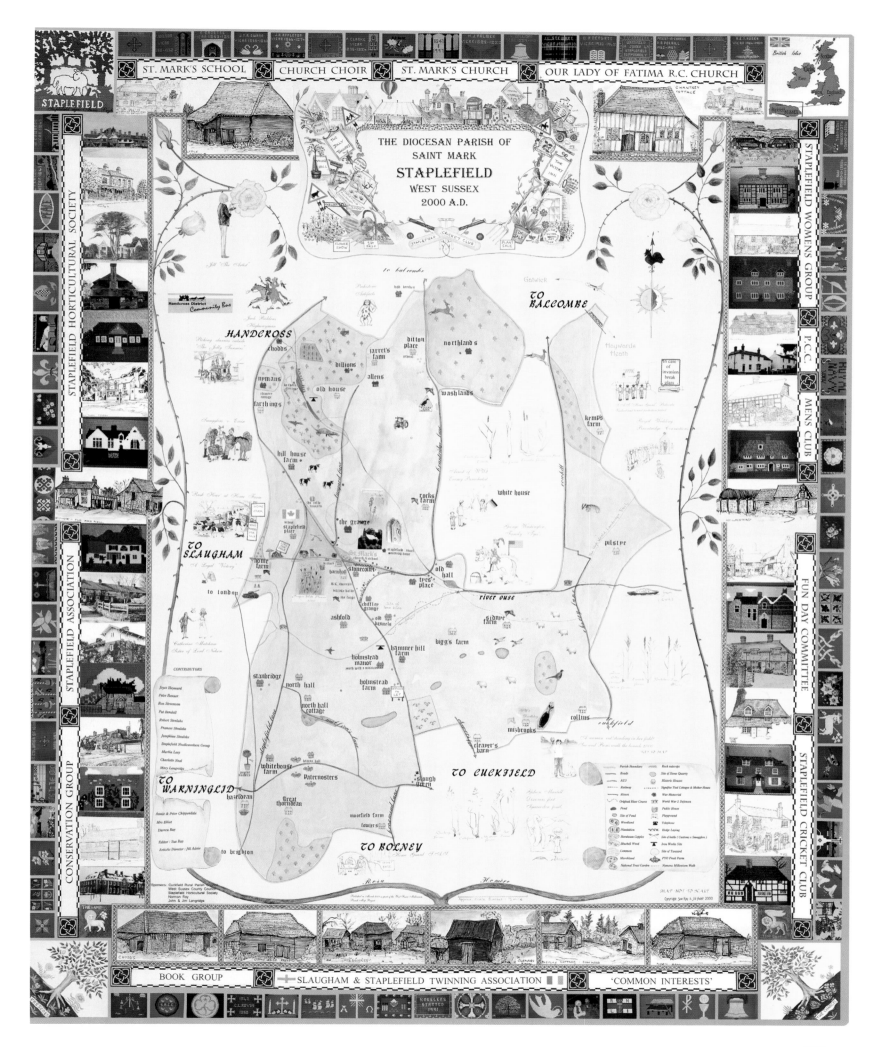

THE DIOCESAN PARISH OF
SAINT MARK
STAPLEFIELD
WEST SUSSEX
2000 A.D.

ST. MARK'S SCHOOL · CHURCH CHOIR · ST. MARK'S CHURCH · OUR LADY OF FATIMA R.C. CHURCH

STAPLEFIELD

STAPLEFIELD HORTICULTURAL SOCIETY

STAPLEFIELD ASSOCIATION

CONSERVATION GROUP

STAPLEFIELD WOMENS GROUP

P.C.C.

MENS CLUB

FUN DAY COMMITTEE

STAPLEFIELD CRICKET CLUB

BOOK GROUP · SLAUGHAM & STAPLEFIELD TWINNING ASSOCIATION · 'COMMON INTERESTS'

231

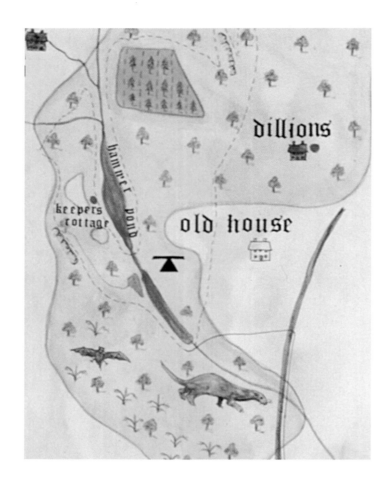

The second, smaller common, has recently been rejuvenated with hedge-laying by a local volunteer group and the reinstatement of a small 'lost' pond. This common is a much quieter place for reflection and a significant habitat for much varied wildlife. What a welcome addition to the village!

But it is well worth making an effort to be a little more adventurous and investigate further afield. To capture the spirit of the place it's essential to abandon the car and the safety of the commons and strike out on foot. Within a short time the explorer is among the woodlands to the north of the village. Typical Sussex ghylls (sometimes spelt gills) – which are streams cut into deep valleys in this part of the High Weald – make the walking interesting, no flat ways here! We go over little footbridges, following ancient tracks. Much of Sussex has lairs belonging to Pook, our local version of the little sprite called Puck. There is no doubt he was here. Maybe he still bides in hidden, secretive places, quietly observing these modern-day folk as they wander around his very special place. Today his magic is to soothe the modern hassled mind.

It was with the idea of encouraging more people to explore and delve into the locality like this that we undertook the parish map project. It also gave us the opportunity to record the essence of the village and the surrounding parish just as it stood at the beginning of the 21st century, with some added pictorial comment on current affairs, such as the lack of a resident vicar and agricultural diversification. Can you spot the clues on the map? Maybe someone in the future will look carefully at some of these clues and start thinking 'I wonder why?'.

SUE RAY

Stedham with Iping

6 ‘GOD BLESS STEDHAM’ proclaims the inscription on the youngest of Stedham's church bells, a prayer surely answered many times over. Like the whole string of Rother Valley villages, Stedham and Iping have been richly blessed. Tied together in the Rother's twists and turns, these quiet and modest neighbours enjoy a pastoral countryside without equal in West Sussex. As their chronicler, Roger Chatterton-Newman, so aptly remarked: ‘If the Rother Valley was set to music it must surely be Beethoven's Symphony No. 6 in F Major – the "Pastoral" ' – inspired by a shady, limpid stream. When Disraeli, the future prime minister, came visiting in 1840, he called it ‘the greenest valley with the prettiest river in the world’.

Their one great blessing is that they are both off the main road, along lanes heading deep into the countryside, narrow and sunken below field level, making their river crossings by some of the finest bridges surviving in southern England. In all their antiquity they symbolise long-gone days in travel and transport. The historian of these Rother bridges – there are fifteen in all – the Reverend A.A. Evans, commented that wherever we find these ancient structures ‘they spring from the waters and span the banks as things of living beauty. They have noble piers, splendid cutwaters, recessed parapets, and, in a wonderful way, blend with surroundings of trees, green banks and running waters.’

The most scenic way to approach both villages is from the north bank across the bridges. Iping, its centre just a little cluster around the church, has seen noisier, busier days when the valley pulsed to the beat of the waterwheel. Just west of the bridge a former watermill went through any number of transformations since first recorded in the 11th century – for grain, malt, fulling (or cleaning) woollen cloth, timber-cutting and most notably paper-making. It was the last paper-making mill in Sussex, in its later years making blotting paper until burnt down in 1925. Feeding the Rother just west of here is

Hammer Stream spilling from Hammer Pond – hence Hammer Lane and Hammerwood; an echo of yet more industry when water-powered hammers forged the iron when Sussex was one of the major concentrations of ironmaking in Britain. It's hard to think that these little lanes took the traffic of all this heavy industry.

It's now a peaceful landscape, yet full of surprises. H.G.Wells played a trick on the village, for good or ill sending its name around the world in his science-fiction thriller *The Invisible Man* (1897). Mayhem and terror concocted by Griffin, ‘experimental investigator’, fell on Iping, but Iping in name only. Wells simply loved teasing readers with his place names. For ‘Iping’ read ‘South Harting’ and then all is clear. (Some local writers want to make it Stedham, but that's a complete red herring.)

Stedham Hall

What Stedham does claim is the best view – from the river – of a huge and picturesque house, a view that has been described as giving ‘a formidable fairy-castle effect’. This is Stedham Hall, at its core centuries old, today very much an early 20th-century rebuild by a wealthy young stockbroker of Scottish descent called John Scrimgeour (1872–1925). He didn't destroy anything of beauty, as a

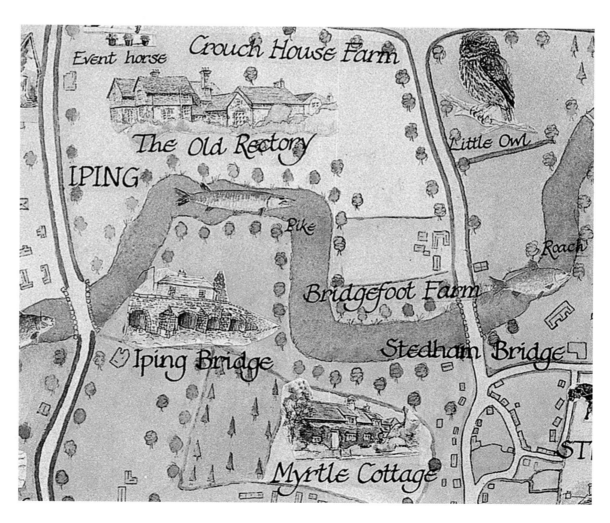

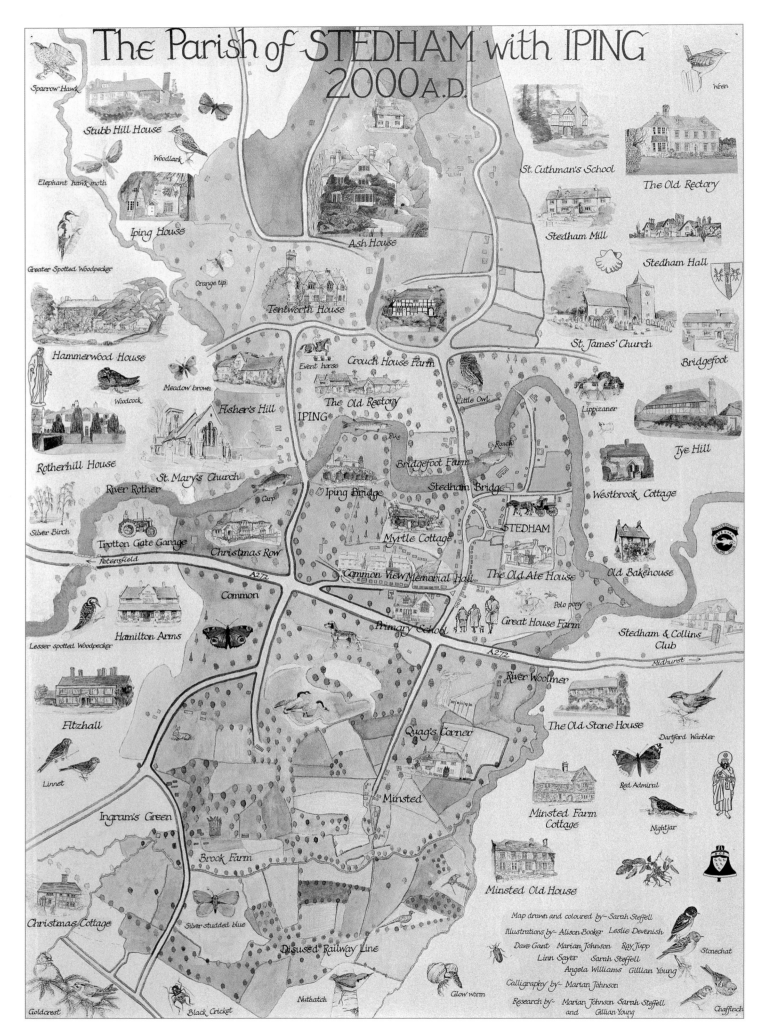

The Parish of STEDHAM with IPING 2000 A.D.

Sparrow Hawk
Wren
Stubb Hill House
Woodlark
St. Cuthman's School
The Old Rectory
Elephant hawk-moth
Iping House
Ash House
Stedham Mill
Stedham Hall
Greater Spotted Woodpecker
Orange tip
Tentworth House
St. James' Church
Bridgefoot
Hammerwood House
Event horse
Crouch House Farm
Little Owl
Lippizaner
Meadow brown
Woodcock
Fisher's Hill
The Old Rectory
IPING
Pike
Roach
Tye Hill
Rotherhill House
St. Mary's Church
Iping Bridge
Bridgefoot Farm
Stedham Bridge
Westbrook Cottage
River Rother
Carp
Silver Birch
Trotton Gate Garage
Christmas Row
Myrtle Cottage
STEDHAM
The Old Ale House
Old Bakehouse
Petersfield
A272
Common View Memorial Hall
Common
Polo pony
Great House Farm
Stedham & Collins Club
Hamilton Arms
Primary School
A272
Midhurst
Lesser spotted Woodpecker
River Woolmer
Fitzhall
Quag's Corner
The Old Stone House
Dartford Warbler
Linnet
Red Admiral
Ingram's Green
Minsted
Minsted Farm Cottage
Nightjar
Brook Farm
Christmas Cottage
Silver studded blue
Minsted Old House
Disused Railway Line

Map drawn and coloured by:- Sarah Steffell
Illustrations by:- Alison Booker   Leslie Devenish
Dave Gant   Marian Johnson   Ray Jupp
Linn Sayer   Sarah Steffell
Angela Williams   Gillian Young
Calligraphy by:- Marian Johnson
Research by:- Marian Johnson   Sarah Steffell
and   Gillian Young

Goldcrest
Black Cricket
Nuthatch
Glow worm
Stonechat
Chaffinch

234

previous owner, a banker with all the skill of an early Victorian vandal, had ruined the place with cement, canvas sheeting and blue paint. With its new ground floor of stone, the upper half-timbered, it dates from 1910–20, but has all the feel of the 1520s.

Scrimgeour wanted to enhance Stedham: his memorial lies all around and is still felt today. As lord of the manor he wanted to build a model village, offering good, well-designed homes and social facilities to his tenants at a time when thousands of villages across the country lacked decent amenities. Through his Stedham Water Company he gave the village its first pumped water supply, he gave a sports club and bath house where villagers could take a free hot bath, provided an eight-acre playing field and new cottage accommodation. The eight semi-detached cottages called

Christmas Row

Christmas Row in School Lane – so called because many of the local Christmas family built them – are some of the best specimens of estate building to be found anywhere, with their decent brickwork, sturdy little porches, eyebrow roof-line and diamond-paned windows. They were built for renting to newly-married couples. (If only a John Scrimgeour could build Christmas Rows all over the land today!)

No wonder that in the parish church there is a handsome memorial to Scrimgeour 'From many who loved him in and around Stedham' and yet again a plaque on the ponderously named Stedham Collins & Sports Club informing that 'This memorial was erected by the ex-servicemen of Stedham in memory of the late Mr A.J. Scrimgeour and of his many kindnesses to them'. In May the village is draped in purple aubretia, his favourite flower, his perennial memorial.

St Cuthman's School

The Hamilton Arms

Even the trees remind us of this enlightened benefactor, like the poplars he planted along the river bank and the fine specimens around that other impressive Scrimgeour residence – Wispers, more lately St Cuthman's School, to the north of Stedham, built for John's father.

Stedham's pride and joy is a single tree, its ancient yew, one of the largest churchyard yews in Sussex, listed as number four out of forty in the county in terms of decrepitude, presence and dimensions. It's the oldest thing alive in Stedham, estimated at some two thousand years old, and nearly 36 feet in circumference, so big that someone once said that you could hold a party in its open bole.

There's a great sense of history here, but equally a very active community living very much in the present. Colin Dunne captured its spirit in his *Downs Country* magazine edited from South View Cottage by the village green. He has told how its vitality has been enriched by incomers like the Australian millionaire Kerry Packer and his polo set. Then there's

Surapee Mudita Karnasuta who owns the village pub, the Hamilton Arms, running one of the best Thai restaurants in the country, centre also for Buddhist festivals – Eastern dance, music and food in a Sussex woodland setting. The village is especially good at organising special events, with firework displays, 'the best in the south', and suppers on the village green. 'No significant anniversary is allowed to slip by without some sort of concert and party, and in between there is a constant string of coffee mornings and bring-and-buys.' This great social life played out in such a wonderful setting – with no through traffic – gives Stedham a personality hard to beat.

KIM LESLIE

St James' Church

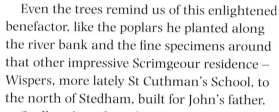

Tangmere

IF EVER THERE WAS A competition for the most world-famous village in West Sussex it would almost certainly be won by Tangmere. Its name became part of the currency of the Second World War and will always remain well-known as long as the heroics of the Battle of Britain are remembered. The Royal Air Force has gone, the airfield demolished, but memories and nostalgia are as much alive today as are some of its very real legacies that still influence present-day life and work in Tangmere. Any talk about the past shaping the present in Sussex villages invariably means a past that is centuries old, but here it's very much about a fairly recent past.

Ordered from on high, Tangmere lost its old identity by compulsory requisition, only to regain another. No wonder that its parish history book was given the sub-title *A Village with two stories*, about stories of war and peace so diametrically different. And now what we see today is yet another identity that has emerged since the Property Services Agency finally auctioned it all off in 1979. The history of what has happened since then is very much the story of Tangmere today. Disused airfields in south-east England rarely go back to green fields.

So the Spitfire sweeping across the village with such prominence is more than just a picture from the past – it's a deep-seated acknowledgement of just how much the Second World War is embedded in the local psyche. Exactly the same message comes through from other images: the RAF crest, several aircraft, the control tower and the Bader Arms pub sign. Douglas Bader, legendary fighter pilot of the war, the first man with artificial legs ever to pass a medical for flying duties, was stationed here. Look closely under the Spitfire's wing to find the picture of

RAF Control Tower

the memorial stone Bader unveiled in 1976; it commemorates the airfield 'manned by Royal Air Force Squadrons whose valiant memory is recorded for all to see at the church of St Andrew'. Inside the church is the Roll of Honour, outside the starkly-white servicemen's graves with a section for German aircrew who perished. 'Ein Deutscher Soldat' says one with some poignancy over the body of an unknown fighter. Here, in death, enemies are united. The windmill at the top of the map – Halnaker Mill – is outside the parish, but has a special place as 'the windmill on the hill', one of the first signs of safety to returning fighter pilots. The comforting sight of the mill-that-meant-home features in quite a few wartime accounts of flying from RAF Tangmere.

Halnaker Mill

TANGMERE AIRFIELD NURSERIES LTD

One way these wartime days are still part of everyday life today is in some of the street names shown on the map. They are commemorative street names, some named after aircraft: Spitfire Court, Wyvern Close, Hampden Place and Lysander Way (Lysanders ferried secret agents and resistance fighters to and from occupied France from Tangmere); others are named after wartime heroes: Gibson Road and Cheshire Crescent (Guy Gibson and Leonard Cheshire). The full story of both aircraft and aircrew is told graphically in Tangmere Military Aviation Museum. At the last annual count the museum brought some twenty-four thousand visitors, many from abroad, through the village.

When the RAF finally left in the 1970s the local population stood at just over eight hundred. By 2001 it was 2,560, a threefold explosion in just thirty years. With one of the fastest growth rates in the area, there inevitably followed some massive implications for community life. The airfield and its decaying buildings had left a vacuum which planners and developers have been filling ever since, bringing housing and light industry to the new hi-tech business park, and over fifty acres of glasshouses spreading across the old concrete runways. There's a major greetings card publisher, a manufacturer of heart-rate monitors and the largest single grower of sweet peppers in the UK, dedicated to the production of green, red, yellow and orange peppers. Huge lorries leave Tangmere with their colourful fruits for every major supermarket chain in the UK. Local employment prospects have vastly improved. Many more jobs are now available in the village than ever before.

But now, after such enormous growth, the hopes and expectations of this new community reflect huge concerns for the future of the village. The local people are proud of its past and are mostly very happy with the present, but what happens tomorrow is the big issue.

The general consensus is that people so far are happy with the way that much of the new housing has harmonised with the rest of the village, as in Churchwood Drive where mature trees and house design are seen to be in keeping with the area. There is a pub, a small village shop, a village hall, plenty of space for playing fields and some parish allotments. Open farmland is close to the village centre,

Old Tangmere

New Tangmere

Alexendra Mackie • Rory Minns • Benjamin Myers • Jason Newell • Siobhan Odell • Lily Peacock • Katy Pennells • Ruby Priestley • Ashley Ives • Jamie Quick • Amy Raybone • Kirsty Raybone • Claire Richards • Louisa-Marie Rutteer • Thomas Simpson • Ella Smith • James Stark • Ruth Stone • Haydon Tuker • McCormick • Samuel McFarlane • Joe Mc Nally • Tracey Minns • Victiria Newton • Thomas Parker • Daniel Porter • Freya Potter • Shane Richards • Samuel Salkeld • Abbey Shrubb • Stephanie Shrubb • Karina Smith • Shane Stapleton • Stacey Stubbington • Alexander Tanser-Pearce • Kristian Tanser-Pearce • Ashleigh Forster • Arnold Fumagall • Jamie Furner • David Blennard • Tiffany Goodacre • Stephanie Haggarty • Grant Hanwell • Martina Holden • Elliott Holyman • Lauren Hopkin • Charmine Albewite • Lauren Bain • Lloyd Beck • Alexander Beer • Courtney Brannigan • John Brazil • Sarah Brennan •

TO GOODWOOD

BOXGROVE

A27 TO CHICHESTER

A27 TO ARUNDEL

OLDE COTTAGE INN

GARLAND SQUARE

PEAR TREE KNAP

CARAVAN PARK

EDWARDS AVENUE

MEADOW WAY

GIBSON ROAD

SCHOOL

EAST HAMPNETT LANE

NETTLETON AVENUE

BISHOPS ROAD

MIDDLETON GARDENS

PLAYING FIELDS

TANGMERE ROAD

HAMPDEN PLACE

CITY FIELDS BUSINESS PARK

CHESTNUT FARM

TENNIS COURTS

PUBLIC HOUSE

OAKWOOD CLOSE

OLDBURY FARM

MEADOWSIDE WALK

CITYFIELDS WAY

DOCTOR / DENTIST SURGERY

VILLAGE CENTRE

JERRARD ROAD

NELSON CLOSE

CANBERRA PLACE

MARSH LANE

MALCOLM ROAD

SPITFIRE COURT

CAMPBELL ROAD

CAEDWALLA DRIVE

SUNDERLAND CLOSE

MANNOCK ROAD

CHESTNUT WALK

DERWENT CLOSE

TAMAR WAY

CHURCHWOOD DRIVE

CHESHIRE CRESENT

HUNTERS GATE

MEADOW WAY

LYSANDER WAY

FULMAR WAY

COPPER BEECH DRIVE

WOODFIELD CLOSE

WYVERN CLOSE

BARNCROFT CLOSE

CHICHESTER DRIVE

BAYLEY ROAD

WHITEBEAM WAY

OLD COTTAGE CLOSE

THE GLEBE

ST. ANDREW'S CHURCH

HALEYBRIDGE WALK

CHURCH LANE

HARESFIELD TERRACE

SAXON MEADOW

HEARN CLOSE

TANGMERE MILITARY AVIATION MUSEUM

GAMECOCK TERRACE

COPSE FARM

TO CHICHESTER

TANGMERE ROAD

BADER ARMS

Adam & Jo Stone

TANGMERE AIRFIELD NURSER

Tangmere Players Est 1988

Tangmere & Boxgrove Rainbows
May 1993 - May 2000
15 Rainbows - 14 Rainbows

1st Tangmere & Boxgrove Brownie Pack
Formed 12 July 1962 with 24 Brownies
May 2000 - 25 Brownies

1st Tangmere & Boxgrove Guide
Formed 12 July 1962 with 22 Guides
May 200 - 6 Guides

ROYAL AIR FORCE
TANGMERE
ATTACK TO DEFEND

Hollie Maynard • Rebecca McCormick • Ellie Moorhouse • Jessica Myers • Alex Peacock • Amber Pettitt • Hannah Ryan • Stuart Samways • Christopher Stone • steven Sutherland • Maxwell Taylor • Bradley Wadey • Aleisha Whitew • Aaron Williams • Matthew Yates • Sophie Arcedeckne-Butler • Joe Bain • Bryan Henderson • Brionie Rowland • Padraic Rutter • emily Showcross • Crag Stapleton • Oliver Stocks • Ryan Wadey • Natalie Werham • James Beaton • Oliver Bone • Oliver Cousins • Jessica Evans • Charles Forster • Sara Frisby • Callum Haggarty • Daniel Hills • Lewis Jelley • Joshua Kershaw • Sand Farhana Rahman • Connor Ryan • Karl Ryan • Eleanor Salkeld • Alexander Simson • Jake Steer • Lewis Walford • Joshua Williams •

many seeing the rural atmosphere all around as important to their well-being. Greenery in the form of trees, grass and gardens all play their part – notice the little photographs of village views on the map, all chosen to make this point. Past developers have made imaginative use of small groups of houses with green open spaces, producing a pleasant and relaxed atmosphere. Two views are particularly cherished: to the north there is the backdrop of the Downs in the direction of Goodwood, and to the west the sight of Chichester Cathedral across open countryside. There have been plenty of successes in modern Tangmere. There is the feeling that what has happened here could well become a beacon for the rest of the county because of the way a populous rural village has provided new homes and work places, at the same time as enhancing an environment valued by its residents.

What the people of Tangmere now want to see is their village protected from further massive growth. They want to preserve its country atmosphere of space and air, they want to preserve the gap and view towards Chichester. They don't want to become a suburb of the city as suggested by the two new commercial areas calling themselves Chichester Business Park and City Fields. They want to be Tangmere in their own right. In the village they don't want to see any more infilling

between properties, especially where it can damage the setting around the older houses. In the view of many residents the character of the village will be irretrievably lost if infilling continues as it has done in recent years. Importantly they feel that the amount of business development so far permitted is as much as this small parish can take without the destruction of its character and identity. They want to see that *their* environment is understood and cared for. If their wishes are granted then Tangmere's face as we know it today – its third identity in less than a hundred years – will have some real prospect of survival. An understanding of what Tangmere people really want for their village will give a fair view of what might be said to make for the ideal community in action – not of some isolated rural idyll, but one firmly set in the workaday world of the 21st century.

KIM LESLIE

RAF Tangmere officially closed with due ceremony on 16th October 1970 after occupying the village for many decades. During these years all the usual village facilities and organisations quietly disappeared. These now had to be replaced 'From swords to Ploughshares' is a very apt quotation. From 1970 the majority of the old RAF buildings became a playground for vandals until 1983 when Seawards Ltd purchased the 37 acre site for development. As part of the contract they built meadowway and new roundabout at its junction with the A27.

The Parish was very fortunate in having Seawards Ltd Estate development and the conversion of old farm buildings in Saxon Meadow by Federated Homes Ltd. These were of such good, practical and pleasant design considerably enhancing the village. Tangmere unlike the majority of Sussex parishes is a village of 'Young Married Families' with young children growing up fast.

In 1977 the Parish council purchased from the RAF/PSA the eleven acre sports field with dilapidated pavilion in Malcolm Road, plus nine acres of land on the old airfield for allotments and amenity use. In 1987 The Parish Council had The Village Centre complex built comprising village hall with usual offices, changing rooms for those using the sportsfield, plus The Medical Centre comprising Doctors surgery, Dispensary, facilities for District Nurse and well equipped Dental surgery.

The airfield proper was sold back to the original farmer owners, farmed and over the years concrete runways, blast walls and pens have been demolished, ground up and used as hardcore for new roads.

In 1989 Tangmere Nurseries Ltd erected seven acres of glass houses for tomato growing. Today year 2000 they have some 48 acres of glasshousing in which the maincrop is 'Peppers', supplying a major part of the English market and being the largest employers in the parish.

The 1939/45 war changed Tangmere. A poignant remembrance of those days is the well kept 'Service Graves' of some 89 Allied and German serviceman buried next to The Parish Church.

David Greenwood

The club started in 1982 at the Pavilion (now the Village Hall). There we had a course of lessons given by Mrs Morris, (a most charming lady, sadly no longer with us). Her fee then was only £5.00 plus £1.00 for flowers and £1.00 for petrol. The cost of the 6 lessons was £3.50 for members and £4.00 for non-members. (What a difference now when a demonstration can cost between £30 and £40).

This Club was formed in 1976 with the help of Age Concern. We have a lively membership who enjoy meeting together each week for games of cards and scrabble and delicious refreshments. We go on outings to the theatre and places of interest. At Christmas we enjoy a meal at a local hostelry. Its is great fun.

It's time to give our Institute its place on the map. If you're needing an interest then we'll fill the gap.

There're speakers and demo's to suit every need. If you've time on your hands, your imagination we'll feed.

Our ladies are friendly and very refined. We're all very helpful and terribly kind.

We've a craft group and darts team, we bake and we sew, Whatever your interest, we'll give it a go

They're trips and three're parties and plenty of fun, We cater for Great Great Grandmas Right down to young Mums.

Our village has history from airmen and planes, To very old buildings that still look the same.

The "Bader" is handy for a meal or a drink, Or just walk on the airfield if you need time to think.

So enjoy the village and do join our team. You might see that WI ladies are not quite what they seem!

Tangmere W.I. 2000

FUNDED BY THE NATIONAL LOTTERY
Millennium Awards
THE MILLENNIUM Awards

Help the Aged Millennium Awards

Tangmere Cricket Club
Tangmere Tennis Club
Tangmere Keep Fit
Tangmere Football Club
Tangmere Horticultural & Allotment Society
Tangmere Twinning Association

Printed by the West Sussex County Council Print Unit

Turners Hill

CARS – VANS – LORRIES – they drive their endless nose-to-tail journeys around the map, symbols of their relentless grip on this crossroads village on the hill. From north, south, east and west, traffic pours through Turners Hill, unhappy hub of a giant web of roads radiating to Crawley, Horsham, East Grinstead, Haywards Heath, Godstone, Lingfield and Edenbridge. Some twenty thousand vehicles pass through the village every day. No wonder the parish council reports that 'Traffic calming, roads, pavements, signs and all things connected continue to take up much of our time' with expressions of 'frightening experiences' from locals going about their daily business. The hero of every school day must surely be the lollipop lady who sorts children from traffic on this blind summit. These vulnerable youngsters feel dwarfed by this menace on their doorstep which is why the parish map – made entirely by pupils at the village school – highlights road vehicles around its borders. It is with some feeling that they show more wheels than buildings.

In this way their perspective on village life is highly significant. And what is more their map is unique: Turners Hill Church of England Primary School is the only school in the county to have made a complete map for the West Sussex Parish Maps Project.

But ignore traffic for a moment as well as the overflying jets – two are painted in the sky from Gatwick Airport just five miles away – and look closely at the map for buildings and green spaces around the village. There are plenty of interesting features, attractive buildings, two good village pubs, a third recently converted into a restaurant, the bonus of wonderful views over four counties, sports and playing facilities and a very active community. Sadly most guide-books tread in the footsteps of their predecessors, ignoring the village altogether. S. P. B. Mais dismissed Turners Hill as just a place 'where there is an inn' (he seems to have missed the others).

But with the children as our guide, what would they, as makers of the map, have us see around their village centre?

Here are just a few of their more noteworthy features:

■ Proudly they would start with their school, the best example in West Sussex of extending a Victorian school sympathetically with its original 19th-century architecture. Once just a single room serving as both church and school before the parish church was built, the Victorian-gothic windows have been copied, roof pitches matched and original proportions carefully maintained in its 1988 extension. And much care has been taken to build the extension in stone, for this is very much a stone village. There were sandstone quarries all round the parish, rocky outcrops can be seen in North Street and Church Road, and some of the older houses are built on solid rock foundations. Sandstone blocks protect the corners of the village green.

The School

■ Opposite the school, again in stone, is the tiny toytown-like fire station, known locally as 'Trumpton' after the puppet community that had its own fire brigade under the incomparable Captain Flack. This is the smallest West Sussex village to retain its own fire station.

Fire Station

■ The Crown at the crossroads is a 17th-century timber-framed farmhouse, later a drovers' inn, refaced in distinctive fishscale-shaped tiles.

The Crown

■ Newstone Cottages in East Street are ten semi-detached stone and timber cottages topped with Tudor-style chimneys built in 1919 for Lord Cowdray's Paddockhurst Estate workers. His monogram decorates the central pair above the little sundial-skirt statue. Designed by Sir Aston Webb – who also designed part of Buckingham Palace – this is aristocratic architecture for working men.

Newstone Cottages

■ The Ark, just beyond the cottages, is the centre of local social life, taking its name from the original parish hall by the school perched on the top of the hill like the biblical ark. This is now the home of any number of clubs and societies, a centre for computer training and home to the village museum. Sheltered housing opposite is called Noah's Court. Both are in Mount Road, an allusion to Mount Ararat!

The Ark

■ The 18th-century Red Lion, a former coaching inn, is in the village centre's quietest road, Lion Street – once the main road before North Street was cut – at the core of the Conservation Area and home to the Turners Hill Tolleymen – marble players who compete on the two rings at the back of the pub and at the annual World Marbles Championships at nearby Tinsley Green. They reached the world semi-finals in 2005. (A tolley is the marble used to shoot opponents' marbles out of the ring.) Several historic houses in this road are protected as grade-two listed buildings.

The Red Lion

■ The late 19th-century stone parish church crowns the highest point of the village, giving extensive views to both the North and South Downs. A good story is told about digging its foundations in the 1890s. The specifications said nothing about where to put the earth being dug out. The foreman, asking where it should go, got the reply: 'Dig a hole and bury it'!

St Leonard's Church

Turners Hill's countryside, part of the High Weald Area of Outstanding Natural Beauty, covers the headwaters of not just one, but three rivers – Mole, Ouse and Medway – the parish straddling three water-catchment areas. Within yards of each other springs and streams burst out to tumble north, south and east. Turners Hill's waters end up as far apart as East Molesey on the Thames (opposite Hampton Court), Newhaven in East Sussex and Sheerness in Kent. Heading for the Ouse, just below the school, is Threepoint Gill, a gill being the ancient name for a stream cut into a deep ravine-like valley.

West of the village is the Benedictine Worth Abbey, its distinguished 19th-century architecture in such contrast to its 1960s–70s circular Abbey Church, of great presence and power. The abbey, part monastery, part school, was originally a private house called Paddockhurst, owned by Robert Whitehead (1823–1905), inventor of the torpedo, and then Lord Cowdray (1856–1927) whose main Sussex property was at Cowdray Park near Midhurst. The Paddockhurst Estate has had a great influence on life in Turners Hill, offering

jobs in farming and forestry, its lands creating a buffer against village expansion, so the village hasn't grown as big as its neighbours, Crawley Down and Copthorne. One of its former properties, now owned by the Beare family, is Tulleys Farm, recently voted UK Farm Retailer of the Year with its thriving pick-your-own business, farmshop, tearoom, children's farm and summertime maize maze. The first farm maze in Sussex, it draws thousands into the parish each year.

On the other side of the village is Turners Hill's prestigious hotel – Alexander House – ancestral home of the Bysshe family that bore the illustrious poet, Percy Bysshe Shelley. Other great names in English literature have come this way. George Bernard Shaw stayed at Wyndham Croft during the First World War where he first met Virginia Woolf at a house party and was inspired to write his play *Heartbreak House*, in what he calls 'The hilly country in the middle of the north edge of Sussex'. He was deeply depressed by the sound of gunfire from France – the 'drumming in the sky' of act three – heard from the terrace. By contrast, Edward Thomas, writer and poet of the countryside (who was killed in the same conflict at Arras), found 'cloistered tranquility' when staying just up the road at Selsfield House. He loved the still quietness, eulogising 'the steep little valley . . . of the Medway' in his classic evocation of the English countryside, *The South Country* (1909). Mantlemas in Lion Street lent its name to the *Mantlemass* historical saga set in Sussex by local children's writer Barbara Willard (1909–94).

With Turners Hill's rich history, its attractive corners, surrounding countryside and lively social scene it's not difficult to understand the great affection felt for the village. 'We are really so proud to live in this wonderful place' says village stalwart and former school head, Eric Dawes, who has given more than half his lifetime to building its community spirit, reflecting maybe the churchyard tribute made nearly a century ago to Cecil Blaker 'who had the happiness of being the first vicar of this parish'.

KIM LESLIE

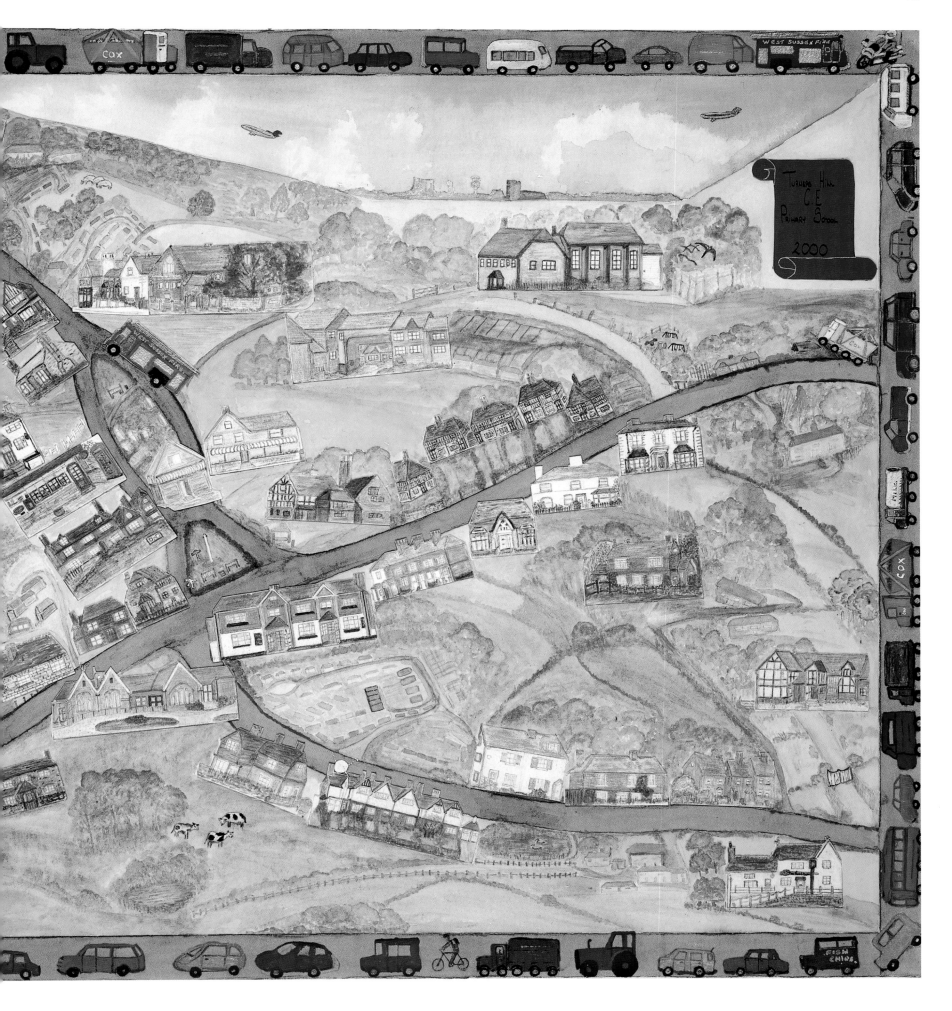

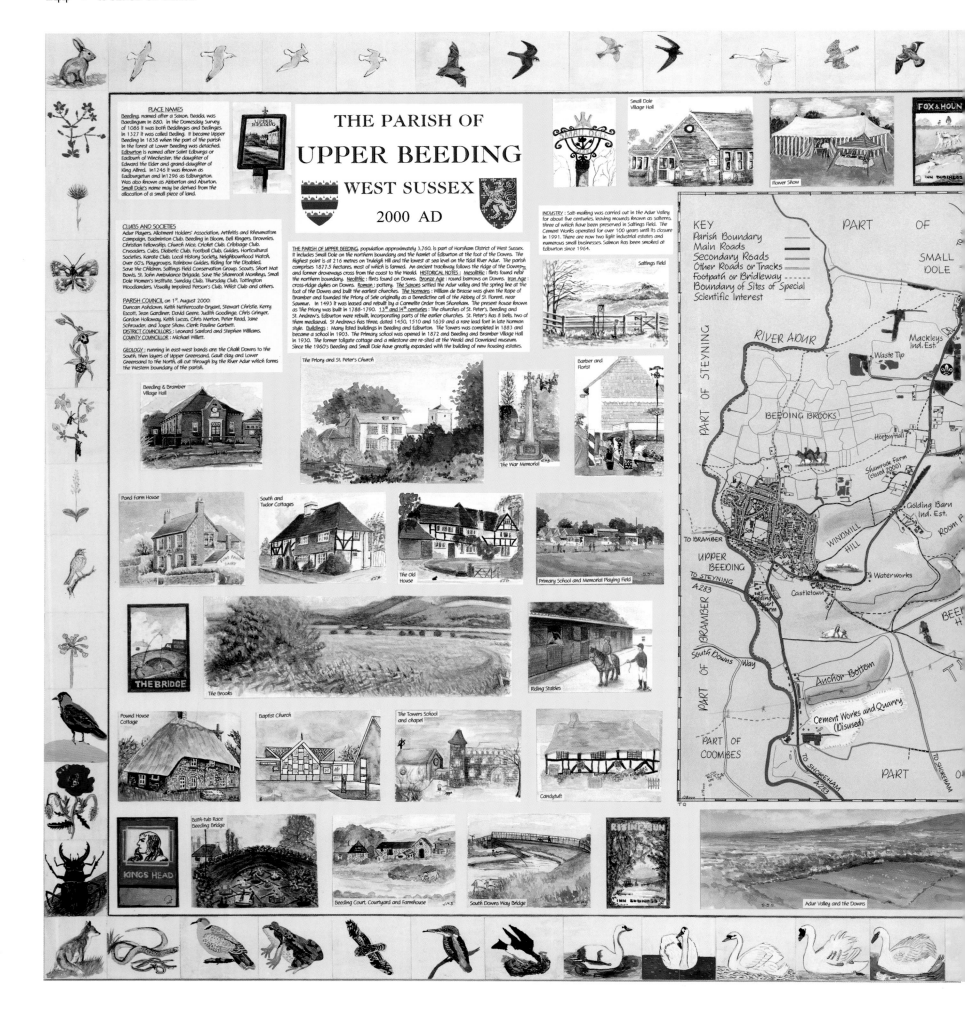

Upper Beeding

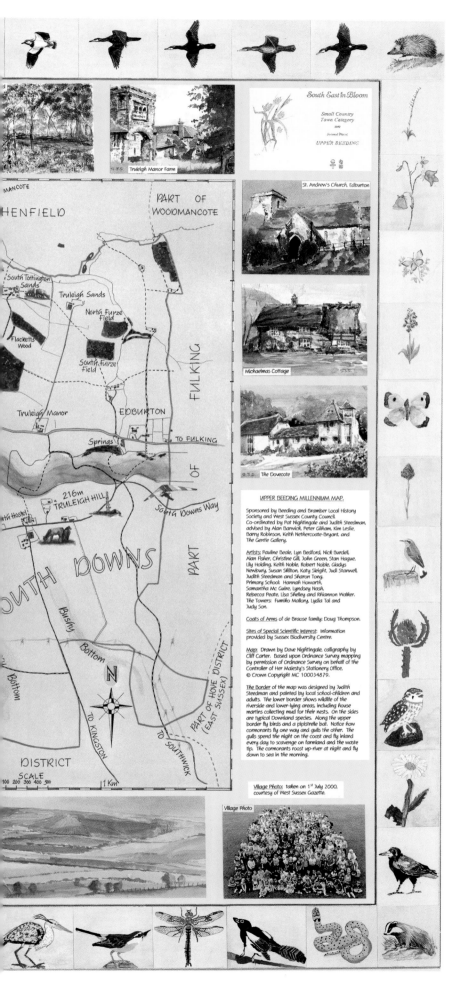

A SUSSEX PUZZLE of *Alice in Wonderland* logic: how comes it that a village called Upper sits lower than its higher namesake Lower, whose waters even flow from lower to upper parts? – a place-name conundrum worthy of a county where its Downs are really its Ups. That guardian of all that made Sussex so special and distinct, Hilaire Belloc, loved oddities like this, playfully remarking that it was Adam who, so as 'to establish by names this good peculiar place, this Eden which is Sussex . . . was to make her names of a sort that should give fools to think. So he laid it down that whatever was high in Sussex should be called low, and whatever was low should be called high', his best example being Lower Beeding on its hilltop, with Upper Beeding almost down at sea level.

The real answer to the puzzle establishes Upper Beeding's importance. In medieval times it was the original mother settlement from where early settlers left to colonise the wilder lands of north Sussex as swine pastures. Although ten miles apart, both places shared their common roots by being named as one – although separated by three other parishes in between. Eventually the original Beeding was called Upper (or 'greater') and its offshoot Lower (or 'lesser') as a way of distinguishing their relative status.

Upper Beeding's superiority is demonstrated by its great antiquity, supported by the evidence of some very fine buildings – many of them listed – in the High Street, down the hollow-way of Hyde Street and around the church by the site of the medieval Sele priory. Cameos around the map highlight some of these older properties, including the delightfully named Candytuft, all of them in traditional materials: brick, timber, stone, flint and thatch.

Candytuft

245

Bath-tub Race
Beeding Bridge

The Towers School
and chapel

Beeding's local importance is suggested by the fact that it even conferred its name on the Beeding river as an alternative to Adur. And before Shoreham's bridges were built in the 18th and 19th centuries, the village stood at the river's lowest bridging point, at a crossroads commanding two vital highways across the county: one forming part of the great east-west route through southern England from Canterbury to Southampton; the other north-south to the coast, and what eventually became one of the earliest London to Brighton roads climbing straight over the steeply-rutted Beeding Bostal. So over the centuries the village has seen a vast amount of passing traffic – including a great number of commercial barges on the river – with the consequence that there are many references to 'travellers' in the parish registers. Since 1981 the village has been bypassed, the main road through the centre now an oasis of calm compared to when it was being used by road freight from Shoreham's port on its way to the Midlands and the North. Sussex writer Ted Walker wrote of pre-bypass days in 1973 when a look at the old houses in the High Street was only 'for the nimble and intrepid who dare to take the risk of being run over or

buried beneath a lorry-load of timber'. Since then things have improved massively for Beeding. Now locals and visitors can take their time with a reasonable chance of survival.

The map gives a superb summary of what it is that makes up the wider community of this big civil parish covering three so very different villages: Upper Beeding itself, plus Small Dole and tiny Edburton, with three quite distinct landscapes: chalk downland, marshy brookland along the river and clay farmland to the north. Two panoramic views offer a good feel for the local scenery dominated by the Downs. And whilst the main village of Beeding is well built-up, what comes over very strongly is that most of the parish is quite free of buildings – in fact only 4 per cent is occupied by the village. For all its modern development, it's very much a rural parish over most of its five thousand acres. And that's exactly what Pat and Dave Nightingale of Beeding and Bramber Local History Society wanted to convey when they started to organise the project. As Pat said: 'We soon saw that it was nearly all open space. Only quite a small area is built on, so we decided to concentrate on the nature and wildlife aspects by emphasising our local birds, animals and wild flowers to make the point.'

THE BRIDGE

Adur Valley and the Downs

Flower Show

Much of the wildlife around the border was painted by girls from Beeding Primary School and The Towers Convent under the direction of designer Judith Steedman. The lower border shows wildlife found by the riverside, including house martins collecting mud for their nests. Cormorants and gulls fly across the top of the map in opposite directions, which is precisely what happens along the river. By day the gulls feed on the landfill site at Small Dole, returning to the coast at dusk, while the cormorants fish on the coast and come over Beeding on their way to their night-time roost at Wyckham Farm, Steyning. Amongst the wild flowers is the best-known of all British orchids, the chalk-loving bee orchid, painted by the oldest artist of the group, 84-year-old Lily Holding. Such a fine collection of wildlife paintings points to an enormously attractive countryside around the village.

Val Booth, who ran the village estate agency in the High Street, was asked for her feelings about the place for a feature in the *West Sussex Gazette*. She mirrored the feelings of so many: 'I love the atmosphere, the community. As an estate agent I sell the village, and I tell people, "if you want the picturesque go to Steyning, if you want a community come to Beeding". People don't often move out of Beeding. If they do, they want to move back after a few years.... We have a lot going for us.'

In fact the map lists thirty-six clubs and societies (scripted, as elsewhere on the map, by calligrapher Cliff Carter) ranging from the

Allotment Holders and Beeding in Bloom to a varied mix of sports through to whist, cribbage, karate and groups such as the bellringers, the Sunday Club, Church Mice and Crusaders. The Saltings Field Conservation Group cares for a small cluster of salt mounds, surviving remnants of the medieval salt industry of the Adur Valley. There's pretty much something for everyone in the village.

Saltings Field

When it was all finished after fifteen months of hard work, lavish praise was heaped on all those who had made it possible, the *County Times* reporting the production as 'fabulous' when it was unveiled. There was a great buzz of excitement when copies went on sale, and as three guests at the ceremony wrote afterwards: 'I knew that this was going to be good, but not this good' – 'A great result from a very ambitious project' – ' What a wonderful keepsake of our parish'.

KIM LESLIE

Village millennium photograph

Walberton and Binsted

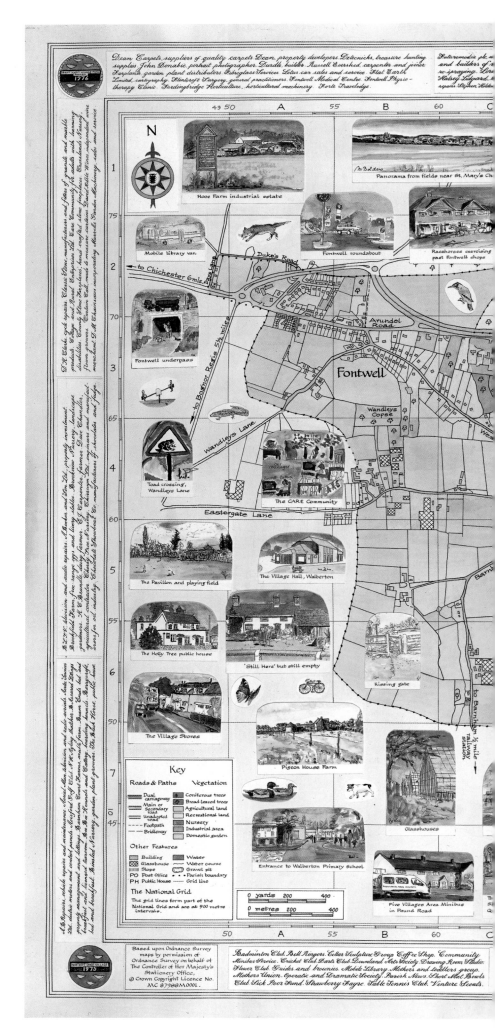

WALBERTON ACTION GROUP – WAG for short – has a bit of a reputation for making maps, not only with this distinctive celebration for the millennium, but also with a whole range of more matter-of-fact utility maps and plans of the civil parish that unites two ancient ecclesiastical parishes – Walberton and Binsted – with their two contrasting modern outposts, Havenwood Park, tucked away in the woods, and most of Fontwell (less the race-course area in another parish that brings fame to its name) up by the A27. WAG's house-name maps, made at the suggestion of a former postmistress, guide postmen around elusive unnumbered properties, and since then have been requested by the ambulance and police services; there are maps showing Walberton village centre and its features not shown or named on any other available maps; another giving local bus routes and destinations (linked to a Bus Fact Sheet), as well as a range of footpath maps opening up the surrounding countryside. The crystal-clear clarity of the parish map, artistic detail kept well apart from cartographic detail, is very much in line with WAG's quest for geographic precision in its work. Its mapping is rooted in a real understanding of local needs and a sense of location.

With all its energetic activities for enhancing and improving life in the parish, WAG certainly lives up to its name as an action group. Its inspiration is grounded in the 1992 Rio Earth Summit to save the planet, with the message that everyone and every place in the world has a part to play in caring for the environment. Care, consideration and understanding for the locality are at the very heart of WAG's initiative and that's why maps for setting the scene and as guides to home surroundings are so significant.

This map was prepared during 1998 and 1999 by members of the Walberton Action Group and others, under the West Sussex Millennium Parish Map Scheme.

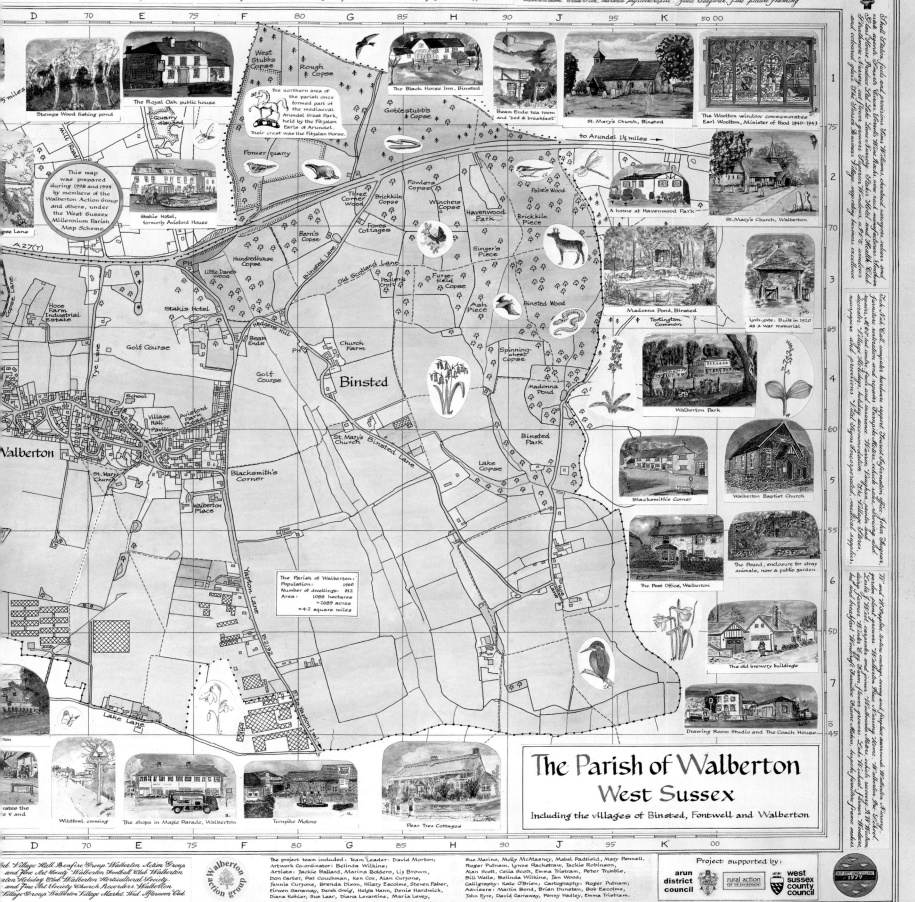

The Parish of Walberton
West Sussex
Including the villages of Binsted, Fontwell and Walberton

The Pond, Walberton

There is a lively conservation programme with landscape-improvement schemes such as pond clearance, planting hedges, trees and bulbs, keeping footpaths in order, the Churchyard Heritage Project and the Parish Hedgerow Survey. And just as WAG spawned the parish map, so out of the map was born the Walberton History Group. And from their interests have come projects to reproduce and interpret 18th- and 19th-century maps as well as a booklet of reminiscences.

In 1997 WAG conducted its Valued Features Survey to find out what local people really valued most about the parish. The features – all 170 of them – give a superb summary of what it is that makes up the distinctive character of Walberton. They represent the very essence of the place. A few examples from each category give a good flavour of the richness of this environment, underlining that it is the very ordinary and everyday features easily taken for granted that really matter to people. Features such as these give Walberton, Binsted and Fontwell their own very special identity.

Flora and Fauna
Cow parsley in spring in Tye Lane and Binsted Lane; the bulbs throughout the village; hedges throughout the parish; horses ridden through the village

Water
Walberton Pond; the Madonna Pond, Binsted; the waterfall and stream in Eastergate Lane; the stream in Spinning Wheel Copse

Woods
Binsted Woods; copses and fields south of St Mary's Church, Walberton; the avenue at Walberton Place Nursing Home; the 'stone pines' at Fontwell (a species of pine, like an umbrella at the top, by the Police House, and also along Fontwell Avenue, just beyond the parish boundary)

Scenes and Land
Views of the Downs and Halnaker Windmill; heathland along the western section of Old Scotland Lane; Binsted Valley; the green verge of Maple Road

Buildings
The succession of Victorian terraces in the Street; the former Baptist chapel, now a garage; the cohesion of old and newer properties in Walberton; the boarded-up house on the village green (known as 'Still Here')

'Still Here' but still empty

Constructions
The Jubilee Arch; the underpass at Fontwell; the Pound; the gate-piers of Walberton Place Nursing Home in Yapton Lane with graffiti by US soldiers stationed here for D-Day, 1944

Footpaths and Lanes
Footpaths: Binsted Rectory to the Madonna Pond; across the fields from Walberton Church to Lake Lane and Barnham;
Lanes: Binsted Lane and Hedgers Hill; unmade Mill Lane and Copse Lane

Madonna Pond, Binsted

Post Office, Walberton

Shops and Services
Walberton's shops; 'our postman'; the garage; the bus services

General Environment
All the Binsted area; the community spirit; Open Gardens Day; 'the compactness of Walberton village centre'

Amenities
The Village Hall, Pavilion, playing fields and play area; the village school; the five ways in and out of the village; Walberton Action Group

Village Hall, Walberton

Miscellaneous
The toad crossing in Wandleys Lane; the sound of the church bells; the bus timetables produced by WAG; lack of street lighting

This wealth of treasures is the very stuff of what life means to local people here; they are some of the myriad threads that bind people to place. What they tell us is a far cry from Arthur Mee's terse 1930s description of Walberton as just 'charming corners on the way to Arundel', its ancient font 'the chief of its possessions'. By highlighting only the church – as typically so many guide-books do when describing villages – Mee missed all the hidden subtleties of the place, the qualities that give atmosphere, like its sounds – the little streams, the horses riding by, the church bells – and the views – of woods, marshland and hills – and all the other incidentals loved by villagers, unnoticed by so many passers-by.

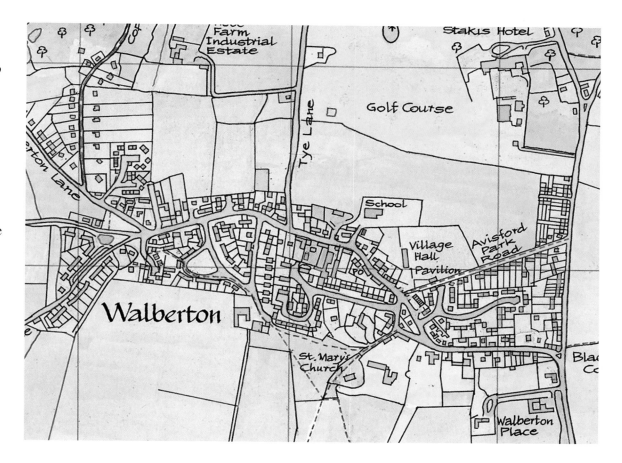

There are so many little hidden places. Take Binsted and Emma Tristram's remarks about its 'secluded atmosphere' protected from the noise and disruption of the A27 by its thick barrier of woodland. She mentions a press article of 1937 – still appropriate for today – referring to 'its silent woods' giving 'this tree-entwined village . . . peace with its isolation'. And in her own words 'the "secret", enclosed fields . . . have a hidden quality. In the Binsted Rife Valley, you feel cut off from human

habitations, as they are hidden by the lie of the land and hedges and trees, though it is within easy walking distance of many houses in Walberton. The layout of Binsted Lane, a horse-shoe "dead-end" for cars, is essential in preserving the sense of enclosure', Emma comments in *Binsted and Beyond*. This beautifully presented book captures the spirit of this atmospheric place. Read it, visit the village, take time and you'll be amply rewarded.

WAG has similarly dug deep into Walberton's spirit with a book of its own. In the pages of *Walberton Past and Present*, contributors convey the enormous variety of the local scenery and its village settlements. To the east there is Binsted amongst the woods and fields, its peaceful, timeless atmosphere and sense of looking back into the past a rare and precious survival of a coastal plain parish. And then to the west – in such contrast – the trunk-road culture of Fontwell, offspring of the A27 with its stop-over traffic for the Travelodge and Little Chef. Sandwiched between at the centre is Walberton itself, the bigger, parent village, ancient and modern side by side, with shops, services, sports field, village hall and school making for a really lively parish.

If it's people that make lively villages, then one of its principal players is Emma Tristram. Having chaired both the parish council and WAG, her finger is very much on the local pulse. 'It is an incredibly vibrant, interesting and friendly place to live. There is so much going on', she says. She loves the place with such a passion and enthusiasm that when recently asked by the local press about village life reportedly 'socked out the goodies like joyful straight lefts'. It's these goodies that ensure that if you are looking for real, living villages, then three are to be found right here amongst some of the most perfect countryside in southern England.

KIM LESLIE

Fontwell roundabout

Racehorses exercising past Fontwell shops

Warningcamp

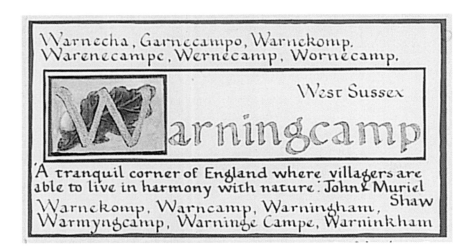

Warnecha, Garnecampo, Warnekomp, Warenecampe, Wernecamp, Wornecamp.

West Sussex

Warningcamp

'A tranquil corner of England where villagers are able to live in harmony with nature.' John & Muriel Shaw

Warnekomp, Warncamp, Warningham, Warmyngcamp, Waninge Campe, Warninkham

River Coppice and The Street

A place we lucky ones discovered and stayed.

The attraction is not so much in the village but in the views to Arundel and walks along the river bank, weather, cows and mud permitting.

railway and offer hospitality at the Youth Hostel.

My birthplace, it has changed so little over the years. It is said that home is where the heart is; mine is here.

'Twixt heaven and earth/ 'Twixt down and town/ No fairer view could I behold . . . .

These are just some of the villagers' recent comments on their lovely downland-riverside home enjoyed quite as much for its scenery as its small village feeling. Its riches are in its surroundings and people rather than any communal facilities that can be simply listed as two telephone boxes, two post boxes and a bus shelter. Without church, school, pub or shop, and with no central focus, it would be easy to write Warningcamp off as deprived. But whatever it might be lacking in these quarters, two extraordinary people prove it's still possible to generate an enormous amount of community spirit from strong and

Arundel Castle from Warningcamp

Woodleighs Hanger – 'Happy Valley'

A tranquil corner where villagers live in harmony with nature.

Warningcamp is a pretty straggle of three hamlets – Upper Warningcamp people have a pond and woods; Middle Warningcamp people have views to Arundel, the Castle and beyond; Lower Warningcamp people have the river and

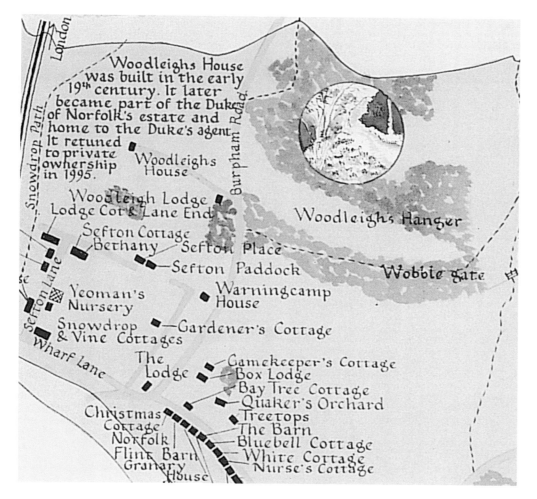

determined leadership; that at the end of the day it's inspirational people rather than any buildings that make a community.

In between working in Madagascar and raising two children, missionary Mary Barber gathered a staggering amount of material about Warningcamp, telling its story in what must rate as one of the most detailed compilations ever written for such a tiny Sussex village – *Warningcamp: The History of a Sussex Community*, published in 2002. This book is certainly no mean feat when it's seen that most Sussex books either omit it completely or dismiss it as having 'nothing of special interest'. The book demonstrates that so much can be discovered from even the most unlikely place, given plenty of time – Mary gathered her information over sixteen years involving so many people in a vast village enterprise – plus everyone's strong attachment to the place. An incredible production of some 350 pages, the book gives new meaning to places where it's said there's 'nothing of interest'.

In setting the scene in her very first chapter called 'What Makes Warningcamp Special?',

Mary's answer is its community coming together as one, expressed through making the parish map. This is where Lou Oakes comes in. A geographer passionate about expressing her Christian faith through art and print-making, Lou swept the village along into quizzes, competitions, walks, wildlife surveys, a questionnaire, a newsletter and Saturday morning workshops, galvanising the village as never before.

She takes up the story when the map was unveiled in Arundel Youth Hostel – which is actually in Warningcamp – in March 2000:

Every now and then this week I've had the feeling that one of the family is missing. But we're all here. What's missing is the map! No, this is not a detective story, but a brief description of how we made the map.

We began by delivering a questionnaire to every household in the village asking what they would like to see commemorated on the map, what their favourite places in the village are and if they would like to take part in a wildlife survey or have a go at calligraphy or painting. To get the children to think a bit more about the village we had a nature walk and quiz – 'How well do you know our village?' – and parents and grandparents came along to help with answers and identify plants and butterflies. It was such a lovely sunny day that everyone was very happy to reach the village pond for refreshments and to compare answers.

The butterfly survey was a bit hampered by the weather earlier in the year. We didn't see many at all but by the time the survey was finished we had 17 different types of butterfly to illustrate. The questionnaires and surveys gave us an idea of what to illustrate, and we had some wonderful photographs to work from. The problem was how to fit it all on to a piece of paper 30 inches by 40 inches. Quite a tricky problem!

Once a rough design was made we had three workshops on Saturday mornings to teach watercolour techniques and calligraphy. We have an amazing resource in our village – 18 artists and calligraphers ready to create something very special. What also gave a head start was all the research into local history that Mary Barber generously shared with us to use for 'snippets' of information on the map.

My studio has been full of papers and sketches for nearly a year now and the project felt like a second child. I've been asked two questions. Did I realise what was involved when I started and if I'd known, would I have done it? Well, the answer to the first question is No, I had no idea, and to the second an emphatic Yes. To coin a phrase, 'It's the journey not the destination'.

Warningcamp's journey with Lou had a fantastic effect in bringing together so many people of all ages. About twenty key volunteers worked directly on the map, but everyone had the chance to get caught up in the barrage of asking, probing and searching. All sorts of favourite locations and much-loved sights like the elusive white deer and Snowdrop Path came out of the questionnaire. The butterfly survey recorded 'scarce' or 'infrequent' varieties like the painted lady, comma, holly blue and ringlet. Perfect ways for raising awareness about local building materials, wildlife and scenery were the village quiz and photographic survey, spotlighting familiar, everyday

Norfolk Flint Barn

features taken so easily for granted that they generally go unnoticed. We find the local version of Pooh Bridge, Kath's Swing in the woods, Wobble Gate, little out of the way secret spots known to the few who love this place. Lou produced an incredibly interesting 'educational' package, some great opportunities – and a lot of fun – in putting Warningcamp on the millennium map.

KIM LESLIE

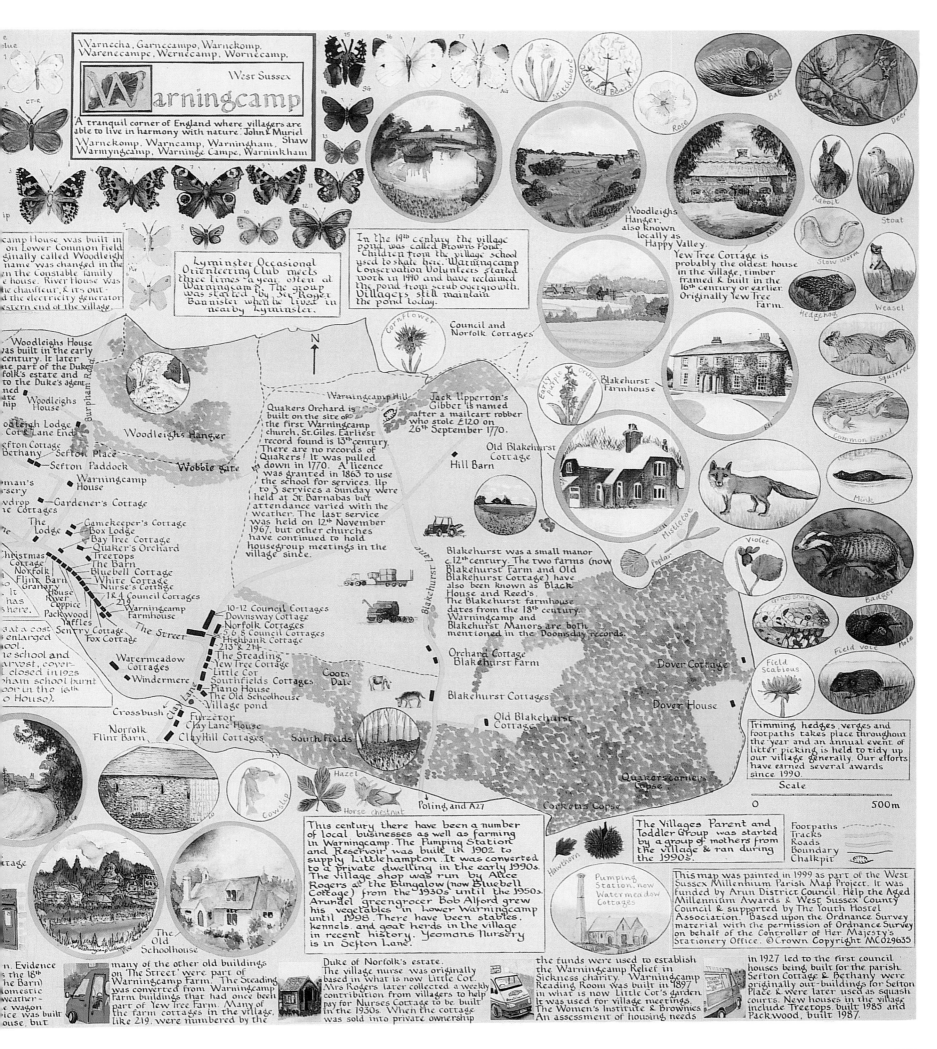

Washington

. . . all along the road under Chanctonbury, that high hill, we went as the morning broadened: along a way that is much older than anything in the world. . . .

So wrote Hilaire Belloc in his fantastical story of *The Four Men*, published in 1912. Belloc bestowed on Washington not only an ancient pedigree, but the ultimate accolade of having an inn, the Frankland Arms, that served the finest beer he had ever tasted. He wrote a hauntingly beautiful account of watching the moon rise over Chanctonbury one cold Halloween night.

So much has changed since Belloc's time. He would be astounded to find the parish bisected by the A24 dual carriageway which cuts deep down into the chalk. The Frankland Arms is still there, but both the rural labourers with whom he talked and Michell's Ale – that 'nectar' which could not be praised enough – have long since passed from memory.

Yet for those sensitive to a place and its past, the spirit of old Washington may not prove as elusive as first impressions might suggest. For just below the surface, beyond the modern façades, out of earshot of passing traffic, there are timeless things to bring reassurance and repose.

The geology of the parish is a lesson in the make-up of south-eastern England, its underlying strata representing both the Weald and Downs in miniature. A traveller coming on the village from the South Downs Way will first pass over the upper chalk, pure white and almost gleaming. Here are found the great flint nodules that for centuries supplied the raw materials for both dwellings and agricultural buildings.

As the walker descends, the flints become sparser and the chalk is of a more greyish hue: this is the lower chalk. Containing a high content of clay, it was known as marl and used as fertilizer on the fields. By the 19th century, lower chalk was being fired in kilns to produce lime. Just off Washington Bostal – to the east of the present A24 – an extensive series of

Rock Mill

disused kilns can still be located, an almost romantic ruin in their dilapidated and overgrown state.

On reaching the village, outcrops of the upper greensand will be seen. The exposed roots of ancient trees have forced this rock to the surface. The percolation of water through the chalk ensures that the sandstone is more grey than green, but its texture is quite different to the chalk, and so are its uses. The eminent houses of the old village have been built on these dependable, well-drained outcrops, while the cottages of the labouring people tended to be built on the gault clay.

This gault clay is a narrow band that runs between the chalk and the greensand. Its course is fairly easy to follow at Washington, especially after heavy rain. Little streams flood out from the hills and pools form where the clay is deepest. Pity the poor cottager who had to contend with these deluges on a regular

basis! At one time the clay was a vital ingredient in the cement-making process, and great vats of slurry were maintained for the purpose.

The A283 Storrington to Steyning road through Washington is built over the gault clay. Cross this busy road onto land known as Rock Common and suddenly you will see a great sand quarry. This sand, ideal for the building trade, is taken from the lower greensand, which again is not green, but a rusty brown. It has a high iron content and from a distance the mottled effect is rather beautiful.

High above the quarry, surrounded by trees, stands Rock Windmill. The sails, or sweeps as they are known in Sussex, were removed nearly a century ago and the mill is now a private residence. Fifty years ago the composer John Ireland (1879–1962) moved here for peace and quiet. It is not difficult to understand his distress as the quarrymen moved in to shatter his rural idyll.

To the west of the A24 and north of the A283 is an area on the edge of Washington parish known as Heath Common. Over the years it has gone under several different names, including Sleepy Hollow and the Sanctuary. It was under this last name that it found notoriety as the home of a back-to-the-land commune founded by a young heiress, Vera Pragnell, in the 1920s. For a decade people of different backgrounds and creeds came together here, united by their wish to turn their backs on the material world.

Roy Armstrong (1902–93), founder of the Open Air Museum at Singleton, was one of the great characters on its fringes. He built his own house with his own hands on Heath Common in 1931, in later life giving part of his large landscaped garden for the establishment of Sandgate Country Park. The gracefully-built bridges across the waters of Sandgate Wood were all his own handwork. During the war in the 1940s, Roy opened his home in Bracken Lane to Jomo Kenyatta when he couldn't return to Africa. Jomo was given his own area

Washington... Wasingetune... From Duha's clearing to the red spring, from the red spring to Leodgeard's hill, from Leodgeard's hill to Tatmonn's apple-tree, from Tatmonn's apple-tree to Peneburh's mound, from Peneburh's mound, from the warriors' battle to Beonna's hill, from the hill to the stony hill, from the stony hill to Hatheburh's mound, from the mound to the entrenchment, from the entrenchment to the two hills, from the two hills to Ramsdean, from Ramsdean to Biggen Holt, from Biggen Holt to the warriors' battle, from

WASHINGTON MILLENIUM MAP   by Alison Milner-Gulland, with Jacqueline Baker, Moya Bevin, Jean Coltman, Paul Coltman, Katherine Goatcher, Geoffrey Goatcher, Rosemary Gregoire, Barbara Lidbetter, Tom Milner-Gulland, Mildred Summertov, Richard Turley, Gina Wilmshurst, Roger Wilmshurst.

Supported by Horsham District Council and West Sussex County Council.

257

labourers. One of these, Rowdell, was demolished in 1959, while the other, Highden, is now Windlesham House School. The gentry families that lived here since Norman times have gone and with them the old feudal order they represented, which in many respects still lingered on at Washington until the middle years of last century.

At the time of writing, in 2005, Washington still numbers amongst its residents men and women who lived and worked under that old order. One of these, Frank Brooks, at the age of 95, is still a bell-ringer at the parish church. Yet most residents today are incomers and the old continuity has been broken, as indeed is the case in most Sussex villages.

That great Sussex landmark, Chanctonbury Ring, dominates Washington. The circular clump of trees, planted by Charles Goring in 1760, was devastated by the 1987 hurricane, but nearly twenty years later, following replanting, it is just beginning to show signs of its familiar outline. Walking alone to this spot, particularly on an evening in autumn, is an experience to excite the senses and evoke fancies of bygone times.

Hilaire Belloc's description of Chanctonbury, viewed from the east on that Halloween night a century ago, has a timeless quality that can still touch us in these modern times:

The moon stood over Chanctonbury, so removed and cold in her silver that you might almost have thought her careless of the follies of men; little clouds, her attendants, shone beneath her worshipping, and they presided together over a general silence. Her light caught the edges of the Downs. There was no mist. She was still frosty-clear when I saw her set behind those hills. The stars were more brilliant after her setting, and deep quiet held the valley of Adur, my little river, slipping at low tide towards the sea.

CHRIS HARE

of scrubland to clear where he grew his own supply of vegetables and kept some chickens. One of Roy's silver birches became his 'sacred tree' through which he communicated with the spirits of his people. From this sanctuary on Heath Common, Kenyatta returned home after the war, eventually becoming first President of Kenya in 1964, but never forgetting his gratitude to Roy during his days of exile.

Amidst the imposing houses of modern-day Heath Common, with their security fencing and CCTV cameras, will be found a few small one-storeyed houses from the old Sanctuary days. Vera Pragnell's dreams were never fulfilled and she died older and wiser, but also sadder, in those innocent days of idealistic expectation.

Washington was once a village in thrall to the great houses of the parish. The men and women of the village worked in these houses as servants or worked in their fields as

West Hoathly

THE PARISH LIES ACROSS a ridge in the High Weald alongside the boundary with East Sussex and a little south of the Surrey border. The ridge forms a watershed: on the north side draining to the infant Medway and eventually the North Sea; to the south, local springs are headwaters of the Ouse that fall into the Channel. Geographically, West Hoathly sits not only on this most important divide, but also on the route of the High Weald Landscape Trail between Horsham and Rye; it passes through a good cross-section of the parish and right along the village street. 'Be prepared to linger in this village' advises the trail's guide-book.

From this hilltop site some six hundred feet above sea level there are spectacular views across four counties seen from the toposcope (or viewing table) on Finche Field. A few of the significant landmarks indicated are Oxted chalk quarries in Surrey to the north; Tunbridge Wells in Kent to the east; Firle Beacon in East Sussex to the south; Chanctonbury Ring in West Sussex to the south-west. All are visible on a good, fine day.

The parish map was designed and overseen by Julia Piqué and Richard Toomer. Twenty-one adults plus children from the primary school contributed their pictures. One unusual addition is the inclusion of the rainfall bar-chart for 2000, highlighting falls of nearly double the average, an incredible year. (West Hoathly is the only West Sussex parish to give such information on its map.) The garland

Jackson Jewsbury
James Johns Judge
Jelly Johnson
Jennings Johnstone
Jennison Jones

enclosing the map includes some of the wildflowers and plants found here, some of them evidence of ancient woodland. Lettering around the border by Bob Sellens records the surnames of all the residents. Roger Bourne, who remembers a happy childhood in the village, drew the map.

Besides the main village, there are three other settlements within the civil parish: Highbrook, Selsfield and Sharpthorne.

Highbrook became a separate ecclesiastical parish in 1884 when All Saints' was built, and is now a joint living with West Hoathly. It retains its separate identity and has made its own parish map (see pages 128–30). Selsfield, with its landmark hundred-year-old water-tower and National Trust common, is an even smaller hamlet. Sharpthorne, much more a village than a hamlet, developed after the railway line and station opened in 1882. The line closed in 1958, the track was removed and the station demolished, but the Bluebell Railway is currently extending its operations to connect with the main-line station at East Grinstead. The whistle of the trains as they approach the long tunnel is a familiar sound. The line here was a setting for scenes in the recent television adaptation of *The Railway Children*.

The sandstones and clays of the High Weald were the basis of local ironworks that flourished here some centuries ago. There was a Tudor furnace at Chiddinglye and an 18th-century gun-making furnace at Gravetye. The industry left a legacy of ponds, place-names and some fine houses built from the profits. In the church are more reminders of this industrial past in the unusual iron grave slabs in the south aisle, memorials to the Infield family, owners of the ironworks at Gravetye.

The local clay is also excellent for brickmaking. In the woods there was oak for building, bark for tanning and coppices of hazel, hornbeam and sweet chestnut for poles and charcoal burning. Remarkably today these resources continue to sustain profitable enterprises, giving employment as in times past.

Philpots Quarry, where dinosaur and fish fossils have been found, is one of the few Wealden quarries still producing building stone. At Sharpthorne, the Ibstock brickworks makes high-quality bricks. Comber's flourishing building business will soon celebrate its centenary. The woodlands, less profitable these days, are alive with deer, badgers, foxes and birds. The overgrown coppices are carpeted with bluebells in the spring. Charges for shooting rights augment diminished returns on farmland and encourage the preservation of woods and shaws. Some beef cattle and flocks of sheep graze the hilly fields but the renowned dairy herds are no longer part of the rural scene.

Philpots Quarry

Hedge-laying

Map of the Parish of West Hoathly 2000 A.D.

There are many good examples of local ironwork, including the West Hoathly village sign made by George Newnham, former blacksmith at the forge in North Lane. The tradition continues: the horse-shoeing forge may be no more, but Anvil Blacksmiths have won awards for wrought ironwork, making gates and decorative pieces today. Near the old forge, a garage specialises in the maintenance and restoration of vintage cars.

When the iron furnaces fell silent, the people relied once more on the fields and woods, familiar to a bedrock of families whose names echo through the ages and who were baptised, married and buried here. They supported church and chapel, caring for the poor and needy. Only when the railway was built towards the end of the 19th century did their way of life start to change. Wealthy newcomers bought land, refurbished old houses and put up new ones. Chiddinglye, a fine Victorian country house, became the home of the Earl of Limerick, whose descendants still live there.

One man who brought fame to the parish was William Robinson (1838–1935) who moved to Gravetye in 1885. He revolutionised the principles of gardening by advocating wild gardening – planting that was allowed to develop its own natural sequence, instead of set-piece formalised carpet-bedding. His books became bibles of gardening, his Gravetye garden their expression. When he died after half a century here, the whole world of gardening far beyond the shores of England mourned: the *New York Times* in its farewell called him 'The World's Grand Old Man of Gardening'. Today his work is still celebrated at Gravetye, his old Elizabethan house, now a hotel of renown.

Many other well-known people have lived around here – writers, artists, actors and musicians, attracted by the scenery and rural tranquillity. Today we are fortunate to have so many talented people in our midst, many of them coming together each year to keep up the traditions of the Stoneland Players. They were originally founded by the family of John Godwin King in 1910 to stage community drama in their barn. King's descendants have their home in the Manor House that he gave to his daughter, Ursula, on her marriage. As the lady of the manor, Ursula Ridley wrote the first popular history of the parish. She died in 1974 but is still remembered as a force to be reckoned with, promoting housing for local people, public footpaths and treating her tenants with generosity. Her influence, and that of her family, in village affairs is recalled in the housing estate called Ridleys. Her son, Jasper, became a well-known historical biographer. It was their family that restored the Priest House and presented it to the Sussex Archaeological Trust for use as a museum.

Thirty-nine societies and clubs are recorded on the millennium map, their activities representing the best of English village life. The community benefits from much voluntary work. The Madeleine Ensemble performs concerts in the church, the Sharpthorne Carol Party raises funds for charity. As our map makes clear, there is something for everyone to enjoy.

KAY COUTIN

The Stoneland Players

The Madeleine Ensemble

The Sharpthorne Carol Party

Woolbeding and Linch

WITHIN THE TRIANGLE formed by Midhurst, Petersfield and Haslemere we are in the remotest corner of the county, a countryside of narrow lanes and isolated farmsteads where villages are few, the enclosing woods thick and deep. There is a remarkable sense of insularity. This is where West Sussex runs out, rolling into Hampshire and Surrey where life splits between three counties. Little wonder that strangers can be unsure about their precise whereabouts. With trains to town and shops and services across the county border, West Sussex is sucked into its neighbours. Liphook in Hampshire looms large in many a Linch household. One grand lady who firmly lived in West Sussex always insisted she lived in Hampshire because her post town was Petersfield. And E.V. Lucas pointed out that any visitor coming by balloon to these northern parts of Sussex – he was writing in 1904 – would be quite puzzled to name the county in which he had alighted.

Boundaries, loyalties and a sense of belonging for those in search of roots, have always been a bit of a problem on this outer edge of West Sussex, no more so than in Linch where territorially local people have been pulled in all sorts of confusing directions over the centuries. Linch children once walked to school in Iping, the rector lived in Fernhurst,

Riding School, Woolbeding

parish boundaries have chopped and changed. Today the ecclesiastical parish of Linch covers the southern part of the civil parish of Milland.

Without a defining centre to Linch, neighbouring Milland plays its part in pulling the area together through the pub, village hall and the school at nearby Wardley (in Milland, but confusingly called Hollycombe from the name of the big house which is in Linch parish). *Milland News*, a remarkably-inspired community newspaper, encourages a strong sense of unity. As Val Porter, its editor, emphasises, people think of Linch as very much part of Milland (yet Linch people are fiercely independent, relishing their separateness through their own parish meeting). In her Milland history, Val points out the importance of 'The Valley' in tying things together. 'Geography wins', she says: 'it is more powerful than the powers that be, whether the Church, the State or wealthy landowners'.

To add to the confusion about its identity, Linch was once even somewhere else. It was six miles away to the south. Take the underdown road westwards from Cocking and there between Bepton and Didling stands the clue – Linch Farm – one of Sussex's deserted medieval villages. Its little Domesday church, lost centuries ago, stood in ground covered by the farmyard where bones and a coffin have been dug up. All traces of the little village have now gone. And rising high above the farm is Linch Down and Linchball Wood.

St Luke's Church, Linch

These three place-names are now the only signs of this little Domesday community. Like so many downland parishes it had an offshoot further north for swine and cattle pastures in the forested Weald and thus the parish developed in two distinct parts, separated by Woolbeding. Whilst the population declined in the south and the church decayed, in the north the scattered settlement grew and a new church – it was called a chapel then – was built in the early 1500s in the part of Linch called Woodmansgreen. Falling into ruins, it lasted less than a century so that parishioners were described as 'straying sheep without a shepherd, sometime to one church and sometime to another, and then put thence to their great grief and vexation'. These poor lost souls finally got another church in the 18th century, Linch's third, and it is this, much restored, that survives as the present parish church of St Luke.

But where's the parish and where are the people? A church is so often in a village centre, but there's no village here at all. By the church there's just a farm and a handful of houses. Where exactly *is* Linch? – indeed *what* is Linch? Ask a stranger to find the place. There's no road sign to say they've arrived here. Try using the most up-to-date OS Explorer map. There's 'Linch Old Rectory' (more than a mile from the church), 'Linch Road' marked by Woolbeding Common and 'Linch CP' – meaning Civil Parish – printed across the fields. Find Hirtwell, Becksfield Farm, Elmers Marsh, Bembrook and Woodmansgreen by the church – these are some of the little places that make up Linch today, still reflecting how the countryside was

Woodmansgreen Farm, Linch

263

colonised centuries ago when woodsmen and swineherds settled in isolated cottages within the dense woodland. A remarkable feature is the large number of tiny scattered settlements, clusters of just a few old houses and cottages to which we owe the maze of ancient footpaths and lanes criss-crossing the countryside. A recently-produced report by the Countryside Commission describes this immediate area as 'a secretive landscape which feels hidden, separate and enclosed. . . . There are many contrasts and surprises; these woodlands are a disorientating maze of lanes, tracks and narrow sunken paths. . . undiscovered, remote and very special.'

These last few words are certainly right for the hamlet of Redford, home to the shop and post office, an amazingly rare survival in such an isolated location. It's now the only shop left in the whole Milland Valley, and although closer to Linch, is actually part of Woolbeding

Redford Stores and Post Office

parish that looks southwards towards the Rother Valley and Midhurst. But Redford people feel proudly independent. They'll tell you that's where they live, not Woolbeding some two miles away down by the Rother – 'another country!' says Val Porter from up in the Milland Valley. But with no meeting place itself, Woolbeding pays its compliments to Redford by coming to Redford Village Hall for its annual parish meeting.

In size, Woolbeding is in no way a village, but a tiny hamlet, beautifully compact, just a church, a big house noble in its bulk and setting, an elegant manor farmhouse and just a handful of farm buildings. It's 'so quiet and secluded', says local author Roger Chatterton-Newman, 'it has the feeling of entering a time

Woolbeding House

warp'. For a short time in the 18th century the big house was home to novelist and poet Charlotte Smith, much admired by Sir Walter Scott and Wordsworth, whose most famous work was *The Old Manor House* (1793).

Other literary connections are in the churchyard. Francis Bourdillon (1818–1912),was once rector, well-known for his popular religious books and his poems in praise of Sussex. His gravestone (south-east of the porch) carries a medallion portrait. Also buried here (on the south side of the church pathway marked by a Celtic-style cross) was his poet son, Francis William (1852–1921), best remembered for his poem *Light*, made famous as a song, beginning 'The night has a thousand eyes, and the day but one'. Father and son loved Woolbeding's inspirational landscape that filled their lives with so much wonder and delight. The rector himself had been all over England after relinquishing his living here, but on his death thirty-seven years later, he came home to Woolbeding, to this little place by the river he had loved so dearly and had never forgotten. The power of place had triumphed.

KIM LESLIE

All Hallows' Church, Woolbeding

Gregory Daulby

Alice Lascelles

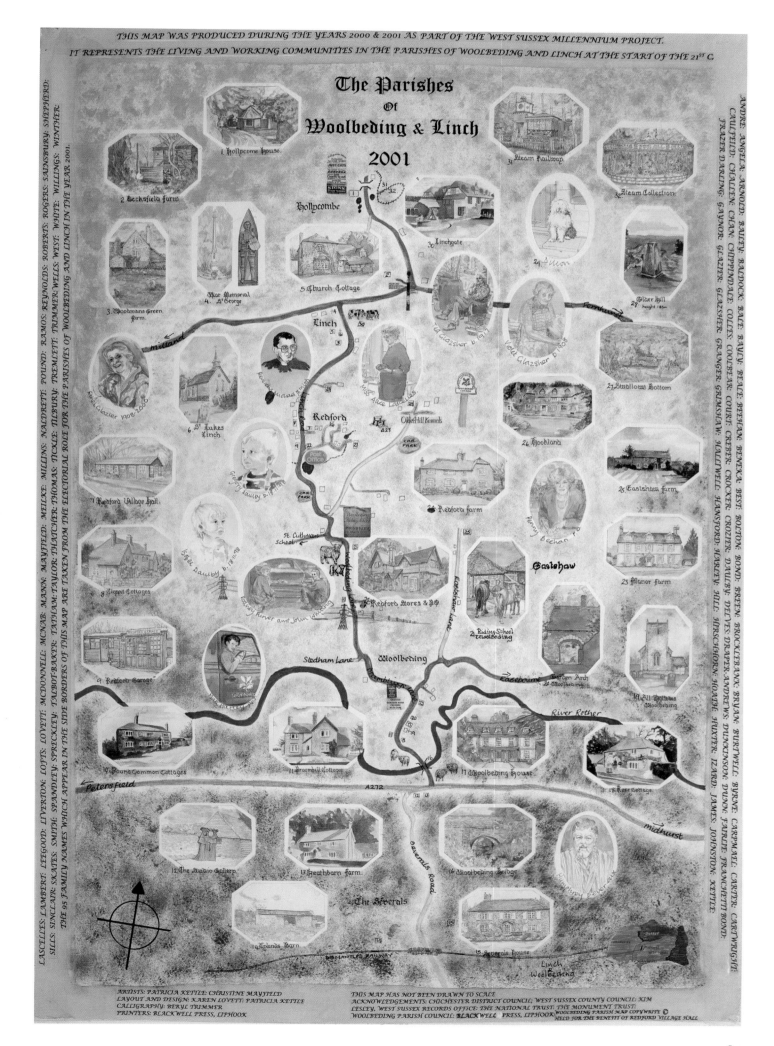

Yapton and Ford

A VISITOR ONCE STOPPED in the village of Yapton and asked for directions to Yapton Road and was stumped when the local replied 'which one?' Each of the four roads leading into Yapton we call Yapton Road: from Barnham in the west, Walberton in the north, Felpham in the south and Climping in the east!

The growth of Yapton in the last hundred years has been tremendous. From a sleepy Sussex village of 543 souls in 1801 the population grew to 715 in 1901 and then to just over three and a half thousand today. Hardly a village any longer, but the designations 'village' and 'town' are founded in the psyche of the inhabitants – Yaptonians definitely view their community as a village. The friendliness and affability of people meeting in the streets attests to the strong sense of community.

The population is an eclectic mix of people: young and old, professional and manual. It is this wide range of people that gives Yapton its vibrancy and liveliness. Children play on the village green whilst the elder generation sit on the benches and discuss the weather. Often this is a repetitious conversation since Yapton is blessed by being located within the same weather 'window' that gives Bognor its famously sunny climate. It hardly ever seems to rain – blue skies are the order of the day, even if only a few miles away thick rain clouds can be seen in every direction. In the 19th century the parish nurtured acres of orchards, encouraged, no doubt, by the mild climate. Sadly none of the orchards exists today – replaced by the endless need for new houses – but the large commercial greenhouses growing cut flowers and pot plants for garden centres and supermarkets are testament to the continuing clement climate.

Looking at all the new homes built in Yapton in the last fifty years, you could be forgiven for thinking that Yapton is a young village. You would be mistaken. The church of St Mary dates from the 12th century, one of its oldest treasures being an early Norman tub font. The village probably dates back to well before the Norman Conquest. Over the centuries it has been known by many different spellings such as Abbiton, Yabeton and Yeapton. The name itself is thought to be a corruption of 'Eappa's Tun', Eappa being one of St Wilfrid's priests who tried to convert the locals to Christianity in the 7th century. Maybe it's the local dialect that causes a problem, but Yaptonians are used to spelling out Y-a-p-t-o-n every time they give their address!

The village of Ford is a more bijou affair with its diminutive church secreted away by the banks of the Arun – its tower was used as a navigation beacon by river shipping on its way to the wharves at Arundel. St Andrew-by-the-Ford is an early Norman church dating from the 11th century and has hardly changed in appearance for the last thousand years. In 1904, E.V. Lucas said that 'popular

'St Mary at Yapton', Church.

'St Andrew by the Ford', Church.

Yapton and Ford Village Hall

rumour has it that its minute and uninteresting church ... was found one day by accident in a bed of nettles'! Small it may be, but it is certainly not uninteresting. During restoration in 1899 and more recent conservation work, a series of medieval wall paintings was uncovered. They are some of the earliest surviving church paintings in Britain. But the church never got around to having electricity so services still take place by candlelight.

Most modern visitors will know Ford for its railway station – it used to be called 'Ford for Littlehampton' because of the spur line to the seaside resort, but sixty years ago it was better known for its aerodrome.

Ford Trimotor at Ford Aerodrome . circa 1931

The origins of Ford's airfield go back to 1917 and its later use as a training station leading up to the Battle of Britain. Known variously as Ford Junction, then RAF Station Ford and from 1939 as HMS *Peregrine* as a naval air station, it was, by all accounts, a popular posting. Airmen frequented the local pub – no surprises there – later renamed the Shaky Doo, referring to a hazardous sortie.

For much of the last two hundred years, Yapton seems to have been a place to pass through rather than linger within. The Portsmouth and Arundel Canal was opened through the centre of the parish in 1823, giving through access by water to London. But

it had little effect on Yapton as there was no wharf here. Overall the canal was a commercial failure and disused by 1847 soon after the opening of the railway. The London, Brighton and South Coast Railway ran through the north of the parish, with Yapton having its own station until 1864 when the much larger Barnham station was opened.

Even today Yapton is full of passing traffic with commuters and business vehicles travelling between Chichester and

Junction of river Arun and canal c. 1823

Former railway station and level crossing

Littlehampton. You don't need to wear a watch in Yapton to tell the time; just listen to the traffic pouring along the road. The change in pace from noisy daytime to undisturbed night-time is eerie.

Being only a mile or so inland and with numerous rifes connecting the village to the sea, tales of smuggling are commonplace. Leave a door open and someone will as likely say 'Do you come from Yapton?'. This doesn't refer to the welcoming inhabitants but to the custom of leaving doors ajar, according to one story so that the ghost of a ferocious black dog could pass unhindered through the village. Bad luck is said to befall anyone who fails in this regard! The Black Dog pub – recently renamed the Olive Branch – is said to have been named after the same beast, once owned by the 18th-century smuggler Thomas Kingsmill of the notorious Hawkhurst Gang.

To the south of the village, but still very much part of the parish, are the two hamlets of Bilsham and Flansham. Bilsham's few houses are scattered around its medieval chapel. Gerard Young (1912–72), writer, journalist and local historian, lived at Flansham which he celebrated in four delightful books full of passion for his surroundings here. In a nutshell he described Flansham thus:

Former Bilsham Chapel.

Like most villages, no one has ever heard of it and no one can ever find it. … It is a dead-end village; two lanes which lead to nowhere, a village which successfully frustrates the summer evening motorists who rattle up the lane with a condescending smile for the men still working in the meadows, and a few minutes later rattle back again without a condescending smile, having landed up in a ploughed field.

Ironically it is these qualities today that are so attractive to the people of Flansham looking for seclusion and tranquillity.

Despite its unassuming appearance and unpretentious nature, Yapton has plenty to boast about:

- Where most villages are content with two or more pubs, Yapton has four including the Shoulder of Mutton & Cucumbers, which has one of the longest pub names in Britain.

- There are two Conservation Areas, fourteen listed buildings and a further thirty-one Buildings of Special Character in the parish.

- Park Lodge in Church Lane was the last home of the noted parson-poet of the countryside, Andrew Young, who died here in 1971.

- The village was also the home of Olympic swimming champion Duncan Goodhew who is commemorated by the naming of Goodhew Close.

- Hobbs Centre at Northwood Farm at Bilsham hosts an annual folk festival.

Undeterred by its size, Yapton still retains its village atmosphere. There are several Yaptonians born and bred in the village who still live here today. Quite simply there is nowhere else they would rather live.

GEOFF WESTCOTT

Yapton

Yapton is a mixture of old and new. The parish includes Bilsham and part of Flansham, and is quite spread out. Many of the older properties are in the vicinity of the church which is dedicated to "St Mary the Virgin".

One of Yapton's claims to fame from the past is being known as the village of "open doors", reputedly to help smugglers evade the attentions of the Excise men, conceal their contraband and make good their escape. It is also the place where a man sold his wife for the sum of 7/6d at the "Shoulder of Mutton and Cucumbers" public house. There are four public houses within the parish.

The Portsmouth to Arundel Canal was constructed through the parish c.1821 and opened to traffic in 1823. However the opening in 1846 of the Shoreham-Chichester railway - which passes to the north of the village - saw its demise. Yapton had a railway station which was operational during 1846-7 and 1849-64. The station buildings are still there at the end of the 20th century (see illustration no. 10).

(9) Coachman's Cottage, Yapton.

Yapton has a varied industrial history; mainly agricultural in earlier times. The Sparks family from Holkham in Norfolk, together with the beginnings of the machine age brought the area to life with the repair and hire of traction engines and agricultural machinery.

Sparks also found the clay around the village was suitable for brick making. John Sparks built cottages such as Holkham Cottages for his workers presumably using local bricks.

The traction repair workshop and foundry became the Village Hall and this served the village until the mid 1980's when it was replaced by the present one located on the King George V Playing Field. The old building became a village convenience store.

'Sparks' Fowler Class BB Plough Engine

(23) Yapton Free Church.

(24) Former Bilsham Chapel.

(25) The Staddle Barn, Flansham.

Downland Shepherd

While stable-boys go thundering by
Slinging dark divots at the sky,
Like a wind-hover he stands still
Beside the sun, late on the hill,
And chin on hands, hands on his crook,
Tegs, shearlings, yoes come like a book
Or sees them pass slow as a cloud,
Four hundred heads with one prayer bowed.

Andrew Young.

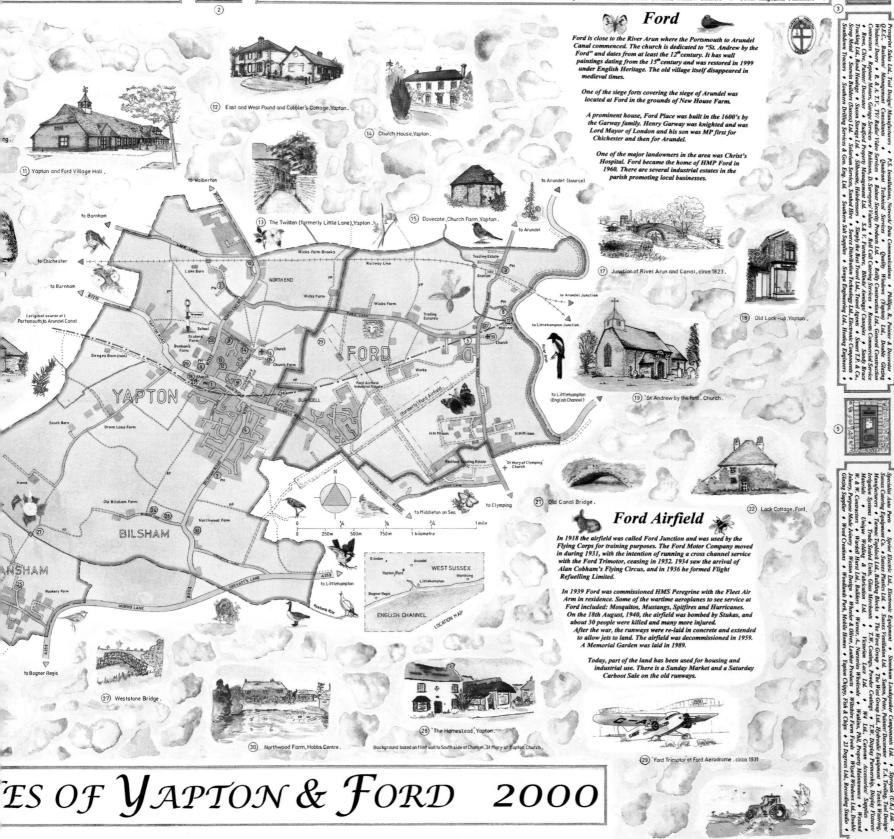

Ford

Ford is close to the River Arun where the Portsmouth to Arundel Canal commenced. The church is dedicated to "St. Andrew by the Ford" and dates from at least the 12th century. It has wall paintings dating from the 15th century and was restored in 1999 under English Heritage. The old village itself disappeared in medieval times.

One of the siege forts covering the siege of Arundel was located at Ford in the grounds of New House Farm.

A prominent house, Ford Place was built in the 1600's by the Garway family. Henry Garway was knighted and was Lord Mayor of London and his son was MP first for Chichester and then for Arundel.

One of the major landowners in the area was Christ's Hospital. Ford became the home of HMP Ford in 1960. There are several industrial estates in the parish promoting local businesses.

Map labels

11 Yapton and Ford Village Hall.
12 East and West Pound and Cobbler's Cottage, Yapton.
14 Church House, Yapton.
13 The Twitten (formerly Little Lane), Yapton.
15 Dovecote, Church Farm, Yapton.
17 Junction of River Arun and Canal, circa 1823.
18 Old Lock-up, Yapton.
19 'St Andrew by the Ford', Church.
21 Old Canal Bridge.
22 Lock Cottage, Ford.
27 Weststone Bridge.
28 'The Homestead', Yapton.
29 'Ford Trimotor at Ford Aerodrome, circa 1931.
30 Northwood Farm, Hobbs Centre.

Background based on flint wall to South side of Chancel, 'St Mary at Yapton Church'.

Ford Airfield

In 1918 the airfield was called Ford Junction and was used by the Flying Corps for training purposes. The Ford Motor Company moved in during 1931, with the intention of running a cross channel service with the Ford Trimotor, ceasing in 1932. 1934 saw the arrival of Alan Cobham's Flying Circus, and in 1936 he formed Flight Refuelling Limited.

In 1939 Ford was commissioned HMS Peregrine with the Fleet Air Arm in residence. Some of the wartime aeroplanes to see service at Ford included: Mosquitos, Mustangs, Spitfires and Hurricanes. On the 18th August, 1940, the airfield was bombed by Stukas, and about 30 people were killed and many more injured. After the war, the runways were re-laid in concrete and extended to allow jets to land. The airfield was decommissioned in 1959. A Memorial Garden was laid in 1989.

Today, part of the land has been used for housing and industrial use. There is a Sunday Market and a Saturday Carboot Sale on the old runways.

Location map

WEST SUSSEX
Arundel
Yapton/Ford
Littlehampton
Worthing
Bognor Regis
ENGLISH CHANNEL
LOCATION MAP

...ES OF YAPTON & FORD 2000

This map was undertaken by the Yapton & Ford Local History Group in conjunction with the West Sussex Millennium Parish Map Scheme and was prepared during 1999/2000.
The Project Team included: Team Leader: Ronald Griffiths, Artists: Sonia Barnett, David Day, Marion Griffiths, Marilyn Hammerton, Dorothy Michell, Graphics: Geoff Westcott, Advisers & Researchers: Janet Phillips, Roy Phillips.

The poem 'Downland Shepherd', reproduced by kind permission of Miss A. Young, was written by her father, Andrew Young, who was a resident of Yapton from 1959 to 1971.

The Project was sponsored by: West Sussex County Council • Arun District Council • Ford Parish Council • Yapton Parish Council • Austin Divall Fabrications Ltd. • Bilsham Stores • Company 'B' • European Stationers plc • Hobbs Centre (Northwood Farm) • K.R. Hocking (Drove Lane Farm) • I.C.S. Electronics • A.C. Langmead (Wicks Farm) • Leeside Toolshop • M.W. Trading • The Page Group • Ship & Anchor • Shoulder of Mutton & Cucumbers • Tarmac Topblock Ltd. • W4 Ltd. • Wardell Hurst Ltd. • A. White (Stakers Farm)

West Sussex County Council • ARUN DISTRICT COUNCIL

Further Reading and Sources by Parish

APTURING A SENSE OF PLACE is inevitably a very personal and impressionistic exercise; the approach used in the previous pages has meant that writers have had to be highly selective in their use of information. To help with the more detailed exploration of each place and the backgrounds against which they can be understood, there follows a selective listing of recommended books for further reading and notes on any other sources used. All the books cited have been published in the UK, except where noted.

Other supplementary sources that may be found useful are county histories and guide-books, local pamphlets and village and town websites. Increasingly coming on stream now are Design Statements and Parish Plans that give a very good feel for a parish – indeed because they assess the character of a community and parish they are very much complementary to parish maps. (Significantly some of these publications incorporate design features taken from the maps.) Some, but not all of those published, are listed below. For further information on their availability see the appropriate parish, or district, council.

In the text accompanying some of the maps there are a few references to Ian Nairn's comments on local architecture. He was responsible for the West Sussex section of the series more popularly known as 'Pevsner'. The source is Ian Nairn and Nikolaus Pevsner, *Sussex* (Penguin Buildings of England series, 1965).

Other authors also quoted for their comments are:
E.V. Lucas, *Highways and Byways in Sussex* (Macmillan, 1904).
S.P.B. Mais, *Sussex* (Richards Press, 1929).
Arthur Mee, *Sussex: The Garden by the Sea* (Hodder and Stoughton, 1937). Part of the King's England series.
Simon Jenkins, *England's Thousand Best Churches* (Allen Lane/Penguin, 1999).

Aldwick

Lindsay Fleming, *History of Pagham in Sussex* (Ditchling Press, three vols, 1949–50). Aldwick was part of Pagham until 1934.

Gwen F. Stabler, *Aldwick and Craigweil Of The Past* (Bognor Regis Local History Society, 2000).

Gwen F. Stabler, *A Pictorial History of Aldwick and Craigweil* (Mulberry Press, n.d. [2002]).

The statement that visitors were safe to enjoy Aldwick 'without the fear of molestation' forms part of a petition to the local justices of the peace in 1875 opposing the licensing of Craigweil House as a private lunatic asylum. The licence was refused. West Sussex Record Office, QAL/1/1/W2(8).

The story of the royal stay is recalled in Rev. John W. Maynard (ed.), *The King and Queen at Craigweil in 1929* (Pagham Parochial Church Council, 1984).

Aldwick through aristocratic eyes is chronicled in three volumes of autobiography by Lady Diana Cooper (in which her seaside home is cavalierly referred to as 'Bognor'): *The Rainbow Comes and Goes* (1958); *The Light of Common Day* (1959) – the source of the two quotations, pp.87–8; *Trumpets from the Steep* (1960), all published by Rupert Hart-Davis.

The notion that the cottages of the Aldwick Bay Estate are 'like overblown strays from an Essex village' is from Ian Nairn in Pevsner's *Sussex*.

The quotation about its exclusivity is from the original prospectus for *The Sussex Riviera: Aldwick Bay Estate* (n.d. c.1929).

The compliment that 'Aldwick will be ever loved and admired' is from Richard Dally, *The Bognor, Arundel and Littlehampton Guide* (1828), p.77.

Apuldram

Richard Ratcliff, *A History of Apuldram* (no publisher given, 1986).

The parish is also covered in three books about the harbour:

Angela Bromley-Martin, *Chichester Harbour Past & Present* (Hughenden Publications, 1991).

John Reger, *Chichester Harbour: A History* (Phillimore, 1996).

Monika Smith, *Chichester Harbour: An informal look at the last hundred years* (Chichester Harbour Conservancy, 2004).

The visual impact of the spire of Chichester Cathedral in the flat landscape is illustrated by a quotation from W.H. Hudson, *Nature in Downland* (Longmans, Green, 4th imp., 1906), pp.253–5.

The story of the sailing barge *Will Everard*, possibly the last commercial craft to use Dell Quay in 1935, is told in Derek Coombe, *Spritsail Bargemen* (Pennant Books, 2003).

Arundel

John Godfrey, *Arundel and the Arun Valley in Old Photographs* (Alan Sutton, 1990).

Joseph H. Preston, Arundel: *A History of the Town and the Castle* (Associated University Presses, Cranbury, USA, 1993).

Tim Hudson, *A History of Arundel* (West Sussex County Council, 2000).

Balcombe

Leslie Fairweather, *Balcombe: The story of a Sussex village* (Balcombe Parish Council, 1981).

For a detailed discussion on the War and Peace frescoes in the Victory Hall see Keith Grieves, 'Neville Lytton, the Balcombe frescoes and the experience of war, 1908–1923' in Sussex Archaeological Collections vol. 134 (1996), pp.197–211.

Balcombe Place, home of Lady Denman and HQ of the Women's Land Army, is described in Gervas Huxley, *Lady Denman, GBE, 1884–1954* (Chatto & Windus, 1961).

E.V. Knox's satire on Balcombe is in his *An Hour from Victoria and some other excursions* (George Allen & Unwin, 1924).

Billingshurst

Wendy Lines, *Billingshurst and Wisborough Green* (Tempus Publishing, 2002). History through photographs.

The Billingshurst Parish Council Guide for Billingshurst (Sussexcoast/Billingshurst Parish Council, 2002).

Bolney

Margaret Burgess & Ian Denyer, *Bolney: Village of a Thousand Years* (Bolney Millennium Committee/Bolney Local History Society, 2000).

The 1930s proposals for turning the parish into a Garden City with its own aerodrome are briefly referred to in Bolney Parish Council Minutes, West Sussex Record Office, Par. 252/49/1, pp.244, 248.

Bosham

Angela Bromley-Martin, *Bygone Bosham* (Phillimore, 1978).

Angela Bromley-Martin, *Around Bosham* (A. Bromley-Martin, n.d.).

Maurice Hall, *Bosham and its Berkeley Barons: A Medieval Manor 1483–1919* (Maurice Hall, 1985).

See also the books on Chichester Harbour listed under Apuldram.

The quotation is from Arthur Stanley Cooke, *Off the Beaten Track in Sussex: Sketches Literary and Artistic* (Combridges, 1911), p.161.

Boxgrove

John Luffingham (ed.), *Boxgrove: History of a Sussex Village* (Boxgrove History Group, 2000).

The two references to the very early playing of cricket at Boxgrove in 1622 are quoted in Timothy J. McCann, *Sussex Cricket in the Eighteenth Century* (Sussex Record Society vol. 88, 2004), pp.xxxi–ii.

Belloc's poem 'Ha'nacker Mill', used as a symbol for his disillusionment with the state of the nation, was published in his *Sonnets and Verse* (Duckworth, 1923), p.119.

Bramber

Alison Noble (ed.), *Bramber: Glimpses of a Village* (Beeding and Bramber Local History Society, 1996).

John Batten's *West Sussex Gazette* article is dated 19 January 1978.

Bramber was described as 'a tea-party paradise' in *Sussex County Magazine* vol. 2 (1928), p.565.

Burgess Hill – Worlds End

There is no specific publication about Worlds End, but its context within Burgess Hill is briefly alluded to in:

Heather Warne, 'The Place Names and Early Topography of Burgess Hill' in *Sussex Archaeological Collections* vol. 123 (1985), pp.127–43.

Hugh Matthews, *Burgess Hill* (Phillimore, 1989). Noteworthy is the reference to unsuccessful attempts to rename Worlds End as North End, p.115.

Burpham

Roger Coleman, *Downland: A Farm and a Village* (Viking Press, New York, 1981).

Chris Hare (ed.), *Good Old, Bad Old Days: The Sussex of Lawrence Graburn* (Southern Heritage Books, 2001). Graburn lived in Burpham, 1881–1965.

Sebastian Peake's *A Child of Bliss: Growing up with Mervyn Peake* (Lennard Publishing, 1989) tells the story of the family's time in Burpham, pp.7–29.

Edward Lear's 'sprain-ancle road' is quoted from Vivien Noakes (ed.), *Edward Lear: Selected Letters* (Clarendon Press, 1988), p.10. For more of Lear on the subject of the bad road to Peppering see 'Edward Lear on Sussex Roads: A Record of 1829' in *Sussex County Magazine* vol. 10 (1936), pp.69–70.

Bury

Lilian E. Brown, *All About Bury* (Combridges, 1948).

Noggie Mann's story and the reference to Elsie and Doris Waters and the radio show *Floggits* are in the Bury and West Burton Women's Institute Scrapbook made in 1958. West Sussex Record Office, Add.Ms. 53, 723, pp.30–1.

Chichester – St John's Street

Alan H.J. Green, *St John's Chapel and the New Town, Chichester* (Phillimore, 2005).

Chichester – Whyke

Maurice Wilson-Voke, *A Walk Through Historic Rumboldswhyke* (Whyke Residents Association, 1999).

Katherine Slay *et al.*, *Aspects of Whyke Through the Ages* (Whyke Residents Association, 2000).

Richard Barnam's gift to the church in 1525 is quoted in R. Garraway Rice, *Transcripts of Sussex Wills vol. IV* (Sussex Record Society vol. 45, 1941), p.42.

Chidham

Doreen Stewart, *Some Aspects of the History of Chidham and Nutbourne* (Doreen Stewart, 1983).

Olga M. Baldwin *et al.*, *We Remember Chidham, Hambrook and Nutbourne 1930 to 1960* (Olga Baldwin *et al.*, 2002).

Chidham and Hambrook Parish Plan (Chidham Parish Council, 2005). The parish map is reproduced on the cover.

See also the books on Chichester Harbour listed under Apuldram.

Clapham and Patching

David Gillard *et al.*, *Bricks & Water: 100 Years of Social History in Clapham & Patching Villages* (David Gillard *et al.*, 2000).

Richard Williamson's quotation is from his article on the villages in the *West Sussex Gazette*, 3 November 1988.

For memories of Miss Collins and Miss Cracknell and their School of Nature Study and Gardening at Clapham see Ros Bayley, 'Wood End School?' in *The Abbey Chronicle* of the Elsie Oxenham Appreciation Society no. 22 (January 1996), pp.18–26.

The Bunny Austin quotation is from *Bricks & Water*, p.142.

Cocking

Naomi Barnett *et al.*, *A Short History of Cocking* (Studio Gallery Publications, 2005).

The Cocking History Column with its two parish maps owes its inspiration to Philip Jackson. The background to his work can be appreciated in Philip Jackson *et al.*, *Philip Jackson Sculpture since 1987* (Studio Gallery Publications, 2002).

Coldwaltham, Watersfield and Hardham

Sandra Saer, *Coldwaltham: a story of three hamlets* (SMH Enterprises, 1987). Covers Coldwaltham, Watersfield and Hardham.

Two books by Marjorie Hessell Tiltman, *Cottage Pie* (1940) and *A Little Place in the Country* (1944), both published by Hodder & Stoughton, evoke Coldwaltham's countryside month by month.

The status of Coldwaltham's churchyard yew is given in Owen Johnson, *The Sussex Tree Book* (Pomegranate Press, 1998), pp.17, 78–80.

The planning and laying out of Champs Hill is described in Alfred H. Bowerman, *Tales of a Grandfather* (A. H. Bowerman, 1980), pp.120–3.

Copthorne

Joy Day *et al.*, *Copthorne: The Story So Far* (Copthorne Village Millennium Group, 1999).

Kipling's reference to the oak as the 'Sussex weed' is from his lines 'I will go north about the shaws/ And the deep ghylls that breed/ Huge oaks and old, the which we hold/ No more than "Sussex weed" ', from *Sea and Sussex* (Macmillan, 1926), p.30. For the oak as metaphor and symbol – as used by the Copthorne map-makers – see Esmond & Jeanette Harris, *Oak: A British History* (Windgather Press, 2003), pp. 131–51.

Valerie Porter's view about the village as 'essentially, its inhabitants' is quoted from her book *English Villagers* (George Philip, 1992), p.10.

The reference to lawless characters is in Mark Antony Lower, *A Compendious History of Sussex: Topographical, Archaeological & Anecdotical* vol. 1 (George P. Bacon, 1870), p.122.

Crawley Down

Pamela Petrie (ed.), *Crawley Down Village and Church . . . The First 150 Years* (All Saints' Parochial Church Council, 1993).

William Cobbett's observation, made in 1823 on one of his frequent visits to Worth, is in his *Rural Rides* (1830), (Dent's Everyman edn., 1957), vol. 1, p.219.

Donnington

Saskia Heasman (ed.), *Donnington: A Brief History* (Chris Heasman, 2000).

David Bathurst, *The Selsey Tram* (Phillimore, 1992).

Alan H. J. Green, *The History of Chichester's Canal* (Sussex Industrial Archaeology Society, 2005).

Easebourne

Sir William H. St. John Hope, *Cowdray and Easebourne Priory in the County of Sussex* (Country Life, 1919).

Derek Russell-Stoneham & Roger Chatterton-Newman, *Polo at Cowdray: Home of English Polo since 1910* (Polo Information Bureau, 1992).

Disraeli's quotation on Cowdray on the occasion of his visit in 1837, is from Christopher Hibbert, *Disraeli: A Personal History* (HarperCollins, 2004), p.107.

For Cowdray and its trees see numerous references in Owen Johnson, *The Sussex Tree Book* (Pomegranate Press, 1998).

Elsted with Treyford cum Didling

R.C. Troke, *Elsted, Treyford and Didling, Sussex* (Courtenay Press, 1967).

The Telegraph House quotation is from *The Autobiography of Bertrand Russell vol. II 1914–1944* (George Allen and Unwin, 1969), p.153.

Felpham

Tim & Ann Hudson (eds.), *Felpham by the Sea: Aspects of History in a Sussex Parish* (T.P. Hudson, 1988).

Sheila Gould, *Felpham Matters: The Growth of a Sussex Coastal Village from 1800–1914* (S.G. Gould, 1996).

For Felpham's impact on Blake see G.E. Bentley, Jr, *The Stranger from Paradise: A Biography of William Blake* (Yale University Press, New Haven, USA, 2001).

Ted Walker's *Bognor Regis Observer* article is dated 27 October 1972.

Fernhurst

Alice M. Tudor, *Fernhurst: The Story of a Sussex Village* (Billing & Sons, 1934;Blackdown Bookshop reprint, 1969).

Brian Silver, *Fernhurst including Kingsley Green and Henley: Pictures and People* (Brian Silver, 1999).

Fernhurst Village Design Statement (Fernhurst Village Design Statement Committee, 1999).

Geoffrey Kavanagh, *Fernhurst Conservation Area Character Appraisal* (Chichester District Council, 2000).

John Magilton *et al.*, *Fernhurst Furnace*, Chichester District Archaeology 2 (Chichester District Council, 2003). With a prologue by Spencer Thomas on 'Settlement in the western Weald', including Fernhurst, pp.9–26.

The quotation about the village green is by Alan Stanley in the *West Sussex Gazette*, 26 June 1997.

Ferring

Ronald Kerridge & Michael Standing, *Ferring Past* (Phillimore, 1993).

J. A. M. Vaughan, *Goring and Ferring Past and Present* (Photrack, 1993).

Ferring Parish Plan 2005 – 2015 (Ferring Parish Council, 2004).

Fishbourne

Rita Blakeney, *Fishbourne: A Village History* (Rita Blakeney, 1984).

Mary Hand (ed.), *The Fishbourne Book* (Fishbourne Book Project Group, 2006).

The WI scrapbooks are in West Sussex Record Office, Add. Ms. 49, 481–3.

Funtington and West Stoke

Nigel Brown *et al.*, *The Parish of Funtington: A History for the Millennium* (Funtington Parish Council, 2000).

Richard Williamson, *The Great Yew Forest: the Natural History of Kingley Vale* (Macmillan, 1978).

The references to country houses and their settings are from James Dallaway, *A History of the Western Division of the County of Sussex* vol. I (1815), pp.107, 108, and the parish history noted above, pp.7, 13.

Goring-by-Sea

Frank Fox-Wilson, *The Story of Goring and Highdown* (Goring Book Association, 1987).

J. A. M. Vaughan, *Goring and Ferring Past and Present* (Photrack, 1993).

John Batten's *West Sussex Gazette* article is dated 31 August 1978.

Goring as the last landfall on bearing south-south-east from the centre of Britain is described and painted by Peter Collyer in *Encompassing Britain: Painting at the Points of the Compass* (Thomas Reed Publications, 2002), pp.79–83.

Graffham, Selham and South Ambersham

Frederick T. Barrett, *Graffham through a thousand years (with notes on Woolavington and Selham)* (Alfred Press, 1953, reprinted 2000).

Harting

Rev. H.D. Gordon, *The History of Harting* (W. Davy & Son, 1877).

E. M. Yates, *A history of the landscapes of the parishes of South Harting and Rogate* (Phillimore, 1972).

D.C.R. Francombe, *Forty Years On – Harting: The story of the post war years* (Harting Society, 1988). Covers 1940s – 80s.

H. G. Wells' comments on Harting are from *The Research Magnificent* (Macmillan, 1915) quoting from Collins' edn., *c.*1922, pp. 115, 184.

A copy of the film *An English Village* (1956) is held by Screen Archive South East in West Sussex Record Office and is available on DVD from Panamint Cinema in Scotland (see www.panamint.co.uk). Reference to the insight it was intended to give 'Africans' and others is from the *Midhurst, Petworth & District Times*, 2 March 1956.

Haywards Heath

Wyn K. Ford & A.C. Gabe, *The Metropolis of Mid Sussex: a History of Haywards Heath* (Charles Clarke, 1981). This includes the local directory for 1879, quoted in this article.

Wyn Ford & Lilian Rogers, *The Story of Haywards Heath* (S.B. Publications, 1998).

Lilian Rogers, *Haywards Heath: Yesterday Remembered* (Lilian Rogers, 1999).

Wilfrid Jackson, *Haywards Heath: A History & Celebration* (Francis Frith, 2005).

For Mark Antony Lower's observations see *A Compendious History of Sussex: Topographical, Archaeological & Anecdotical* vol. 1 (George P. Bacon, 1870), p.225.

For Anna Sewell and her family's home at Petlands see Adrienne E. Gavin, *Dark Horse: A Life of Anna Sewell* (Sutton Publishing, 2004).

Muster Green Conservation Area (Mid Sussex District Council, 1979).

The 'magic carpet' reference is from the *Official Guide to Haywards Heath, Cuckfield and Lindfield* (Haywards Heath Chamber of Commerce, 1946), p.6.

Mary Stott, *Organisation Woman: The Story of the National Union of Townswomen's Guilds* (William Heinemann, 1978), gives the story of the first guild formed in the country at Haywards Heath in 1929, pp.11, 26–8.

Henfield

Henry de Candole, *The Story of Henfield* (Combridges, 1947; Henfield Ratepayers and Residents Association reprint, 1976).

Marjorie Carreck & Alan Barwick, *Henfield: A Sussex Village* (Phillimore, 2002).

Heyshott

Ronnie Palmer, *Heyshott 2000BC – AD 2000* (Heyshott History Society, 1999).

Richard Cobden's quotation on the beauty of Heyshott's setting is given in the above book, p.147.

Betty Murray's contribution to Heyshott and public life in West Sussex is recounted in Paul Foster *et al.*, *Flints, Ports, Otters & Threads: A Tribute to K.M. Elizabeth Murray 1909–1998* (Chichester Institute of Higher Education, Otter Memorial Paper 12, 1998). She lived at Upper Cranmore in the parish.

Highbrook

Martyn Hodgson, *Heart & Soul: All Saints Church Highbrook: A History 1884 to 2000* (M.L. Hodgson, 2001). This substantial history, unusual for a church, puts All Saints' at the focus of this tiny community.

Hunston

Iain McGowan & Geoff Girling (eds.), *Mundham, Runcton & Hunston: An Early Photographic Record: Photographs of the Reverend Edward Outram* (Mundham Golden Jubilee Appeal Committee, 2002).

Hurstpierpoint and Sayers Common

Ian Nelson (ed.), *Hurstpierpoint – kind and charitable* (Ditchling Press, 2001).

Parish of Hurstpierpoint and Sayers Common Design Statement (Hurstpierpoint and Sayers Common Parish Council, 2004).

For the two local diarists see:

Anthony Bower (ed.), *A fine day in Hurstpierpoint – the diary of Thomas Marchant 1714–1728* (Hurst History Study Group, 2005).

Ian Nelson (ed.), *The Weekes Diaries: 19th century Hurstpierpoint seen through the eyes of the medical practioners Richard and George Weekes 1800–1872* (Hurst History Study Group, 2005).

Itchenor

Irene Wilson (ed.), *Memories of Itchenor* (no publisher given, 1975).

West Itchenor Village Design Statement 2004 (Itchenor Society, 2004).

See also the books on Chichester Harbour listed under Apuldram.

Lavant

Ken Newbury, *The River Lavant* (Phillimore, 2nd edn., 2000).

Elizabeth Woodford (ed.), *Lavant, A Century of Change* (Lavant History Group, 2000).

For references to Blake and his visits to Lavant see G. E. Bentley, Jr, *The Stranger from Paradise: A Biography of William Blake* (Yale University Press, New Haven, USA, 2001).

Lindfield

Helena Hall, *Lindfield Past and Present* (Charles Clarke, 1960).

Gwyn Mansfield, *Lindfield: A Village Scrapbook* (G. Mansfield, 2004).

John Batten's *West Sussex Gazette* article is dated 14 November 1974. The following three quotations are, in order, from Mais, p.138; Tony Wales, *The West Sussex Village Book* (Countryside Books, 1984), p.120; Charles Fleet, *Glimpses of our Ancestors in Sussex* (Farncombe, 2nd series, 1883), p.204.

Conservation: The Journal of the Society for the Preservation of Lindfield. The reference to natural and man-made features is from issue number 1 (October 1973).

Littlehampton

D. Robert Elleray, *Littlehampton: A Pictorial History* (Phillimore, 1991).

Arthur Ransome's connection with Littlehampton and Hillyards is given in Roger Wardale (ed.), *Ransome at Sea: Notes from the Chart Table: A transcription of Arthur Ransome's various logbooks from 1920 to 1954* (Amazon Publications, 1995).

Osbert Lancaster's reference to the town's 'homely charm' is from his *With An Eye to the Future* (John Murray, 1967), p.31. His comment about 'unbutlined Littlehampton' is from his *All Done From Memory* (John Murray, 1963), p.46.

Lodsworth

Martyn Hepworth & A.E. Marshall, *Lodsworth: The Story of an English Village* (Weald and Downland Open Air Museum, 1995).

John Rickman, *The Land of Lod* (Peggy Rickman, 1998).

John Fellows (ed.), *The Parish & Liberty of Lodsworth: notes to accompany the Lodsworth Millennium Map 2001* (Lodsworth Map Group, 2001).

The quotation 'another of the nooks and corners …' is from Louis J. Jennings, *Field Paths and Green Lanes in Surrey and Sussex* (John Murray, 1877), pp.121–2.

For E.H. Shepard's home at Lodsworth see Rawle Knox, *The Work of E.H. Shepard* (Methuen, 1979); Arthur R. Chandler, *The Story of E.H. Shepard: The Man who drew Pooh* (Jaydem Books, 2000).

Loxwood

John C. Buckwell, 'Stories of Loxwood' in *Sussex Archaeological Collections* vol. 56 (1914), pp.161–91.

P.A.L. Vine, *London's Lost Route to the Sea* (David & Charles, 4th edn., 1986). The Wey and Arun Canal and Loxwood.

C.H. Bayley, *Ifold, Loxwood & Plaistow: Forgotten border villages* (Ifold and District Local History Society, 1988).

Peter Jerrome, *John Sirgood's Way: The Story of the Loxwood Dependants* (Window Press, 1998).

Lurgashall

Dorothy F.P. Heathcote & G.R. Rolston, *Lurgashall: An Old Sussex Parish* (no publisher given, 1950).

H.S. Roots, *A View of Edwardian Lurgashall* (Window Press, 2000).

Lurgashall Design Statement (Lurgashall Parish Council, 2004).

For Tennyson and his home at Aldworth see Robert Bernard Martin, *Tennyson: The Unquiet Heart* (Clarendon Press/ Faber and Faber, 1980).

John Magilton *et al.*, *Fernhurst Furnace*, Chichester District Archaeology 2 (Chichester District Council, 2003). Includes a history of 'The Yaldwyns of Blackdown and Heath Hall' by Spencer Thomas, pp.75–82.

The lines quoted at the end of this article are from Rupert Brooke's poem 'The Soldier' (1914).

Lyminster

An Old Churchwarden, *Lyminster Parish and Church* (E. Carlton Holmes, 1906).

Local opposition to the new telephone system and also the need to change the parish's name is recorded in the Lyminster Vestry Minutes, 6, 20 December 1888; West Sussex Record Office, Par. 131/12/1, pp.149–51.

For the legend of the Knucker Hole see Tony Wales, *Sussex Customs, Curiosities & Country Lore* (Ensign Publications, 1990): 'Here be Dragons: The Knucker Hole Monster', pp.68–9; Jennifer Westwood, *Albion: A Guide to Legendary Britain* (Granada, 1985), pp.94–6.

For Edward Lear's visits to three local houses – Batworth, Brookfield and Calceto – see Vivien Noakes (ed.), *Edward Lear: Selected Letters* (Clarendon Press, 1988), pp.6,7,10, 285.

Lynchmere

Michael & Anne Tibbs, *A Look at Lynchmere From the Vicarage in the thirties and early forties* (M.& A. Tibbs, 1990).

Michael & Anne Tibbs, *Another Look at Lynchmere: A Village Scrap Book* (M. & A. Tibbs, 2004).

Madehurst

For farming in the parish see Nick Adames, *The Life and Times of a 20th Century Farmer's Boy* (Woodfield Publishing, 2002).

Belloc's quotation 'strongholds of silence and of desertion' is from his anonymously written *Sussex* (Adam & Charles Black, 1906), p.168, and 'where the passage of strangers is rare and unperceived' from his essay 'The Mowing of a Field' in *Hills and the Sea* (Methuen, 18th edn., 1927), p.197.

The two Edmund Cooper science-fiction books set in and around Madehurst are *The Cloud Walker* (1973) and *Prisoner of Fire* (1974), both published by Hodder & Stoughton.

Horsfield's quotation is from his *The History, Antiquities, and Topography of the County of Sussex* vol. 2 (Baxter, 1835), p.120.

Midhurst

Charles White, *19th & early 20th Century Midhurst in old photographs* (Charles White, 1972).

Vic & Barbara Mitchell, *Midhurst Town – Then and Now* (Middleton Press, 1983).

Frances Johnson-Davies, *Midhurst: A Brief History* (Midhurst Society, 1996).

John Magilton & Spencer Thomas, *Midhurst*, Chichester District Archaeology 1 (Chichester District Council, 2001).

Milland

Val Porter, *Milland: The Book* (Milland Memories Group, 2003).

Val Porter, *Milland: Living Memories* (Milland Memories Group, 2003).

Flora Thompson's writings abut the district were published in the *Guide to Liphook, Bramshott and Neighbourhood* (F. Williams, 1925). The quotations are from p.37.

Northchapel

Pamela Bruce, *Northchapel: A Parish History* (Northchapel Parish Council, 2000).

For the Northchapel Dependants see Peter Jerrome, *John Sirgood's Way: The Story of the Loxwood Dependants* (Window Press, 1998).

North Mundham

John Hole & Iain McGowan, *Mundham & Runcton: A Portrait of a Sussex Parish AD2000* (Mundham Millennium Map and Book Committee, 2000).

Iain McGowan & Geoff Girling (eds.), *Mundham, Runcton & Hunston: An Early Photographic Record: Photographs of the Reverend Edward Outram* (Mundham Golden Jubilee Appeal Committee, 2002).

The horticultural statistics are from company websites and conversations with staff.

Pagham

Lindsay Fleming, *History of Pagham in Sussex* (Ditchling Press, three vols, 1949–50).

The Pagham Parish Plan (Pagham Parish Council, 2004). The plan incorporates elements from the parish map.

For the background and context to Pagham's 'plotland culture' see Dennis Hardy & Colin Ward, *Arcadia for All: The Legacy of a Makeshift Landscape* (Mansell Publishing, 1984).

For King George V's recuperation see Rev. John W. Maynard (ed.), *The King and Queen at Craigweil in 1929* (Pagham Parochial Church Council, 1984).

For the Knox quotations see A.E.Knox, *Ornithological Rambles in Sussex...* (John Van Voorst, 2nd edn, 1850), pp.7–8.

Parham

[J. Wentworth-Fitzwilliam], *Parham in Sussex* (Batsford, 1947). About the house and manor.

On Humphrey's Homestead see Viola Meynell, *Alice Meynell: A Memoir* (Jonathan Cape, 2nd imp., 1933), chapter XVII: Greatham, pp.271–94; Francis Meynell, *My Lives* (Bodley Head, 1976).

The first two D.H. Lawrence quotations are taken from Aldous Huxley (ed.), *The Letters of D.H. Lawrence* (William Heinemann, 1932), pp.219, 244. The quotation from Lawrence's *England, My England* is from the Penguin edn. (1982), p.7. This book of short stories was originally published in 1924.

The Farjeon reference to the little Rackham cottage and to walking on the Downs is from Eleanor Farjeon, *Edward Thomas: The Last Four Years* (Sutton Publishing, rev'd edn., 1997), pp.129, 134–5. Eleanor was enchanted by the whole area. The Arun Valley south of Adversane to the Downs is the setting for two of her fantasy books: *Martin Pippin in the Apple-Orchard* (Collins, 1921) and *Martin Pippin in the Daisy-Field* (Michael Joseph, 1937). See Kim Leslie, 'Eleanor Farjeon's Sussex' in the *West Sussex Gazette*, 13 November 2003.

Parham's outstanding embroidery is illustrated and described in Mary Gostelow, *Art of Embroidery: Great Needlework Collections of Britain and the United States* (Weidenfeld and Nicolson, 1979), pp.170–85.

Petworth

Peter Jerrome & Jonathan Newdick, *Petworth Time Out Of Mind* (Window Press, 1982).

Peter Jerrome, *Tread Lightly Here: An affectionate look at Petworth's ancient streets* (Window Press, 1990).

Peter Jerrome, *Petworth from the beginnings to 1660* (Window Press, 2002). A subsequent and final volume bringing the story down to the present is in preparation.

Geoffrey Kavanagh, *Petworth Conservation Area Character Appraisal* (Chichester District Council, 2000).

The lampooning of Petworth by the anonymous visitor of 1824 is quoted from *The Petworth Society Magazine*, no.65 (September 1991), pp.14–15.

The story of the Jackdaws' Parliament is told in the *West Sussex Gazette*, 16 June 1870.

Plaistow

C.H. Bayley, *Ifold, Loxwood & Plaistow: Forgotten border villages* (Ifold and District Local History Society, 1988).

Janet Austin, *Kirdford: The Old Parish Discovered* (Ifold and District Local History Society, n.d.). Plaistow was formerly part of Kirdford.

The Archbishop's dispensation to reduce the frequency of church services at Plaistow because of the poor state of the roads is recorded in Kirdford's parish register in 1768; West Sussex Record Office, Par. 116/1/1/3, f.35.

For a brief reference to the Ifold plotlanders see Dennis Hardy & Colin Ward, *Arcadia for All: The Legacy of a Makeshift Landscape* (Mansell Publishing, 1984). This study puts the whole plotland movement in context.

Poling

The 1919 quotation is from Philip Manwaring Johnston, 'Poling and the Knights Hospitallers' in *Sussex Archaeological Collections* vol. 60 (1919), pp.67–91.

The naming of Winnie-the-Pooh after a swan called Pooh on the Decoy Pond is explained by A.A. Milne in his introductions to *When We Were Very Young* (1921) and *Winnie-the-Pooh* (1926), both published by Methuen.

Pulborough

Winifred L. Cousins, *Memories of Pulborough* (D.J. Ellis, 1980).

Ivy Linda Strudwick, *Pulborough: A Pictorial History* (Phillimore, 1983).

P.A.L. Vine, *Images of England: Around Pulborough* (Tempus, 2002).

Robert H. Goodsall, *The Arun and Western Rother* (Constable, 1962).

The other four delicacies making up the Seven Good Things of Sussex are Chichester Lobster, Selsey Cockle, Eastbourne Wheatear and Rye Herring. See Admiral Chambers, 'Gastronomic Sussex: Being a Dissertation on the "Seven Good Things" and Some Others' in *Sussex County Magazine* vol. 10 (1936), pp.18–22.

The reference to the water-bailiff and his work on the Arun is from Joseph Fowler (ed.), *A Description of the High Stream of Arundel ... (c. 1637*, reprinted by the Nature and Archaeology Circle, Littlehampton, 1929), pp.43,45.

The references to eating stewed eel, and to flooding and the use of duckboards in the Arun Valley, are from Marjorie Hessell Tiltman, *Cottage Pie* (Hodder & Stoughton, 1940), pp.66, 261.

Rogate

E.M. Yates, *A history of the landscapes of the parishes of South Harting and Rogate* (Phillimore, 1972).

Roger Chatterton-Newman, *Betwixt Petersfield and Midhurst* (Middleton Press, 1991).

The reference to Wenham is in E.L. Grant Watson, *Walking with Fancy* (Country Life, 1943).

For Canon Simpson's Sussex background, his investigations into the tuning of bells and his commemoration at Rogate see George P. Elphick, *Sussex Bells and Belfries* (Phillimore, 1970), pp.19–22, 373.

Selsey

Frances Mee, *A History of Selsey* (Phillimore, 1988).

David Bathurst, *The Selsey Tram* (Phillimore, 1992).

Alan Stanley's quotation is taken from the *West Sussex Gazette*, 12 December 1996.

The press report on the completed map was published in the *Chichester Observer*, 24 May 2001.

Shipley

M.M. Hickman, *The History of Shipley: A Wealden Village* (Greenfields, 1947).

Richard Anniss, *Shipley and Associations: A Millennium Ramble* (Whitehall Publications, 2000).

The green lane at Crookhorn Farm is said to be the 'finest preserved' drove road in the area. See Peter Brandon, *The Kent & Sussex Weald* (Phillimore, 2003), p.16.

Eleanor and Reginald Jebb, *Testimony to Hilaire Belloc* (Methuen, 1956). Personal family insights by his daughter and son-in-law.

The anecdote about Belloc and the motor-cycle noise is from Bob Copper, *Across Sussex with Belloc: In The Footsteps of 'The Four Men'* (Alan Sutton, 1994), pp.54–5.

For the composer John Ireland and the influence of West Sussex on his work see John Burke, *Musical Landscapes* (Webb & Bower, 1983), pp.67–72.

Sidlesham

Rev. H.W. Haynes, *Sidlesham Past and Present* (Southern Publishing, 1946).

George Torrance *et al.*, *Sidlesham ... into the year 2000* (Sidlesham Parish Council, 1988). The quote by Robin Knox-Johnston is given on p.8.

Hans Florin *et al.*, *Sidlesham: A look at the Past* (Sidlesham Parochial Church Council, 2000).

Ted Walker's article was published in the *Chichester Observer* of 13 April 1973.

Singleton

Ian Serraillier, *All Change at Singleton for Charlton, Goodwood, East & West Dean* (Phillimore, 1979).

Elizabeth Doff, *No Misery to be Seen: A brief history of the Parish of Singleton and its people* (Elizabeth Doff, 1998).

An outline of the history of the museum is given in Kim Leslie, *Weald & Downland Open Air Museum: The Founding Years 1965–1970* published by the museum in 1990.

Slinfold

Diana Chatwin, *Slinfold Street: The Development of a Village in the Sussex Weald* (Slinfold Society, 2000).

Slinfold Parish Design Statement: Final Draft (Slinfold Parish Council, 2005).

South Stoke

The Constable quotations starting ' I long to be...' is from Leslie Parris & Ian Fleming-Williams, *Constable* ((Tate Gallery, 1991), p.482; 'The trees hang....' is from Graham Reynolds, *Catalogue of the Constable Collection* (Victoria & Albert Museum, 2nd edn., 1973), p.219.

Michael de Larrabeiti, *Foxes' Oven* (Robert Hale,2002).

C.E.M. Joad, *Folly Farm* (Faber and Faber, 1954).

The George Herbert quotation is from his advice on how to be a model country parson in *A Priest to the Temple* (1652): chapter xxxv: 'The Parson's Condescending'.

Staplefield

There is no published parish history, but as it was carved out of Cuckfield in 1848 see Rev. Canon J.H. Cooper, *A History of the Parish of Cuckfield* (C. Clarke, 1912).

A section on Staplefield is included in Roger Ray, *Handcross Over the Years* (Roger Ray, 1991), pp.61–70.

Stedham with Iping

Robert H. Goodsall, *The Arun and Western Rother* (Constable, 1962).

Roger Chatterton-Newman, *Betwixt Petersfield and Midhurst* (Middleton Press, 1991).

Kenneth Hellrich *et al.*, *Stedham and Iping: The Story of Two Sussex Villages* (Stedham Parish Council, 2000).

Disraeli's praise of the Rother as 'the greenest valley with the prettiest river in the world' on the occasion of his staying nearby at Woolbeding in 1840, is quoted in Christopher Hibbert, *Disraeli: A Personal History* (HarperCollins, 2004), p.143.

A.A. Evans' study of the Rother bridges is in his book *By Weald and Down* (Methuen, 1939), pp.151–60.

Michael Gates, *A Brief History of the Wispers Estate and St Cuthman's School* (Michael Gates, 2004).

For Stedham's churchyard yew, and its ranking as one of the largest in the county, see Owen Johnson, *The Sussex Tree Book* (Pomegranate Press, 1998), pp.42,80.

Tangmere

George Harper, *Tangmere: A Village with two stories* (Phillimore, 1983).

Andy Saunders, *RAF Tangmere in old photographs* (Alan Sutton, 1992).

For a detailed outline history of flying at Tangmere see Chris Ashworth, *Action Stations 9: Military airfields of the Central South and South-East* (Patrick Stephens, 1985), pp.265–74.

Wing Commander H. R. (Dizzy) Allen, DFC, *Fighter Station Supreme: RAF Tangmere* (Panther Books/Granada Publishing, 1985).

Tangmere Village Design Statement (Tangmere Parish Council, 2002).

Turners Hill

Eric Dawes (ed.), *St Leonard's: Turners Hill Parish Church 1895–1995* (Turners Hill Parochial Church Council, 1995).

Eric Dawes, *Crossroads Village* (Turners Hill Village Museum, 2001).

Eric Dawes, *Postcard Village* (Turners Hill Village Museum, 2003).

The source of the Medway is explored in R.H. Goodsall, *The Medway and its tributaries* (Constable, 1955).

For the Wyndham Croft reference see George Bernard Shaw, *Heartbreak House* (Constable, 3rd imp., 1921), pp.1, 90; and Michael Holroyd, *Bernard Shaw, vol. III, 1918–1950: The Lure of Fantasy* (Chatto & Windus, 1991), pp.18–19.

The 'cloistered tranquility [sic]' quotation is from Eleanor Farjeon, *Edward Thomas: The Last Four Years* (Sutton Publishing , 1997 rev'd edn.), p.46. His reference to the Medway is from *The South Country* (Dent, 1984 edn.), p.112.

Upper Beeding

Alison Noble (ed.), *Beeding: History of a Village* (Beeding and Bramber Local History Society, 1998).

Hilaire Belloc's playful remarks on the highs and lows of Sussex place-names is from *The Four Men: A Farrago* (Thomas Nelson, 1912), p.84.

Ted Walker's *West Sussex Gazette* article is dated 8 February 1973.

The Val Booth comment is from the *West Sussex Gazette*, 10 October 1991.

Under the by-line 'Eco-map for village', the unveiling ceremony was reported in the *West Sussex County Times*, 23 August 2001.

Walberton and Binsted

Brenda Dixon, *Unknown to History & Fame: A collection of prose, poetry and photographs from 19th century Walberton, West Sussex* (Woodfield Publishing, 1992).

Emma Tristram (ed.), *Walberton Past and Present: Aspects of Walberton Parish as seen by local people* (Walberton Action Group, 1999).

Emma Tristram (ed.), *Binsted and Beyond: Portrait of a Sussex Village* (Friends of Binsted Church, 2002).

Emma's up-beat remarks on village life were published in Alan Stanley's article 'Walberton – a REAL Village' in the *West Sussex Gazette*, 12 February 1998.

Warningcamp

Mary Barber, *Warningcamp: The History of a Sussex Community* (Woodfield Publishing, 2002).

Lou Oakes' parish-map story is reprinted from *The Bell* (Arundel's quarterley magazine) vol. v, no.2 (Spring 2000), pp.10–11.

Washington

Chris Hare, *The Washington Story: the forgotten history of a downland village* (Washington Parish Council, 2000).

Alison Milner-Gulland (ed.), *Washington Parish Alphabet* (no publisher given, 2006).

The opening and closing quotations are from Hilaire Belloc, *The Four Men: A Farrago* (Thomas Nelson, 1912), pp.160, 132–3.

For John Ireland see under notes for Shipley.

Roy Armstrong's Heath Common community of the 1930s inspired the chapter 'Sussex and Bloomsbury' in Reginald Reynolds' book *My Life and Crimes* (Jarrolds, 1956) where he (Roy), 'in some indefinable way "presided" over the clique, [and] preached and practised a tolerance which was all-embracing' (p.92).

West Hoathly

Ursula Ridley, *The Story of a Forest Village: West Hoathly* (Friends of the Priest House, 1971).

Kay Coutin (ed.), *Out and About in West Hoathly West Sussex from Early Days to Modern Times* (West Hoathly Local History Group, 2005).

Mea Allen, *William Robinson 1838–1935: Father of the English Flower Garden* (Faber and Faber, 1982).

Woolbeding and Linch

Roger Chatterton-Newman, *Betwixt Petersfield and Midhurst* (Middleton Press, 1991).

Val Porter, *Milland: The Book* (Milland Memories Group, 2003). Covers Linch.

Val Porter, *Milland: Living Memories* (Milland Memories Group, 2003). Covers Linch.

F. Vere Hodge & W.R. Farwell, *The Parish Church of St Luke* (Linch Parochial Church Council, 2nd edn, 2005).

Woolbeding Parish Action Plan (Woolbeding Parish Council, 2006).

Linch parishioners were described as 'straying sheep' by the rector of the neighbouring parish of Lynchmere in 1635; West Sussex Record Office, Par. 124/1/1/1, f.35v.

The Countryside Commission quotation is from *The Landscape of the Sussex Downs Area of Outstanding Natural Beauty* (Countryside Commission/Sussex Downs Conservation Board, 1996), p.40.

Yapton and Ford

For a detailed outline history of flying at Ford see Chris Ashworth, *Action Stations 9: Military airfields of the Central South and South-East* (Patrick Stephens, 1985), pp.107–15.

For the canal see P.A.L. Vine, *London's Lost Route to Portsmouth* (Phillimore, 2005).

The Gerard Young quotation is from his book *Come into the Country* (Samuel Walker, 1943), p.9. He also wrote *The Cottage in the Fields* (Samuel Walker, 1945); *The Chronicle of a Country Cottage* (Samuel Walker, n.d.); *Down Hoe Lane* (Arundel Press, 1950).

The pub spelt out as 'The Shoulder of Mutton and Cucumbers Inn' was recorded as the longest UK pub name in *The Guinness Book of Records* for 1969, p.152. This claim has since been superseded.

2 – Books on the Concept of Place

Edward Relph, *Place and Placelessness* (Pion, 1976). First systematic examination of the many forms and essential features creating a sense of place and the forces working towards placelessness.

Ronald Lee Fleming & Renata von Scharner, *Place Makers: Public Art That Tells You Where You Are* (Townscape Institute, Cambridge,USA/Hastings House Publishers, New York, 1981).

Paul Cloke *et al.*, *Writing the Rural: five cultural geographies* (Paul Chapman Publishing, 1994). Includes a lengthy discussion on the work of Common Ground and its work for local distinctiveness.

Robert M. Hamma, *Landscapes of the soul: a spirituality of place* (Ave Maria Press, Notre Dame, USA, 1999). Explores the idea that place matters and what is involved in developing a sense of place.

Tacita Dean & Jeremy Millar, *Place* (Thames & Hudson, 2005). How do we recognise place as being significant and not just a space?

Kay Dunbar (ed.), *Landscape into Literature : A Writer's Anthology* (Green Books, 2005). The mysterious chemistry between landscape and fiction.

Sue Clifford & Angela King, *England in Particular: A celebration of the commonplace, the local, the vernacular and the distinctive* (Hodder & Stoughton, 2006). By the founders of Common Ground.

3 – Books on Pictorial and Parish Maps

Angela King & Sue Clifford, *Holding Your Ground: An action guide to local conservation* (Maurice Temple Smith, 1985). How to look after your locality with ideas for projects, including parish maps.

Nigel Holmes, *Pictorial Maps* (Herbert Press, 1992). Much emphasis on modern graphic art and unconventional mapping as opposed to atlas-type maps.

Doug Aberley (ed.), *Boundaries of Home: Mapping for Local Empowerment* (New Society Publishers, Gabriola Island, Canada, 1993). 'Maps are invaluable and enjoyable tools for learning about and communicating the intricacies of place, but they are too often controlled by distant bureaucrats or companies. The 15 contributors ... introduce a wide range of home-grown creative maps that show more than roads and political boundaries...'

Sue Clifford & Angela King (eds.), *from place to PLACE: maps and Parish Maps* (Common Ground, 1996). The basic text on parish mapping.

Katherine Harmon, *You are Here, Personal Geographies and other Maps of the Imagination* (Princeton Architectural Press, New York, 2004). Pictorial maps to stimulate the imagination.

Peter Barber, *The Map Book* (Weidenfeld & Nicolson, 2005). In emphasising that maps are not just diagrams of the route from A to B, charts the way the world has been mapped in beautiful works of art from the very local to the global.

West Sussex Parish Maps Project – the project unfolds

The starting point

West Sussex County Council circulated a fact sheet offering the idea of making parish maps as a way of celebrating the millennium:

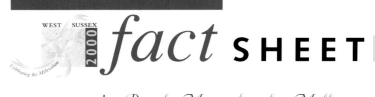

WEST SUSSEX 2000 *Celebrating the Millennium*

fact SHEET

Painted Maps • Quilted Maps • Ceramic Maps • Woven Maps

Parish Maps for the Millennium

Making a pictorial parish map is an ideal way to celebrate the millennium by recording what it is that local people think about where they live.

West Sussex County Council is promoting the parish map scheme initiated by the environmental/educational charity Common Ground. Throughout the country, hundreds of maps have already been made under this scheme by a wide range of organisations such as parish councils, Women's Institutes, historical and amenity societies and schools. In some cases, individuals working by themselves have created their own maps.

The maps are not constrained by conventional map-making methods. Some are drawn and painted, others woven, embroidered, quilted, and even knitted or made in ceramic form. They are colourful and vibrant expressions of key features that make a community what it is today.

They celebrate local distinctiveness and local identity - usually with a strong feeling for history, topography and wildlife - so that people can identify what is particular and special about their home surroundings.

Common Ground's commentary on a parish map for Muchelney in Somerset well conveys something of the background thinking and its translation into pictorial form:

Everywhere means something to someone. You don't have to own it, or even visit it often for a place to be significant to you. Starting with the question "what do you VALUE in your place?" turns everyone into experts, no one else can tell you what is important to you. The smallest of details and the most enduring stories can be important - the lovely doors along the row, Geoff's hedge and how he keeps the holly trimmed, the pollarded willows, the sluice gates, orchards and wandering chickens; seasonal things - such as where the best blackberries or mushrooms can be found, Jim ploughing that way, where the toads spawn, the floods; events that have become stories - "do you remember when the lightning struck the holm oak?". All of these and many more are captured by Gordon Young in his map of Muchelney. It could not be anywhere else.

The process of making a parish map needs community involvement - for meetings, discussion and action. There will be crucial debates on what to put in and what to leave out, about what is important and should be highlighted.

fact SHEET *continued ......*

Many parishes have found that the parish map has acted as a spur for creative action within the community. They have created agendas for action: over footpaths, the bus shelter that doesn't exist, open spaces, derelict buildings and eyesores, and opportunities to look at local history to enhance what is worth preserving today. The finished map need not be an end in itself.

The parish map should be displayed in a public place - the village hall, library, community centre, museum, church or pub - to act as a constant stimulus to discussion and musing, inspiring people to look again at what is so easily taken for granted just because it is so local and familiar.

Maps have been turned into posters and postcards which have helped them reach many more people and also generated income for community projects. One village has used the profits to fund a village sign, another to create a wild flower meadow.

Locally, grants may be available to assist in the creation of parish maps from Rural Action for the Environment. Up to £2,000 is available to each project and can help cover the costs of specialist technical advice, provision of materials and display. While a 50 per cent contribution must be made to any grant, this can be met through the time volunteers give to work on the project, so no actual fund-raising is necessary. Schools and educational establishments are not eligible.

Contact Box

For advice on all grants contact:

MIKE GRIFFIN
Sussex Rural Community Council
212 High Street
Lewes
BN7 2NH
Tel: 01273 473422

If you would like a list of publications about parish maps send a stamped addressed envelope to:

COMMON GROUND
Seven Dials Warehouse
44 Earlham Street
London
WC2H 9LA

If you, or an organisation to which you belong, would like to arrange an illustrated talk about how to go about making a parish map, or would like any further information about the West Sussex Millennium Parish Map Scheme, contact:

KIM LESLIE
West Sussex Record Office
County Hall
Chichester
PO19 1RN
Tel: 01243 533911

WEST SUSSEX 2000 *Celebrating the Millennium*

Issued by the West Sussex Millennium Forum

Designed by *The Design Unit · County Hall · Chichester · West Sussex PO19 1RQ* • **Printed by** *LES Printing · Hazelwood Close · Hazelwood Trading Estate · Worthing · West Sussex BN14 8NP*

> **Note:** since this fact sheet was printed some of the information in the Contact Box has changed:
> The Sussex Rural Community Council is now Action in Rural Sussex at the same address.
> The contact for grants is now Tammi Dallaston-Wood.
> Common Ground is now at Gold Hill House, 21 High Street, Shaftesbury, Dorset SP7 8JE. Telephone 01747 850820.
> West Sussex Record Office telephone is now 01243 753602.

Parishes responded to the fact sheet

by taking up the offer of having a talk and presentation:

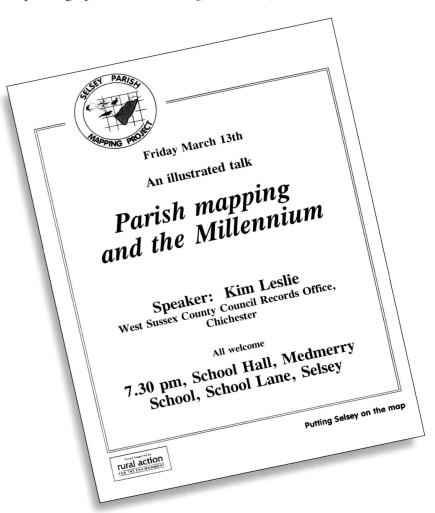

Talks were offered to any organisation willing to make the local arrangements. They were generally given under the auspices of parish councils, WIs, preservation and amenity societies and in some cases brand new groups. Audiences varied from three to about seventy – low numbers meant nothing, the crucial issue being the enthusiasm to take up the challenge and the coming forward of one key person – a local leader/co-ordinator. Without this person there was never a map. About five parishes stalled and in every case this was because such a person could not be found.

Prints of parish maps from other counties in the country were displayed at each presentation. Ten maps were shown, selected for their variety; they had all been laminated in thick transparent plastic with rounded corners for safety. They survive well after over a hundred presentations and exhibitions.

Abbots Langley, Hertfordshire	Mere, Wiltshire
Aveton Gifford, Devon	Osmington, Dorset
Aylesbeare, Devon	Rattery, Devon
Charlbury, Oxfordshire	Welford, Berkshire
Elham, Kent	Wonersh, Surrey

35mm slides were professionally made to enlarge the detail of each map. Using a Kodak Carousel projector with a zoom lens, great magnification was possible at each presentation. Today, PowerPoint is increasingly used.

To emphasise key points – and stimulate discussion – the following information was made into four display sheets:

- Parish Maps have three essential elements: (1) mainly about the present (2) something about the past (3) wildlife

- Parish Maps celebrate local distinctiveness and local identity

- Parish Maps: we need to ask some questions: What is particular and special about the parish? What makes it different and recognisable from other places? How do you know where you are?

- Parish Maps: consider the usefulness of adding (1) a scale, even if approximate (2) a north point (3) the year of publication (4) the names of contributors and sponsors (5) a location map in context of the UK

At the end of each talk and presentation organisers were encouraged to collect names, addresses and telephone numbers of all those expressing an interest in the project.

Involving the community

Once an embryonic map group had been formed then appeals for help went out, calling for artists, researchers, technical experts and those who know about their community – for anyone with skills, knowledge and enthusiasm:

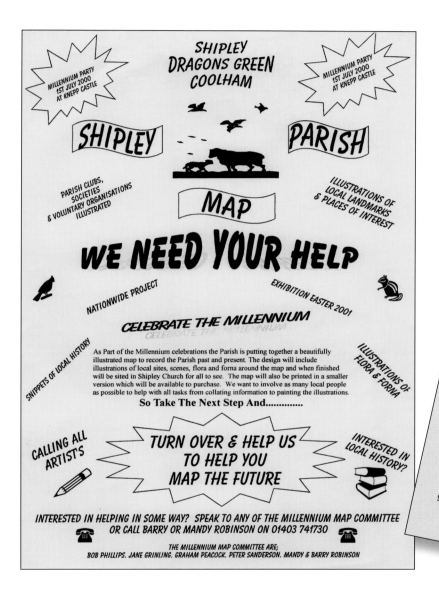

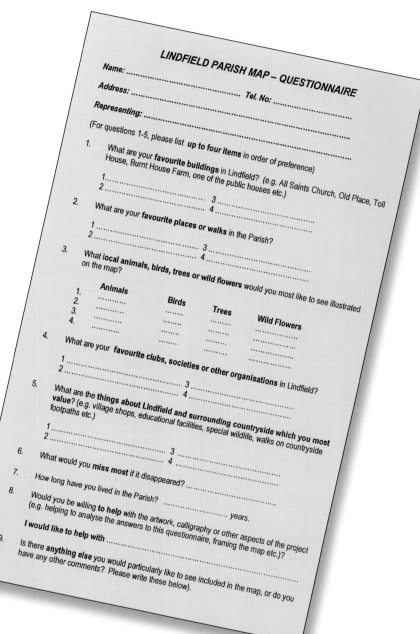

Questionnaires are always important as a way of finding out what people – especially those outside the map group – would like to see on *their* parish map. In some parishes they have been distributed to every household. It ensured that everyone had a chance to contribute their ideas so that what is produced is a democratically-made community map.

Sharing experiences

We organised a well-attended day conference to bring together experience from a wide variety of backgrounds, offering inspiration, new ideas and the opportunity for map-makers from a wide area to meet together for the first time. It started a strong feature of the West Sussex project – liaison between parishes, sharing experiences and even equipment:

*Detail from the Charlbury (Oxfordshire) Parish Map
– an inspirational map in the West Sussex project*

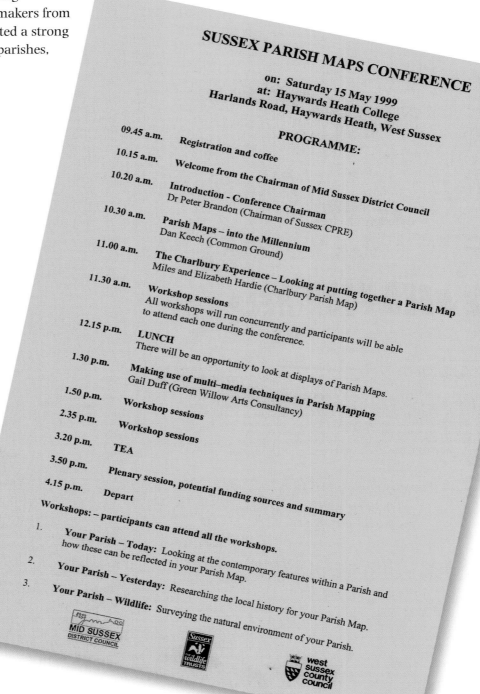

SUSSEX PARISH MAPS CONFERENCE

on: Saturday 15 May 1999
at: Haywards Heath College
Harlands Road, Haywards Heath, West Sussex

PROGRAMME:

09.45 a.m.	Registration and coffee
10.15 a.m.	Welcome from the Chairman of Mid Sussex District Council
10.20 a.m.	Introduction - Conference Chairman Dr Peter Brandon (Chairman of Sussex CPRE)
10.30 a.m.	Parish Maps – into the Millennium Dan Keech (Common Ground)
11.00 a.m.	The Charlbury Experience – Looking at putting together a Parish Map Miles and Elizabeth Hardie (Charlbury Parish Map)
11.30 a.m.	Workshop sessions All workshops will run concurrently and participants will be able to attend each one during the conference.
12.15 p.m.	LUNCH There will be an opportunity to look at displays of Parish Maps.
1.30 p.m.	Making use of multi–media techniques in Parish Mapping Gail Duff (Green Willow Arts Consultancy)
1.50 p.m.	Workshop sessions
2.35 p.m.	Workshop sessions
3.20 p.m.	TEA
3.50 p.m.	Plenary session, potential funding sources and summary
4.15 p.m.	Depart

Workshops: – participants can attend all the workshops.

1. **Your Parish – Today:** Looking at the contemporary features within a Parish and how these can be reflected in your Parish Map.
2. **Your Parish – Yesterday:** Researching the local history for your Parish Map.
3. **Your Parish – Wildlife:** Surveying the natural environment of your Parish.

MID SUSSEX DISTRICT COUNCIL   Sussex wildlife trusts   west sussex county council

Parish Map Conference at Haywards Heath, an interesting day which sparked off some more ideas and consolidated others. Also useful for networking with other villages and sources of help.

From Pru Hart's Graffham Parish Map Diary

Keeping in touch

Newsletters have been produced to keep everyone in touch, publicising ideas, meetings and all sorts of activities from ploughman's suppers, quiz nights for fund-raising, walks and competitions. Everyone felt part of a united enterprise:

As well as a county-wide newsletter, some parishes produced their own:

WEST SUSSEX PARISH MAPS PROJECT

NEWSLETTER 3   **JULY 2002**

Edited by Kim Leslie

With more parishes coming on board, the project continues, but now without 'Millennium' in the title.

Quite a few developments have taken place since the Worthing exhibition and so this Newsletter has been produced to keep everyone fully informed. Much more information will be available at the meetings planned for ⸻ber and October.

⸻meantime do have a good summer.

⸻EFING UPDATE

⸻ies of afternoon meetings will be held this autumn at West Sussex ⸻rd Office with the following identical programme:

> Welcome and Introduction
>
> The Italian West Sussex Presentation (pages 2-4)
>
> Tea
>
> Feedback from Parish Map Groups
>
> What Next?
> Common Ground's Parish Alphabet Project (pages 7-8)
> Proposal for a West Sussex Parish Maps Book
>
> End of Meeting

WARNINGCAMP
Parish Map Newsletter

July 1999

************SURVEYS**************

Over the summer months various people will be out and about with their cameras having offered to take photographs of the village and surroundings, so if you see someone clicking away you'll know what they're up to! Thank you to all of them and also thank you to all those who are butterfly spotting and keeping notes of the wildlife they see. May and June were disappointing months for butterflies, but now we're in July more seem to be about, so keep up the spotting!

***********COMPETITION************

Congratulations to Muriel and John Shaw, from Nurses Cottage, who were the winners of the competition on the parish map questionnaire. Their winning entry will be used on the map. Catherine Davies chose their entry as it summed up what she felt when she lived here. They wrote, ' A tranquil corner of England where the villagers are able to live in harmony with nature'. We had some lovely quotes and even a poem. All of the entries will be kept in a scrapbook that we are putting together for the project as an archive.

Hurst Millennium Parish Map Project

NEWSLETTER

November 1999

A great deal of work has been going on behind the scenes by the Working Group. One of our artists has generously offered us the use of her studio as a base for our meetings and it seems a very appropriate venue for working on the artistic design and content of the map.

The size of the finished Parish Map will be approximately 5' x 3' 6". We ⸻

days as an historical document in the Archives of West Sussex Records Office, Chichester.

Our map will have a painting in each of the corners depicting the four seasons. Because we have a large Parish area, we will show an enlarged view of the centre of Hurst village to give more detail. We have agreed a colour palette of soft transparent earth colours for the backdrop and tone of the map.

The Working Group has started on a full scale rough draft of the map, which is a very satisfying stage to reach. Our progress is on schedule, and we still expect to call upon our artists early in the new year. The Newsletter after Christmas will be more informative about what ⸻

Making the map

All the maps were made in the absence of any rules and framework imposed from on high. This is not Common Ground's style, although at Kim Leslie's talks and presentations some suggestions were always offered for consideration and discussion, see this appendix, page 280.

Two groups – Fernhurst and Walberton – made reports on their work which they then made available to other map groups. Copies are held in the project's archive in West Sussex Record Office. We give here Walberton's list of materials and equipment, noting the need to use materials to conservation standards if the originals are going to last. Further information on conservation materials and stockists is available from the Conservation Section of West Sussex Record Office.

Photo: Steve Robbards

The Lindfield team – led by Margaret Nicolle (front left) and Gwyn Mansfield (front right) taking advice from Dennis Webb, from the printers EMS International of East Grinstead, at the layout stage.

Walberton and Binsted Parish Map – Materials and Equipment

Display of map during its preparation

- Folding easel made in-house
- 9mm Sundeala board
- 3Ms Remount Creative Adhesive
- Bostik Blu-Tack

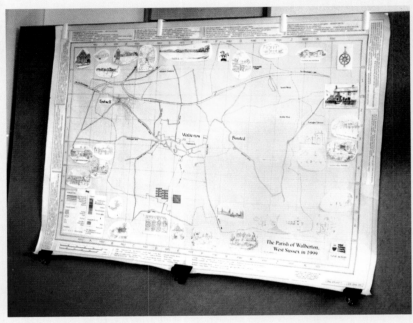

The draft map takes shape

Preparation of map

- A0 sheet of Saunders Waterford acid-free, hot-pressed, watercolour paper made by St Cuthbert's Mill, supplied by Frank Herring & Sons of Dorchester
- Supplies of Fabriano hot-pressed watercolour paper for illustrations and panels of names
- Japanese Shohfu paste for fixing the illustrations and panels of lettering to the map
- Drawing pens, eg Pilot DR and Edding 1800 of various sizes and colours
- Calligraphy pens
- Camera for photography of key features
- Artists' quality watercolour paints and watercolour brushes

- AO drawing board on tubular stand with parallel motion
- AO light box, made in-house
- Access to a photocopier with reduction facility, capable of copying on to watercolour paper
- Word processor for arranging text for calligraphy
- Weights and pieces of hardboard to form pressure pads to facilitate pasting-up
- Use of a spacious artist's studio for public meetings to view early drafts, for map assembly work, for artists' signing session and other occasions

Framing the AO map

- Mitre-cutting equipment
- Bevelled-edge mount cutter
- Moulding for frame: 2m × 3m lengths
- Heritage conservation board for mount and backing
- Evacon conservation adhesive for fixing two sheets of mount board together and for glueing wooden beading into position
- Wooden beading to increase the air gap between glazing and map
- Blue acrylic paint for colouring wooden beading
- Shellac-based primer paint for treating all internal wooden surfaces

- Archival framing tape for fixing the map to its mount
- 6mm Perspex sheet for glazing
- Clear silicon sealant containing fungicide for sealing the sheet of Perspex into the frame
- Sheet of archival barrier paper and joining tape
- PVA glue for corners of frame
- Corner cramps
- Brackets for reinforcing corners of frame
- Brass sheet for engraving the name plaque
- Mirror plates for fixing frame to wall

Artist's drawing reduced by photocopier to a standard size

The design team – led by Belinda Wilkins (left) – makes final adjustments

After pasting on all the details around the map, weights – using bricks – were set on a layer of tissue and hardboard strips

Photos: David Morton

Mapping the parish boundaries

Parish map-makers need to know the limits of their parish through finding its boundaries. Hence the opportunity to revive the ancient custom of beating the bounds. South Stoke beat its parish bounds by water and footpath as reported in the *West Sussex Gazette* of 27 May 1999:

■ South Stoke parishioners beat the boundary along the Arun.

Villagers revive bounds tradition

By Phil Hewitt

SOUTH STOKE'S bounds were beaten for the first time in living memory as preparation for the village's millennium map.

More than 40 people of all ages, representing almost the entire population of South Stoke and Offham, plus two boats, dogs and a pony played a part in the revival of the centuries-old ceremony.

Last November there was great support in the parish for the setting up of a millennium map project as part of the county-wide initiative.

A parish map group was created, but when the group first started to look at the boundaries of South Stoke and Offham, they realised that they weren't sure exactly where the boundaries ran.

The decision was taken to revive the traditional ceremony of beating the bounds.

Traditionally boundaries were walked at Rogation time, and this year the weekend of May 15 and 16.

George Herbert, 17th Century poet and populist, described the benefits of the ceremony as including "a blessing of God for the fruits of the field, justice in the preservation of bounds".

The beautiful South Stoke parish includes the river and wetlands as well as woods, farmland, downland and part of Arundel Park.

The sheer variety of the environment and the inaccessibility of some areas meant it made sense to spread the walk over two days.

As part of the boundary runs along the middle of the River Arun, Martin Earp from the Black Rabbit Inn at Offham came up trumps with his boat Britannia.

Originally a fireboat in London more than a century ago, Britannia's colourful history includes guiding square-riggers into port at Littlehampton and helping with the evacuations at Dunkirk.

The first day's beating included the old river beds in the wetlands. Beating sticks were hazel branches.

The most inaccessible part of the boundary was covered by gaining access from a smaller, flat-bottomed boat.

Sunday's beating began at the Chapel Barn at South Stoke Farm for a traditional ploughman's lunch with ginger beer.

The fitter members of the community set off for South Wood to follow the boundary up the steep slope from the river to the top of the Downs in Arundel Park. The line goes close to the Roman road which descended from the top of the Downs to the river, fording the Arun opposite North Stoke.

The boundary was eventually followed along the Gallops to Swanbourne Lake where other parishioners met the group for the final stretch around the Wildfowl Trust and up to Offham with a brief stop at the Black Rabbit Inn.

Throughout the weekend, points of historical interest along the boundary enriched the walk and led to lively discussions.

The Rogation service for the blessing of the fields was held in South Field in Offham. It was conducted by the Rector of South Stoke, Father Keith Richards. Traditional hymns were sung, and Father Keith blessed the barley crop.

■ The Rogation Service for blessing the fields at Offham. Picture shows Father Keith Richards, rector of South Stoke, with Chris Clarke plaing the hymns.

■ Leaving the chapel barn at South Stoke to beat the boundary over the farmland, woods, dow

Left: reprinted by permission of the Editor

Below: all participants were given a certificate

Photo: Kim Leslie

Victoria Leslie discovers the parish and county boundary stone at Ditcham, marking the division between Harting, West Sussex and Buriton, Hampshire

This certificate is awarded to

Kim Leslie

to commemorate his participation when the parishioners of South Stoke and Offham joined together in the Rogation Tide tradition of Beating the Bounds. "A blessing of God for the fruits of the field; Justice in the preservation of bounds; Charitie in living, walking and neighbourly accompanying one another".

May 1999

The Millennium Map Group

Unveiling the map

After many months of work the great day arrived
and the map was finally unveiled. . . .

Jan Elliott, co-ordinator of
the Singleton Parish Map,
presents a copy to Kim Leslie
for the Record Office

Photo: Chichester Observer

**BOXGROVE PARISH MAP
UNVEILING**
(Copies of The Map will be on sale after the Fireworks)

By the Duke of Richmond

**WEDNESDAY
20th DECEMBER**
at
6.00pm in the

VILLAGE HALL
Followed by

FIREWORKS

A free drink and food.
The bar will be open too.

Millennium Map

Unveiling and Exhibition

INVITATION

Haven Centre Hall,
Hophurst Lane, Crawley Down
Thursday 31st August 2000
7pm-9pm
(Unveiling at 8 pm)

Kim Leslie

We do hope you will be able to come

RSVP: 01342 712401

Friday, December 14, 2001   www.horshamtoday.co.uk   **WEST SUSSEX COUNTY TIMES**

Putting Coldwaltham on the map

A RECEPTION to mark the official launch of Coldwaltham's Millennium parish map was held last Thursday at Sandham Hall.

"I think the map is very beautiful," said Sandra Sear, who helped co-ordinate the project.

"A Millennium map is something that is there forever," she added.

The Coldwaltham Map group, consisting of Donovan Brown, Anne Dicken, Annie Nelson, Tony Spackman and Sandra, was present to welcome friends and supporters, including parish chairman Peter Beresford, fellow councillors and Parochial Church Council members.

Guest of honour at the launch was Kim Leslie, of West Sussex Record Office, whose strenuous efforts to spearhead the making of West Sussex parish maps culminated in an exhibition of some 87 maps, currently being held at Worthing Museum and Art Gallery until February 2.

"The mix of talent is really something," Sandra said.

In September 1999, Mr Leslie met the parish council and from this came the idea of a Millennium map covering Coldwaltham, Watersfield and Hardham.

"I got together a very good group of people," said Sandra.

Mark Weston, who painted the map using watercolours, was also at the launch. He was commissioned to do the work after successful applications for funding were made to Horsham District Council, West Sussex County Council, Coldwaltham Parish Council and Awards for All.

"Mark used to live in the parish. He's really talented and we could not believe how good the map was when we saw it laid out on my coffee table," added Sandra.

Artists Kay Saunders, Annie Nelson, Joan Watts and Graham Barber donated further paintings that were used to surround the map.

"A lot of people have worked very hard to get the whole thing off the ground," she added.

Copies of the map are currently on sale priced at £3.50 and can be bought from the sub-post office in Coldwaltham. Alternatively, they can be bought by either calling Sandra on 01798 831260 or Annie Nelson on 01798 873363.

PICTURE of the present: (from left) Anne Dickin, Kim Leslie, Annie Nelson, Sandra Saer, Tony Spackman and artist Mark Weston with the map (also top right).   No 374

reproduced by permission of the Editor

Parish map exhibition at Worthing Museum and Art Gallery

The exhibition marked the culmination of the West Sussex Millennium Parish Maps Project. Since then the project has continued, but without 'millennium' in the title.

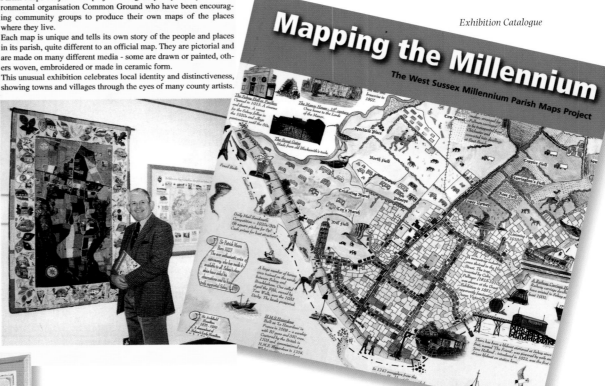

Sussex Life, January 2002 – reproduced by permission of the Editor

Mapping the Millennium

Sixty - six West Sussex parish maps are being exhibited in the Art Gallery and the Norwood Gallery at Worthing Museum until 2nd February 2002.

The spectacular maps are the result of the West Sussex Millennium Parish Maps Project. The project was greatly inspired by the environmental organisation Common Ground who have been encouraging community groups to produce their own maps of the places where they live.

Each map is unique and tells its own story of the people and places in its parish, quite different to an official map. They are pictorial and are made on many different media - some are drawn or painted, others woven, embroidered or made in ceramic form.

This unusual exhibition celebrates local identity and distinctiveness, showing towns and villages through the eyes of many county artists.

Photos: Monika Smith

What's On Guide

At the launch of the exhibition, by the stunning Fishbourne Map, which was created by the Fishbourne Women's Institutes. It is a hanging fabric, hand-painted on linen with fine embroidery, applique and gold work, with fringing and beading at the base.
Pictured are Directors of Common Ground, initiators of the National Parish Maps scheme and Christopher Sedgwick, Vice Chairman of West Sussex County Council.
To the right is Kim Leslie, co-ordinator of the project.
Mapping West Sussex
Worthing Museum and Art Gallery
Chapel Road, Worthing
Now until 2nd February Admission Free
NB when in the Art Gallery, don't forget to continue into the Norwood Gallery for further maps

Exhibition Catalogue

Mapping the Millennium
The West Sussex Millennium Parish Maps Project

Photo: Kim Leslie

Photo: Kim Leslie

These are just a few of the visitors' comments on seeing the maps brought together for the first time:

A lovely journey through our native county

Stunning from every point of view

What a marvellous way to catch the past and present for future generations

Happy memories of our many, many walks in and around Sussex

These wonderful maps show what talent there is in West Sussex

The Italian experience

Through the initiative of the Istituto di Ricerche Economico Sociali in Piedmont, the West Sussex Parish Maps Project has been represented at Italian conferences promoting local identity held in Turin, Biella, Genoa and Argenta.

A widespread network of contacts has been established linking West Sussex with projects in Italy, Poland and Spain.

LE PARISH MAPS
DEL WEST SUSSEX

LYMINSTER

MAPPE CULTURALI
PERSONE E LUOGHI

HARTING

ECOMUSEO DELLA PASTORIZIA

REGIONE PIEMONTE

Convegno

Ecomuseo: mappa
di una cultura

Pietraporzio
Pontebernardo

Venerdì 10 e Sabato 11
maggio 2002

PROGETTO DI RICERCA MIUR 03
La costruzione di scenari strategici per la pianificazione del territorio: metodi e tecniche
coordinatore nazionale: Alberto Magnaghi

UNITA' DI RICERCA LOCALE
Costruzione di scenari strategici: teorie metodi e strumenti per il dialogo e l'integrazione tra i linguaggi della pianificazione e quelli del senso comune
responsabile: Mariolina Besio

DOTTORATO IN SCIENZE STORICHE
indirizzo: geografia storica per la valorizzazione del patrimonio storico-ambientale
coordinatore: Massimo Quaini

seminario di studio

SAPERE TECNICO SAPERE LOCALE

per la costruzione di scenari di progetto

a cura di Franca Balletti

Facoltà di Architettura di Genova
Dipartimento POLIS
Aula Edoardo Benvenuto
18 febbraio 2005 ore 9.30

Mercoledì 15 giugno / ore 15.00
ARGENTA (FE) / Museo della Bonifica - Impianto idrovoro di Saiarino

MAPPE CULTURALI DEL TERRITORIO FERRARESE
Tavola rotonda
Saluti   **Agostino Parigi**
                  Direttore generale Consorzio di Bonifica Renana
Introduce e coordina   **Andrea Veronese**
                  Assessore alla cultura della Provincia di Ferrara

Sono invitati per un contributo gli Assessori alla cultura dei Comuni della Provincia di Ferrara
Intervengono arrecando il contributo di esperienze già avviate
- **Kim Leslie** - West Sussex Record Office
- **Maurizio Maggi** - Ires Piemonte
- **Donatella Murtas** - Ecomuseo dei Terrazzamenti
- **Fiorenza Bortolotti** - Ecomuseo del paesaggio Orvietano
- **Andrea Ross** - Ecomuseo del Casentino

Sera: Arrivo dei partecipanti al workshop, con sistemazione all'Ostello di Campotto

As a tangent to the Turin Conference in 2002 a pilot study was set up to produce a *mappa di comunità* at Pietraporzio in the Italian Alps.

Photo: Kim Leslie

Here villagers of Pietraporzio listen to Sue Clifford of Common Ground and Kim Leslie. At the back of the room is a display of West Sussex parish maps.

Parish maps as creative inspiration

Parish maps have inspired a variety of by-products . . .

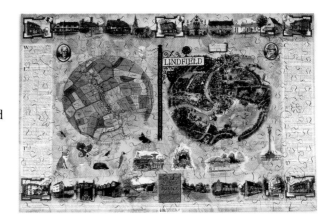

jigsaws for Lindfield

and for Clapham
and Patching

Map of Clapham and Patching

and an inlay for
a coffee table at
Lindfield

and a cover for
a video about
Felpham . . .

... as well as postcards for Chidham, notelets for
Poling and calendars for Chichester District Council

Chidham and Hambrook
Parish Plan

and setting the scene for parish plans – Chidham and Hambrook's
conveys the feel for homes and land bounded by fields and water.

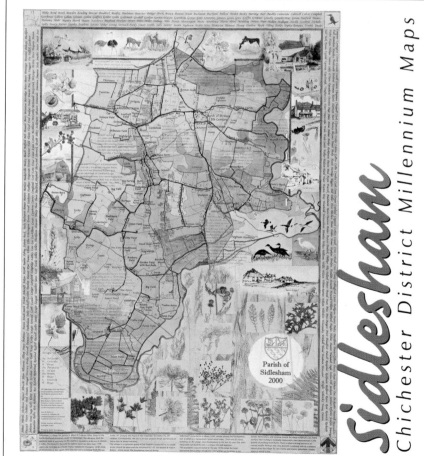

Action Point Schedule

*Design details taken from the map add local
colour to the text of the Parish Plan*

Questionnaire Results

Sidlesham
Chichester District Millennium Maps

SEPTEMBER *2002*

Mon	Tues	Wed	Thurs	Fri	Sat	Sun
2	3	4	5	6	7	1
9	10	11	12	13	14	8
16	17	18	19	20	21	15
23	24	25	26	27	28	22
30						29

Parish mapping and new directions

A great deal has been written about the influence of parish mapping in making people much more aware of their surroundings, raising issues about the built environment and our stewardship of the landscape and its wildlife.

But what of its influence on individual lives, on people themselves? A great many West Sussex people have reported on the real positive effects they have experienced from taking part in the project.

Fiona Gowar contributed to Easebourne's map. Here she describes its influence on her own work:

The map project was the start of a new phase in my career as an artist as it was the beginning of my drawing and painting buildings. I now work part of the time on commercial 'artist's impressions' for building developments, which has stemmed directly from my work on the Easebourne map project. The enthusiasm of working with a group who are all talented artists makes one realise that the possibilities are almost endless!

I now work on commissions for portraits of houses and cars, loving going out to see people and talking to them about what they care about most, and then doing a painting for them.

Working on the map project widened my range of work and ambition, for which I am very grateful.

I trained in textile and fashion design and then worked for many years in the industry, always doing illustrations as part of my work; understanding, from the contact with textiles, how much surface texture matters – and this feeling for surfaces gave me my love of working in water colour with the wonderful feeling you get when a brush full of some beautiful wet colour is applied in a soft sweep to creamy thick textured paper leaving a mark that is always a little unpredictable – and therefore always interesting – especially as it always dries to a different shade to that which was put on wet.

My fascination with textiles, combined with my watercolour work, led to producing designs for tapestry kneelers in the church at Easebourne featuring the birds and flowers of the parish, which again brings my connection round to the millennium map.

Some years ago I was asked to do some illustrations for the Roseland magazine in Cornwall. I went down to stay with some good friends in St Mawes and drove around to get a feeling for the place and take some photographs. It is the most beautiful area, and over the years since then we have spent much time down there, always with the most wonderful excuse that I had to go down to do some more work! It was these drawings for the Roseland magazine - of monuments, churches, cottages, butterflies, spiders, schools, the country and seaside – that I showed to the artists at Easebourne when the map group was being formed. And so I joined the group. . . .

Fiona Gowar in her studio

Photo: Barney Gowar

Details from Easebourne Parish Map

And finally . . .

The whole story of the project is documented in great detail in the files of the West Sussex Parish Maps Project Archive.

This is held at West Sussex Record Office and is divided into three parts:

- Printed copies of parish maps, with disks and transparencies used for printing
- WSCC files created by Kim Leslie relating to the overall organisation, 1997 to date
- Parish files created by a representative number of map groups: Arundel; Graffham, Selham and South Ambersham; Haywards Heath; Lavant; Petworth; Walberton and Binsted; Warningcamp

West Sussex Parish Maps Data

The following list gives:

- An asterisk * after the parish name indicating that printed copies have been published. A leaflet giving the price and contact address for each map *still in print in 2006* is available from West Sussex Record Office, County Hall, Chichester, PO19 1RN

- The medium/media used

- The abbreviation 'ca' meaning 'computer assembled' for maps with their hand-created elements scanned and put together by computer

- The measurements referring to the size of the original, or the size of the computer-assembled copy, given in inches, height first, width second

- The location of the original, or, if computer assembled, the location of a copy on public display

Aldwick*: watercolour; ca; 20 × 27; Parish Council Office.

Amberley: in progress.

Apuldram*: watercolour, oil and photographs; ca; 16 × 23; Parish Church.

Ardingly: watercolour, pen and pastel; ca; 56 × 32; St Peter's Primary School.

Arundel*: watercolour and photographs; ca; 38 × 50; Library.

Ashington: embroidery; 55 × 41; Community Centre.

Balcombe*: gouache, coloured pencil, watercolour, pen and ink; 37 × 76; Victory Hall.

Billingshurst*: mixed media, mostly watercolour; 36 × 48; Village Hall.

Birdham: embroidery and appliqué; 48 × 72; Parish Church.

Bolney*: watercolour; 37 × 51; Parish Church.

Bosham*: watercolour; 40 × 30; Village Hall.

Boxgrove*: watercolour; 34 × 54; Village Hall.

Bramber*: watercolour; 36 × 50; St Mary's House.

Burgess Hill – Worlds End*: watercolour and photographs; 36 × 48; Ryder Hall Lounge, St Andrew's Church.

Burpham*: coloured graphite and photographs; 37 × 51; Village Hall.

Bury*: watercolour; 41 × 28; Village Hall.

Chichester – Parklands: in progress.

Chichester – St John's Street*: photographs, Lazertran on foam board; 30 × 97; St John's Chapel.

Chichester – Whyke*: watercolour, pen and ink and photograph; ca; 16 × 23; St George's Parish Centre.

Chidham*: fabric painting, patchwork, embroidery and appliqué; 63 × 43; Parish Church.

Clapham and Patching*: watercolour; 53 × 39; Village Hall, Patching.

Cocking History Column: bronze column on a Portland stone base; 15 feet high; two bronze maps in relief at base, each 23 × 23; signposted near bend at foot of Cocking Hill.

Coldwaltham, Watersfield and Hardham*: watercolour and photographs; 38 × 48; Sandham Hall.

Copthorne*: watercolour, pen and ink; ca; 22 × 32; Parish Church.

Crawley Down*: watercolour, pen and ink and pencil; 36 × 50; Haven Community Centre.

Donnington*: watercolour and photographs; ca; 34 × 24; Parish Hall.

Easebourne*: watercolour; ca; 50 × 36; Easebourne Priory.

Eastergate*: watercolour, oil and photograph; ca; 16 × 23; Parish Hall.

East Preston: watercolour, pen and ink; ca; 35 × 48; free-standing noticeboard by shopping parade near post office.

Elsted with Treyford cum Didling*: watercolour; 33 × 50; Elsted Village Hall.

Felpham*: watercolour, acrylic, pen and ink; 53 × 77; St Mary's Centre.

Fernhurst*: watercolour; 35 × 26; Village Hall.

Ferring*: watercolour; ca; 28 × 21; Library.

Fishbourne*: fabric hanging, hand painted on linen with embroidery, appliqué and gold work, fringing and beading at base, supported by an oak pole with hand-carved dolphin finials at each side; 72 × 45; Fishbourne Roman Palace.

Funtington and West Stoke*: watercolour; 26 × 36; West Ashling Village Hall.

Goring-by-Sea*: watercolour; 32 × 46; Library.

Graffham, Selham and South Ambersham*: watercolour, pen and ink; 33 × 46; Empire Hall, Graffham.

Harting*: watercolour; 36 × 47; Community Hall.

Haywards Heath*: watercolour; ca; 31 × 41; Town Hall.

Henfield*: watercolour, pen and ink; 49 × 36; Henfield Hall.

Heyshott: gouache; 24 × 52; Village Hall.

Highbrook*: watercolour; 72 × 48; Village Hall.

Hunston: fabric collage, fabric paints and embroidery; 38 × 56; Village Hall.

Hurstpierpoint and Sayers Common*: watercolour; 46 × 64; Hurstpierpoint Library.

Itchenor: painted linen with embroidery; 38 × 27; Memorial Hall.

Lavant*: watercolour; 29 × 41; Memorial Hall.

Lindfield*: watercolour, pen and ink; 28 × 35; King Edward Hall.

Lindfield Rural*: watercolour; 54 × 42; Scaynes Hill New Millennium Village Centre.

Littlehampton*: watercolour; 44 × 59; Town Council Offices.

Lodsworth*: watercolour; 47 × 35; Recreation Hall.

Loxwood*: watercolour and acrylic; 42 × 28; Village Hall.

Lurgashall*: watercolour; 33 × 23; Village Hall.

Lyminster*: watercolour and photographs; 30 × 42; Parish Church.

Lynchmere*: watercolour; 39 × 51; Parish Church.

Madehurst*: watercolour; 49 × 33; Parish Church.

Midhurst*: gouache; 54 × 40; Town Council Office.

Milland*: watercolour; ca; 48 × 60; Memorial Hall.

Northchapel*: watercolour; 36 × 27; Village Hall.

North Mundham*: watercolour; 42 × 29; Village Hall.

Oving: in progress.

Pagham*: watercolour, pen and ink; 43 × 33; Village Hall.

Parham*: watercolour; 54 × 43; Parham House.

Petworth*: watercolour, pen and ink; 44 × 55; Leconfield Hall.

Plaistow*: watercolour; 18 × 25; Winterton Hall.

Poling*: watercolour; 53 × 43; Parish Church.

Pulborough*: watercolour; 41 × 28; Social Centre.

Rogate*: watercolour; 52 × 36; Village Hall.

Rustington*: watercolour, pen and ink; 26 × 35; Library.

Selsey*: watercolour; 54 × 41; Town Hall.

Shipley*: watercolour; 48 × 36; Parish Church.

Sidlesham*: watercolour and collage; 49 × 36; private address, copy in Parish Church.

Singleton*: watercolour; 24 × 17; Village Hall.

Slindon*: watercolour; 84 × 120; Coronation Hall.

Slinfold: embroidery; 42 × 53; Village Hall.

Sompting: in progress.

South Stoke*: watercolour; 39 × 52; private address.

Southwater: embroidery; 54 × 82; Village Hall.

Staplefield*: watercolour, pen and ink and photographs; 76 × 62; Village Hall.

Stedham with Iping*: watercolour; 33 × 23; Memorial Hall, Stedham.

Sutton and Bignor: embroidery and appliqué; 55 × 88; Parish Church, Sutton.

Tangmere*: watercolour; ca; 34 × 48; Village Centre.

Turners Hill*: watercolour; 28 × 35; Primary School.

Upper Beeding*: watercolour; 44 × 60; Village Hall.

Walberton and Binsted*: watercolour; 36 × 49; Village Hall.

Warningcamp*: watercolour; 33 × 45; Youth Hostel.

Washington*: mono-print, watercolour, pen and ink, embroidery, photographs, stained glass, computer work and silkscreen; 60 × 48; Village Hall.

Westbourne: in progress.

West Hoathly*: watercolour; 65 × 51; Village Hall.

Woolbeding and Linch*: watercolour, gouache and ink; 41 × 31; Redford Village Hall.

Worthing – West Tarring: watercolour; 32 × 22; private address.

Yapton and Ford*: watercolour; 33 × 48; Village Hall, Yapton.

Petworth

West Sussex Parish Maps Project – List of Contributors

The co-ordinator(s)/leader(s) for each map group is/are shown in italics

Aldwick
Ray Burt
Sue Kidd
Gwen Stabler
Aldwick Parish
  Council

Amberley
At start-up, March
  2006
Elizabeth Butler
Margaret Butler
Pat Chapman
Vincent Dane
Melanie Edge
Jim Endacott
John Gillings
Neill Hill
Pam Keeble
Steve Kennet
David Lyon
Antonia Maas
Dorothy Olney
Claire Seymour
Graham Stevenson
James Tolson
Jenny Toynbee
Mike Toynbee
Mike Wright

Apuldram
John Bassett
Fred Dickin
Jill Dickin
Suzanna Gayford
John Gostlin
Tom Groom
Natalie John
Chris Keville
Ginny Keville
Ian Manning
Bill Mason
Sally Mason
Linda Wilkinson

Ardingly
Simon Allaby
Michael Atkins
Joy Broughton
Audrey Caisley
John Caisley
John Carpenter
Michael Denman
Clive Izzard
Rosemary Maloney
Olive Saltmarsh
Roy Tester
Margaret Veasey
Lyn Wood

Arundel
Bill Beere
Mary Cable
Rosemary Hagedorn
Chris Halls
Pauline Halls
James Kenny
Frank Penfold
Roland Puttock
Sarah Rodger
Pamela Umbima
Jean Wolfenden
Matthew Woods
Arundel Agenda 21
Arundel Art Society
Arundel CE Primary
  School
Arundel St Philip's
  RC Primary School
Green Lane WI

Ashington
Julia Abel
Cathy Clark
Yvonne Cliff
Margaret Crofts
Alan Davis
Mary Davis
Margaret Dyson
Wendy Head
Velda James
Mary Laker
Brenda Lelliott
Ann Marchant
Greta Meeten
Marion Meeten
Sylvia Metcalfe
Brian Norton
Daphne Norton
Wendy Proctor
Joyce Roberts
Daphne Stokes
Shirley Webb

Balcombe
Joan Dutton
Isobel Gordon
Kenneth Jackson
Alan Jones
Tessa Land-Smith
John Lewis
Michael Noble
Peter Pope
Roger Reese
Balcombe clubs
Balcombe Estate
Balcombe Parish
  Council

Billingshurst
George Baczowski
David Barker
Hazel Barnes
Judy Beckwith
Margaret Berry
Rhon Daniel
Nevin Davies
Daphne Fielding
Laurie Gillett
Alice Goring
Terry Griffin
Caroline Holmes
John Hurd
Valerie Jennings
Jan Jewkes
Joan Jones
June Kiddell
Gillian Knight
Jane le Cluse
Kim Leslie
Wendy Lines
Barbara McIntosh
Irene Marshall
Pippa Masters
Stuart Pullen
Chris Rainer
Brenda Richards
Sheila Shannon
Joan Sibson
Gordon Simkin
Sylvia Simkin
Irene Stallard
Aileen Walker
Madeleine Woods

Birdham
Bryan Arthur
Rosemary Arthur
Marie Berry
Barbara Blay
Wendy Breeze
Sylvia Druce
Liz Fecher
Chris Fridlington
Beryl Garlick
Frankie Gibbs
Hilary Lambert
Wynne McRae
Mair Mills
Pam Purse
Alison Watts
Gwen Wilson
Joan Wright
All members of
  Birdham WI added
  at least one stitch to
  the embroidery

Bolney
Marielle Carr
Angela Davies
Bryan Davies
Lawrence Evans
Ann Gardiner
Joan Higinbotham
Emily Hutchings
Barbara Robins
Janine Scola
Maggie Smith

Bosham
Jean Armstrong
Joyce Baines
*Angela Bromley-
  Martin*
Pamela Challenor
Rita Gilby
Tom Groome
Doreen Hedley
Jules Hoare
Trevor Ingham
Brenda Lismer
Bill Mahoney
Roseanne Miller
Hazel Rouse

Boxgrove
Brenda Atlee
David Brecknell
Nick Brooks
Hugo Cobham
Chris Grant-Smith
John Greenaway
Kim Leslie
Tim McCann
Ken Meads
Elaine Pearce
Vera Quinton
Mark Roberts
Rose Savage
Lilian Trowsdale
Nancy Tunbridge
Dione Venables
Geoff Woods
Boxgrove CE Primary
  School
Goodwood Estate

Bramber
Ron Balaam
Rosemary Cole
Geoff Denby
Peter Firth
Sally Firth
Alan Fisher
John Green
Janice Griffiths
Daphne Jones
Alison Noble
Keith Noble
Robert Noble
Jeannette O'Reilly
Sarah Page
Betty Peirce
Elma Pendennis
Diana Schuler
Penny Schuler
Sue Skilton
Katy Sleight
Sue Smith

Burgess Hill – Worlds End
Gerry Canning
John Hayward
Hagop Kasparian
Ronald Rankin

Burpham
Nicola Young

Bury
Dorothy Bishop
Chris Briggs
Arthur Byng
Hugo Dunnell
Barbara Godwin
Ron Kirby
Abigail Lerche
Olivia Lerche
Tess Pendry
Joyce Reynolds
Jan Sitwell

Gwen Squire
Janet Thomas
Eleanor Ward
Melanie Ward

Chichester – Parklands

At start-up, March 2006
Catherine Batchelor
Glenwys Beaton
Nigel Beaton
Paula Chatfield
Ian Clark
Richard Cole
Richard Crossley
Enid Davies
Benedict Goddard
Jessica Goddard
Judith Goddard
Georgina Godfrey
Heather Hide
Jean Howlett
Chris Hughes
Jeannette Knott
John Knott
Frances Lansley
Peter Lansley
Michael Merritt
Barbara Pennicott
Christine Phillippo
Graham Phillippo
Ann Stewart
Beryl Turner
Pat Turner
Peg Wagstaff
Beryl Webster
Joan Whibley

Chichester – St John's Street

Deborah Mitchelson
Jane Weeks

Chichester – Whyke

Barbara Booth
Roger Clark
Jo Denton
Marigold Durnford
Peter Etheridge

Freddie Fielden
Geoff King
Monica Maloney
Pauline Newton
Jo Patten
Katherine Slay
Bunny Williams

Chidham

Lynda Aplin
Cliff Archer
Delph Archer
Edna Bailey
Olga Baldwin
Nina Bates
Joy Beech
Geoff Bell
Anna Blencowe
Gay Cardwell
Sandra Cheeseman
Adrian Davis
Caroline Davis
Pam Dimmock
Lin Dimon
Jenny Doland
Janet Dummer
Gillian Edom
John Edom
Jane Evans
Nita Fielder
Phoebe Fisher
Linda Green
Sheila Highfield
Alyzn Johnson
Kim Leslie
Lyn Mooney
Virginia Patterson
June Phillips
Catherine Rossiter
John Simpson
Ann Smallbone
Margaret Strange
Debbie Thompson
Jackie Thompson
Desmond Tubby
Marlene Whalen
Barry Wood
Polly Young
Many villagers each stitched one railway sleeper

Clapham and Patching

Mollie Cormick
Tony Crowther
Jane Dahill
Grace Foyle
David Gillard
Suzanne Gillard
Wendy Hodges
Malcolm Jacob
Sonia Jacob
Ron Olley
Margaret Rogers
Terry Rogers
Richenda Warriner
Irene Wood

Cocking History Column

Naomi Barnett
Clarissa Bewley
Colin Bradley
Carla Burley
Michael Carter
Yvonne Carter
Lady Cowdray
Juliet Crawford
Patrick Crawford
Jackie Eastman
Edney family
Guy Goodens
Greenhough family
Isabel Heller
Jamie Jackson
Jean Jackson
Philip Jackson
Jim Jarrad
Juliet Kay
Bet Kidd
Tom Kidd
Angus Manson
Aubrey Marks
Joy Marks
Chloe Pargenter
Judy Perry
Myfanwy Rogers
June Rolls
Karen Smith
Frances Wall
Marion Whitehorn
Morris Singer
   Foundry, Lasham

Coldwaltham, Watersfield and Hardham

Donovan Brown
Anne Dickin
Annie Nelson
Sandra Saer
Tony Spackman
Mark Weston

Copthorne

Christine Cheesmur
Gwyn Cheesmur
Colin Clarke
Joy Day
Ann Easton
Sue Kernohan
Pam Norman
Eileen Tulley
Paula Wood

Crawley Down

Richard Allen
Fred Baker
Rachel Bicker
Sandy Bushaway
David Carter
Sharon Cook
Hannah Cornell
Valerie Greenhalgh
Nichola Hardy
Dorothy Hatswell
Jeremy Hodgkinson
Jean Hopkins
Reg Houghton
Alison Hunt
Lorraine Kelly
David Lane
Brenda Law
Susannah Legg
Brian Leslie
Conrad Lowell
Grace Meldrum
Bob Mitchell
Jonathan Ogilvy
Jack Pope
Nick Powell
Janet Reeves
Alan Roberts
Katherine Rowley
Elaine Ruby

Eric Saunders
Jane Saunders
Mereith Saunders-Gale
Melanie Spencer
Charles Swingler
Rebecca Tammadge
Ian Tester
Sarah Thouless
Kim Walker
Noemie Watts
Ben Weaver

Donnington

Sylvia Arden-Brown
Edna Atkins
Hugh Brown
Ron Clarke
Cynthia Coates
Colin Doyle
Janet Doyle
Hugh Fleming
Lucy Harris
Mary Harris
Chris Heasman
Saskia Heasman
Mark Hewitt
Jeanne Higby
Owen Higby
Les Howick
Ted Humphrey
Bunty Ison
Carol Keet
Lucy McGairl
Isobel Perry
Mike Perry
Ebbi Ridd
John Ridd
Marjorie Sell
Mervyn Stacey
Pearl Stewart
Brian Turberfield
Jo Ward
Ron Wayne

Easebourne

Tina Ealovega
Zoe Edgington
Fiona Gowar
Patricia Luke
Sabrina Percy

Mary Shotter
Tom Smith
John Stringer
Jeanette Sutton
Danny Warner
Frank White
Emma Williams

Eastergate

Mary Botting
Janet Carter
Peter Carter
Rosemary Collins
Eastergate Parish Council

East Preston

Sally Stevens
Richenda Warriner

Elsted with Treyford cum Didling

Terence Allan
Michael Casement
Colin Coulson
Heather Coulson
Penny Fenn
Kenneth Higton
Maggie Mockett
Seona Rivett
June Rolls
John Saunders
Andrew Shaxson
Jenny Shaxson
Jill Wallace

Felpham

Eric Bobby
Brian Cage
Harold Checkley
Colin Clark
Jeanette Clark
Roy Clark
Sheila Gould
Mary Hite
Peter Lambert
May Newnham
John Roberts
Annie Rolls

Steve Streeter
Gwendolyn Tapp
Diana Wade
Geoffrey Willis
Artwork from 18
  parish groups
Bishop Tufnell CE
  Infant School
Bishop Tufnell CE
  Junior School
Downview Primary
  School
Felpham and
  Middleton History
  Workshop
Felpham Parish
  Council

Fernhurst

Pat Adsett
John Cooper
Lizzie Gould
Marjory Heaton
Jane Hudson
Peter Hudson
Nick Jackman
Mike Johnston
Roy Kelly
Pat Kettle
Jackie Knight
Phil Knight
Sandy Livingstone
Ann McLaughlin
Arnold Madgwick
Christine Maynard
Jeremy Miller
Jean Moreton
Helen Ouin
Ken Ouin
Angela Parrott
Laura Ponsonby
Lynn Rackham
Glenis Taylor
Rachel Taylor
John Tucker
Judith Turner
Charlotte Willson-
  Pepper
Patrick Wright

Ferring

Roy Aldam
David Barber
Oliver Barleycorn
Perry Charrington
Charmain Cooney
Joyce Cooper
Michael Cooper
Joan Cornwell
John Creasey
Malcolm Crowlie
Barbara Davies
Jo Dommett
Barbara Doyle
Joan Evershed
Christy Hall
Ann Hedges
Frank Leeson
Gill Kirk
Sandra Martin
Michael Parkin
Edna Parsons
Joy Rennard
Rachel Richards
Sue Robinson
Brian Rolf
Wendy Ross
Roy Rouse
Kathryn Sloane
Pauline Smith
Jenny Stenner
Michael Tanner
Sally Tanner
Ben Tapernier
Marcus Vince
Dora White
Janet Wright
Jean Writer

Fishbourne

Nick Benn
Margaret Borsberry
Les Eames
Edna Franklin
Denise Hughes
Patsy Johnson
Kirsten Kryger
Pearl Moore
Benny Paxton
Joyce Smith
Vi Waller
Patsy West

Hazel Young
Liz Young

**Funtington and
West Stoke**

Val Bateman
Nigel Brown
Gina Burt
Brian Coles
Frank Garrett
Sybil Grindrod
Robert Headley
Monty Lemmon
Margaret McMullen
Laura Mason
Charles Pritchard
Colin Robinson
Dawn Robinson
Mandy Shepherd
Dennis Ward

Goring-by-Sea

Jane Allen
Jill Anstey
Jane Bond
Robin Bradley
Michael Ebeling
Janet Hannant
Vivienne Hooker
Irene Kitto
Graham Redman
Gertrude Sanders
Pauline Smith

**Graffham, Selham
and South
Ambersham**

Ed Austin
Diana Bellis
Maureen Boulton
Marion Bowley
Betty Bradley
Ina Bridger
Michael Bridger
Paula Burke
Dick Challen
June Challen
Wendy Challen
Shelagh Chapman
Roger Clarke
Peter Cotton

John Fellows
Pru Hart
Barbara Kemp
Diana Kingsmill
Stuart LeFevre
Kim Leslie
Tim Morton
Phyll Nicholl
Robert Ralph
Rosemary Robson
Andrew Shilcock
Anny Spilberg
Elly Spilberg
Mike Spilberg
Daphne Taylor
Mary Taylor
Teresa Whittington
Diana Williams
Graffham First School
Seaford College

Harting

Heather Bushell
Christina Casement
Judy Dobson
Jane Healey
Roger Holmes
Bill Hopkins
Stephanie Morgan
Sally Pringle
John Sladden
Doreen Smith

Haywards Heath

Margaret Baker
Richard Bates
William Coleman
Penny Jennings
Margaret Joss
Christine McLean
Debby Matthews
Carole Morgan
Jane Reid
Neville Way
Yvonne Wemyss
Ann Went

Henfield

Alan Barwick
Annette Blair-Fish
Marjorie Carreck

Monica Copley
Pauline Fisher
Mary Garside
Mary Rose Hardy
David Hill
Joan Hill
Brenda Hobbs
Jean Huggett
Kathy Lancashire
Sylvia Macintosh
Mike Morgan
Geraldine Pullin
Mike Russell
Anne Ryall
Al Salvage
John Squire
Gladys Wilkins
John Willis

Heyshott

Olwyn Bowey
Vivian Palmer

Highbrook

Peter Browne
John Downe
Brett Hudson

Hunston

Joyce Blair
Heather Crate
Joan Duberley
Anne Duffy
Anne Hack
Jill Hodnett
Mavis Kirkland
Betty Pennicott
Di Redford
Gwen Stubbington
Mary Watson
Margaret Wuyts

**Hurstpierpoint and
Sayers Common**

John Avis
Ben Awcock
Mickie Bennett
Gillian Black
Joan Booker
Evelyn Bowles

Geoffrey Bowles
Michael Cheetham
Kay Cogan
Sally Coleman
Joyce Creaton
Cameron Cresswell-
  Falvey
Margaret Edwards
Peter Fry
Beverley George
Paul Hartley
Bryony Hill
Mary Faux Jackson
Suzanna Kemp
Natalie Miller
Jan Morley
Valerie Olszewski
Bill Parrott
Sue Pendred
Derek Rogers
Susan Skinner
Bill Swallow
Sylvia Thornhill
Maxine Tyler
Angela Wade
June Ward
Daisy Ware

Itchenor

Veronica Ferguson
Pam Gibson
Sybella McCann
Petra Rook
Janie Strachan
Sissy Thompson
Hilary Wright

Lavant

Michael Burton
Geoffrey Claridge
Ronnie Cowan
Glen Dixon
John Farren
Penny Goldring
Peter Grant
Jane Hall
Judith Hayter
Natalie King
Rebekah Naylor
Bob Pine
Adam Power

Jenifer Pressdee
Rhoda Robinson
Mandy Shepherd
Ted Squires
Rod Stern
Kimberley Stewart
Robert Tedman
Diana Thomas
Jeremy Thomas
Elizabeth Woodford

Lindfield

Trevor Bashford
Yvonne Bee
Betty Billins
Roy Billins
Chris Bosker
Sally Dew
Peter Duncan
Veronica Eleleman
Brian Field
Claudia Gaukroger
Christine Giltrow
Dave Hill
Sue Hipperson
William Hipperson
Gwyn Mansfield
Margaret Nicolle
Pamela Pound
Andy Powell
Alan Sawyer
Charles Smith
John Stephens
Dorothy Taylor
Janet Wade
Tony Way
Dennis Webb
Yvonne Wemyss
Mollie Whitten
Blackthorns
   Community
   Primary School
Lindfield Primary
   School

Lindfield Rural

Angela Barton-Smith
Matilda Bevan
Doris Buswell
Ron Buswell
Carol Campbell

Sally Church
Sally Fodder
Charles Harris
Janet Harris
Arthur McCulloch
Graham Mitchell
Patrick Pilcher
Sheila Pilcher
Lyn Watkins
Tony Way
Great Walstead
   School
St Augustine's CE
   Primary School,
   Scaynes Hill
Scaynes Hill clubs
   and societies

Littlehampton

Eric Burchell
Olivia Crane
Audrey Daggett
Wilfred Daggett
Lynne Friel
Barbara Hughes
Betty Jones
Lynette Nicholson
Sally Stevens
Joyce Thorn
Paula Thrift
Richenda Warriner

Lodsworth

Patrick Atkins
Vanessa Atkins
Brian Baker
Vera Baker
Joan Corbett
John Fellows
Sarah Fellows
Kim Leslie
Anne McKee
Gerard McKee
Steve Morley
Lord Nathan
Jack Osborn
Nevil Phillips
Peter Ricketts
Betty Simmonds
Fiona Stephens

Loxwood

Pamela Davis
Ron Davis
James Jarrad
Dena Kitchener
John Kitchener
Len Milsom
Steve Parsons

Lurgashall

Pam Bruce
Caroline Wilding
Peter Wilding

Lyminster

Sue Bingham
Anthea Blackmore
Liam Bligh
Verity Bligh
Alan Burnett
John White

Lynchmere

Emily Alderton
Yvonne Beresford
Jim Bound
Daniel Brown
Sheila Burkitt
Kathleen Calverley
Katherine Crompton
Sally Crosthwaite
Hayley Denny
Freddie Ellis
Anna Gregory
George Hanbury
James Harthill
John Hooker
Mary Jane House
Ben Irwin-Brown
Mark Kimber
David Lipscombe
Gay Loades-Carter
Ellie Lusona-Sears
Toby McCallum
Henry Marks
Lucy Mildren
Rory Millar
Alasdair Mitchell
Molly Monks
Alex Moore
Fiona Musson

Katherine Nkosi
John Northway
Tom Parkes
Ben Pite
Harriet Russell
Janet Sears
Murray Sears
Sarah Sears
Edward Sherlock
Jo Smith
Anne Marie Sturt
Francasca Swan
Anne Tibbs
Eleonora Tibbs
Frederick Tibbs
Geoffrey Tibbs
Michael Tibbs
Holly Vowels
Archie Watson
Catherine White
George Williams

Madehurst

Nicholas Adames
Elizabeth Bratley
Sarah Clilverd
Andrew Cossar
Mandy Faulkner
Robert Green
Gay Maclaren
Joyce Newman
Peggy Newman
Gail Simmons
Peter Simmons
Annie Simson
Deborah Thornton
Jane Thorpe
David Tod
Graham Tooley
Ann Wakelin
Anne Wilson

Midhurst

Ron Carver
Michael Chevis
Susan Haines
John Harrison
Colin Hughes
Estelle Morris
John Morris
Stuart Neal

Mary West
Max Wholey

Milland

William Barker
Sir Hubert Bennett
Bob Farwell
Lorraine Grocott
Simon Hobson
Jane Pask
David Risley
Maureen Truss

Northchapel

Frances Abraham
Pam Bruce
Sarah Callingham
Laura Dadswell
Sarah Harding
Julie King
Kim Leslie
Denise Lunn
Sarah Payne
Caroline Wilding

North Mundham

John Hole
Arnold Hooton

Oving

Roger Baynham
Sandra Baynham
Janie Brierley
Anne-Marie Dales
Sue England
Janet Johnstone
Sue Millard
Brian Nesbitt
Karen Nesbitt
Karena Shaw

Pagham

Angie Hancock
Sue Kidd
Lesley King
Michael King
Geoff Longlands
Gina Marley
John Maynard
Val Ryan

Stanley Sharp
Byron Stroud
June Widdowson
David Woodall
Irma Wunderlick

Parham

Marion Batchelor
Tessa Mackie
Glenys Rowe
Jennifer Sadler
Mark Weston

Petworth

Jacqueline Golden
Lewis Golden
John Humphry
Eileen Lintill
Clive McBain
Stefan Oliver
Don Simpson
Jean Simpson

Plaistow

Janet Austin
Ann Brooks
Jo Goulder
Peggy Harman
Gwen Millichamp
Wendy Rapley
Stella Ribbens
Maureen Tully
Eileen Wright
Ifold Local History
   Society

Poling

Jill Adams
Alec Butcher
Bryan Curtis
Helen Curtis
Verity Curtis
Yvette Curtis
Mandy Harding
Jenny Inglis
Sandy Kent
Carla Lander
Peter Lander
Nan Liddersdale
Pam May

Penny May
Billy Maynard
Lucinda O'Neill
Diana Parkin
Lorraine Read
Philip Read
Chloe Richards
Gareth Richards
Norman Shepherd
Valerie Shepherd
David Turgoose
Gwen Turgoose
Tim Worley

Pulborough

Debbie Bath
Chris Briggs
Alan Cook
Biddy Hutcheson
Andy Leese

Rogate

John Ashton
John Aslett
Richard Barber
Kathleen Bell
Margaret Berendt
Neville Conder
Susan Conder
Rena Cook
Linda Ellingham
Susan Erskine
Shirley Gatehouse
David James
Jacky Leonard
Margery Sadler

Rustington

Sheila Bolton
Betty Breward
Daphne Brotherston
Harry Clark
Ann Diacon
Pauline Druiff
Ian Ennis
Joan King
Elizabeth Leach
Lynette Nicholson
Sue Oldfield
Kay Sear
Elizabeth Thornton

Dennis Wakeling
Dot Woosnam

Selsey

Jean Bankes
Cliff Fidler
Robert Francis
Bob Holcombe
Eileen Savill
Joe Savill
Jill Sutcliffe
Moira Torrance
Peter White
Sarah White
Selsey Society
Groups and
    organisations

Shipley

Hariot Anniss
David Bucks
Charles Burrell
Ann Clarke
Sarah Delaney
Mike Gibson
Ann Green
Jane Grinling
Deanna Hilder
Phyllis Humphrey
Pat Lawrence
Brian Lee
Kim Leslie
Graham Peacock
Bob Philips
John Redman
Joy Redman
Barry Robinson
Mandy Robinson
Zar Roggendorff
Peter Sanderson
Claire Searle

Sidlesham

Gina Carrington
Brigitte Crafer
Joyce Fairbairn
Adrian Harland
Lawrence Holloway
Marjorie Lytton
Margaret Moorhouse
Jill Richards

David Scott
Elizabeth Smart
Geoffrey Spiby
Sally Tynan
Numerous other
    parishioners

Singleton

Jan Elliott
Norah Godber
Olwyn Gudgeon
June Hampton
John Lamb
Sheila Mcdonald
Ann Pollock
Maurice Pollock
Rosemary Staples
Bill Stewart

Slindon

Katy Armstrong
Richard Atkinson
Bonny Beere
Juliet Bray
Molly Burchell
Sam Coates
Alice Colling
Charlotte Colling
Ken Dale
Martin Denyer
Mandy Faulkner
Saska Fenton
Lou Friend
Margaret Gibbons
Faith Harris
Ben Harvey
Daniel Harvey
Mick Hutton
Sandra Izard
Luke Jacobs
Sam Johnson
Lorna Kirkby
John Lewis
Dominic Moor
Mary Moor
Maggie North
Anita Pascall
Kate Procter
Phillipa Redman
Cameron Rowell-
    Jones

Ashely Rule
Lesley Smith
Joan Spofforth
Elizabeth Thomas
Marie Tinker
Anne Waters
Alyx Wood
Jack Yates
CARE Community,
    Walberton
St Mary's CE Primary
    School
Slindon College

Slinfold

Beatrice Baldwin
Peggy Blackhurst
Janet Chisholm
Daphne Cowan
Margaret Dunkerton
Joan Esdale
Valerie Harrison
Nina Hopkins
Pansy James
Valerie Leslie
Joan Puttock

Sompting

At start-up, March
    2006
Tim Clarke
Tracey Clarke
Eileen Colwell
Bill Lindfield
Mike Prince
Martin Snow
Mike Tristram

South Stoke

Chris Clarke
Jayne Cooper
Phyllis Dyson
Charlotte Earp
Harriet Earp
Jill Earp
Martin Earp
Conor Haydon
Jackie Haydon
Lorna Haydon
Ryan Haydon
David Julian

Sahda Lemoine
Karen Lowater
Gaynor Marsh
Peter Marsh
Alex Mills
Kelly Mills
Dominic Munns
Oliver Munns
Sarah Rodger
Emma Rowley
Sue Rowley
Ben Wintour
Mary Wintour

Southwater

Jessica Amos
Gladys Andrews
Margaret Birchmore
Audrey Broad
Janice Bull
Marilyn Dias
Caroline Foster
Sheila Griffiths
Alison Hendra
Wendy Hunt
Anne Jones
Frances Lines
Eunice Pearson
Doris Pierce
Robert Piper
Sue Rowe
Barbara Smith
Villagers who worked
    on the logos

Staplefield

Jill Adair
Pat Bendall
Peter Benner
Annie Chippendale
Peter Chippendale
Penny Elliot
Joyce Hayward
Mary Langridge
Martin Levy
Charlotte Neal
Darren Ray
Sue Ray
Frances Stenlake
Josephine Stenlake
Robert Stenlake

Ron Stevenson
Staplefield
    Needleworkers
    Group

Stedham with Iping

Alison Booker
Leslie Devenish
Dave Gant
Marian Johnson
Ray Jupp
Linn Sayer
Sarah Steffell
Angela Williams
Gillian Young

Sutton and Bignor

Sarah Ackner
David Armstrong
Barbara Bertram
Jill Biggs
Alison Boreham
Priscilla Burfield
Susan Dudman
Margaret Eatock
Fiona Elliot
Geraldine Elliot
Pam Fenner
Toni Green
Marion Hobbs
Brianne Holdsworth
Jane Hoyle
Steve Jackman
Becky Kingdom-
    Butcher
Jane Lawes
Allyson McDermott
Tara Marshall
Anne Mills
Susan Parker
Anne Poulter
Anthea Pratt
Toni Richmond
Anne Rowe
Joan Rudd-Jones
Susan Venning
Joan Verrall
Susan Vince
Betty Wade
Catherine Wapshott

Pat White
Sue Wilson
Nicky Young

Tangmere

Vicky Anderson
Joan Cook
Travers G. Johnson
Bill Malloy
Betty Rudkin
John Rudkin
Phillip Saunders
Patience Skelton
John Stapleford
David Tyler

Turners Hill

Edward Armstrong
Thelma Blezard
Laura Botting
Maddy Cooper
Jonathan Warren

Upper Beeding

Alan Barwick
Pauline Beale
Lyn Bedford
Nick Burdell
Cliff Carter
Alan Fisher
Peter Gilham
Christine Gill
John Green
Stan Hague
Lily Holding

Hannah Howarth
Kim Leslie
Samantha McGuire
Fumiko Mallory
Lyndsey Nash
Keith Nethercoate-
  Bryant
Gladys Newbury
Dave Nightingale
Pat Nightingale
Keith Noble
Robert Noble
Rebecca Peate
Barry Robinson
Lisa Shelley
Susan Skilton
Katy Sleight
Judy Son
Judi Stanwell
Judith Steedman
Lydia Tai
Doug Thompson
Sharon Tong
Rhiannon Walker

**Walberton and
  Binsted**

Jackie Ballard
Marina Boldero
Martin Bond
Liz Brown
Don Carter
Pat Couchman
Ken Cox
Alan Curzons
Jennie Curzons

Brenda Dixon
Brian Dunstan
Bob Escolme
Hilary Escolme
John Eyre
Steven Faber
David Garraway
Eirwen Garraway
Derek Greig
Penny Hadley
Helga Hann
Denis Hardwick
Diana Kohler
Sue Lear
Diana Levantine
Maria Levey
Molly McAtasney
Sue Marino
David Morton
Kate O'Brien
Mabel Padfield
Mary Pennell
Roger Putnam
Lynne Rackstraw
Jackie Robinson
Alan Scott
Celia Scott
Emma Tristram
Peter Trumble
Bill Wells
Belinda Wilkins
Jan Wood

Warningcamp

Chris Austen
Becky Barber

Mary Barber
Brian Bull
Alan Chapman
Gillie Fox
Alison Groves
Pippa Groves
Simon Groves
Tim Groves
Audrey Hall
Jack Harry
Rosalind Holden
Alan Howard
Sally-Jane Howard
Lou Oakes
Peter O'Shea
Claudia Taylor-
  Roberts
Matthew Taylor-
  Roberts
Chris Warren-
  Adamson
Paul Winner
Numerous children
  took part in the
  butterfly and
  wildlife surveys

Washington

Jacqueline Baker
Moya Bevan
Jean Coltman
Paul Coltman
Geoffrey Goatcher
Katherine Goatcher
Rosemary Gregoire
Barbara Lidbetter

Alison Milner-Gulland
Tom Milner-Gulland
Mildred Summerton
Richard Turley
Gina Wilmshurst
Roger Wilmshurst

Westbourne

Margaret Anthony
Peter Barge
Thomas Blower
Elisabeth Kinloch
Frieda Lawes
Tony Lawes
Piers Mason
Jenny Stewart
John Veltom
Peter Wilkinson

West Hoathly

Tony Blunt
Roger Bourne
Marion Briggs
Richard Coleman
Richard Comber
Terry Cooper
Basil Cridland
Enid Cridland
Nick des Forges
Bill Fish
Peter Hulbert
Sally Lambert
Ian Linnett
Tim Linnett
Sarah Merrifield
Alan Piqué

Julia Piqué
Bob Sellens
Shirley Shier
Antony Smith
Richard Toomer
Nick Wavish
Vin Whitmarsh
West Hoathly CE
  Primary School

**Woolbeding and
  Linch**

Pat Kettle
Karen Lovett
Christine Mayfield
Beryl Trimmer

**Worthing – West
  Tarring**

Ruby Nelson

Yapton and Ford

Joan Alnutt
Sonya Barnett
Kelvin Briscoe
David Day
Marion Griffiths
Ronald Griffiths
Marilyn Hammerton
Alan Misselbrook
Janet Phillips
Roy Phillips
Geoff Westcott

South Stoke

Index

This index excludes all personal names in Appendix Four – List of Contributors.